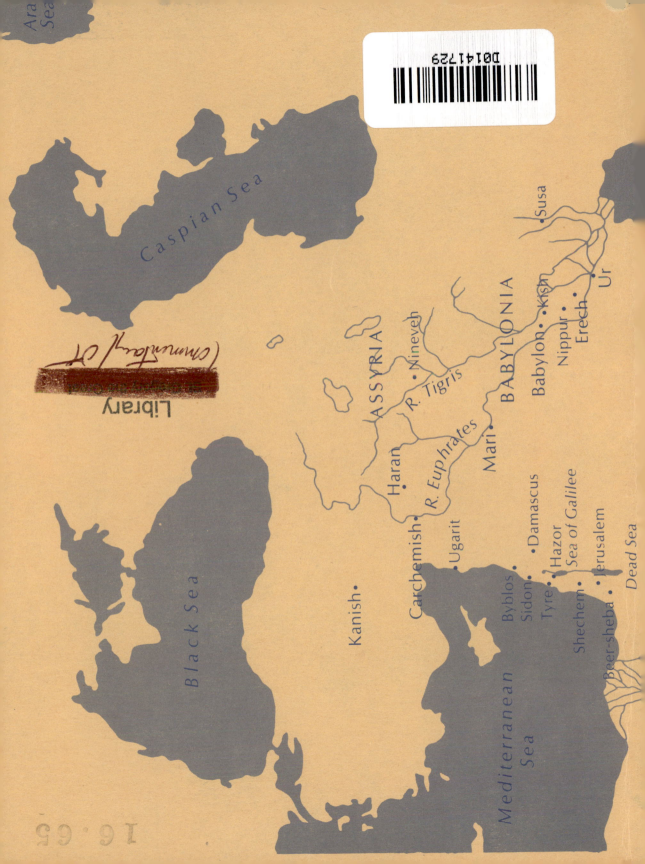

Ara
Sea

Caspian Sea

Black Sea

Mediterranean
Sea

Kanish•

Carchemish•

•Ugarit

Byblos•
Sidon•
Tyre•
Hazor•
Sea of Galilee
Shechem•
Jerusalem•
Beer-sheba•

•Damascus

Dead Sea

Haran•

ASSYRIA

R. Euphrates

•Nineveh

R. Tigris

Mari•

BABYLONIA

Babylon• •Kish
Nippur•
Erech•
Ur•

•Susa

CRISIS AND STORY: INTRODUCTION
TO THE
OLD TESTAMENT

CRISIS

Mayfield Publishing Company

AND STORY:

INTRODUCTION
TO THE
OLD TESTAMENT

W. LEE HUMPHREYS
University of Tennessee

COVER: Old Testament lands photographed from space: Egypt in fore-ground, with Sinai peninsula surrounded by Mediterranean Sea (*left*), Gulfs of Suez and Aqaba (*center*), and Red Sea (*right*). In the center background, the Dead Sea marks the border between present-day Israel and Jordan. Photograph courtesy of NASA.

Library of Congress Catalog Card Number: 78–64594
International Standard Book Number: 0-87484-437-1

Manufactured in the United States of America
Mayfield Publishing Company, 285 Hamilton Avenue, Palo Alto, California 94301

This book was set in TxT Elegante with Zenith and Basilea display type by
Dharma Press and was printed and bound by Haddon Craftsmen.
Sponsoring editor was Alden C. Paine, Carole Norton supervised editing, and
Barbara Pronin was manuscript editor. Michelle Hogan supervised
production, the book was designed by Nancy Sears, maps were prepared by
Janet Ralston, and sketches were prepared by Ireta Cooper.

To my family—
Alberta and Cecil Humphreys
Laurey
Laurie and Christopher Lee
And especially to Rebecca Leah
whose life became proof of the
vitality and beauty
found in memories

CONTENTS

MAPS

PREFACE

During the past decade or so several giants in the field of the Old Testament and early Jewish studies have passed away—among them, Martin Noth, William Foxwell Albright, Nelson Glueck, Roland de Vaux, Gerhard von Rad, and G. Ernest Wright. While it is not yet apparent who will fill their places, there is much movement in the field today, and a number of basic shifts are taking place. In America, for example, Bible study is no longer centered primarily in theological seminaries or church-related colleges but is also to be found in secular institutions where it takes its place among all the world's religions, both ancient and contemporary, as well as amid the humanities as a whole.

This introduction to the Old Testament and to other early Jewish writings seeks to provide enough breadth of coverage to be useful in all these contexts. The approach is broadly historical, not theological, and is based on the several critical methods that have been brought to biblical studies during the past century. Its goal is to foster understanding of how and why the people of ancient Israel and the adherents of early Judaism expressed their beliefs and ordered their lives about them. Other approaches are possible, however, and, while the scope of the text permits supplementation by other books and articles, as well as by classroom lectures and discussions, the author hopes that its completeness will enable it to stand together with the Bible as a sole basic resource. A more intensive study of limited segments of the Bible should form the subject of more advanced courses.

The primary readings listed at the beginning of each chapter include almost all the Old Testament, large selections from the Apocrypha, and material from Qumran, although not all need to be covered in utilizing this text. They are placed at the head of each chapter, however, because they should be read first. Although students need interpretative help in initially confronting the Old Testament, I believe that the Bible can be read with some initial comprehension which will then be enriched by the text, while introducing the text first would necessitate retelling a great deal of what is in the Bible. Ideally, segments of the readings should be reread during the study of the text and long afterward as well.

Coworkers in the field will be well aware of my scholarly debts throughout the text, but footnotes have here been dispensed with in favor of chapter bibliographic notes which offer suggestions for those who seek greater depth in some area of study. The notes concentrate on basic recent works in English, many of which contain further bibliographic references, and the classroom instructor should supplement these as new works appear. Finally, maps, chronological charts, illustrations, and a glossary have been included, the latter, especially, to serve as a continuing source of student reference.

Here I wish to express my gratitude to the many students who have passed through my classes over the past eight years at the University of Tennessee; to my colleagues in the Department of Religious Studies, who provide the proper balance of challenge and support; and especially to Professor Stan Lusby, who, as department head, so effectively facilitates the teaching and writing done by his coworkers. In addition, I wish to thank my own teachers: Professor R. Lansing Hicks, who introduced me to the field, and Professors Samuel L. Terrien, James A. Sanders, George M. Landes, and Moshe Held, who guided my further study.

I am grateful to Cecille Tobin, Joan Reidl, and Karen Dotson, who graciously saw several versions of the text through typing; to Janet Ralston who produced the maps; and to the staff at Mayfield Publishing Company—especially Carole Norton; Barbara Pronin, under whose skilled editorial hand this text has become a far stronger and finer work; and Nancy Sears and Michelle Hogan, who designed and brought the book through production. I owe a special debt of thanks to Alden C. Paine, recently retired as an editor at Mayfield, who from our first chance meeting has been a source of encouragement and valued criticism.

To others, who need not be named but who have shared in the excitement and labor of preparing this text and who have in many ways enriched my life, I trust that my gratitude is clear. Finally, I wish to express thanks to my parents, my wife Laurey, my daughters, and my son, who have not only helped greatly in the writing of this text but have encouraged me in a life of teaching. To them I dedicate this book.

INTRODUCTION: PATTERNS OF MEMORY

THE NATURE AND FUNCTION OF RELIGIOUS TRADITION

A few years ago an author and teacher who is an American Indian addressed a group of scholars on the subject of "A Man Made of Words." In speaking of the creation of a full human life, he meant more than the creation of a biological organism. He talked about his own life, that of a unique individual with values and dreams, likes and dislikes, loves and fears. He spoke of storytelling, observing that some stories passed from one generation to another are reformed as they are remembered and retold. Some become special treasures that are preserved by individuals and communities because they are a vital part of life. He spoke of how such stories can mean very different things to the father who tells them and to the son who hears them and may in time tell them in his own way to his own son. He spoke of the past and the present, of remembering and imagination.

These stories—and I believe that we all have them—are powerful creative forces. They become constitutive of an individual, a community, or a nation. As they are taken into our lives they impart a particular shape, an identity, a structure; and as we accept and pass them on, as we preserve and transform them, we become men and women made of words. We are informed and enlivened by this heritage of ancestral memories. Our unique character as individuals and communities is given shape, as are our relations with the world around us. Such stories build a foundation for our interaction with other individuals and communities and with the very earth upon which we live.

I am thinking here of stories that engage more than our intellectual curiosity and certainly more than our passing interest. These stories are not conveyed by an inert mechanical TV receiver that makes us detached spectators of the pseudolives of imaginary people, nor are they the artistically impressive stories that one sometimes encounters in books. These are stories that engage the whole person, that grasp us and make us a part of the action. We are not outside observers but live ourselves in the telling of them. Especially in the case of those belonging to communities and nations, such stories are often told in special places and at particular times, accompanied by distinct actions and forms of ceremony which bring the story into the present experience of those who hear it and take part in the activity. When stories become so well known that they are an essential part of us, the actions or ceremonies may come to predominate so that the story is told either in brief outline or is implied rather than spoken aloud.

In America, for example, the story of the Pilgrims and of Plymouth Colony has, since the Civil War at least, been retold and reenacted at a particular time of year by families gathered about a bountiful table of feasting. The Thanksgiving story tells of an attempt to form a new society that would allow and even encourage the search for religious and political freedom. It is the story of the special relationship of this community with others, with the natives of the new land, with the land itself, and with their god. Within the framework of the Thanksgiving meal the story is retold each year, or perhaps only implied, for words are not always needed. As a part of America's past is relived in this special way at a time set apart for remembering, an essential ingredient in the American character is reaffirmed, renewed, and enlivened.

Myths and Stories

In the study of religions these stories are sometimes called *myths*; but this is a loaded term, and even the term *story* bears negative connotations for many. Scholars differ widely concerning what constitutes myths, how they have functioned among various peoples, and how they may most fruitfully be understood. On the more popular level the term suggests a fiction, a falsehood, or a simple explanation that serves to satisfy a primitive or childlike mind. This last connotation we owe to the ancient Greeks, whose myths are perhaps the best known. When Socrates encountered a man named Euthyphro shortly before his famous trial, the latter offered to share with the philosopher some of his rich store of myths about the gods. If Plato's account can be believed, Socrates not only found it remarkable that there were people who still believed such things but dismissed the whole business as being inconsequential to serious study. "Save them for another time," he said, "when we have the leisure."

Even then ages old, Euthyphro's stories were devoid of value to Socrates and to others of his day. Not only were they dead but it was hard to see how some of them could ever have been believed, have given life to people, and have had the power to shape lives. Yet they had been living, dynamic, organic things; as such, however, they could also die. As changing currents in the history and intellectual life of Greece radically altered the political, social, philosophical, and religious foundations upon which these myths had been formed and supported, they slowly died or became quaint relics out of the past, detached from the rituals that had accompanied and brought them to life. They became stories for children or poets. We must remember, however, that children and poets often have insights possessed by few others.

The question of historical factualness forces myths into a mold that ill suits them because myths do more than merely relate past happenings, and in that respect they transcend the narrow strictures of historiography. A moment of retelling, of reliving, of remembering, taking over, and passing on the past as story or myth is a creative force for life, and at that level historical factualness is a secondary, not a central concern. The stories told to us by our parents and grandparents are treasured, but not primarily because they preserve a factual account of what really happened. Indeed, we often cherish our own memories even when we suspect that they have gone far beyond what we know to have actually occurred.

In their pursuit of historical accuracy many recent books that treat the Pilgrims and the Plymouth Colony in a nonidealized manner have not taken into account the role and impact of the Thanksgiving story on the formation and preservation of the American character or its values and goals. That the motives that brought these early settlers to our shores were mixed and varied, that there was disharmony within the colony at Plymouth, and that the relation of the colonists to the natives of the land was at times deplorable has been shown with increasing force in recent studies, and these studies may have a profound effect on the vitality of the Thanksgiving myth. They may, in fact, reflect a changed climate of opinion in which the older myth cannot survive. For many today the meaning and impact of Thanksgiving in America has already been diluted or lost.

Thus, as the terms *story* and *myth* are used in this book, the question of historical factualness will not be prejudged. Some stories may now seem to us pure fantasy; others may conceal actual events of human history or tell of nature's rhythmic cycles behind a screen of scarcely penetrable symbols; still others may provide excellent source material for historical reconstruction. For us, however, the terms will serve simply to emphasize that particular memories are set apart from others and are recited again and again by an individual or community because they are found still to live and to give life when recalled and recited.

An Israelite and Jewish Story

The ancient Israelites and early Jewish communities had many stories of this kind, many memories, and many forms for each, but the most cherished story of all told in ceaseless variation of how their ancestors had once escaped bondage to the king of Egypt by crying out to their god for release. Their god had heard them and, through Moses, had brought about their deliverance with terrifying signs and wonders. Saved at the sea from the pursuing Egyptians, the slaves had fled to the wilderness and come to Mount Sinai. There, through the mediation of Moses, the law of their savior god had been offered to them and accepted. From the mountain they had moved slowly toward the land that they believed had been promised by this same god to their ancestors generations earlier. In time they were able to enter and take possession of that land.

Even today Jewish families gather about the dining table for the Seder on the eve of Passover to tell the story of slaves who fled from Egyptian bondage, and in doing this they do what in one form or another Jews, and Israelites before them, have done for millenia. The story is retold in actions and words, through ceremonies and special meanings given to items of food and drink, in questions and answers, sometimes in free and rousing debate and song. It is actually relived as it is retold, and the community of Jews is reformed and rebuilt at Passover. Individuals find an identity and place in this community, sharing its experiences in this dramatic retelling of the story, taking on for themselves its values and ideals, affirmations and hopes, obligations and privileges. Jews by birth or conversion, they now become Jews by affirmation and experience. They become men and women made of words. The past forms and reforms the present moment of telling, even as the present telling gives ever new forms to the remembered past.

Ancient Israel and early Judaism had other stories as well, which took many forms through the vicissitudes of the people who treasured them. Some of the stories died in time; sometimes crises called for a radical reformation or rejection of the old stories. It is this cherished story of deliverance from slavery, together with the other stories that we shall meet in the course of these pages, that constitute what we call the religious traditions of ancient Israel and Judaism. We will center our attention on their nature and content, their forms of telling and presentation, their birth, life, and sometimes their death, for stories and myths, like persons and nations, have lives and histories of their own. We will study the history of some forms of the remembered past, not just to learn what once actually happened, but first and foremost to learn how and why the memory of the past has taken the forms in which it has come down to us in the Bible and other writings.

We will not seek to adopt or relive one or another story for ourselves but will attempt rather to understand how and why individuals, communities, and nations told and treasured their stories. We will not be theologians, although we will look at some of the ways in which certain people formed their theologies. We will not speak of God but will look at ways in which different people who composed the ancient nation of Israel and the early Jewish communities spoke of their god or gods. We will not seek to be confessional—that is, to give our allegiance to the stories—but instead will look at some of the forms of confession or allegiance that individuals and communities once made.

In all this our task is historical. We want to study and understand the historical development, growth, change, and sometimes decline of these stories or religious traditions of ancient Israel and early Judaism. For those who stand within the currents of Western culture—whether or not we stand within any of the forms of Western religion—these stories or traditions form one of our basic historical foundations. To understand their origins, shapes, and preservation is to learn about ourselves. Whether we accept or reject our past, whether we attempt to build on this heritage or turn from it, we should understand it as fully as we can, for whatever response we make to it—and respond we must—will constitute the most critical and far-reaching of decisions.

It was well known in old Israel that words had real and immediate power, especially words spoken at particular times and places by special persons. Names given at birth, deathbed blessings, the words of oaths or curses, the words of prophets, priests, or kings, the sayings of wise teachers—all were believed to be filled with power capable of creating or destroying, altering or reforming lives. The stories that we shall study were for many people formed of such words. They enlivened and informed individuals and communities and were in turn reshaped by men and women whose lives were thereby made of words.

ORIGINS OF ISRAEL'S STORY

Because some stories or myths are rooted in particular events, the historian can attempt to recover them. The story recited and relived at Passover, for example, originated in events that occurred in the Near East from about 2100 to 1200 B.C.E. (the Middle and Late Bronze Ages) when a group of slaves in Egypt fled bondage into the wilderness of Sinai under the leadership of a man named Moses. From Sinai, in the course of time, their descendants entered southern Palestine and became a constituent part of the nation that was to be called Israel. Those Israelite forefathers, led by Moses and Aaron and to a lesser degree the figures of the patriarchs Abraham, Isaac, and Jacob before them, have been broadly set upon the stage of ancient history. From this distance, however, we cannot focus upon them too sharply because there is no reference to them in the numerous written records from Egypt, Mesopotamia, or Palestine or to events or persons

ANCIENT NEAR EAST in the MIDDLE and LATE BRONZE AGES

B.C.E.	Egypt	Palestine	Mesopotamia
2000	TWELFTH DYNASTY (1991–1786)	MIDDLE BRONZE AGE (2100–1550)	UR III (2060–1950)
1900		Patriarchs	
1800			I BABYLON (1830–1530)
1700	SECOND INTERMEDIATE (18th–16th centuries)		Mari age Hammurabi (1728–1686)
1600			
1500	EIGHTEENTH DYNASTY (1552–1306)	LATE BRONZE AGE (1550–1200)	
1400	Thutmosis III (1490–1436)		
1300	Akhenaton (1364–1347) NINETEENTH DYNASTY (1306–1200) Sethos I (1305–1290) Rameses II (1290–1224)	Hebrews in Egypt	
1200	Mer-ni-ptah (1224–1211) TWENTIETH DYNASTY (1180–1069)	Exodus IRON AGE I (1200–1000)	
1100			
1000	TWENTY-FIRST DYNASTY (1069–935)	Philistines Federation	

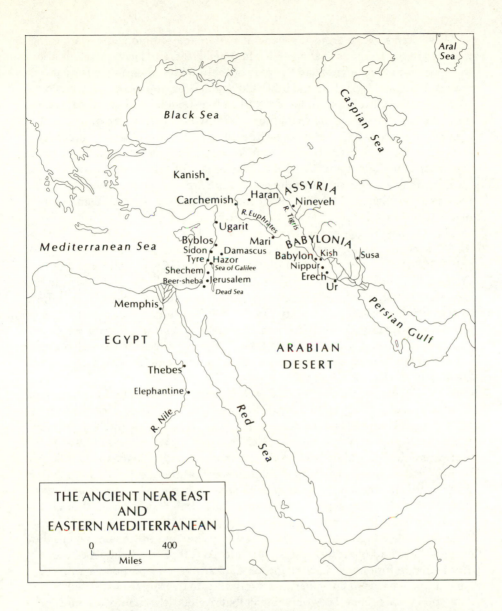

Aral Sea

Black Sea

Caspian Sea

Kanish.

Carchemish. Haran. ASSYRIA
•Nineveh

R. Euphrates

R. Tigris

•Ugarit

Mediterranean Sea

Byblos• Mari• BABYLONIA
Sidon• •Damascus
Tyre• •Hazor Babylon• Kish• •Susa
Shechem• Sea of Galilee Nippur•
Beer-sheba• •Jerusalem Erech• •
Dead Sea Ur•

Persian Gulf

Memphis•

EGYPT ARABIAN
DESERT

Thebes•

Elephantine•

R. Nile

Red Sea

THE ANCIENT NEAR EAST
AND
EASTERN MEDITERRANEAN

0   400
Miles

associated with them in the biblical material. From archaeological investigations carried out over the last century in the Near East and from the decipherment and study of many written materials, an ever enlarging picture of the social, political, economic, cultural, and religious life of that era and areas has begun to emerge. Although there are many disagreements with regard to particulars and large gaps remain in our knowledge, many scholars believe that various items in Genesis, for example, can be set firmly into this picture.

These items range from the general pattern of seminomadic wanderings reflected in the accounts dealing with Abraham, Isaac, and Jacob to details about the nature of their religion and the type of their deities, their name formations, marriage customs, adoption and inheritance practices, and other social customs. Many of these customs seem linked with similar familial and social patterns in the northern Mesopotamian cities of Mari (which was at its height in the eighteenth century B.C.E.) and Nuzi (fifteenth century B.C.E.), where archaeologists have found thousands of written records that have enabled them to reconstruct many aspects of the life of that time. All this helps to confirm the tradition that Mesopotamia was the homeland of the patriarchal ancestors of the Israelites (see Genesis 11:26–32 and Joshua 24:2–3), even though their seminomadic lives caused them to leave little imprint behind them.

The bondage in and escape from Egypt have been set securely in the time of the Nineteenth Dynasty in Egypt during the long reign of Pharoah Rameses II (1290–1224 B.C.E.) and possibly during the shorter reigns of Seti I and Mer-ne-Ptah which bracket it. In this period new building projects were begun in the Egyptian delta region where the Nile branches into several channels as it flows to the Mediterranean Sea. Located in the northeastern delta are the cities of Pithom and Raamses, which are named in Exodus as the cities on which the Israelites worked as slaves (Exodus 1:8–11). Egyptian records have also established that the Egyptians employed foreign slaves, some of whom came from Syria-Palestine to escape famine. Although Israelites are not mentioned specifically in these records, let alone a child or man Moses in the Egyptian royal court, this should not lead to a denial that one group of slaves escaped from its labor camps. Under Moses' leadership, it appears that a group did flee, probably across the Reed Sea (as it is called in Hebrew) into the wilderness of Sinai to the east where they would be well off the commercial and military roads followed by Egyptian traders and armies. Perhaps it was the stratagem of taking a course through the marshes in the eastern delta area that frustrated Egyptian pursuit. Historical probability suggests that some such event took place, though the details are not fully recoverable now.

In time these fugitives made their way into the land of Canaan where they seem to have had older ties and found kindred folk. Some schools of thought affirm that before entering the land of Canaan these same people suffered a generation of hardship in wilderness wandering, in the course of which they had a religious experience at Mount Sinai that welded them into a community bound in covenant to each other and to a god. This god was named Yahweh and appears to be linked with the sacred mountain upon which he appeared. Moses, who mediated the encounter between the people and the deity, is said to have met him earlier when he was living in that same region with his father-in-law, Jethro. Some suggest that Yahweh was the god of Midianite and Kenite tribal groups to which Jethro belonged. Through the efforts of Moses it appears possible that some early legal materials (based perhaps on some form of the Ten Commandments) were given to and accepted by the people. Following ancient Near Eastern models, these legal formulations were understood as commands of the deity. Thus a basic structure was given to the community, and a rudimentary administrative apparatus was formed (Exodus 18).

Other scholars suggest that the accounts of the trials in the wilderness, the events at Mount Sinai, and the conquest of the land of Canaan from the east reflect the experiences of different groups that only later came together in Canaan to form the nation-state of Israel. After the several groups were joined, their individual accounts of their experiences were slowly linked with the account of the group that had escaped Egyptian slavery, forming an extended narrative that runs from the patriarchs through Egyptian bondage and escape to the conquest of the land. In this way individual narratives became the common possession of all Israel and received in turn a larger all-Israel cast.

Debate over these differing points of view, as well as over many particulars relating to the prehistory of Israel, is very lively and is likely to remain so for some time. New evidence emerges slowly from the archaeologist's dig and the scholar's analysis of clay tablets and papyrus, while sides are drawn with a fervor that at times goes beyond evidence and supporting data. To attempt a more fully detailed reconstruction of Israel's prehistory is to enter an area of extreme speculation and confusion for a beginning student of the Old Testament.

In spite of the rich extrabiblical material at hand and still emerging, the biblical record itself must serve as a primary source for any historical reconstruction of the period. That there is a history to be reconstructed is not in doubt, but the historian must first determine the nature, intention, and context of his sources. These biblical sources, along with later Jewish writings, reflect distinct stages in the history of Israelite and Jewish religious traditions. They are often forms of story or myth that took their present shape many centuries after the events of which they tell. The biblical materials as we now have them are in some cases the result of a complex and lengthy process of retelling.

The overall picture presented in the books of Genesis through Joshua is often strikingly different from that offered by many scholars who would reconstruct Israel's prehistory from them, for these books contain material that is the product of individuals and groups who sought more than an accurate record of the past. They must be studied first and foremost as stories of the struggle of believing individuals and communities to express and live their faith in clear-sighted engagement with their present realities. They must be considered in light of the time, place, and persons who produced them, of others who re-formed and retold them, of others who treasured them, and of some who rejected them. Even though the story is rooted in actual historical events, those who remembered this past, recited the story, and relived it in varied ways were not antiquarians but people in search of identity, directions, and goals. Especially at times of crisis they recalled the past because it provided a rudder for safe passage through troubled waters.

This book will consider how a people's religious traditions informed and molded their character, values, institutions, and culture and shaped both their early and later history. It will study how, what, and why a people remembered, how their memories shaped their present, and how the remembering often reshaped the past. In short, it will show how certain individuals and communities were made out of words.

TRADITION AND CRISIS

A theological or confessional thrust gave the story of the fugitive slaves the unique potential to inform the lives of many in ancient Israel and early Judaism. Quite possibly this thrust was provided by Moses, and it may have been his most essential contribution to the tradition. For the claim was made as the story took shape that it was not human initiative and ingenuity that freed the slaves from Egypt, preserved them in the wilderness, and enabled them to take the land. In response to a cry of human distress, it was the god named Yahweh who did all this.

This claim is not to be judged by the canons of modern historical study; a deity is not a datum used for historical research and reconstruction as these are defined today. It is a theological interpretation placed on a narrative of events in human history, transforming the narrative into a story in which later generations found life and identity. That such a theological interpretation was made *is* a historical datum because people and their deeds are the materials with which historians work. As historians, we must acknowledge the claim that the god Yahweh freed the slaves without judging the claim as true or false. We will attempt rather to discover how, why, when, and where different Israelites and Jews understood this confession for themselves.

The confession made the narrative a sacred story. Over several centuries it would form and reform a federation of tribes in southern Palestine, which would then become an empire reaching from the border of Egypt to the River Euphrates and then become two small states holding tenuously to life on the edges of the mighty and expanding empires of Assyria and Babylon to the north and east. In new forms the story would later give structure and identity to communities of Jews who lived as exiles in the alien land of Babylon, and then to scattered communities in the Persian, Hellenistic, and Roman empires, as well as to some attempts to reconstruct the nation of old. The story is found in words of prophetic critique as well as priestly instruction and blessing. It inspired ancient theologians to produce epic narratives. It stood in the background of those who were taught by wise men and addressed by philosophers. In all this the sacred story was retold, reformed, reordered, expanded, and abridged time and again.

The complex history of this story of the deliverance from Egyptian slavery can be structured by centering attention on three crises in the history of the city of Jerusalem. The first crisis was the capture of the older Canaanite city of Jerusalem by King David, who, with his son Solomon, made it the administrative and cultural center of Israel by building there a temple and fixing a cult for the god Yahweh. This event climaxed a radical and extremely rapid transition that Israel underwent in the last decades of the eleventh century B.C.E. In a single generation Israel moved from a small and loose federation of semiindependent tribes in the hill country of lower Palestine to a tightly knit, centralized monarchy and empire with a new and impressive capital. Could the older forms of the sacred story that had united and supported a small collection of tribes expand with the empire?

As the empire grew under David, new groups of people were brought into Israel, each with its own stories and culture. What relations might older Israelites have with them? Suddenly it seemed that former enemies had become friends, and kindred folk at times seemed enemies. Could one speak of Egypt's villainies in the court of Solomon whose bride was an Egyptian princess? Was all this the god's doing as well? Was this part of his care for his chosen people? Was the deity of the federation also the god of the empire? What was his relation to the deities of other peoples with whom contact was now becoming close and vital? It would take centuries to form and fully digest the varied and sometimes conflicting responses to these questions. The old story would live on but in different forms and settings, and other stories would come to stand with it.

The second crisis occurred in the years 598–587 B.C.E. when Nebuchadnezzar, king of Babylon, captured, sacked, and destroyed Jerusalem. The temple was looted and leveled; many were killed or exiled; the land was incorporated into the provincial system of the Babylonian empire; and in these events the historical life of the ancient nation Israel ended. What now of the deity who had formed and preserved old Israel? What now of the chosen people, scattered and scared? Was Yahweh dead? Was he impotent before the might of Babylon and its gods? Did he not care, or was he angry? If so, what had caused such anger? And what about the land of promise, the gift of Yahweh?

For those in exile as well as for those remaining in the ruins of the lost homeland, there were questions after the initial shock had passed and the weeping subsided. What now? How shall we live? Can we worship without a temple? How can we retain our identity and unity? What institutions and structures can we build for this? What is to be our relation with the people among whom we now find ourselves? Again it took eventful centuries to respond to this crisis, the responses were many, and the stories were transformed.

12   By some they were rejected; others found in them new direction for the present and future.

The third crisis occurred in the years 66–70 C.E. when the province of Judaea, in the land that had once been the nation Israel, rebelled against its Roman masters. In the year 70, Jerusalem was again captured and destroyed; the temple, which had been rebuilt, was once again gone; and many of the old questions returned in a new context. Where was the hand of the deity in this? The revolt was sparked in part by some unique ways of retelling the old stories, by some remarkable interpretations of their god's actions in the history of the people. Because some of these had fragmented Judaism, however, they now seemed dangerous. How could they be blunted and guarded against in the future? How were Jews now to live under Roman authority? How could the god be served? How could identity be maintained? As before, some ways of telling and living the old stories were rejected and others were reaffirmed.

These three crises in the history of Jerusalem broke over the people with such force that they seemed to shatter the religious traditions of the past. They were periods of crisis not just because they resulted in radical changes in social, political, or economic structures but because the remembered past, the sacred story, had given these structures a vital religious foundation. We may well designate these crises by the Greek term *kairotic*—that is, as times filled with more than ordinary significance—because they not only raised new questions but changed the very terms in which the questions were asked and answered. They demanded rigorous self-scrutiny by individuals and communities alike. They made decisive action necessary to save or to restore the nation, the community, and the individual. New recitations of the sacred story were needed because the past could not now be remembered as before.

These three crises provide the framework for the chapters that follow. David's capture of Jerusalem opens Part 1. The crisis of 598–587 B.C.E. provides the transition between Parts 1 and 2, bringing to an end the story of ancient Israel and opening that of early Judaism. The third crisis closes Part 2. The several attempts to deal with these crises and with other events will be discussed throughout the book. In this way the biblical and other early Judaic traditions are treated above all as religious tradition, as the living, enlivening remembrance of a people's past.

Not all material in the Old Testament deals directly with these crises, nor does all retell or build upon a form of the sacred story. Israel and early Judaism were too rich and varied in their religious and cultural expression to fit fully into any system. But by centering attention on the essential stories, by considering their formation, development, reformation, and decay as direct or indirect reactions to the three crises in Jerusalem's history, we plunge to the normative heart of Israelite and early Jewish religious tradition.

Toward the end of a course sequence on ancient Israelite and early Jewish religious traditions a student once remarked that "they were always rewriting their history." In studying this process we will encounter a particular relationship between the remembered past and the experienced present. It is one in which the past informs the present, while at the same time the nature and form of the remembrance of the past is a product of the present and determined by it. Our study will uncover some distinct patterns of memory.

BIBLIOGRAPHIC NOTE

This introductory Bibliographic Note lists general works dealing with the Old Testament, Apocrypha, and related writings and with the methods employed in studying them. The notes appended to individual chapters will be confined to selected works treating the specific topics covered in those chapters, though, for full coverage of the subject, reference should also be made to the works presented here. A very useful set of volumes covering the full range of biblical studies is *The Interpreter's Dictionary of the Bible*, 4 vols., and its *Supplementary Volume*, ed. George A. Buttrick (Nashville: Abingdon Press, 1962 and 1976). Many specific articles from this work will be cited in the notes following each chapter, but other useful articles are to be found there as well.

Translations of the Bible

> *The Jerusalem Bible.* Garden City, N.Y.: Doubleday & Co., 1966. A translation by Roman Catholic scholars.

> *The New American Bible.* Translated by the Catholic Biblical Association of America. New York: P. J. Kenedy & Sons, 1970.

> *The New English Bible with the Apocrypha: Oxford Study Edition.* Edited by Samuel Sandmel. New York: Oxford University Press, 1976.

> *The New Oxford Annotated Bible with the Apocrypha: Expanded Edition.* Edited by Herbert G. May and Bruce M. Metzger. New York: Oxford University Press, 1977. A study edition of the Revised Standard Version.

Ancient Near Eastern Sources for Bible Study

> Pritchard, James B., ed. *Ancient Near Eastern Texts relating to the Old Testament.* 3d ed., supp. Princeton: Princeton University Press, 1969.

> ———. *The Ancient Near East in Pictures relating to the Old Testament.* Princeton: Princeton University Press, 1965.

> ———. *The Ancient Near East: An Anthology of Texts and Pictures.* Princeton: Princeton University Press, 1965. Selections from the above two studies, handy for classroom use.

Methods Used in Bible Study

> Coats, George W. "Tradition Criticism, OT." In *The Interpreter's Dictionary of the Bible: Supplementary Volume*, pp. 912–14. Nashville: Abingdon Press, 1976.

> Habel, Norman. *Literary Criticism of the Old Testament.* Philadelphia: Fortress Press, 1971.

Hayes, John H., ed. *Old Testament Form Criticism*. San Antonio: Trinity University Press, 1974.

Klein, Ralph W. *Textual Criticism of the Old Testament*. Philadelphia: Fortress Press, 1974.

Koch, Klaus. *The Growth of the Biblical Tradition: The Form Critical Method*. New York: Charles Scribner's Sons, 1969.

Miller, J. Maxwell. *The Old Testament and the Historian*. Philadelphia: Fortress Press, 1976.

Rast, Walter E. *Tradition, History, and the Old Testament*. Philadelphia: Fortress Press, 1972.

Roberts, B. J. "Text, OT." In *The Interpreter's Dictionary of the Bible*, vol. 4, pp. 580–94. Nashville: Abingdon Press, 1962.

Robertson, D. "Literature, The Bible as." In *The Interpreter's Dictionary of the Bible: Supplementary Volume*, pp. 547–51. Nashville: Abingdon Press, 1976.

————. *The Old Testament and the Literary Critic*. Philadelphia: Fortress Press, 1977.

Thompson, J. A. "Textual Criticism, OT." In *The Interpreter's Dictionary of the Bible: Supplementary Volume*, pp. 886–91. Nashville: Abingdon Press, 1976.

Tucker, Gene M. *Form Criticism of the Old Testament*. Philadelphia: Fortress Press, 1971.

————. "Form Criticism, OT." In *The Interpreter's Dictionary of the Bible: Supplementary Volume*, pp. 342–45. Nashville: Abingdon Press, 1976.

Literary Introductions to the Old Testament and Apocrypha

Eissfeldt, Otto. *The Old Testament: An Introduction*. New York: Harper & Row, 1965. The standard work in the field.

Fohrer, Georg. *Introduction to the Old Testament*. Nashville: Abingdon Press, 1968. A useful revision of an older work by Ernst Sellin.

Kaiser, Otto. *Introduction to the Old Testament: A Presentation of Its Results and Problems*. Minneapolis: Augsburg, 1974.

Soggin, J. Alberto. *Introduction to the Old Testament*. Philadelphia: Westminster Press, 1976.

Weiser, Artur. *The Old Testament: Its Formation and Development*. New York: Association Press, 1961. A work that has had great influence on scholarship.

Background on the World of Ancient Israel and Early Judaism

Aharoni, Yohanan. *The Land of the Bible: A Historical Geography*. Philadelphia: Westminster Press, 1967.

————, and Avi-Yonah, Michael. *The Macmillan Bible Atlas*. New York: Macmillan Co., 1968. Comprehensive and very attractive.

Baly, Denis. *The Geography of the Bible*. New York: Harper & Row, 1974.

de Vaux, Roland. *Ancient Israel: Its Life and Institutions*. New York: McGraw-Hill, 1961. A standard reference work by a great French archaeologist and biblical scholar.

Gaster, Theodor H. *Myth, Legend, and Custom in the Old Testament*. New York: Harper & Row, 1969.

Gray, John. *Archaeology and the Old Testament World*. London: Thomas Nelson & Sons, 1962.

The Interpreter's Dictionary of the Bible. Edited by George A. Buttrick. Nashville: Abingdon Press, 1962 (Volumes 1–4), 1976 (Supplementary Volume). An illustrated encyclopedia with many excellent articles.

Kenyon, Kathleen. *Archaeology in the Holy Land*. New York: Praeger, 1970.

May, Herbert G. *Oxford Bible Atlas*. London: Oxford University Press, 1962.

National Geographic Society. *Everyday Life in Bible Times*. Washington, D.C.: National Geographic Society, n.d.

Noth, Martin. *The Old Testament World*. Philadelphia: Fortress Press, 1966.

Pedersen, Johannes. *Israel: Its Life and Culture*. London: Oxford University Press, 1926 (Volumes 1–2), 1940 (Volumes 3–4). A useful focus on the psychological characteristics of ancient Israel.

Thomas, D. Winton, ed. *Archaeology and Old Testament Study*. London: Clarendon Press, 1967.

Wolff, Hans Walter. *Anthropology of the Old Testament*. Philadelphia: Fortress Press, 1974.

Wright, G. Ernest. *Biblical Archaeology*. Philadelphia: Westminster Press, 1962.

Histories of Ancient Israel and Early Judaism

Albright, W. F. *The Biblical Period from Abraham to Ezra*. New York: Harper & Row, 1963. A brief hand-survey that is useful if dated and polemical at points.

Bright, John. *A History of Israel*. Philadelphia: Westminster Press, 1972. A standard in the field reflecting the so-called Albright point of view.

de Vaux, Roland. *The Early History of Israel: To the Period of the Judges*. Philadelphia: Westminster Press, 1976.

Hayes, John H., and Miller, J. Maxwell, eds. *Israelite and Judaean History*. Philadelphia: Westminster Press, 1977. Contributions by several experts, most up to date, providing extensive bibliography.

Herrmann, Siegfried. *A History of Israel in Old Testament Times*. Philadelphia: Fortress Press, 1975.

Noth, Martin. *The History of Israel*. New York: Harper & Brothers, 1960. A second standard in the field providing a perspective distinct from that of Bright.

Orlinsky, Harry M. *Ancient Israel*. Ithaca, N.Y.: Cornell University Press, 1960. A brief overview.

Old Testament Religion and Theology

Albright, W. F. *From the Stone Age to Christianity*. Garden City, N. Y.: Doubleday & Co., 1957.

Childs, Brevard S. *Biblical Theology in Crisis*. Philadelphia: Westminster Press, 1970. Review of past theologies and introduction of a new approach called "canonical criticism."

Cross, Frank Moore. *Canaanite Myth and Hebrew Epic: Essays in the History and the Religion of Israel*. Cambridge, Mass.: Harvard University Press, 1973.

Dentan, Robert C. *Preface to Old Testament Theology*. New York: Seabury Press, 1963.

Eichrodt, Walther. *Theology of the Old Testament*. Philadelphia: Westminster Press, 1961 (Volume 1), 1967 (Volume 2). A classic.

Fohrer, Georg. *History of Israelite Religion*. Nashville: Abingdon Press, 1972.

Hasel, Gerhard. *Old Testament Theology: Basic Issues in the Current Debate*. Grand Rapids, Mich.: William B. Eerdmans Publishing Co., 1972. This and the Dentan volume offer reviews of past theologies and suggestions for the future.

Kaufmann, Yehezkel. *The Religion of Israel: From Its Beginnings to the Babylonian Exile*. Chicago: University of Chicago Press, 1960. Abridgment of a basic work by an Israeli scholar.

Kraus, Hans-Joachim. *Worship in Israel*. Richmond, Va.: John Knox Press, 1966. A history of worship and the cult of ancient Israel and early Judaism.

McKenzie, John L. *A Theology of the Old Testament*. Garden City, N.Y.: Doubleday & Co., 1974.

Ringgren, Helmer. *Israelite Religion*. Philadelphia: Fortress Press, 1966.

Rowley, H. H. *Worship in Ancient Israel: Its Form and Meaning*. Philadelphia: Fortress Press, 1967.

von Rad, Gerhard. *Old Testament Theology*. New York: Harper & Brothers, 1962 (Volume 1), 1965 (Volume 2). Most important.

————. *The Problem of the Hexateuch and Other Essays*. New York: McGraw-Hill, 1966.

Vriezen, T. C. *The Religion of Ancient Israel*. Philadelphia: Westminster Press, 1967.

Wright, G. Ernest. *The Old Testament and Theology*. New York: Harper & Row, 1969.

The Wilderness as seen from the base of Mount Sinai

Nowitz/FPG

PART 1
THE RELIGIOUS TRADITIONS OF ANCIENT ISRAEL

The land of the Old Testament is not a gentle land. It is a land of stretching sands and rocky outcroppings laid bare by wind and sun, a scorched land with only a few scattered sites made green by the miracle of water. Such a place yields grudgingly to human aspirations, and any blessing it bestows is cause for wonder. Here three of the world's great religions were born: Judaism, Christianity, and Islam.

This book tells of the oldest of those faiths and of the ideas that inspired its adherents. In the pictures that accompany the text, one glimpses something of their physical world: the works wrought by their hands to sustain both life and faith, the spiritual and temporal enemies they faced, the contending civilizations that rose and fell about them . . . and the harsh, loved land they looked upon each day.

**Colossi of Ramesses II forming facade
of Great Temple at Abu Simbel**

Reitz/Leo de Wys

**A bend in the Jordan River, believed
near the site of Christ's baptism**

Gerling/FPG

**Fishermen on the River Jordan where it
flows into the Sea of Galilee**

Religious News Service

Stone bas relief of warrior on camel, ca. 1000 B.C.E.

Walters Art Gallery, Baltimore

Desert nomads traverse the land today as their forebears did in Biblical times

Raynor/Leo de Wys

Clay cuneiform tablet, part of the Epic of Gilgamesh, which relates the story of a Great Flood, similar to the account of Noah, ca. 17th century B.C.E.

Reproduced by courtesy of the Trustees of the British Museum

"Horned" altar of limestone from Megiddo, ca. 900 B.C.E.

Courtesy of the Oriental Institute, University of Chicago

Desert nomads gathered at Jacob's Well, Shechem, photographed ca. 1870

The Bettmann Archive

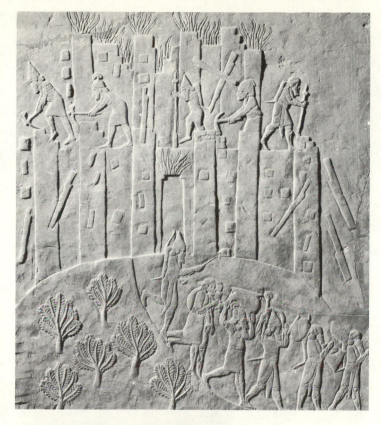

The road from Beersheba to Sodom. The Dead Sea, almost 1300 feet below sea level, can be seen at the bottom of the valley.

Goldman/FPG

Stone mold, at least 3500 years old, of figurine of Astarte, Canaanite fertility goddess

By courtesy of the Israel Department of Antiquities and Museums

Gold-plated bronze figure of Ba'al, Canaanite storm and fertility god

Courtesy of the Oriental Institute, University of Chicago

Assyrian troops destroy a city in this relief from Ashurbanipal's palace, 7th century, B.C.E.

Reproduced by courtesy of the Trustees of the British Museum

Siloam tunnel, built in the 7th century B.C.E. to channel water into Jerusalem in preparation for a possible Assyrian siege

By courtesy of the Israel Department of Antiquities and Museums

Part of a bas relief of King Ashurbanipal, Assyria's last king, 7th century, B.C.E.

Reproduced by courtesy of the Trustees of the British Musuem

Absalom's tomb

Reitz/Leo de Wys

PROLOGUE TO PART 1

Primary readings: *Deuteronomy 26; Joshua 24*
                          Joshua 1–24
                          Judges 1–16

ORIGINS OF ANCIENT ISRAEL

The origins of the ancient nation of Israel are obscure, and its composition, even at the earliest stages, is complex. Tradition suggests that the nation can trace its bloodline back through many generations to twelve sons of a man named Jacob (who was also called Israel), himself the grandson of Abraham who first roamed over the land that the nation would later occupy. But historical probability and an ever enlarging picture of Palestine in the Middle and Late Bronze Age (2000–1200 B.C.E.) combine with biblical tradition to suggest that the composition of earliest Israel was richly diverse and that the story of its origins was more complex than that of fugitive slaves fleeing Egyptian bondage and suddenly conquering Canaan to seize the land for themselves.

To most of those who study the archaeological and literary data it has become apparent that the source of earliest Israel's unity and common identity was not blood kinship. Indeed, many historians suggest that it is impossible to isolate a political, social, cultural, or religious entity that can be called Israel before the actual formation of the state at the end of the Late Bronze Age in southern Palestine. That elements of later Israel existed earlier and elsewhere, perhaps in some instances bearing the name Israel, is not doubted, but the new compound that these elements came to form is believed to have had no prior existence apart from the land of Canaan. Thus, despite religious traditions that trace the seed of Israel back to Abraham, historians of ancient Israel, and especially of its religious traditions, must begin with the formation of a distinctive national and political entity in the land of Canaan toward the end of the thirteenth century B.C.E. The question of Israel's earliest composition and structure is rooted in the problem of the conquest, and several divergent reconstructions have been proposed for that event.

Theories about the Conquest

A Process of Slow Migration   One point of view, perhaps most firmly associated with the German biblical scholar Martin Noth, rejects the picture of the conquest gained from the Book of Joshua, which is said to be a later idealization from an all-Israelite perspective. Noth holds that over centuries, and from several directions, groups of seminomadic pastoralists settled into the agricultural lands of southern Palestine, taking first the marginal land of the hill country and later the richer land of the valleys, coastal foothills, and plain. In the Book of Genesis the patriarchs Abraham, Isaac, and Jacob are depicted as wanderers through the land, setting roots slowly and living largely in peace with the native Canaanite inhabitants. The political structure assumed by these newcomers, the so-called Twelve Tribes, took shape only after settlement. Some tribes flourished and vanished before others had even taken shape, and some older tribes merged with newer groups.

Each of these diverse components of early Israel brought with them their particular heritage, their stories of their past, their religious traditions and practices. As different groups settled and met others in the land of Canaan, their varied traditions were combined, reworked, unified, and harmonized into the all-Israelite composition now found in the books of Genesis through Joshua. The rich tapestry that was then created is now revealing parts of its diversity to the critical methods of biblical scholarship.

External Attack   A second school of thought, fully developed in the historical studies of the American scholar John Bright, gives more credence to the picture presented in the Book of Joshua, especially as this picture relates to archaeological evidence. This school of thought admits that the process was more complex than that presented in Joshua but affirms that the events depicted there —the sudden conquest of Jerico, Ai, and Bethel and the defense of Gibeon, followed by the conquest of the south and then the north—essentially reflect historical reality. Certainly not all who later composed Israel were fugitives from Egypt with Moses and Joshua, for the wilderness could never have supported so many.

Those who came as a conquering army out of the wilderness from the east were joined by kindred groups already in the land and settled in places that therefore had not to be conquered (for example, the city of Shechem, the important religious and political center in the central hill country). However, a significant group of people did conquer much of the land of Canaan in a series of quick effective military thrusts under the leadership of Joshua, upon whom authority lay after the death of Moses. This wilderness group was already organized into a political structure that recognized the existence of several tribal groupings and was united in a common covenant with the deity Yahweh through the mediation of Moses. Into their structure were absorbed the kindred people already in the land. Archaeological evidence of a sudden and violent destruction in the thirteenth century of several sites, which were rebuilt in some cases by a people with an inferior quality of private and public structures and common artifacts, is further witness to this rapid and violent conquest.

Internal Uprising A third reconstruction of the conquest recently brought forth by George Mendenhall has found tentative acceptance among some scholars and seems at first glance to be a combination of the two theories presented above. Mendenhall brings together an extensive group already in the land of Canaan with a small but vital group of fugitive slaves who brought with them an account of deliverance from bondage by the god Yahweh and a remarkable political structure that centered in covenant allegiance to this deity.

This reconstruction overturns several assumptions supporting the first two theories, however. First, the previous theories both develop an antithesis between the seminomadic herdsman, his desire for rich land and a settled life, and the farmer. While acknowledging that such tensions did exist (note Cain and Abel in Genesis 3), Mendenhall suggests that the pastoralist and agriculturalist stood together in common antagonism against the city dweller (Cain and Abel were *brothers*). Second, Mendenhall challenges the presupposition that the people of Israel came into the land from somewhere else. In his view the distinction between Israelite and Canaanite was not based on divergent racial, linguistic, or historical origins but on religious and political allegiance.

Mendenhall observes that Late Bronze Age Palestine was composed of a number of semiindependent city-states—that is, walled cities often built on hills, controlling a range of agricultural land and villages beneath them—in which a sharp social stratification separated the king, court, and urban population from the rural farmer and herdsman. But the city lived to a great extent off the labor of the latter, who saw increasingly less benefit coming his way in return. For the peasant farmer the city and its royal administration were often represented by the tax official who took most of his produce and left him little on which to survive, especially when intercity warfare not only increased taxation but ravaged the countryside. The gain in royal prestige that might come from such wars meant little to country folk.

Thus there emerged within the Canaanite population of Palestine an alienated element that Mendenhall identifies with the Habiru mentioned in contemporary Near Eastern documents. The term *Habiru* is related to the word *Hebrew* and is found in texts from a number of dates and places in the Near East. It designates a person or group that stood outside the normative legal and social structures and can be translated as "outlaw." Habiru were those who had been driven or had withdrawn their allegiance from the political and legal system in which they lived. Sometimes the withdrawal was physical, sometimes it was in terms of values and loyalties.

Into this volatile setting came a small group of fugitives from Egyptian slavery. It was to the alienated peasant farmers, with their burden of oppressive servitude to the city-state king and his court, that they appealed with their story of a god who delivers his own from an alien bondage, and it was an appeal reinforced by initial successes in combat with kings east of the Jordan (Numbers 21–24) and in defense of the allies from Gibeon (Joshua 10). In this story of release from slavery the Habiru saw prefigured their own experience, condition, and aspirations. The story ignited a revolt. Some city-states were overthrown; territory was captured from others; a few survived unharmed. The result was the formation in southern Palestine of a new religious/political entity called Israel, even though some Canaanite urban enclaves, such as Jerusalem, remained. Israelites were those who gave their allegiance to the god Yahweh who overturned the established social structure; Canaanites remained loyal to the city-state king and to the religious and political structures that supported him.

Shape of the Federation

Whatever theory on the origin of ancient Israel seems most compelling—and scholarship is likely to be divided on this for the foreseeable future—there is now broad agreement that the nation's earliest form was that of a loosely bound federation of tribes. Some recognizable entity called Israel must have existed in Palestine by about 1230 B.C.E., because it is mentioned in a victory hymn of the Egyptian Pharaoh Mer-ne-Ptah from that year. A careful reading of several units that are strung together in the Book of Judges suggests that, even when threatened by destruction from peoples around and among them, each Israelite tribe relied on its own resources and leadership, at best receiving aid from neighboring tribes that were also endangered. The song of Deborah in Judges 5 calls pointed attention to those tribes that did not respond to her rallying summons (Judges 5:15–17, 5:23). Each tribe had largely to hold and defend its own territory, and one tribe, that of Dan, lost its original place to the Philistines, a group that entered southwestern Palestine at about this same period and also sought a place for settlement.

Little can be said of intratribal political, social, and legal structure during this period. Those persons designated "judges" appear for the most part to have been charismatic leaders who rose to the occasion as if inspired and led their

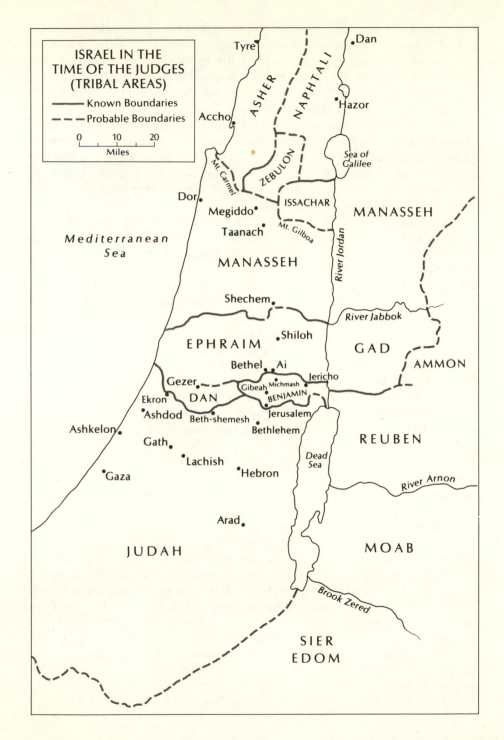

ISRAEL IN THE
TIME OF THE JUDGES
(TRIBAL AREAS)

—— Known Boundaries

- - - Probable Boundaries

0   10   20

Miles

Tyre

Dan

ASHER

NAPHTALI

Accho

Hazor

Mt. Carmel

ZEBULON

Sea of
Galilee

Dor

ISSACHAR

MANASSEH

Megiddo

Taanach

Mt. Gilboa

Mediterranean
Sea

MANASSEH

River Jordan

Shechem

River Jabbok

Shiloh

EPHRAIM

GAD

Bethel   Ai

AMMON

Gezer

Jericho

Ekron

Gibeah Michmash

DAN

BENJAMIN

Ashdod

Beth-shemesh

Jerusalem

Ashkelon

Bethlehem

REUBEN

Gath

Dead
Sea

Lachish

Hebron

River Arnon

Gaza

Arad

MOAB

JUDAH

Brook Zered

SIER
EDOM

endangered tribes through some immediate crisis. Thus Othniel of Caleb's clan is said to have prevailed over an otherwise unknown Cushanrishathaim from Mesopotamia (Judges 3:7–11), and Ehud the Benjaminite deceived and slew Eglon, king of the Moabites, who with the help of others had harassed the tribe of Benjamin (Judges 3:12–30). In Judges 4 we have a fuller account of the victorious engagement of Deborah and Barak, from the central tribe of Ephraim, with the Canaanites who remained in southern Palestine around the city of Hazor. Judges 5 preserves a victory song, among the oldest surviving pieces of Hebrew poetry, that was sung in celebration of this important event. Judges 6–8 presents several incidents from the life of Gideon (who also bears the Canaanite name Jerubbaal), centering about his defeat of camel-riding Midianite raiders from the east who plagued his kinfolk.

Further indications of the turmoil of the federation period are found in the report of an abortive but destructive attempt by Gideon's son Abimelech to rule as king over the important city of Shechem (Judges 9). Jepthah, of whom we learn next, was of the territory of Gilead east of the Jordan River and, before being summoned to aid his people in their conflict with the neighboring Ammonites, appears to have been an outlaw held in disgrace by his family. His unfortunate oath, its fulfillment, and his conflict with the Ephraimites suggest something of the desperateness of the situation he faced and of the inner tensions of the federation of tribes (Judges 11–12).

In Samson we meet another sort of leader from this early period in Israel's history. Said to be a Nazirite, which bound him to abstain from cutting his hair and from drinking wine, Samson's special vows and manner of life set him apart as devoted to his god (Judges 13:2–7; 16:17). In Judges 14–16 he appears as a sort of guerrilla fighter for his people and god, single-handedly taking on the Philistines who were encroaching on the territory of the tribe of Dan. A number of skirmishes as well as more friendly contacts occur, of which the outcome is twofold: the Philistines are chastened and held at bay, but in the struggle Samson loses his life at his own hands. Samson was a well-intended but only partly effective leader, certainly not one to whom the future stability of a people could be entrusted.

Each tribe seems to have had complete autonomy with regard to its internal life, with leadership and legal procedures determined by ancient local practice and custom. It is possible that the persons called "minor judges" provided continuing if limited intertribal authority and legal guidance (Judges 10:1–5; 12:8–15), although the nature of their activity is not specified. In sum, there appears to have been little effective central authority binding the tribes to a common purpose, structure, and mutual aid from about 1200–1000 B.C.E. Like the early United States of America under the Articles of Confederation immediately following the Revolution, each unit pursued the course it found best, while a force for disintegration was ever present. Yet the Israelite federation lasted about two centuries; the federation of the United States, but a few years.

Furthermore, the topography of southern Palestine did not lend itself to political unification. The older Canaanite city-states were never united into a national structure.

What held this loose federation together for the first two centuries of Israel's life? What was it that overcame the fragmenting geographic and political forces that had hitherto conditioned the structure of Palestine? In the turbulent years marking the transition from the Bronze to the Early Iron Age (1200–1000 B.C.E.) in Palestine, forces for fragmentation seemed to grow even stronger. The Near Eastern power centers of Egypt and Mesopotamia appeared impotent in that period, and Palestine seemed up for grabs among Israelites, Philistines, remaining Canaanites, the smaller nations of Edom and Moab, the Ammonites, and even Bedouin Midianite raiders. What united these Israelite tribes long enough to permit them to exist as a federation for two centuries of internal and external upheaval that would finally bring about a transformation resulting in a monarchy and empire?

TRIBAL UNITY AND RELIGIOUS TRADITIONS

The answer to these questions lay in a story that spoke of a god who delivered slaves from bondage, formed them into a community, preserved them as his chosen people in the face of grave dangers, and in turn commanded their full allegiance as their only sovereign. It was this story, in Mendenhall's view, that empowered the peasants to rise up in independence from their oppressors. Forms of the story, which are at the heart of the Jewish Passover even today, are rooted in certain reconstructable events that were part of the history of some of those who would come to comprise the nation Israel. We must now consider how the story was recited by, how it informed and enlivened, that nation during its initial federation period.

Early Creedlike Formulations

In biblical studies a method called *form criticism* seeks to isolate and define small or larger whole units that have similar structure. The form critic analyzes that structure in terms of its component parts and their interrelations and then attempts to describe the life setting of that form and its function in that setting. Critical analysis of chapter 26 of Deuteronomy and chapter 24 of Joshua has isolated short creedlike recitals of the basic story of Israel's origins, and we will here consider some of its results.

The critical events in Israel's story are recited in just five verses in Deuteronomy (26:5–9); in Joshua the recital is extended to twelve verses (24:2–13) as each central theme or event is fleshed out with a few more details; but the extent of each recital is the same. Although now set in context with legal or historical material, each creedlike recital finds its most immediate association with some form of cultic activity. Deuteronomy 26 is set within the ceremony of offering the first fruits of the harvest at the altar of Yahweh; Joshua 24 is found in what appears to be a renewal at the city of Shechem of the covenant made at Mount Sinai. In each case the recital has a programmatic function similar to the recital of a creed in certain contemporary forms of worship; that is, it sets the immediate occasion against a broader background that provides the basis for the relation between worshiper and deity. The creed supplies the vital story (myth) that gives shape and life to the acts (ritual or ceremony) engaged in as an act of worship.

The Sacred Story

Each creedlike recital begins with a reference to the patriarchal forebears from whom Israel traces its line. In Deuteronomy 26 there is but the terse mention of "a wandering Aramaean" who is Jacob. But in Joshua 24, Abraham, Isaac, and Jacob are all mentioned along with such ancillary figures as Terah, Abraham's father; Abraham's brother Nahor; and Jacob's brother Esau. At the heart of each recital is the bondage in Egypt, the slaves' cry of distress, and the deliverance or exodus with signs and wonders upon Egypt and pharaoh. Again, Joshua 24 enlarges the brief references in Deuteronomy with specific mention of the pursuit of the fugitives by Egyptian chariotry, the darkness that fell on them, and the sudden destruction of the Egyptian host at the sea. In each recital, however, the period of wilderness wandering is passed over quickly, which stands in striking contrast to the later fully developed form of the story in the books of Genesis through Joshua.

The recital concludes with the taking of the land of Canaan and settlement in this land "flowing with milk and honey." Joshua 24 is once again fuller, with reference to the defeat of the Amorite kingdoms in the area east of the Jordan River, to the ineffective curses of Balaam, and to the crossing of the Jordan near Jericho. Yet the basic themes are the same in each: forefathers, Egyptian slavery, deliverance, wilderness passage, and conquest of Canaan; this is the skeletal structure upon which further details are hung. It is a story that ranges over centuries, but it revolves about the central theme of oppression and freedom.

As befits a creedlike recital of a sacred story, the subject of most of the important verbs of summons, response, deliverance, sustenance, and giving is the deity. Abraham, Isaac, Jacob, even Moses and Aaron, indeed the people as a whole are all secondary. Moses is not named in Deuteronomy 26, nor is Abraham; Joshua is named in neither recital. Yahweh alone stands forth in these creeds. It is Yahweh who is said to have called Abraham from Mesopotamia and led him through Canaan, Yahweh who heard the cry of distress from the brickworks in Egypt, who freed the slaves, who overwhelmed the Egyptians at the sea with signs and terrors, who took and gave the land of Canaan to Israel.

And *I* gave them into your hand. And *I* sent the hornet before you, which drove them out before you, the two kings of the Amorites; *it was not by your sword or by your bow. I* gave you a land on which you had not labored, and cities which you had not built, and you dwell therein; you eat the fruit of vineyards and of olive yards which you did not plant.

(Joshua 24:11–13, italics added)

These recitals are in essence theological, dealing not just with the actions of men and women but with the events through which Yahweh became the god of Israel. This is not secular human history but sacred history, a narrative not of human initiative and action but of the intersection of the divine and the human. It is this story of Yahweh that Joshua and the groups following him brought into the land they conquered, that traveled with one or another group of seminomads as it slowly migrated into the land, and that served as the spark with which a small but critical core of fugitive slaves ignited a revolution in southern Palestine at the end of the Late Bronze Age.

Covenant Renewal

Another striking feature in these credal confessions is the appearance within the recitation of sudden shifts from past to present, from objective to subjective, from dead ancestors to the living community. There is a marked jump in Deuteronomy 26 from the "wandering Aramaean who went down to Egypt" to the "us" of the remainder of the unit: "And the Egyptians treated *us* harshly, and afflicted *us*. . . . Then *we* cried to Yahweh. . . . Yahweh heard *our* voice, and saw *our* affliction, *our* toil, and *our* oppression; and Yahweh brought *us* out of Egypt" (italics added). This same interchange is found in Joshua 24, which also begins with objective reference to past generations, then moves to the subjective present, then back, then forward again:

And I sent Moses and Aaron, and I plagued Egypt with what I did in the midst of it; and afterwards I brought *you* out. Then I brought *your fathers* out of Egypt, and *you* came to the sea; and the Egyptians pursued *your fathers*. . . . And when they cried to Yahweh, he put darkness between *you* and the Egyptians, and made the sea come upon them and cover them; and *your eyes saw what I did to Egypt.*

(Joshua 24:5–7, italics added)

The full narrative of Genesis through Joshua makes it clear in several places that, of the generation that left Egypt, all but Joshua and Caleb perished in the wilderness and that only their descendants, a new generation, entered Canaan (Numbers 14:26–38; Deuteronomy 1:34–40; Joshua 5:2–7). The shorter creeds may reflect a tradition in which the generation of the exodus was that of the conquest as well. That these creeds appear to stand in tension with the larger framework in which they are now embedded may be due to the combination of different versions of Israel's origins, but this fails to account for the several interchanges found within only three verses of Joshua 24.

Approaching the problem from another perspective, it has been noted that both creeds are set in the midst of cultic acts. Joshua 24, for example, is set in what appears to be a renewal of the covenant first made with Yahweh at Sinai in the wilderness. Several scholars suggest that underlying this presentation is a pattern for a regular, perhaps annual, form of cultic service in which the covenant that bound Israel to Yahweh and Israelites to one another was renewed and taken up afresh. It has become a commonplace in discussion of the federation period to refer to the twelve-tribe structure and unity as an *amphictyony*, a Greek word denoting a six- or twelve-member league of tribes, cities, or other human groups. Such amphictyonies were bound into a distinct unit by common allegiance and service to a cultic center and deity. In short, an amphictyony was a religious as well as a political structure, and during the two-century period of the federation Israel was such an amphictyony, united in its allegiance to and service of the god Yahweh and his cult.

It is not easy to pinpoint the location of this cult, nor is it certain that the cult was ever restricted to one place. At one time or another, Gilgal, Shechem, Bethel, and Shiloh seem to have provided centers for cultic reaffirmation of allegiance to Yahweh and the covenant. But these and no doubt other creedlike formulations of the sacred story once stood as part of a service of covenant renewal that took place at these sites. The creedlike formulations functioned as the cult's myths, informing the cultic actions and ritual of the service and providing the foundation for the relationship between Yahweh and Israel that the service expressed and effected anew. At each service of renewal new generations and others who entered the sphere of ancient Israel became Israelites, entering for themselves the covenant that bound Israel in allegiance to its god.

The definite form of this covenant and the service of its renewal became clear to scholars when Mendenhall compared Joshua 24 (as well as other segments of the Bible, such as Exodus 20–24 and the Book of Deuteronomy) with ancient Hittite vassal treaties. In the Late Bronze Age the Hittites formed a powerful kingdom in much of what is today Turkey, and treaties exist in which the Hittite king bound other rulers to him in a suzerain-vassal relationship. These were not treaties between equals. The two parties did not stand in a parity relationship, and only the vassal explicitly took obligations upon himself. The structure of the treaties is revealing.

They begin with a preamble which introduces the suzerain: "Thus says so-and-so, the great king, king of the Hittites. . . ." (Compare Joshua 24:2: "Thus says Yahweh, the God of Israel.") This leads into a historical prologue reviewing the previous relations between the two parties, with emphasis placed on the suzerain's benevolent deeds on behalf of the vassal. The review of past relations is so cast as to evoke feelings of gratitude and dependence in the vassal. This is precisely the nature and thrust of Joshua 24:2–13, the recital of the sacred story, which tells of Yahweh's past gracious actions for Israel's benefit.

Following the historical prologue are the stipulations of the treaty, the definition of specifics in the future relationship between vassal and suzerain and between different vassals of the same suzerain. Alliances with other rulers, for example, are prohibited in the strongest terms. With this one might compare Joshua 24:14: "Now therefore fear Yahweh, and serve him in sincerity and in faithfulness; put away the gods which your fathers served beyond the River, and in Egypt, and serve Yahweh." This is the only stipulation in Joshua 24, but some have suggested that at this point an early form of the Ten Commandments (see Exodus 20:1–17; Deuteronomy 5:6–21) might have found recital. The stipulations form the heart and substance of the treaty, but it is because of the relationship already acknowledged in the historical recital of the suzerain's past acts that the vassal freely accepts the stipulations as binding (see especially Joshua 24:16–18). Thus the ethical thrust of early Israelite religious tradition, the moral quality revealed in the stipulations of Yahweh for his people, is a function of this covenant form by which Israelites bound themselves to Yahweh and to one another.

Next there is a provision for the deposit of some written form of the treaty in a sacred place and for its periodic public reading (compare Joshua 24:26–27; Deuteronomy 31:9–13). The treaties conclude with a list of deities as witnesses, who thereby lend their authority to the preservation of the relationship, and the stipulations are further reinforced by lists of blessings and curses that will result from fidelity or infidelity to the treaty. While the internal logic of Joshua 24 prohibits the introduction of any other deities as witnesses, attention must be called to verse 22: "You are witnesses against yourselves that you have chosen Yahweh, to serve him." The people then acknowledge that this is so (see also Joshua 24:27). Lists of curses and blessings are also found in chapter 28 of Deuteronomy. A record of the treaty or covenant was deposited at the sacred site (Joshua 24:26) and, quite likely, some form of sacrificial rite would accompany ratification (compare Exodus 24:3–8).

This is how many scholars reconstruct the basic form for the covenant that bound the tribes to Yahweh and held the amphictyony together, a form rooted in cultic actions by which the covenant was ratified and renewed. It must be emphasized that this is a theoretical reconstruction from evidence that was in part reformed and reshaped as it was handed on through generations. In this reconstruction a vital place is provided for the creedlike recitals and a basis is given for understanding their interchange between past and present, objective and subjective. It was on the basis of what Yahweh had done for Israel that the stipulations were willingly accepted and the covenant relationship affirmed.

But Yahweh's saving actions had to have been experienced for this to happen, if not firsthand ("historically," we might say), then cultically, for the essence of cult lies in its particular blending of the recital of a story (myth) and symbolic actions (ritual). The ritual makes the myth real, present, and experienced, while the myth provides meaning for the acts of ritual and the symbols employed in the cult. In ritual, the story or myth is experienced as present. Time and space are for the moment transcended, and you can confess that *you* are in Egyptian

38 bondage, *your* cry goes forth and is heard, *your* eyes see the signs and wonders of Yahweh upon pharaoh and Egypt.

It has been suggested that some such form for the acting out of this story of bondage and freedom lies behind the account of the crossing of the Jordan and conquest of Jericho found in Joshua 1:3–6, 8:30–35, and chapter 24. This account has not the usual quality of a battle report, detailing the movement of armies or the fighting for and destruction of a city. It seems rather a cultic reenactment of not just one battle for one city but of the essential sacred story as found in Deuteronomy 26:5–9 and Joshua 24:2–13. All the trappings of religious pageantry are there in the extensive preparations for the procession with the ark and the Levites. Then follows the passage through the divided river (the Jordan? or the Reed Sea relived?), the gathering of huge stones and construction of a sacred site, the circumcision of males, the ringing of Jericho for seven days, the blowing of rams' horns, and the announcement of the city's fall. Here in word and action is affirmed the experience of all who find deliverance from bondage and new possibilities for enriched lives.

Through cultic reenactment of this sacred story all who entered the fold of Israel experienced bondage and release. Through this experience, the covenant allegiance to Yahweh, and his stipulations based upon it, Israel was ever reformed and renewed. A common past and a common experience relived provided the basis for the federation's unity and a foundation for the identity of both community and individual. The covenant was renewed again and again in the affirmation and blessing, "You shall be my people, and I shall be your god." The land upon which they lived was the deity's gift to them, and their relationship with one another was defined by their common allegiance to this god as their only overlord.

That fundamental religious allegiance was the foundation for earliest Israel's unity and identity cannot be overemphasized. This is the issue in Joshua 24: "Choose this day whom you will serve." Will it be the gods of the ancestors, the Canaanite deities of the land, or Yahweh alone? But if it is a matter of fundamental religious allegiance, it is a political matter as well, for religious and political spheres were seldom kept distinct and separate in the ancient Near East. Kings ruled either as gods, as in Egypt, or as the chosen of the gods, as in Mesopotamia. Allegiance to the gods of Canaan meant allegiance to the Canaanite city-state kings, who had founded their authority on the divine sphere and had cloaked their political structures within religious traditions and cultic panoply.

Here we might recall Mendenhall's observation that it was a distinction of allegiance—political and religious—that separated Israelite from Canaanite. In Joshua 24 and in the service of covenant renewal that stands behind it, no human figure is found between the deity and the people. Allegiance is given to Yahweh and to no mortal leader. Leaders summoned by Yahweh would emerge in times of crisis, but they were restricted to meeting the immediate crisis; any attempt to perpetuate or institutionalize this leadership or even to pass it on to one's sons was doomed to failure. This is the lesson of the Abimelech episode in Judges 9. In time prophets, kings, and priests would attempt to represent the deity before the people and rule in his authority. How their claims would be made and adjudicated will be explored in some of the chapters that follow.

For about two centuries the sacred story and its reenactment united the federation of tribes that first composed the nation Israel. Even when internal and external stresses threatened to shatter that unity, and when in response to such stresses Israel was forced to undergo extensive change in shape and size, the story continued to be reworked and to provide a basis for judgment and support for prophet's oracle, historian's lesson, and priest's blessing. When in time some would reject or forget this story, their action appears shocking precisely because the story had stood so long at the heart of ancient Israel's and early Judaism's unifying identity. It is to the retellings, reformations, and rejections of the story that this book now turns.

BIBLIOGRAPHIC NOTE

The Israelite Conquest of Palestine and the Federation

Different reconstructions of the so-called conquest and formation of the state of Israel are found in Martin Noth, *The History of Israel* (New York: Harper & Brothers, 1960); John Bright, *A History of Israel* (Philadelphia: Westminster Press, 1972); John H. Hayes and J. Maxwell Miller, eds., *Israelite and Judaean History* (Philadelphia: Westminster Press, 1977); and Siegfried Herrmann, *A History of Israel in Old Testament Times* (Philadelphia: Fortress Press, 1975). G. E. Mendenhall's article on the "Hebrew Conquest of Palestine" is conveniently found in *The Biblical Archaeologist Reader 3*, ed. Edward F. Campbell and David Noel Freedman (Garden City, N.Y.: Doubleday & Co., 1970). The same volume contains two other formative studies by Mendenhall: "Ancient Oriental and Biblical Law" and "Covenant Forms in Israelite Tradition."

Mazar, Benjamin. *Judges.* In *The World History of the Jewish People*, vol. 3. New Brunswick, N.J.: Rutgers University Press, 1971. Covers the period of formation and the federation.

McCarthy. D. J. *Old Testament Covenant: A Survey of Current Opinions.* Richmond, Va.: John Knox Press, 1972.

Mendenhall, G. E. "Covenant." In *The Interpreter's Dictionary of the Bible*, vol. 1, pp. 714–23. Nashville: Abingdon Press, 1962.

Riemann, P. A. "Covenant, Mosaic." In *The Interpreter's Dictionary of the Bible: Supplementary Volume*, pp. 192–97. Nashville: Abingdon Press, 1976.

von Rad, Gerhard. "The Form-Critical Problem of the Hexateuch." In *The Problem of the Hexateuch and Other Essays*, pp. 1–78. New York: McGraw-Hill, 1966. A discussion of the early creeds.

Weippert, Manfred. "Canaan, Conquest, and Settlement." In *The Interpreter's Dictionary of the Bible: Supplementary Volume*, pp. 125–30. Nashville: Abingdon Press, 1976.

————. *The Settlement of the Israelite Tribes in Palestine*. Studies in Biblical Theology, no. 21. London: SCM Press, 1971. A critical review of recent historical reconstructions.

The Book of Joshua

Good, E. M. "Joshua, Book of." In *The Interpreter's Dictionary of the Bible*, vol. 2, pp. 988–95. Nashville: Abingdon Press, 1962.

Miller, J. M. "Joshua, Book of." In *The Interpreter's Dictionary of the Bible: Supplementary Volume*, pp. 493–96. Nashville: Abingdon Press, 1976.

Soggin, J. Alberto. *Joshua*. Philadelphia: Westminster Press, 1972.

The Book of Judges

Boling, Robert G. *Judges*. Garden City, N.Y.: Doubleday & Co., 1975.

Kraft, C. F. "Judges, Book of." In *The Interpreter's Dictionary of the Bible*, vol. 2, pp. 1013–23. Nashville: Abingdon Press, 1962.

Rogers, M. G. "Judges, Book of." In *The Interpreter's Dictionary of the Bible: Supplementary Volume*, pp. 509–14. Nashville: Abingdon Press, 1976.

SECTION 1
THE EMPIRE OF DAVID AND SOLOMON

Nineteenth century photograph of Jerusalem

The Bettmann Archive

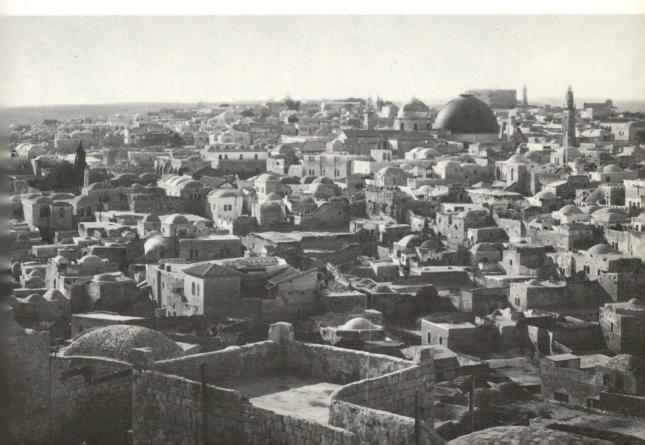

THE FIRST CRISIS

1

Primary readings: *Judges 17–21*
                         1 Sameul 1–31
                         2 Samuel 1–24
                         1 Kings 1–11

FORMATION OF THE EMPIRE

Forces for Dissolution

By the second half of the eleventh century B.C.E. internal and external pressures on early Israel were building to dangerous levels. The Philistines, who applied the external pressure, were groups of people who had moved from the Aegean area and settled in the southern Palestinian coastal plain at about the same time the Israelite federation took shape. In time they sought more territory, though initial skirmishes with Israel (reflected in the Samson narratives of Judges 13–16) seem to have ended in a draw. Soon, however, from their five base cities near the Mediterranean coast, they became such a menace to the tribe of Dan that the latter had to relocate on new land far to the north (Judges 18). The threat expanded to other tribes as well (1 Samuel 4), and, in a crucial battle at Aphek in the central hills, the sacred ark, the symbol of Yahweh's presence in Israel, was lost.

This new external danger to the federation was no longer the localized threat of the period of the judges. Although a charismatic local figure might rally some of the tribes for a single decisive battle, the Philistines, momentarily checked as

43

44   in 1 Samuel 7, would return. Constant preparedness required a standing professional military force made up of men free from obligations to the family farm, and the levy or draft, by which a citizen's army had been raised in the federation, could no longer meet the need. In addition, new forms of leadership were required—specifically, a leader who could serve for extended periods and support himself and his administrative and military establishments through some form of taxation.

As Philistine pressure increased, a crisis of internal leadership developed as well. The amphictyonic structure of Israel's federation of tribes, whose unity was founded on a common allegiance to Yahweh, his cult, and his story, left each member largely free from supratribal forms of human authority. Allegiance was reaffirmed each year in covenant renewal to Yahweh alone. Internal tribal governance was a matter of local custom administered by local leaders. But this system, which lasted more than two centuries and would remain an ideal for some in future centuries, also had weaknesses which become apparent in an examination of Judges 17–21.

Through these chapters runs an editorial theme summarized in the statement: "In those days there was no king in Israel; every man did what was right in his own eyes" (Judges 17:6; 18:1; 19:1; 21:25). On the one hand, this statement could be interpreted as a vision of an ideal time of individual freedom from all external political restraints—of freedom from service to the Canaanite king and his court, for example. It could be the rallying cry of those who valued individual freedom and who sought a world in which no man was denied full range for self-expression and development. On the other hand, it could be a terse description of social and political chaos.

The material found in Judges 17–21 suggests that the latter interpretation may have been intended. These chapters tell of a son's theft of his mother's silver, of the construction of an image from some of this silver, of how the tribe of Dan stole the image from the man's private shrine and lured away its priest (Judges 17–18). We then learn of the rape and murder of a man's concubine by some Benjaminites in the city of Gibeah. No one could by virtue of official authority compel the Benjaminites to deliver up the men guilty of this outrage (Judges 20:12–14); the only recourse was all-out warfare between tribes, great loss of life on all sides, and near destruction of the tribe of Benjamin (Judges 19–20). The tribe is restored only when the city of Jabesh-gilead is wiped out through the organized abduction of the young women of Shiloh. In short, Judges 17–21 does not offer an appealing picture. Certain fundamental crises could not be met without chaos in early Israel, and in this respect the federation structure contained the seeds of its own potential destruction.

Both new leaders and new forms of leadership would come at a cost—a cost that some felt was not commensurate with the results and which some would refuse to pay. But of necessity change did come and with remarkable speed, for both the external threat from the Philistines and the threat of internal dissolution demanded radical changes in Israel's political, social, economic, cultural, and especially its religious structures. Over the last forty or fifty years of the eleventh century B.C.E. Israel was transformed from a loose federation of separate tribes located for the most part in the central hills of southern Palestine into a monarchy and empire whose military authority and commercial reach extended from Egypt and Arabia to the River Euphrates (1 Kings 4:20–21).

In those critical decades of growth and change, an Israelite who had been born in a rural village could reach old age in a cosmopolitan city whose horizons seemed to reach to the ends of the earth. None of the varied materials found in 1 and 2 Samuel and in the first part of 1 Kings attempts to present an objective picture of the events involved in this transformation; the issues were too immediate and important for a stance of neutral objectivity. Still, a reasonably clear picture of the course of events can be extracted from these materials, and a historical outline of them will be presented in this chapter.

EMPIRE of DAVID and SOLOMON			
B.C.E.	**Egypt**	**Israel**	**Phoenicia**
	TWENTY-FIRST DYNASTY (1069–935)		
1050			
		Fall of Shiloh Samuel Saul (1020–1000)	
1000		David (1000–961)	
			Hiram of Tyre (969–936)
		Solomon (961–922)	
950			
	TWENTY-SECOND DYNASTY (935–725) Shishak (935–914)	Schism (922)	
900			

Samuel perhaps epitomizes the strengths and weaknesses of the older type of charismatic leader. Appearing in the line of earlier judges, he could momentarily check but not remove the Philistine threat (1 Samuel 7:3–14); he could serve Israel (or that part of it centered around the tribes of Benjamin) and lower Ephraim with great integrity (1 Samuel 7:15–17); but he could not ensure the continuance of such leadership even through his own sons. Unlike earlier judges, Samuel appears more as a legal arbitrator (like Deborah in Judges 4:5–6) than as a military leader, and he seems to have sought to institutionalize and pass on his office in a clear line of succession. He appears as a priest as well, reared at the federation's central sanctuary, which was then at Shiloh (1 Samuel 3; 7:5–11; 10:11–18; 13:8–13). But charismatic authority is not transmitted through the genes. Samuel's sons were corrupt (1 Samuel 8:1–3), and the popular cry went up, "Appoint for us a king to govern us like all the nations" (1 Samuel 8:5).

More was at stake here than bribes and perverted justice. A king would provide continued vigilance and protection against the Philistines; he would also be an extratribal authority and therefore a force for internal stability. But such vigilance and stability would have to be supported through taxation on produce and persons. Moreover, no longer would each person be free to do what was right in his own eyes. The presence of a king augured deep-seated potential for change in all areas of life, and, as the earlier episodes dealing with Gideon and Abimelech clearly indicate (Judges 8:22–23; 9:1–57), it was not a course to be undertaken lightly.

A fundamental reordering of allegiance was involved: a mortal would now stand between Yahweh and the individual Israelite, even if he were a mortal cloaked in the deity's legitimating authority. 1 Samuel 8–12 offers two distinct evaluations of kingship. In one case (1 Samuel 8; 10:17–27; 12) Samuel emphasizes the burdens and dangers of kingship; both the prophet and his deity only grudgingly accede to the popular request. In the other case (1 Samuel 9:1–10:16; 11) Samuel willingly makes the selection of a king. Although both presentations are, in part, later reflections on the monarchy by different circles within Israel, both reflect the tensions that ran deep within the tribal federation at this critical juncture in Israel's history.

The man whom Samuel selected was Saul, a complex person who also exhibited some of the imposing qualities of earlier judges. His spontaneous response to the danger confronting Jabesh-gilead and the rallying of the tribes to its defense are in the classic mold (1 Samuel 11) and led to public confirmation of his kingship. But soon there were hints of disintegration. A spontaneous oath sworn by Saul in the heat of conflict (1 Samuel 14) resulted in only a limited victory over the Philistines, who lost the battle but would regroup and return. Moreover, the victory was as much that of Saul's son Jonathan as his own.

Samuel and Saul represented two groups seeking to govern Israel as well as two distinct views of how Israel should be governed. Samuel represented the older federation patterns of freedom from royal authority and the claims of early prophetic circles to represent the will of the deity.On a very limited scale, Saul sought to take the lines of political, military, and—most essential in the ancient world—religious authority into his own hands, and in so doing he came into conflict with Samuel. Such issues as who would offer sacrifices (1 Samuel 12:8–15) or determine the course and outcome of a war (1 Samuel 15) went to the heart of the crisis of transition. A break had to come, and, after it had come, Saul disintegrated as a person.

Trapped between the old world of the federation and the not-yet-formed monarchy, he was asked to perform within the limits of the former in meeting the tasks of the latter. This external pressure, combined with a personal instability, caused Saul to go insane. It might be said that in Saul the reverse of charisma was madness, for the same charismatic powers that had led him to rally the tribes in defense of Jabesh-gilead finally led to mad obsessions that drove from him all personal, family, and political support. Seeking to accomplish what he had initially been summoned to do, he met the Philistines again at Mount Gilboa, and when the battle was lost and his sons slain he took his own life (1 Samuel 31:1–7). The burial honors given him by the people of Jabesh-gilead were perhaps well deserved (1 Samuel 31:8–13), but they served also to underscore his failures.

Initial Success

Samuel and the older federation structures that he represented failed as well. Tradition presents Samuel as not only rejecting Saul but, as his last act before death, anointing David as future king of Israel (1 Samuel 16:1–13). In David, kingship reached full bloom. In his deeds he vastly surpassed what Saul had but hesitantly attempted, and in his hands all lines of kingly authority came together. Early in his career David demonstrated that artful blend of good luck, pragmatic self-service, and deep commitment to causes and persons that leads to political success. But his initial successes in Saul's army and court, his marriage to the king's daughter, his close friendship with Jonathan (1 Samuel 19:1–7; 20), and the strong bonds between king and protégé seemed to turn to disaster when he was driven from the mad Saul.

For a time David lived as an outlaw (1 Samuel 23) in the wilderness of eastern and central Judah and even became a vassal of the enemy Philistines (1 Samuel 27). Hounded by Saul, to whom his destruction had become an obsession (1 Samuel 22; 23:19–29; 24; 26), he not only avoided Saul's wrath but turned their encounters to his own advantage. Surviving as an outlaw, he gathered others about him and even appears as selling protection to local herdsmen in the wilderness of Judah (1 Samuel 25). At the last moment he was released from his obligation to fight with the Philistines against Israel at Mount Gilboa (1 Samuel 29), an event that would have cut him off irrevocably from any future relationship with the Israelites. The deaths of Saul and Jonathan moved him deeply—his lament (2 Samuel 1:19–27) shows David at his best—but the defeat of Israel and the death of Saul also provided the occasion for his rise to the throne.

With a base in Hebron, he won the allegiance of his own tribe of Judah (2 Samuel 2:1–11). When the group that had formed about Saul disintegrated into an internecine struggle that brought all other claimants to the vestiges of Saul's power to their death (2 Samuel 2:11–4:12), the remaining tribes came to David to make him their king as well (2 Samuel 2:1–5:5). With this base of power, he formally broke ties with the Philistines, defeated them (2 Samuel 5:17–25; 21:15–20; 23:8–29), then employed Philistine contingents in his growing standing army.

In a bold stroke he captured the Canaanite city of Jerusalem, which had until now remained an independent enclave in the midst of the federation of tribes (2 Samuel 5:6–9; compare Judges 19:10–12), and moved his administrative activities to this new capital. From this point on, Jerusalem would be the "city of David." Taking the initial steps that would lead to its becoming the religious center of Israel and later Judaism, he brought the ark—the focal Yahwistic symbol of the old federation—to a hill adjoining the city and initiated plans to build a temple and establish a formal cult for Yahweh on this site.

Through military conquest and commercial negotiations, David built an empire that extended Israelite authority from one end of Syria-Palestine to the other. In some cases, military conquest resulted in brutal subjection; in others, it led to treaties (see the summary in 2 Samuel 8). The relationship with some states, especially that of the Phoenicians of Tyre (2 Samuel 5:11–12), was commercially advantageous to both parties. From Jerusalem, David came to rule an empire composed of varied units tied to him personally. *He* was the thread of unity, in him was completed the transition from a system of tribes to an empire composed of units bound essentially through common allegiance to a king.

But David could not rule his own house. Internal conflict and fratricide, the disputed succession, and the brutal but effective emergence of Solomon in firm control of the throne form a remarkable narrative (2 Samuel 9–20; 1 Kings 1–2) that will be considered in chapter 4. Within his own household and with his own sons, this man of decisive action appeared strangely passive and malleable (see 2 Samuel 19 and 1 Kings 1). His attachment was strongest and most complex toward Absalom, whose every action seemed directed toward his father's downfall (2 Samuel 15–19). From the notice of Michal's barrenness (a son from this daughter of Saul would have been the perfect heir, uniting in his blood Judah and the northern tribes) to Solomon's execution of Adonijah, David's family appeared ill-fated. Finally only Solomon remained.

Consolidation and Realization

In the forty years traditionally assigned to his reign (1000–960 B.C.E.), David built an empire which he handed over to his son, who, in about four decades (960–922

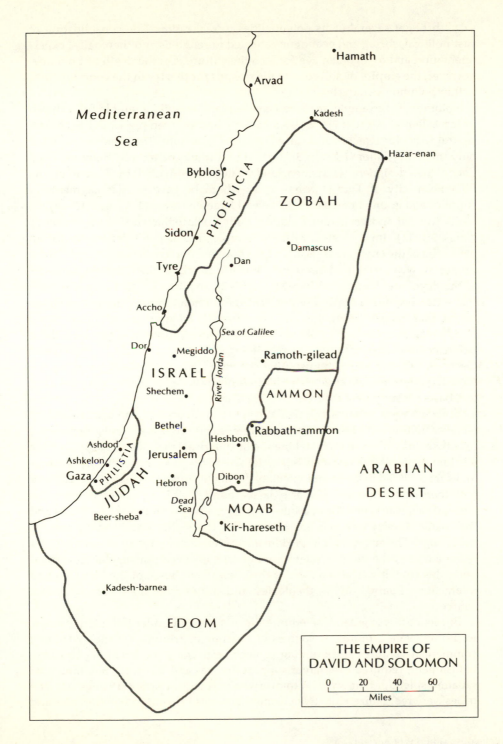

Mediterranean

Sea

• Hamath

• Arvad

• Byblos

PHOENICIA

• Sidon

• Tyre

Accho •

Dor •

Dan •

Sea of Galilee

• Megiddo

ISRAEL

Shechem •

Bethel •

Ashdod •

Ashkelon •

Gaza •

PHILISTIA

JUDAH

Jerusalem •

Hebron •

Beer-sheba •

Dead
Sea

• Kadesh-barnea

EDOM

• Kadesh

• Hazar-enan

ZOBAH

• Damascus

River Jordan

• Ramoth-gilead

AMMON

• Rabbath-ammon

Heshbon •

• Dibon

MOAB

• Kir-hareseth

ARABIAN

DESERT

THE EMPIRE OF
DAVID AND SOLOMON

0   20   40   60
Miles

B.C.E.) brought several of its potentialities to realization. The consolidation of vast political, social, and economic gains led to religious and theological experimentation and to a golden age for Israelite culture. On the death of Solomon, however, the empire dissolved, and the reasons for this lay in the contradictions within Solomon's character.

Solomon, for example, realized David's plans to build a temple for Yahweh in Jerusalem (2 Samuel 7:1–3; 1 Kings 5–8), and this temple would become a central focus for Israelite and early Jewish religious life. Yet Israelites supplied only the heavy labor (1 Kings 5:13–18). In building the temple, Solomon used Phoenician designers, craftsmen, and materials provided by Hiram of the Phoenician city of Tyre (1 Kings 5), to whom he gave regular payments in supplies and granted possession of several Israelite towns (1 Kings 9:10–14).

For himself and his harem, Solomon built a palace that rivaled the temple (1 Kings 7:1–12). Incorporated with the temple into David's Jerusalem by an extension of the city walls, this more than doubled the size of the city. Solomon's numerous wives, acquired through diplomatic marriages, included the daughter of the Egyptian pharaoh (1 Kings 11:13; 3:1–2), an alliance which, together with that with Hiram of Tyre and others, laid the foundation for commercial enterprises that ranged from seagoing ventures (1 Kings 9:26) to becoming a middleman in armaments (1 Kings 10:26–29). In addition, he strengthened the defensive structure of the realm, rebuilding the cities of Megiddo, Hazor, and Gezer as military and administrative centers (1 Kings 10:15–16), making the standing army the sole effective military force in Israel, and relegating the draft to a basis for supplying laborers.

Still, Solomon remains an enigmatic figure, both praised and condemned by Israelite tradition. Some recent scholars refer to his reign as an "enlightenment"; for others his ruthlessness on taking the throne rivals that of any despot; yet his wisdom, especially as revealed in judicial sensitivity, became legendary (1 Kings 3). Wars declined in scope and intensity during his reign (1 Kings 10:14–23), and with increased economic prosperity Israel found itself in a position to enjoy the cultural riches that now flowed into Jerusalem along with foreign courtiers and merchants, their wives and entourages. For Israel this was in many ways a golden age. The encyclopedic wisdom attributed to Solomon in 1 Kings 4:29–34 is but a hint of the literary, scientific, and artistic developments that flourished under his rule. It was also a time of theological synthesis, of the blending and interaction of varied myths, theologies, and stories from many, often foreign, sources.

But its cost was great. The empire did not expand under Solomon; no new territories were acquired as sources of revenue or tribute. Yet the expanding commercial ventures and building projects, especially the enlarging court establishment, required ever larger support in taxes and labor, for Solomon now sat amid splendor that was said to overwhelm foreign visitors (1 Kings 10). The tribes were reorganized into twelve units, at points breaking old boundaries and bringing in new groups of people, and each unit was assigned the task of supplying the enlarged royal court for one month a year (1 Kings 4:7–19). This virtually parodies the older amphictyonic structure in which each tribe was to serve the central cult and the god Yahweh on a monthly rotation. Overseers were appointed to administer the new system. Forced labor levies were gathered to carry out the heavy work of the building projects and were placed under the authority of an official in the king's cabinet (1 Kings 4:6). Also incorporated into the royal administration and cabinet were the religious leaders, the priests and prophets (1 Kings 4:1–6).

Thus tensions grew as court expansion outran its tax and labor base and as some classes saw increasingly less in the central government that would be of benefit to them. Although Solomon held the empire together for his lifetime, he could not pass it on to his son. On his death the empire fell apart and Israel suddenly became two small kingdoms. The stresses that were already observable in the days of David—not only in the inner dynastic rebellion of Absalom but also in Shebna's attempted secession of the northern tribes—now tore Israel asunder. As Ahijah, the prophet from the old federation center at Shiloh, tore his robe apart, so the empire was rent, and its glory passed into a dream for future generations.

FROM AGRARIAN TRIBALISM TO COSMOPOLITAN URBANISM

Saul worked for his family on what must have been at best a small estate. He plowed his own fields (1 Samuel 11:5) and went himself with but one attendant in search of lost livestock (1 Samuel 9:3). Archaeologists have shown his capital at Gibeah to have been very rustic, yet by Samuel and others he was considered to have overstepped himself in his reach for royal authority. As a youth, even David had been a shepherd growing up in rural Bethlehem at the edge of the grazing land and the wilderness south of Jerusalem. Solomon, however, was born and reared in a royal palace and a rich urban setting, which, though forever lost to archaeologists, must have been lavish. On the streets of his Jerusalem could be heard all the tongues of the known world; people could be seen in the rich colors and garb of many nations; varied cultural and religious forms mixed and intermingled as royalty, diplomats, merchants, and courtiers visited from different parts of the world. Although only a few decades separated Saul and Solomon, the cultural difference between rural Gibeah and cosmopolitan Jerusalem was vast.

Political, Economic, and Social Developments

From a loosely structured, decentralized federation bound together only by allegiance to a deity and a sacred story, Israel was transformed in a few years into a monarchy exhibiting ever increasing political, military, social, economic, and religious authority. By way of illustration, Saul's standing army had been made up of a few personal recruits (1 Samuel 14:52); he had been dependent on the levy, and his forces had functioned within the restrictions of the federation and its limited forms of warfare. Within a few years, however, the tribal draft had become an outmoded vestige at best. David was able to bring into his military establishment whole companies of foreign mercenaries and to have his own elite guard (1 Samuel 23:8–39), while Solomon established military and administrative centers in strategic parts of the land (1 Kings 9:15–19).

For another illustration, whereas Samuel had rejected Saul for daring to offer sacrifices in critical circumstances brought on by Samuel's own tardiness (1 Samuel 13:8–15), David brought the ark of the covenant with Yahweh into his city (2 Samuel 6), and Solomon not only built a temple to house the ark but restructured Yahweh's cult. Both David and Solomon included the clergy among their official administrative personnel (2 Samuel 8:16–18; 20:23–26; 1 Kings 4:2–6). Though at one point Nathan, the court prophet, fearlessly rebuked King David (2 Samuel 12:1–14), he appears later as but another scheming courtier, vying for authority and craftily using it in an intradynasty power play whose stakes are life or death (1 Kings 1–2).

If Saul went out personally in search of his father's livestock, an exotic delegation led by the Arabian Queen of Sheba paid court on Solomon to negotiate a trade agreement and to stand in awe before his splendor. In short, in only a few years all lines of authority came to center in the figure of the king, who held complete control over the military, political, legal, economic, and religious structures of Israel. Solomon in his temple and palace complex was very much like the Late Bronze Age Canaanite king in his walled city on the hill, against whom, according to one theory of Israel's origins, disenchanted peasants had revolted years earlier.

Although details are elusive, it is clear that this rapid transformation brought about radical social changes as well. For some people, older styles of life defined by clan or family or by geographical proximity gave way to newer styles in urban cosmopolitan Jerusalem. Lines of authority and loyalty in the city differed greatly from those on the rural homestead, and they focused ultimately on one man. Although wealth flowed into Israel during the time of David and Solomon (1 Kings 10), the flow was uneven. Full-time specialists who served the state in various offices had to be supported by taxes on produce and labor, and this brought about divisions—between city and country, between those closely connected to royal power and those not, between levels of income and possessions, between professional soldier and draftee, between merchant and self-sufficient family homesteader, between the taxed and the tax collector. Such divisions cut through the old lines that had previously bound Israel together. Social distinctions were often marked by inequities in power, wealth, visions or hopes for the future and therefore in commitment to the new order. In short, the transformation was radical, but its impact was felt in different ways and its benefits were unevenly distributed.

Into the fold of Israel David brought whole groups of new peoples, of whom the Jebusites (the Canaanite inhabitants of Jerusalem) were only one. Solomon not only further incorporated new groups but developed windows onto alien vistas as well. To Jerusalem and other royal cities these new peoples brought their arts, customs, and values, their stories and myths, and their gods. Although these new elements would attract some and repel others, all would have to come to terms with them; all would have to justify the radical changes or control or condemn them. Using Phoenician designers and artists in building the temple and palace, comparing Solomon's wisdom with that of Egypt or the peoples of the east—both bespeak a contemporary appreciation of the cultural products and expressions of foreign peoples. The later disapproval of Solomon's marriages, on the other hand, may reflect the attitude of those in the Israel of his day who were less in sympathy with seemingly alien innovations (1 Kings 11:1–13).

Whatever critical judgments were made of this new Israel, the cultural and religious materials at hand were decidedly richer and more complex than they had been only a few years before. That Israel's horizons had been radically extended could not be ignored, however it might be evaluated. New stories, new myths, new religious practices and forms could be brought to bear on the traditions of the federation. But there were central questions to be answered. Was this Yahweh's doing? Was this transformation the work of the god of the federation? Was this a continuation of his action on Israel's behalf of which they sang and spoke in the ceremony of covenant renewal?

Further, was the king a gift of the god (1 Samuel 9:15–17), or was he a symbol of the people's rejection of Yahweh's claims to sole allegiance (1 Samuel 8)? Was the king's relation to Yahweh different from that of other mortals (2 Samuel 7:8–16)? Was this new and strange temple the home of Yahweh, or was it an attempt to imprison a deity who older traditions said would never give up his freedom to move about as he wished (2 Samuel 7:1–7)? What obligations came with power? What were the checks on such power? Who spoke for Yahweh?

These and other questions engaged a generation and more during a creative period that compares with few others in world history. It was a period in which several paths were followed and several new lines staked out, and it determined the limits within which Israel would live the remainder of its life. New stories were adopted while the old story of the federation was retold, reformed to fit the new situation, and plumbed for new depths. Some stories sought to tell of the transformation itself, of the events and persons involved, and to offer insights into the ways of Israel's god with human beings. This richly diverse period of David and Solomon has been called an "enlightenment." While the term may not be wholly appropriate in light of some of Solomon's harsh policies, it does point to a highly formative period in the development of Israelite religious traditions and, beyond these, to the religious traditions of the Western world as a whole.

The Period of the Empire

Along with the histories listed in the introductory Bibliographic Note, see Eugene H. Maly, *The World of David and Solomon* (Englewood Cliffs, N.J.: Prentice-Hall, 1965) and E. W. Heaton, *Solomon's New Men: The Emergence of Ancient Israel as a National State* (New York: Pica Press, 1974).

Myers, J. M. "David," "Saul, Son of Kish," and "Solomon." In *The Interpreter's Dictionary of the Bible*, vol. 1, pp. 771–78; vol. 4, pp. 228–33 and 399–408. Nashville: Abingdon Press, 1962.

The Books of 1 and 2 Samuel

Hertzberg, Hans Wilhelm. *I and II Samuel*. Philadelphia: Westminster Press, 1964.

Szikszai, S. "I and II Samuel." In *The Interpreter's Dictionary of the Bible*, vol. 4, pp. 202–9. Nashville: Abingdon Press, 1962.

Tsevat, M. "I and II Samuel." In *The Interpreter's Dictionary of the Bible: Supplementary Volume*, pp. 777–81. Nashville: Abingdon Press, 1976.

The Books of 1 and 2 Kings

Ackroyd, Peter R. "I and II Kings." In *The Interpreter's Dictionary of the Bible: Supplementary Volume*, pp. 516–19. Nashville: Abingdon Press, 1976.

Gray, Josh. *I and II Kings*. Philadelphia: Westminster Press, 1970.

Szikszai, S. "I and II Kings." In *The Interpreter's Dictionary of the Bible*, vol. 3, pp. 26–35. Nashville: Abingdon Press, 1962.

THE DAVIDIC AND ZION TRADITIONS

2

Primary readings: *Genesis 14*
2 Samuel 5:6–10; 7:1–17; 22:1–23:7
Psalms 2, 18, 20, 21, 45–48, 76, 84, 87,
101, 110, 132, 144

A second story came into Israel's possession with David's capture of the city of Jerusalem, for it is in connection with that city, which is also called Zion, and with King David and his dynasty that it is firmly linked. This second story differs in two important respects from the older sacred story of the tribal federation. First, unlike the latter, whose most prominent expressions are found in creedlike units in Deuteronomy 26 and Joshua 24, this story is found in no single summary unit but is pieced together from allusions, from seemingly isolated motifs, and from a few blessings, narratives, and hymns. For this reason our reconstruction of it will be hypothetical and probably incomplete. Second, the story of Yahweh's deliverance of the slaves and gift of the land was rooted in the historical experience of a particular people; it spoke of particular events that occurred at distinct places and in historical time. The second story, however, speaks of the creation of the universe. It tells how this world order came to be and how it is sustained; but it also speaks of bonds linking the deity who is said to be the creator with the city of Jerusalem and its royal family. For ancient Israel the creator deity would be Yahweh, and the royal family would be that of David.

In capturing Canaanite Jerusalem, David was engaged not in a holy war but in acquiring an administrative center and governing apparatus for his organization of an empire. Certainly an administrative system would be needed quickly, and it was not to be found in the older patterns of the federation. Once the loyalty of the northern tribes was secure, Hebron, in the heart of the southern tribe of Judah, could no longer serve as his capital (2 Samuel 2:1–4). By taking Jerusalem and living therein David assured that no one tribe could appear to have undue influence over the king or appear overly favored by him, for the city stood between and outside the tribal system. So he took Jerusalem (then also called Jebus) in a manner that is not made wholly clear in the preserved report of the event in 2 Samuel 5:6–10 (see also 1 Chronicles 11:4–9). There is no suggestion that David slaughtered all the Canaanites who lived in this remnant of Canaan's old city-state structure (compare Joshua 6 and Samuel's demands on Saul in 1 Samuel 15) or that he destroyed the city itself. The city appears to have fallen into his hands intact, providing a functioning city-state to serve as a basis for his organization of the empire. The building activities that David and especially Solomon carried out appear to have been expansionistic projects aimed at enlarging and strengthening the city, not the repair or reconstruction of a city destroyed in warfare.

From Jerusalem David sent forth his army and diplomatic missions that were to build the empire; and as Jerusalem became the political, commercial, economic, military, and cultural center for the state, it became the religious center as well. David brought the ark of Yahweh into the city with a grand procession, thereby placing the prestige of this old federation symbol of Yahweh's presence in his service. As the example of Saul had made tragically clear, however, federation traditions alone could not support a strong monarchy; so the old ark and the old story were encompassed by another set of traditions and symbols that were more supportive of royal claims. On the physical level, David proposed and Solomon executed plans to build a temple that would house the ark. The site selected was the threshing floor of Araunah the Jebusite. David acquired the non-Israelite site (2 Samuel 24:15–25), and upon it Solomon built a temple. Here Yahweh would dwell as lord of the empire in a home built on foreign modes by foreign designers.

In this new setting Yahweh was served by a priesthood that had roots both in federation Israel and in Jebusite/Canaanite soil as well. Two priests appeared in David's court: Abiathar had been with him since his outlaw days, but Zadok appeared only after Jerusalem had been taken. Some have suggested that Zadok was a Jebusite and that he may have been priest of the god of Jerusalem before the city's capture. Study of Israel's cultic practices, such as the pattern of festivals, and of the orders for daily and special sacrificial offerings suggests that Canaanite influence was formative.

Beyond this it appears that a new and distinct set of traditions arose alongside the older story of the federation. For a time some Israelites believed that these new traditions and the new story could be brought into harmony with, and even inform, the older story. The next chapter will consider a remarkable attempt to combine the old and new; later we will see how the new tradition informed the words of a prophet named Isaiah and possibly another prophet named Hananiah, who would come into conflict with Jeremiah. This conflict reflects a tension between the two stories that would slowly grow until the newer story shattered in the crisis of 598–587 B.C.E., which ended the kingdom of David and the historical life of old Israel. Only pieces of this story would remain, and from these we will now attempt its reconstruction.

JERUSALEM AND ITS GOD

An Inviolable City

The description in 2 Samuel 5:6–10 of the capture of Jerusalem is terse to the point of obscurity. David and his men march upon the city where the people call out mockingly that they cannot come into it for "the blind and the lame will ward you off." This, the narrator suggests, indicates that they thought "David cannot come in here." But David took the stronghold of Zion, possibly by locating the outer end of a water shaft and tunnel through which either his men entered the city or by means of which its water supply was cut off.

For defensive purposes, ancient walled cities were often built on hills. In times of siege it would be impossible to go outside the walls to get water. For this reason, water shafts would begin within the walls in the form of a stepped tunnel down and then out to a spring outside the city walls, permitting tunnel access to water which would flow from the spring into an area beneath the city. The outer spring could then be hidden, and the city's water supply would be secure in case of a siege. Traces of such a tunnel have been located, along with one built later by King Hezekiah, which it is possible to walk through today. Other such water systems have been found in several sites in Palestine. They were necessary if a city was to withstand a conventional siege, but if discovered they might also afford easy access to an enemy. Thus the text states: "David said on that day, 'Whoever would smite the Jebusites, let him get up the water shaft to attack the lame and the blind.' " By some such unconventional means David may have taken the city.

But what are we to make of this reference to the blind and the lame which has puzzled interpreters since early times. If 2 Samuel 5:6–10 contains a couple of attempts at interpretation, the later book of 1 Chronicles omits the statement altogether (1 Chronicles 11:4–9). In 2 Samuel 5:6 we are told that this was intended to mean that David could never take the city, which may be a correct interpretation in one respect. These words of the Jebusites may reflect an old adage giving picturesque expression to a belief that Jerusalem was inviolable: the city could not fall to an attack; even the handicapped could defend it.

In verse 8 this saying is taken literally, and David is presented as actually suggesting an attack on the blind and lame—either that or he here takes up the imagery of the Jebusites and turns it back on them. But the addition of the striking phrase, "who are hated by David's soul," appears to be a literal interpretation of his words and seeks to explain such a harsh statement. The next phrase in verse 8 offers a different sort of explanation, linking some later prohibition regarding the temple to David's remark. These attempts by a later editorial hand to interpret a figurative saying literally only confuse the picture. In any event, verse 9 states clearly that "David dwelt in the stronghold, and called it the city of David."

If it is correct that the picturesque adage of the Jebusites reflects an older tradition about Jerusalem's inviolability, upon what would this belief rest? Perhaps it was based in part on Jerusalem's physical situation. The city was built on a hill—in David's time just the southeastern spur of the hill that is today wholly covered by the city. Well protected by steep slopes to valleys on the east and south and to a lesser degree on the west, its natural defenses were weak only to the north, and here the strongest defensive walls would be set. But a belief that the city could not fall would be based on more than this. It may well be founded on belief in a divine promise of protection and in that respect be linked to the deity of Canaanite Jerusalem.

El Elyon

Who was this deity, and upon what might his promises be based? What would certify them? For answers we must turn to a series of scattered references to Jerusalem and to several figures associated with that city to learn more about the religious traditions of the Jebusites who dwelt there before David's arrival.

El as Creator   In the latter part of Genesis 14 the revered patriarch Abraham is returning from a successful military counterattack on four kings from the east from whom he has just rescued his nephew Lot, among others. He is met by a figure named Melchizedek, who is identified as king of Salem and priest of El Elyon ("God Most High" is a common English translation). The word *el*, like the English word *god*, is used both as a generic term to designate a class of beings (for example, Yahweh is a god; Zeus is a god) and as the proper denotation (often with a capital *G*) for the deity worshiped by Jews and Christians.

Thus the term *El* is, on the one hand, the common word for *god* in the language of the land of Canaan. It appears in a plural form, *elohim*, in the Old Testament and generally refers to Yahweh, the god of Israel, but is also used in reference to deities of other peoples and lands. On the other hand, El is also the name of the high god of the Canaanite pantheon. *Salem* appears to be a designation for Jerusalem, as, for example, in Psalm 76:2, where it is identified with Zion.

Melchizedek offers Abraham bread and wine and then blesses him in the name of his deity. Abraham in turn gives him a tenth of everything he has taken in battle. Melchizedek's blessing tells us something about this god named El who is linked here with Jerusalem:

> Blessed be Abram by El Elyon,
> maker of heaven and earth;
> and blessed be El Elyon,
> who has delivered your
> enemies into your hand.

Here El Elyon is said to be the creator of heaven and earth. The term translated "created" is the Hebrew word *qanah* and has within its range of meanings the sense of "giving birth." The use of this term in the formula of blessing to describe the work of El may reflect an older Canaanite belief in which, as elsewhere in ancient Near Eastern mythology, creation is presented as a process of birth. El begat heaven and earth, to use an old biblical term.

Furthermore, creation is not understood in Near Eastern mythology as a one-time event; it is depicted as a deity's bringing of order to what is disordered or chaotic. The process is never ending, for the created order, both in terms of nature's rhythms and in terms of human political and legal structures, must always be renewed and sustained in the face of an ever present potential for disorder and chaos. Creation and re-creation go hand in hand. Creation myths did not serve primarily to answer the questions of where, when, and how things first came into being. They did not exist to fill an essentially intellectual gap but had a more immediate and vital function. They dealt with how this tenuous order in which human beings live is to be sustained in the face of chaos and how it can be renewed periodically. Creation stories as recited even provided an essential role for the human community in that renewal. El as creator is therefore the one who at all times upholds and reinforces the natural and human patterns, rhythms, and structures that make life possible.

Harmony and Righteousness   Aspects of El's creative and sustaining activity become more apparent on observing certain names that are linked with Jerusalem and with the family of David. These names fall into two sets: in one set there is the element *z-d-k*; in the other, the element *sh-l-m*.

The element *z-d-k* forms the basis for several words in Hebrew denoting "righteousness, justice, integrity, correctness, or truth"—the proper order or harmony on the social level of human life. The name Melchizedek (in Hebrew, *malki-zedek*, meaning "my king is zedek") contains this element, as does the name of another king of Jerusalem, Adonizedek (meaning "my lord is zedek"), mentioned in Joshua 10:1. There is also the name of Zadok, the priest who appears in David's entourage only after the capture of Jerusalem and who plays a major part in Solomon's succession to the throne, in this way displacing his rival Abiathar (1 Kings 1–2). The element *sh-l-m* is found in Hebrew terms denoting "peace, harmony, integrity, wholeness, completeness." In Genesis 14 and in Psalm 76 the city of Jerusalem is called Salem, but the element appears in the name Jerusalem itself, which seems to mean "foundation for shalem." David's sons Solomon and Absalom, apparently born after he had taken the city, both have this element in their names.

These two terms, z-d-k and sh-l-m, essentially denote the harmony, integrity, and wholeness of the created order as sustained by the creator god, and in this respect they can be understood as basic theological terms in Canaanite tradition associated with El in and around Jerusalem in the period predating David. They would denote both critical aspects and results of the god's sustaining creative action. They may also reflect theological speculation by ancient Canaanites about this deity: he is creator—that is, he is the fountainhead for the harmony and righteousness that characterize the created order and nurture life within it. Certainly any claim that Jerusalem was inviolable would carry far more conviction if the deity who defended and supported the city were believed to be the creator and sustainer of all heaven and earth.

El and Yahweh　In rejecting an offer of the spoils taken in the battle with the kings from the east, Abraham reinforced his words with an oath sworn to "Yahweh El Elyon, creator of heaven and earth" (Genesis 14:22). Clearly the phrase "creator of heaven and earth" was a common formula linked to El, but in this oath El Elyon is identified with Yahweh. This may be an instance of such an identification being made within royal and religious circles in David's Jerusalem and read back into Abraham's time. It has already been noted that Zadok may have been a priest of El in Jerusalem before David brought him into the religious structure that he established. In any event, such an identification of the two deities served to enrich and enlarge understanding of Yahweh by the Israelites. Yahweh became the creator as well as the savior from Egyptian bondage.

If, as some scholars suggest, the term *Yahweh* is in Hebrew the causative form of a verb meaning "to be" and therefore has the sense of "to bring into being, to create," the association of Yahweh and El Elyon would be quite natural. Some scholars have even suggested that *Yahweh* was originally an epithet of the Canaanite El—that is, a descriptive term attached to his name and defining some aspect of his character or activity. Since *Elyon* is likewise such an epithet, the identification would again be natural, and taking it back to Abraham would stamp it with the legitimacy of remote antiquity.

The Place of Creation　Scholarship now recognizes the Book of Psalms as a rich collection of ancient Israelite and early Jewish songs that individuals and groups used for worship in the temple and later in the synagogue. Several hymns in this book bring the motifs of creation and sustenance together with a celebration of the city of Jerusalem. Some hymns sing of the unique position of Zion: clear examples are Psalms 46, 48, 76, 87, and 98. While not all such psalms come from the time of David, they nevertheless reflect themes that were first current in ancient Israel at that time. Psalm 46, for example, celebrates the deity's victory over political and natural forces that threaten Zion with chaos. Psalm 48 combines this motif with a celebration of the city's grandeur. In this psalm the deity is referred to as Elyon and then identified as Yahweh, and the identification is clearly intended throughout.

Some scholars have suggested that these psalms were first composed for use in a cultic celebration of the New Year in Jerusalem during which the deity's creation/re-creation of the universe was celebrated as well. Cultic festivals renewing and reliving creation were the focal point of the religious year in Mesopotamia, in Egypt, and probably in Canaan as well. In Babylon the festival included a dramatic procession and a mock combat between creator god and personified chaos; it also involved enthroning Marduk, the city's god, in his temple and the reordering of natural and political rhythms and life for the coming year. These activities climaxed in a joyous celebration, with food and drink for everyone, in thanksgiving for the preservation of life and order.

In a festival of this type the new story of Yahweh's creation would receive the sort of dramatic presentation that was earlier given the older story of the federation. In temple ritual, in pilgrimages to the city (Psalm 84), in processions about and through the city, in some form of mock battle or dramatic presentation of the stilling and binding of chaos, in recital and in song, Israel would annually relive and experience the new story of El/Yahweh, of his creation and sustenance, as well as of his selection and protection of Jerusalem. Yahweh the creator would be recognized as king of all the earth (Psalm 47).

This New Year's festival is a hypothetical reconstruction based in part on ancient Near Eastern patterns, for we have little firsthand information about the cultic forms and feasts that marked the critical points of the year as celebrated in the temple in Jerusalem. Such Near Eastern patterns suggest, however, that the king was officially enthroned at the New Year's festival, and it may be that this coronation was in some cases reenacted each year as well. This introduces another aspect of Canaanite tradition linked with Jerusalem and taken over by David into Israelite Yahwism.

El, Yahweh, and the Dynasty of David

In 2 Samuel 7 there is a unit that is critical for understanding the place of King David's dynasty in ancient Israel. The context of this unit is a rejection, delivered by the court prophet Nathan, of David's desire to build a temple for Yahweh. In the midst of this rejection or postponement of the king's plans a promise is made to David and his offspring:

> I took you from the pasture, from following the sheep, that you should be prince over my people Israel. . . . I have been with you wherever you went, and have cut off all your enemies from before you; and I will make for you a great name, like the name of the great ones of the earth. . . . I will give you

rest from all your enemies. . . . When your days are fulfilled and you lie down with your fathers, I will raise up your offspring after you, who shall come forth from your body, and I will establish his·kingdom. . . . I will establish his throne forever. I will be his father, and he shall be my son. When he commits iniquity, I will chasten him . . . but I will not take my steadfast love from him. . . . Your house and your kingdom shall be made sure forever before me; your throne shall be established forever.

(2 Samuel 7:8–16)

Here Yahweh of Israel singles out one man and makes the promise, hedged by no clear conditions, that he and his offspring shall stand as king over Israel forever (see also 2 Samuel 23:1–7). The phraseology used at one point is striking, especially when set against current Near Eastern theories of kingship: "I will be his father, and he shall be my son." Of no other Israelite is this ever said. This is not to suggest that the king is in any way to be considered the physical son of the deity or that he himself is divine, as was the case, for example, in Egypt. Yet these words of promise, in that period and part of the world, would clearly set the king apart from all other men in a remarkable manner.

In the Psalter similar phraseology and motifs appear in relation to the royal dynasty of David, often in conjunction with other themes associated with El/Yahweh and Jerusalem. In this regard, Psalms 2 and 110 are the most informative, but Psalms 18, 20, 21, 45, 72, 101, 132, and 144 also deal with divine support for the king. In Psalm 2, following a depiction of threatening chaos taking the form of political conspiracy, the divine promise is affirmed:

> I have set my king
>   on Zion, my holy hill.
>
> I will tell of the decree of Yahweh:
>   He said to me, "*You are my son,*
>   *today have I begotten you.*
> Ask of me, and I will make the nations
>   your heritage,
>   and the ends of the earth your possession."

(Psalm 2:6–8, italics added)

The rulers of all the earth are advised to pay homage to the king, who governs with divine authority from the city of El, the creator of heaven and earth. The promise made here is as expansive as was the empire of David and Solomon: all the earth shall be subject to Yahweh's king.

Such divine certification of the king at his enthronement or annual reenthronement was an element of the royal coronation ritual in ancient Egypt and possibly elsewhere as well. A formal decree would be presented in the name of the god declaring this figure to be his chosen king. On this divine decree royal authority would rest. As a part of the Babylonian New Year celebration of re-creation, the king was first stripped of all royal authority and then restored anew to the throne. When a new man became king upon the death of the old, the official coronation was celebrated at the time of, and as part of, next year's festival.

In Psalm 110 several of these motifs reappear. The Davidic king is promised universal rule; from Zion his authority shall extend to the ends of the earth. In verse 4 the royal line is linked with that of Melchizedek, also affirming that the king is, like Melchizedek, also a priest of his god. Again the king's assumption of authority is linked with the stilling of a chaotic threat to the political and natural order. Armed with divine might and promise, the king becomes an instrument in the god's creative and sustaining action. That this action sometimes involves violence is not surprising. It is a common motif in ancient Near Eastern creation theology that forces for chaos on both the political and natural level had to be defeated in pitched battle. The king's exercise of rule and judgment would always involve an element of force. Parts of Psalm 110 are not now wholly clear because in the course of its transmission the Hebrew text became disordered. About the basic themes presented, however, there can be little doubt.

In these psalms the royalist claims of the house of David have been caught up in the confluence of creation motifs associated with El/Yahweh, as well as with traditions telling of the election and inviolability of Zion. The king is lifted out of the human historical sphere and placed in the transcendental sphere of the creator god himself, and his authority is presented as a given part of the created universal pattern, not as a human accommodation or perversion of the divine will (compare 1 Samuel 8:7–9). In the time of David and Solomon such worldwide claims came closest to reality in terms of the actual extent of Israel's authority and influence. The radical transition from federation to monarchy, with its dislocations in all areas of life, made essential the need for founding the king's authority on some basic divine order. It would seem that the initial impetus for this development came from the Canaanite Jerusalem setting in which David founded his dynasty. The roots are here, even if particular expressions of this tradition in psalms and other units reflect later statements by descendants of the Davidic circles.

In summary, we find in this reconstruction of the Davidic and Zion traditions a story that brings three items into a mutually supportive relationship: (1) a creative sustaining deity named El, who is identified with Yahweh; (2) the election and protection of Jerusalem/Zion as the home of this deity; and (3) the universal rule of this deity as this is reflected in the rule of his king whose throne is on Zion. The city and royal dynasty are both inviolable because they stand under the protection of the creator god.

Woven together, these motifs comprise a complex of traditions or a story that is quite distinct from that of the federation. The source of this complex of traditions appears to be older Canaanite Jerusalem, which entered the Israelite sphere under David's kingship and came into contact, in time into conflict, with the older federation complex of traditions. Before pursuing the development of this conflict, we must consider an attempt to bring the stories together, an attempt that was first made during the period of David or Solomon by an unknown historian and theologian who saw in each story motifs that informed the other.

BIBLIOGRAPHIC NOTE

Aspects of the David-Zion Story

> Cross, Frank Moore. "The Ideologies of Kingship in the Era of the Empire: Conditional Covenant and Eternal Decree." In *Canaanite Myth and Hebrew Epic*, pp. 219–73. Cambridge, Mass.: Harvard University Press, 1973.
>
> Engnell, I. *Studies in Divine Kingship in the Ancient Near East*. Oxford : Basil Blackwell, 1967.
>
> Hayes, John H. "The Tradition of Zion's Inviolability." *Journal of Biblical Literature* 82 (1963): 419–62.
>
> Johnson, A. R. *Sacral Kingship in Ancient Israel*. Cardiff: University of Wales Press, 1967.
>
> Noth, Martin. "God, King, and Nation in the Old Testament." In *The Laws in the Pentateuch and Other Studies*, pp. 145–78. Philadelphia: Fortress Press, 1967.
>
> Roberts, J. J. M. "The Davidic Origin of the Zion Tradition." *Journal of Biblical Literature* 92 (1973): 329–44.
>
> _____. "Zion Tradition." In *The Interpreter's Dictionary of the Bible: Supplementary Volume*, pp. 985–87. Nashville: Abingdon Press, 1976.
>
> Szikszai, S. "King, Kingship." In *The Interpreter's Dictionary of the Bible*, vol. 3, pp. 11–17. Nashville: Abingdon Press, 1962.
>
> von Rad, Gerhard. *Old Testament Theology*. New York: Harper & Brothers, 1962 (Volume 1), 1965 (Volume 2).
>
> Weinfeld, Moshe. "Covenant, Davidic." In *The Interpreter's Dictionary of the Bible: Supplementary Volume*, pp. 188–92. Nashville: Abingdon Press, 1976.

Selected Psalms

> Mowinckel, Sigmund. *The Psalms in Israel's Worship*. Nashville: Abingdon Press, 1962.
>
> Weiser, Artur. *The Psalms*. Philadelphia: Westminster Press, 1962.

THE YAHWIST

3

Primary readings: *Genesis 2–11, 12–16, 18–22, 24–34, 38, 49*
                       Exodus 1–24, 32, 34
                       Numbers 11–12, 14, 20–25
                       Judges 1

During the reign of Solomon the sacred story of the federation was boldly recast by someone whose name is not known. He seems to have lived and written in proximity to the royal establishment and to have been influenced by the Zion story, for he produced an epic that enveloped the federation's story within Zion themes. Both historical and theological, his epic tells of Israel's origins and formation, tracing the hand of Yahweh in all these events. In addressing the empire and monarchy he sought in the past for goals, direction, and an identity for the Israel of his own day. Scholars today designate him as the "Yahwist" or refer to him and his work as J. Because neither designation is well known to many who read the Bible, however, it is helpful at this point to look at some results of nineteenth-century critical study of the Old Testament.

LITERARY CRITICAL STUDY OF THE PENTATEUCH

Probably by the time of Ezra in the late fifth century B.C.E. it was generally believed within Judaism that Moses was the primary author of the first five

66   books of the Bible, the so-called Pentateuch or Torah. Certainly this was the common belief in the time of Jesus. During the last few centuries, however, some have doubted the theory of Mosaic authorship. Even before the development and application to the Bible of modern literary critical methods, it was pointed out that the narrative always speaks of Moses in the third person and that his death is recounted in the last chapter of Deuteronomy. The application to the Bible of critical methods for the study of literature brought to attention certain anachronisms, repeated narrative units or doublets, seeming contradictions, variety in subject matter, marked changes in literary style, vocabulary, and syntax, as well as quite distinct and varied theological perspectives. All this suggested that the Pentateuch was a rich, many-layered document and that a long and complex history stood behind its development into its present form.

The Documentary Hypothesis

Over the course of the last century and a half, such observations have enabled students of the Old Testament to isolate four strata or documents within Genesis through Deuteronomy, noting sudden changes in style and vocabulary, as well as in subject and perspective, that could not be explained in terms of the supposed intent of a single author. Foremost among these changes is an alternation of the name *Yahweh* (a specific proper name for the god of Israel) and the term *Elohim* (a general term meaning "god") when speaking of the deity.

Associated with these designations are other characteristic variations in vocabulary. Where the name *Yahweh* is employed, for example, Moses' father-in-law is called Reuel, the sacred mountain is called Sinai, and the natives of Palestine are called Canaanites. Where the term *Elohim* is used, Moses' father-in-law is called Jethro, the mountain is Horeb, and the inhabitants of Palestine are Amorites. Accompanying these vocabulary patterns are marked stylistic changes, only some of which may be accounted for by changes in subject matter; in other instances different writers appear to have been at work. Thus there is in Genesis 1:1–2:4 a highly structured, repetitious, semipoetic account of the creation of the universe by Elohim. In Genesis 2:5–25, however, there appears another account of creation in which the deity is Yahweh, the order of events differs, and the style is much more prosaic.

The appearance of several accounts of the same or very similar events must be noted as well. Not only are there two accounts of creation in the first two chapters of Genesis, but one of the patriarchs appears three times to deceive a foreign ruler about his relationship to his wife (Genesis 12:10–20; 20; 26:1–11). Twice Abraham is involved, and twice the foreign king is Abimelek the Philistine. In other instances two accounts seem to be interwoven. In the flood narrative, for example, the number of animals brought on board the ark, the length of the period of rain and flood, and certain key terms change, suggesting that two once-independent narratives were woven together to form the present complex.

Striking differences in the presentation of the deity and of human beings provide another line of evidence. Sometimes the deity seems directly present to mortals, walking, talking, even debating with them. At other points he communicates with them only through intermediaries, such as angels, or through visions or dreams. In Genesis 18–19, for example, Yahweh appears directly to Abraham, engages him in conversation, offers him a promise, reveals his plans, and debates with him over the fate of Sodom (Genesis 18:1, 18:3, 18:10–15, and 18:17–21). Yet mixed with this is an appearance of three men (18:2, 18:4–8, 18:9, 18:16) and then of two men or angels with Yahweh seemingly making the third (Genesis 18:22; 19:1). These unexpected alternations are not what one would expect from a single writer but could be visible seams in a composite formed of different accounts of the same basic events.

At some points in the Pentateuch narratives the deity is described in human terms; at other points there are attempts to avoid such gross anthropomorphism. The patriarchs are sometimes presented as deceiving, lying, or vengeful; in other instances efforts are made to mitigate such an impression. Thus in Genesis 12 Abraham appears to lie when he says that Sarah is his sister. But in chapter 20 he is presented as technically within the letter, if not the spirit, of the truth, for it is stated that Sarah was his half-sister. (This tradition is supported nowhere else in the biblical tradition, and later law—e.g., Leviticus 18:9, 18:11, 20:17—appears not to allow marriage in such relationships.)

In isolation, no single item or line of evidence is conclusive, but viewed as a whole these varied observations fall into patterns that have led scholars to distinguish within the Pentateuch four strata that are now so intermixed that precise separation is not possible. The first document is called J (after the German spelling of Yahweh as "Jahweh") in recognition of its use of this name for the deity throughout. J is generally dated to about 950 B.C.E. and will be our primary concern in this chapter. The second document is dated about a century later and is called E because of its preference for the term Elohim before the god reveals his name as Yahweh in Exodus 3. E will be studied in chapter 5.

Deuteronomy (D), a body of material that is dated in its present form to about 620–570 B.C.E., is the work of a distinct circle that lived through the last years and destruction of the nation Israel. This work will concern us at the end of this study of ancient Israel's religious tradition. The final and still later document is called P because of its interest in cultic and other priestly concerns. All these documents were in time combined, J and E probably toward the end of the eighth century B.C.E. Into this newly formed narrative (called R^{JE}—R standing for "redactor" or "editor") D was inserted about a century later. Still later P was added, and the Pentateuch came to have its present form.

The strata called J, E, D, and P tell each in its own way the sacred story of oldest Israel already encountered in the creedlike units in Deuteronomy 26 and

Joshua 24. Each represents an attempt to find in this story themes that address the specific needs, concerns, and crises of distinct generations of Israelites and Jews. In this respect the full Pentateuch reflects centuries of development and reformation of Israelite tradition. It is a multilayered repository of storytelling and a treasure house for those who seek to understand the history of ancient Israelite and Jewish religious traditions.

Tetrateuch, Pentateuch, or Hexateuch

Contemporary biblical scholarship is divided over the scope of these several strata. Applying literary, stylistic, and other criteria, scholars have generally succeeded in distinguishing J, E, and P in the books of Genesis through Numbers (D is, of course, Deuteronomy, and its presence in any of the other books is doubtful). These first four books are known collectively as the Tetrateuch. Although all scholars agree that J begins with the creation as recounted in Genesis 2:4–24 and that E begins with the call of Abraham, some feel that none of these documents extends farther than the Tetrateuch, while others believe that J and E once extended into Joshua and Judges.

The first view takes the position that J and E carry the narrative only as far as the wilderness wandering following the covenant at Sinai. At best they offer only a foretaste of the conquest when they tell of the taking of land east of the Jordan River. The account of the conquest of Canaan in Joshua and Judges 1 is in this view part of another great historical narrative that extends through 2 Kings and reviews the history of Israel from the conquest through the monarchy. This great history takes its theological stance in themes that are developed in Deuteronomy and is therefore called the deuteronomistic history.

The other view suggests that J and E at one time extended into Joshua, Judges, and possibly into 1 and 2 Samuel, for these books, too, indicate complex sources behind the material's present form. Some believe there is good evidence that J and E once included an account of the conquest of Canaan. They argue further that it was P, the last document, that excluded any notice of the conquest and that the end was cut from their version of the story at the time of P's incorporation into the other documents. Thus, in the study of J and E we must look to a Hexateuch (Genesis through Joshua), while with P we must limit ourselves to the Pentateuch (Genesis through Deuteronomy) or Tetrateuch (Genesis through Numbers).

Promise and Fulfillment

The narrative outline that underlies the Pentateuch does appear to be open-ended or incomplete. This is essentially the outline found in the federation's sacred story as presented in Deuteronomy 26 or Joshua 24 which first spoke of the election of the patriarchs and of promises made to them by their god. These promises seem to find realization in the conquest of the land of Canaan, but in the Pentateuch this fulfillment is cut off. At the end of Deuter-

onomy the Israelites are still in the wilderness, having taken only some land east
of the Jordan River; the full conquest of the land of Israel lies in the future.

As we shall see, the situation of those who produced the P stratum demanded
this cutting off, for the priestly circle was working to preserve its people in exile,
removed from the land of promise by force of arms. It is our position that J and
E in their full form told of the conquest. Only later was their natural end cut off
and either lost or, as some suspect, caught up into the deuteronomistic history
in the books of Joshua and Judges.

The Yahwist's epic therefore ranged from promise to fulfillment, from creation to conquest, reforming or transforming the older federation story in two
ways. First, it expanded each segment of the older story with a rich variety of
legends and sagas that tell of the patriarchs, the bondage in Egypt, the exodus,
the wandering in the wilderness, and the conquest. Most of these additions deal
with the patriarchs, for what was only an introductory theme in the early
federation's creeds became the focal point in the Yahwist's narrative. Second,
the Yahwist added new themes that were not mentioned in the older story. The
account of the creation and the Garden of Eden, the story of the fall, of Cain and
Abel, of the flood, and of the Tower of Babel—all stand as a prologue to the
story of Israel. Included, too, are the encounter with Yahweh at Sinai and the
formation of the covenant, whose absence from the older story was probably a
result of their setting and use in a cultic action that was itself a reexperiencing
and renewal of the covenant first made at Sinai.

The Yahwist removed the sacred story from this setting in a cultic event.
With the many additions to its basic themes and with the further expansions of
the old story, the brief creedlike recitals became an extended literary unit of epic
quality and an extended theological history divorced from close attachment to a
cultic service. Building on the older story, the Yahwist sought to affirm that
Israel's sudden and complete transition from federation to empire was Yahweh's doing. The Israel of the empire was, he affirmed, Yahweh's creation for
which Yahweh had a mission.

THE YAHWIST'S EPIC

Adopting the outline of the federation's story, the Yahwist brought to it a variety
of seemingly new materials that were, in part, not new at all. A full store of
accounts belonging to one or more of the older tribal groups would form a rich
source for expanding and enriching the older story outline. Also available to
him were themes and motifs developed in the theology and mythology of the
ancient Near Eastern environment in which Israel lived. From material of the
latter type would come the blocks with which he built the prologue to Israel's
story found in Genesis 2–11.

It is likely that these threads all came together in Jerusalem, the cosmopolitan
city of David and Solomon. Here was now housed the ark of the federation;

here, too, was access to older stories of tribal heroes and their adventures, of the events that made some places sacred, of past encounters between forefathers and deities, and of the many incidents involved in the escape from Egypt and of life in the wilderness.

Here in this new urban setting would also be found a freedom to reuse these older materials in new ways. With its intermingling of foreign and native courtiers, merchants, diplomats, royal wives and their entourages, this royal city would provide access to the literary and religious traditions of a world far beyond the borders of the older federation. From Jerusalem one's horizons reached beyond the central hills of southern Palestine to the ends of the earth. In Jerusalem one found Israel caught up in new directions and concerns that had to be comprehended, certified, and directed. The Yahwist addressed his narrative to this new and larger Israel by beginning his epic not with the patriarchs but with creation itself, to which he added a series of remarkable narrative units telling about the human family in general. By centering his attention on all the families of the earth, he set the federation story within a universal perspective.

Israel's Charter and Mission

Creation and Disintegration   From chapter 2 through chapter 11 of Genesis a rich tapestry is woven out of motifs and themes drawn in part from a wide variety of ancient Near Eastern materials, forming a prologue to Israel's own story. The prologue opens with the presentation of a fully integrated, harmonious created order (Genesis 2:4–24) which disintegrates because of an act of human disobedience. The harmony is shattered; what was once a blessed state becomes cursed. The depth of this reversal is then developed in a series of scenes illustrating the disintegration. In this tapestry the Yahwist offers not merely an account of the past but presents his vision of the human situation of this day as he perceives it from his vantage point.

Adam and Eve are driven from the garden and must thereafter scratch out a living from the ground by hard labor (Genesis 3). In time they must die, for they no longer have access to the tree of life. The disorder intensifies as brother turns against brother. First Cain slays Abel (Genesis 4:1–16), then man is set against man in a blood feud (Genesis 4:23–24). The boundary demarking the divine and the human is trespassed in a terse and obscure account of the mating of sons of the god/gods with mortal women (Genesis 6:1–4). Because of human perverseness, nature and the deity destroy humankind in a flood (Genesis 6–9). Finally, an attempt by humans to overreach themselves with their tower results in a scattering of nations and confusion of tongues (Genesis 11:1–9). The human family grows ever more alienated from the deity and from one another until the harmonious order has in every way dissolved. The state of blessing found in the garden has become one of curse. Supportive relationships have become centers for conflict; lines of distinction have turned into barriers. The result is a virtual return to chaos.

Many of the Yahwist's themes appear in the literature and mythology of the Near East, especially in that of ancient Mesopotamia, and in unearthing this corpus of ancient material during the past century, archaeologists have provided a background that gives new dimensions to the Yahwist's work. In a great Mesopotamian epic that deals with a legendary king named Gilgamesh and his tragic search for immortality, for example, we find not only a form of the flood story but also the motif of a serpent who deprives human beings of a plant or tree of life. The same epic contains an account of lost innocence that is associated with a mature awareness of human sexuality and human limitations.

Mesopotamian tradition elsewhere pictures the formation of an ideal gardenlike land through the bringing of fresh water to a barren waste. In Mesopotamia this paradise, called Dilmun, is the home of a man and wife who are immortal, as Adam and Eve are immortal so long as they reside in the garden and have access to the tree of life. Mesopotamian tradition also offers accounts of a shepherd-farmer conflict not unlike that between Cain and Abel. The Tower of Babel, too, may reflect an attempt to explain the truncated stepped tower called a ziggurat that was part of the temple complex in the city of Babylon. These are only samples of the vast resources available to the Yahwist in cosmopolitan Jerusalem.

A study of the opening to the Yahwist's epic in relation to this material reveals his unique creativity in adapting and bringing a unified structure to diverse materials. In Mesopotamian tradition, for example, human mortality is seemingly the result of divine whim; the flood is a tragic event whose causes, which are not clearly stated, lie beyond human comprehension. In the Yahwist's epic, death becomes the human fate because of an act of human disobedience; the flood is just punishment by a deity whose creation has turned against him. In Mesopotamian tradition, too, many deities intimately associated with the forces of nature appear set against one another in conflicts that overwhelm human beings and exceed mortal understanding. Although traces of a polytheistic background are still to be found in Genesis 3:22, 6:1–4, and 11:7, it is clear that one deity alone is the center of all interest and authority in the Yahwist's epic, demonstrating once again that he not only recast the traditions available to him but wove many of them into a unique new construction.

Finally, although the overall vision of Genesis 2–11 is one of paradise lost, there is within it a note of relenting grace on the part of the deity. Fated to die on the day they eat of the forbidden fruit, Adam and Eve do not die until later and only after they have borne children, reflecting Israel's belief that immortality was achieved first and foremost through one's offspring. Thus the real end of the Eden story is found in the notice of the birth of Cain and Abel (Genesis 4:1–2). Further, because Cain slew his brother and became an outlaw, anyone could kill him with impunity. To prevent this, however, he is marked by the deity as being under divine protection. Still later, one man and his family are spared in the flood to preserve life and to rebuild. Thus this account of the passage from blessing to curse retains a small note of preserved and continuing blessing.

Israel's Call and Task   Although a note of blessing appears to be absent from the conclusion of the Tower of Babel episode, the range of vision abruptly narrows at this point. From a universal perspective taking in all nations and peoples, the narrative suddenly focuses on one family and then on one man, Abraham, who is called to leave his Mesopotamian homeland and his kinfolk to become a wanderer through the land of Canaan. An alien having only limited contact with the natives and setting but shallow roots, he lives with a promise that alone sustains him. This is a promise given by his god, who in the Yahwist's narrative is the god of creation, and the promise is the note of grace that attaches to the story of the cursed and scattered nations in the account of the Tower of Babel.

Says Yahweh to Abraham, "Go from your country and your kindred and your father's house to the land that I will show you," but go with this promise and blessing:

> I will make of you a great nation,
>   and I will bless you;
> And make your name great,
>   so that you will be a blessing.
> I will bless all who bless you,
>   but him who curses you I will curse.
> And by you all the families of the earth shall bless themselves.
>
> (Genesis 12:1–3)

According to the Yahwist, Abraham left his home and the social structures that supported and protected him and became a type of outlaw. In time the deity's blessing and charge were transferred to his son Isaac, then to Jacob, and through Jacob to the Twelve Tribes that are said to spring from him. By implication, the blessing and charge passed from the Twelve Tribes to the Israel of David and Solomon.

The form of the promise is very old, and parts of it are probably deeply rooted in Israelite history and tradition. It is the sort of promise that a semino-madic wanderer might carry with him or that the revered founder of a tribe or clan might have been said to have received from his god, and the story of its reception would be remembered by later generations as a source of identity and continued relationship with the god. Thus we may have here traces of some account of how a father met and was blessed by his deity at a place that would thereby become sacred to his heirs who would preserve the story and tell it when they gathered at the sacred place (compare such units as Genesis 15; 28:10–22; 32:24–32).

But in this old blessing the Yahwist saw meaning that far transcended a nomad's hope for offspring and land upon which he could settle; he saw expressed a vision, a goal, and a charter for his people. He found elements of both support and judgment, and upon these themes he built the remainder of his narrative. There is the promise of greatness, of unconditional protection and support, and in the last clause a mission is expressed for Israel: "By you all the families of the earth shall bless themselves."

It should be observed that while the narrative focus has narrowed to one man, all the human families of the earth still remain in view. In this way Israel's story is linked to that of all humankind, and here is the final note of grace. In Abraham and his seed these human families will all find blessing; the curse upon all peoples will be overcome. This is Israel's mission and the reason for its existence. But when a nation is given a mission, a basis is also established for judging that nation. Next we will examine the nation's support, then the potential for judgment.

Support for the Nation   Yahweh's promise to Abraham recalls the promise made through Nathan the court prophet to David in 2 Samuel 7:9: "I will make for you a great name, like the name of the great ones of the earth." Thus the promise to Abraham would seem to find full realization in the empire of David and Solomon because in that period only did Israel's authority encompass the full extent of the land wandered by Abraham. Whether or not Genesis 12:1–3 is to be understood as a conscious recollection of the promise in 2 Samuel 7:9, the Yahwist and the people of his day would probably have understood these words as having been addressed to them through Abraham, for the Yahwist implies that the empire and monarchy are not a departure from Yahweh's ways but are the fulfillment of his actions in Israel's behalf. In this way divine certification was provided for the work of David and Solomon in empire building and establishing their kingship.

From all the nations and peoples of the earth, the Yahwist asserts, one man was selected to carry a promise as full and unconditional as that given in the name of Yahweh to David. Contrary to all that is probable, in the face of unimagined dangers and obstacles, even when the bearer of the promise seemed to doubt the promise, Yahweh supported and upheld him. Even when in the face of famine Abraham took matters into his own hands and left the land of promise for Egypt and food only to face a very different danger, he was still delivered by Yahweh and even came away from Egypt with increased wealth (Genesis 12:10–20). The childless Abraham and Sarah were not abandoned by the deity even when they again took matters into their own hands and sought to get a child either by means of adoption (Genesis 15:1–4) or through a servant girl (Genesis 16). Although time and again they appear unworthy, in their old age they were given a son, and Isaac in turn became the heir of the promise (Genesis 26:1–5).

In time the promise passed to Jacob, who, as the narrative develops, appears the most unworthy of all. The material about Jacob is presented in two interlocking cycles of which the cycle dealing with him and his brother Esau enframes that dealing with him and his uncle Laban. At first this forefather and bearer of the name Israel is presented as an out-and-out rogue. He is a cheat and a liar who steals his brother's birthright and obtains his father's deathbed blessing by deceit. While there is an element of quid pro quo in his dealings with Laban, he is still scarcely a model of rectitude. Yet even as Jacob flees the land of promise and his brother's anger, the promise is renewed for him in a dream at Bethel (Genesis 28:10–17). As he flees Laban and faces Esau years later and as he returns to the land of promise, a parallel scene is enacted in the strange nighttime encounter at Peniel (Genesis 32:22–32). His name is changed, as he has changed, and he is blessed.

First, then, the Yahwist focused attention on just one man, then on twelve sons of that man's grandson, then on a band of slaves in Egypt, then on fugitives in Sinai's wastes. Repeatedly endangered, seemingly about to vanish on many occasions, small, weak, and often unworthy, these ancestors of the Israelite empire of David and Solomon were sustained again and again, even in the land of the god-king pharaoh, because they were a chosen people, elected by a god who upheld and preserved them. In the varied tales of the past, including the cycle of plagues and the account of deliverance, older forms of which were still remembered and relived in cultic celebration, the Yahwist found models for a message of hope and support addressed to the Israelite empire of his own day. On such a precedent his people could place confident trust in the ever renewed and affirmed promise and support of their god Yahweh.

Universalism and Judgment The older federation story that had served to unify a small group of loosely bound tribes in the hill country of southern Palestine was essentially nationalistic. It asserted that Israel had been born in an escape from foreign slavery that had pitted the fugitives and their god against the Egyptians and their god-king pharaoh. It drew clear and sharp lines between insider and outsider, and the lines were defined by mutual hostilities (Joshua 24:2–15). That other nations and peoples were generally experienced as hostile and threatening to Israel's existence the Book of Judges makes most clear. Basically the story affirmed that the deity Yahweh was a national god who fought for and sustained his chosen people. While powerful in Egypt as well as in Canaan, he was comprehended and experienced in terms of the formation and protection of the nation Israel.

The Yahwist reaffirmed these claims of national support and related them to the empire of his day, but he went beyond them and asked why. Why did Yahweh elect, form, support, sustain, and reaffirm Israel? This basic question seems almost forced upon him by the context (Genesis 2–11) into which he placed his account of Israel's history and the vision of his god that is offered there, for his is a god of all peoples, creator of all and concerned with all. From the perspective of the prologue in Genesis 2–11, the question leaps forth: Why did the god of all the families of the earth focus on this one family of Abraham and his seed? Creation and a universal perspective are not part of the federation's creed-like confessions and recitals.

In that early period the assurance of divine protection and support had been enough; self-preservation was then a full-time preoccupation. But the situation changed dramatically with the rapid and thoroughgoing transition to empire. When old enemies became allies or subjects, new modes of relationship and new attitudes were needed. Setting the old story within the perspective of all creation expanded its horizons to match the empire's expanded reach. Hence the old story of national support was both affirmed and provided with a radical new thrust, for Israel is now to be not only Yahweh's chosen people but the instrument by which his blessing as creator god shall come to all the families of the earth. At the end of the account of the Tower of Babel all nations and peoples are cursed, but in Abraham all families are to find blessing; his promise is their promise of grace as well. In the context of the prologue and its depiction of worldwide dissolution, it is clear that Israel is to be the instrument by which the creator god will restore his created universe. The statement that Yahweh created Israel for a purpose enframes the nationalistic thrust of the older story.

To be Yahweh's instrument of blessing, to be the vehicle for life, peace, integrity, and harmony in the created order, to reverse the currents set in motion by the first human act of disobedience—this is the vision the Yahwist held out to the empire of David and Solomon, and in this a potential for judgment is implied. The statement made to Abraham that in him all the families of the earth will find blessing is an assertion, and it is assumed that it will happen, but it also holds up a standard by which the empire itself might be measured.

For example, the account of David's taking of Bathsheba, the future queen mother, and his disposal of her husband Uriah would be well known, if not openly discussed, in Solomon's court and royal city. Who in that setting would fail to compare the actions and motives that Abraham attributes to the Egyptian king (Genesis 12:10–20) with the actions and motives of King David of Israel? But the foreign king, on learning the true relation of Sarah to Abraham, does not kill the patriarch; he sends him away with both lavish gifts and his wife. Quite the opposite is true of David's treatment of Uriah, the Hittite soldier in his army. Abraham was hardly a vehicle for blessing for the Egyptians in his encounter, nor was Jacob later in his relationship with his brother and uncle (see also Genesis 34). Judgment is evoked from the reader on these actions and thereby on more current events as well.

In other situations, however, Abraham is a force for life and blessing. In Genesis 18 he intercedes for the alien city of Sodom; elsewhere he argues with his god over the fate of other human beings (Genesis 13; 26:26–33; 33; in this respect Exodus 12:29–33 should be examined as well). The challenge is there, more often implied than openly stated (see, however, Genesis 18:18; 28:14; Exodus 12:32), to an empire that was too often carved out with a ruthless sword and that seemed to bring death and not life, chaos and not harmony (see 2 Samuel 8). The Yahwist does not moralize openly or state applications to his own day, however. He often allows his sources to address their own varied concerns in their own diverse ways, and as a body they offer a rich mixture of traditions; Israel's past is here preserved in all its complexity and many voices.

The Yahwist seems rarely to have reworked his material internally; it is in the larger structure and in transitions between units that his vision comes through. For this theological epic of Israel is constructed in such a way as both to legitimize the empire and to offer a challenging vision of its larger task in the divine plan for the world. Israel in all its Solomonic grandeur, he asserted, is the deity's force for life, harmony, integrity, and peace in this world. The nationalistic thrust of his epic is thus subsumed by, and made to serve a larger universal vision of, Yahweh's intention for the whole creation. In this way he allowed neither the nation nor the empire at its greatest to become an end in itself. He would not allow the court in Jerusalem to sit in smug satisfaction or to center their worship on the nation as the product of their own efforts.

SYNTHESIS OF THE MOSES-SINAI AND DAVID-ZION TRADITIONS

The Yahwist thoroughly transformed the old story of the federation, recasting it, taking it out of its cultic setting and limited creedlike form, and producing from the older skeleton a complex and richly varied epic. Although he gave a place to the event at Mount Sinai, its place was limited and the legal stipulations in his work are few (Exodus 34 is about all). The covenant made at Sinai and even the exodus event came to be overshadowed by the promise made to the patriarchs, which provides the controlling theme of the epic. In the older creeds the patriarchs are but a prelude to the exodus, but the Yahwist links to Abraham his fundamental confessional formula of support and mission. All that follows in his recital of Israel's history is illustration of Genesis 12:1–3. In giving priority to the patriarchs and to Yahweh's promise to them, and even more in prefacing Israel's story with the universal perspective provided in Genesis 2–11, he essentially altered the thrust of the old story.

In both its content and unconditional quality, the promise made to Abraham echoes that made to David. The deity puts forth no specific stipulations as conditions upon which divine support will rest; the promise is offered without strings and can only be accepted. Even when most unworthy, the patriarchs are not abandoned. "I will make of you a great nation. . . . and make your name great"; "I will make for you a great name. . . . Your house and your kingdom shall be made sure before me forever"—these assurances found in Genesis 12:2 and 2 Samuel 7:9–16 carry the force of certainty, of actions already coming into effect. Beyond this, the extension of Yahweh's concern to the very ends of the created universe and the vision of the deity as creator and sustainer all echo the traditions associated with Zion and David.

In his epic the Yahwist brought together the older story of the federation with formative themes from the newer story that was linked to Jerusalem and its king, the latter providing the epic's overarching and controlling thrust. The two stories are harmonized; no tension is permitted to surface between them. The emphasis on national support does not conflict with the challenge of Israel's mission; both legitimization and judgment are brought together into a larger unified vision.

Although failures to live up to the challenge are noted repeatedly, the certainty of divine support is nevertheless affirmed. Even the challenge finds expression as a statement of fact; it *will* take place: "By you all the families of the earth shall bless themselves." The Yahwist had no doubt that, in spite of human failures, the people of Israel would fill their role in the divine plan that he has set forth. In this respect, too, he reflects the heady days of the empire when briefly under David, and especially under Solomon, all things seemed possible. For a time Israel would shine forth like a light, revealing Yahweh's concern for all the nations of the earth.

Because it was a remarkable vision it is not surprising that not everyone would so understand Yahweh's relation with the Davidic dynasty and the empire or so evaluate the monarchy and the fundamental changes it brought about. Not all would perceive the light, and within Israel tensions were building that would soon dim the brightness of Solomonic Jerusalem and the empire. Of this, however, there is no hint in the Yahwist's work. In the end the nation would not fail, however often it fell short in the meanwhile. But the grandeur would dissolve in time, and tensions between the two stories would become marked. Finally they would be pitted against each other in open conflict, upon the outcome of which would hang the fate of the nation.

BIBLIOGRAPHIC NOTE

The Documentary Hypothesis

The history and current status of the documentary hypothesis is discussed in the Literary Introductions section of the introductory Bibliographic Note.

> Habel, Norman. *Literary Criticism of the Old Testament*. Philadelphia: Fortress Press, 1971.

Prehistory of the Material in Genesis

> Gunkel, Hermann. *The Legends of Genesis: The Biblical Saga and History*. New York: Schocken Books, 1964. A reedition of a still formative older work of 1901.

> Noth, Martin. *A History of Pentateuchal Traditions*. Englewood Cliffs, N.J.: Prentice-Hall, 1972.

78   Pritchard, James B., ed. *Ancient Near Eastern Texts relating to the Old Testament*. 3d ed., supp. Princeton: Princeton University Press, 1969. Source material from the Near East at large.

The Book of Genesis

Eissfeldt, Otto. "Genesis." In *The Interpreter's Dictionary of the Bible*, vol. 2, pp. 366–80. Nashville: Abingdon Press, 1962.

Sarna, Nahum M. *Understanding Genesis*. New York: Schocken Books, 1970.

Speiser, E. A. *Genesis*. Garden City, N.Y.: Doubleday & Co., 1964.

von Rad, Gerhard. *Genesis*. Philadelphia: Westminster Press, 1972. A classic.

Westermann, C., and Alberts, R. "Genesis." In *The Interpreter's Dictionary of the Bible: Supplementary Volume*, pp. 356–61. Nashville: Abingdon Press, 1976.

The Book of Exodus

Childs, Brevard S. *The Book of Exodus*. Philadelphia: Westminster Press, 1974. An excellent commentary.

Clements, Ronald E. "Exodus, Book of." In *The Interpreter's Dictionary of the Bible: Supplementary Volume*, pp. 310–12. Nashville: Abingdon Press, 1976.

Noth, Martin. *Exodus*. Philadelphia: Westminster Press, 1962.

Wright, G. Ernest. "Exodus, Book of." In *The Interpreter's Dictionary of the Bible*, vol. 2, pp. 188–97. Nashville: Abingdon Press, 1962.

The Yahwist

Brueggemann, Walter. "Yahwist." In *The Interpreter's Dictionary of the Bible: Supplementary Volume*, pp. 971–75. Nashville: Abingdon Press, 1976.

Ellis, Peter. *The Yahwist: The Bible's First Theologian*. Notre Dame, Ind.: Fides, 1968.

Wolff, Hans Walter. "The Kerygma of the Yahwist." In *The Vitality of Old Testament Traditions*, edited by Walter Brueggemann and Hans Walter Wolff, pp. 41–66. Atlanta: John Knox Press, 1975.

VISIONS OF THE WAYS OF GOD WITH MAN

4

Primary readings: 2 Samuel 7–20; 1 Kings 1–2
Proverbs 10–31
Genesis 37, 39–48, 50
1 Samuel 9–31

Before taking up the further history of the David-Zion and Moses-Sinai stories we will here focus on several literary products of the reigns of David and Solomon. These materials are of interest not only because they tell about critical events in Israel's history but also because of what they reveal about the literary and theological excitement and creative experimentation during this formative period. Fundamental in all these works are visions of the relationship between the deity and human beings.

Three narratives will be considered as products of the age of Solomon, each of which, like the Yahwist's epic, utilizes older materials as sources, though they rework and reform their sources much more thoroughly. Each offers a distinctive point of view, a controlling plot, and unified though complex character development. Where the Yahwist often allows his source material to speak for itself, confining his contribution to the ordering of units and to transitions between them, the authors of these narratives fully control and shape their material. Their work is therefore more focused and concentrated, offering stories that are both well told and entertaining. In time each narrative is taken up into a larger context and assumes its place in 1 or 2 Samuel or Genesis.

THE SUCCESSION NARRATIVE
2 Samuel 7–20
1 Kings 1–2

The succession narrative, which tells of events closest to the time of its author, is so named because it deals broadly with the question of which of David's sons will follow him on the throne in Jerusalem and how this will come about. The narrative also provides unusual insight into the inner life of David's court and family. Within this matrix of complex and savage political maneuverings and intrigues and within the context of this star-crossed family, we are offered a fascinating portrait of David as king, father, husband, and as a man before his god. Around this central portrait move a number of lesser but also finely drawn figures. The narrative presents a subtle discourse on power, its acquisition and retention, its use and abuse, at the same time that it develops a striking vision of the controlling action of the deity in the course of human history.

Who Will Succeed David?

Whether the narrative opens with 2 Samuel 7 or 2 Samuel 9, the central issue—Yahweh's promise to David of an everlasting dynasty—is clear. The question is how this will come about, or, more immediately, which of his sons will succeed him. From David's first wife, Michal, there was to be no heir who would unite in his veins the blood of the families of Saul and David (2 Samuel 6:23), but David has several other sons by several other wives.

At all events, the complexity of David's character and motives finds expression at the very outset. The king's kindness toward Jonathan's lame son appears to be an act of devotion to the dead father, who was David's close friend (1 Samuel 18:1–4; 19:1–7; 20:1–42), as well as a sign of compassion for the son. But it also places this last member of the house of Saul firmly under David's control. There will be no threat to his right to rule Israel from this quarter.

In the well-known story of David and Bathsheba, which is presented against the background of a war between the Ammonites and Israel (2 Samuel 11), King David now appears as a despot who so abuses his power as to take another man's wife and murder her husband, a foreigner in his service who appears in every way to be nobler than the king. At the same time, however, David shows admirable humility in accepting the prophetic rebuke in Nathan's parable (2 Samuel 12). When divine punishment follows and the first son of this union dies, the king displays a strength of character that mystifies his courtiers (2 Samuel 12:15–25). Then from this union, which has heretofore brought nothing but death, is born the future heir to the throne (2 Samuel 12:24–25). This second son, however, slips unobtrusively into the background as the original act of violence and abuse of authority recoil on David's family. Amnon rapes his half-sister Tamar and, when David does nothing about this for a long period, is murdered by her brother Absalom (2 Samuel 13) who must then flee the country. Through the offices of Joab, Absalom is eventually allowed to return, only to spark a civil war that places him in his father's position in Jerusalem and David in flight (2 Samuel 15).

Throughout these events the complexity of David's character is again striking. His hesitancy to punish Amnon had provoked Absalom and set in motion the events that drove him from the throne; and Absalom's critique of his father's administration of justice must have had some foundation, for he "stole the hearts of the men of Israel" (2 Samuel 15:1–6). Still, this seemingly defeated and impotent king is able to attract to his side in exile many who must have been there out of a strong personal attachment to him (2 Samuel 15:13–37). Once again the king recognizes his limitations and leaves the issue to Yahweh; this is most clearly demonstrated in his response to the curse of the Benjaminite Shimei (2 Samuel 16:5–14). At the same time, however, he seems much too quick to believe the charges of Ziba (2 Samuel 16:1–4).

The attempted coup is put down through Hushai's intrigue (2 Samuel 16:15–17:20) and Joab's military leadership. Joab executes Absalom against David's command. News of his son's death brings an anguished outcry from his father, which leads to a remarkable encounter between the king and his oldest supporter (2 Samuel 19:1–8). Only the coldest of hearts could be unmoved by David's cry, "O my son Absalom, my son, my son Absalom." Yet the force of pragmatic necessity is likewise compelling in Joab's rebuke, "Today you have covered with shame the faces of all your servants, who have today saved your life, and the lives of your sons and your daughters, and the lives of your wives and your concubines" (2 Samuel 19:6). The necessities of political power and its retention win the day but not without further trouble from some northern groups sparked by one Sheba (2 Samuel 20). As the incident between Joab and Amasa suggests, tensions also build within the official family (2 Samuel 20:1–10).

The narrative ends with the passage of power to Solomon, this almost forgotten second son of Bathsheba, on the death of his father. The final scene is one of pure power politics as sides form around Adonijah and Solomon. Demonstrating a political guile that seems incongruous with his earlier moral rebuke, the prophet Nathan carefully orchestrates the presentation of Solomon's claims in 1 Kings 1 (it should be noted that there is no earlier reference in the narrative to this promise which Nathan has Bathsheba "recall" for the king). In short order the new king ruthlessly removes all opposition, and with the aid of Benaiah, his new enforcer, "the kingdom was established in the hands of Solomon" (1 Kings 2). The question posed at the outset has been answered. Solomon has succeeded his father and in a manner most remarkable, for after his birth notice he remains unmentioned and forgotten until the final scene. Nevertheless, David's son now sits on the throne, and the kingdom and dynasty are secure.

But the cost of all this in human life and suffering is great, and the final scene, which offers an unappealing picture of scheming courtiers and family members, also depicts a weak old man at the end of his life. Yet that old man is the hero of the narrative. Again and again he stands above all others, often strong though not ideal. If David's portrait is muted by shadows, the figures acting about him are also complex and real people—ambitious, selfish, cruel, scared, grieved, loyal, humble, noble—who cannot easily be judged. Ambiguities, motives sometimes unspoken and perhaps unconscious, interlace the narrative. Within the royal court where there is power to be seized, perhaps it must be seized but its service can bring death in many forms and can rend the heart of a king who is also a father.

A Concept of Providence

In this narrative the deity makes an appearance only in the oracles of Nathan and in two brief but significant asides by the author. The first aside appears in the notice that because Yahweh loved the second son of David and Bathsheba, the son was called Jedidiah, "beloved of Yahweh" (2 Samuel 12:24–25). Although this infant seemingly disappears from the narrative, the notice leaps suddenly to the fore again when the child is mature and on the throne. The second aside occurs when Hushai's advice is taken over that of Ahitophel. This is a critical moment in Absalom's rebellion, for here the initiative returns to David. Although this event takes place within the tensions and dynamics of court life, the reader is told that it was Yahweh's doing, "for Yahweh had ordained to defeat the good counsel of Ahitophel, so that Yahweh might bring evil upon Absalom" (2 Samuel 17:14).

These brief references to Yahweh do not change what is essentially a secular narrative; they rather underscore the fact that events flow here on the level of human intentionality and initiative. Although the author affirms a vision of divine control over the course of human history, it is not the divine control manifest in the federation traditions, many of which were preserved by the Yahwist. In this older material the deity was highly present and visible, meeting directly with mortals, talking and debating with them, and on more than one occasion intervening in the course of events with a miracle. Indeed, the normal order of nature and human events is violently disrupted in the older traditions as Yahweh splits the sea, sends plagues, rains fire from heaven, pulls down walls, and pours destruction and panic on enemy forces. The author of the succession narrative, however, offers a new vision of divine action which allows full range to human motivation and intention and requires from men and women full accountability for their deeds. Just as David and his family bear the curse of the king's violent taking of a woman and murder of her husband, for example, so Amnon's violence brings violence upon him.

It is affirmed that there is a form of divine control or providence in and behind these events that orders them in ways not always apparent to human beings caught up in the course of their lives. Nevertheless, it is always present, in even the most sordid and ignoble of human events. A vision is developed of a deity who allows full scope to human beings but who catches up human deeds and motives in all their grayness and ambiguity and uses them for good. In short, human lives are caught up in a larger, if not always comprehended, frame of control that will ultimately order events for good. The royal line is preserved, the throne secure, and the promise fulfilled. The child of a destructive mating is the beloved one who becomes the king, but human freedom and responsibility, are retained in this vision.

The succession narrative affirms Solomon's divine right to David's throne, but it also contains a muted warning about the obligations of this position. Although the author supports the royal claims of the Davidic house, he presents the new king as immediately engaging in acts that lead, even in the context of ancient oriental courts and pragmatic politics, to the edge of self-serving abuse of power, and he sounds a distinct note of judgment. It is possible that this narrative was written early in Solomon's reign. If so, it ends with questions that are broader than those with which it began. Will this son of David learn from his father's example, from his mistakes, and from those moments in which he became aware of the limits on human comprehension, ability, and the use of power?

WISDOM AND KING SOLOMON

Proverbs and Wise Men

Statements about Solomon's wisdom and the development of several forms of learning in his court (1 Kings 4:29–34) indicate his patronage of a royal educational establishment. Such establishments, in which officials were trained, were found in most royal courts in the ancient Near East, and collections of brief sayings and admonitions were products of these centers. Those who taught in the court educational centers, were called "wise men," although the designation was also applied to those skilled in various crafts and trades as well as to those who were simply clever (see Exodus 28:3; 35:25; Jeremiah 10:9; Ezekiel 27:8; Psalm 107:27; 2 Samuel 13:14). The several collections found in Proverbs 10–31 seem to reflect the work of court wisdom establishments that flourished throughout the Davidic monarchy. One collection, Proverbs 22:17–24:22, is modeled on an Egyptian collection of didactic sayings called the "Instruction of Amen-em-opet," and all offer practical advice on how to live the good life.

Wise Sayings   In even the earliest human communities there were men and women who were especially adept at expressing experience in words that seized the heart and mind and were readily retainable. Especially if these people had lived long and fully, if their experiences had been both wide and deep, they could give expression to what they knew so that others could profitably build upon it by applying it to both similar and different situations.

The most fundamental step in this process consisted simply in applying words to things and experiences, for naming affixes a handle to a thing, establishing a distance and partial control over it. Once named, it can be compared with other things or events; similarities and dissimilarities can be noted; and patterns can be sought and expressed where formerly all had seemed disjointed. Naming and ordering, often using numbers and lists, were the primary concerns of the oldest sayings, and in bringing together things from quite different spheres of life it was often found that, for all their distinctness, they shared some essential element in common. Sometimes they have no further lesson to teach:

> Three things are never satisfied;
>   four never say, "Enough":
> Sheol, the barren womb,
>   the earth ever thirsty for water,
>   and the fire which never says "Enough."
>
> Three things are too wonderful for me;
>   four I do not understand:
> the way of an eagle in the sky,
>   the way of a serpent on a rock,
> the way of a ship on the high seas,
>   and the way of a man with a maiden.
>
> (Proverbs 30:15-16, 18-19)

The line between this predidactic form of wisdom and the more openly didactic use of sayings is not always apparent now. It was at first more a matter of intention and use than of form. The delightful observations of the effect of strong drink in Proverbs 23:29-35, for example, could serve simply as a description of the mysterious and somewhat frightening powers of alcohol; by giving comic distance to this human experience, it affords some sense of mastery as well. In the mouth of a parent or teacher, however, the same description could serve as a direct, openly didactic warning against excessive imbibing.

Although many admonitions in Proverbs 10-15, 16-22, and 28-29 are objective third-person statements about experience, as now gathered they seem to serve a didactic purpose, and this didactic intent would lead to the formation of other sayings that make a more direct appeal in the imperative mood or in second-person forms of address. Motives would be appealed to through a description of rewards and results. Material in Proverbs 22:17-24, 24:35 and 25-27 reveals this range of forms. At first such teachings were probably localized and informal, based largely in the family or clan; but in time, especially in the urban and court centers, more formal educational establishments would take shape, and tradition places Solomon's Jerusalem in the forefront of these developments. Although anyone could benefit from the teaching offered, the adolescents of the city, youths seeking training for careers in government, commerce, or the state religious cult, were the primary addressees.

The foundations for the work of the court wise men were deeply set in the simplest and earliest forms of human community. The sayings themselves are terse, usually consisting of two parallel lines that compare or contrast things or actions. In the original Hebrew the lines have a regular meter; sometimes they are built on rhymes for purposes of easy recall. On first reading they appear to be commonplace, worldly, and utilitarian; it is suggested that following their advice will assure a long happy life and a share of the good things of the world.

The advice, too, is often situational, recognizing that different circumstances demand different responses. In Proverbs 26:4–5, for example, two sayings stand together:

> Answer not a fool according to his folly,
>   lest you be like him yourself.

> Answer a fool according to his folly,
>   lest he be wise in his own eyes.

This is not muddled thinking. It is a recognition that fools are sometimes dangerous and must be answered, while to debate with fools at other times can only lead oneself into foolish statements and actions. It is not the word of a god that is offered here but the words of experienced, sensitive human beings, and on this basis the sayings are to be considered, weighed against other experience, and accepted or rejected.

World View of Wisdom   Underlying these observations, sayings, and teachings of ancient Israel is a strong belief in an all-pervading divine order and a clear theological affirmation. Life is seen not as disjointed, disconnected, or chaotic but as structured in a way that rewards virtue and overturns evil:

> He who digs a pit will fall into it,
>   and a stone will come back upon
>   him who starts it rolling.

> (Proverbs 26:27)

With effort, human beings can gain a partial knowledge that will enable them to live in harmony and integrity with these patterns. Experience, careful observation, and reflection open one to this wisdom, which can lead in turn to a full, rich, creative life. In these sayings, then, human beings attempt to perceive and express their understanding of Yahweh's will as it is reflected in the ordered structures and patterns of life. The wise seek to apply to the immediacy of daily life a belief in a creator who forms and sustains the universe in a manner that is oriented toward human wholeness.

The sayings must not, however, be seen as limiting the deity's freedom;

Yahweh does not become locked into a particular pattern of human perception. The wise are not blind to the unknowable or the mysterious in human experience. They fully recognize that there are limits to human perception, and they give conscious expression to divine freedom:

> The plans of the mind belong to man,
>   but the answer of the tongue is from Yahweh.
> All the ways of a man are pure in his own eyes,
>   but Yahweh weighs the spirit.
>
> (Proverbs 16:1–2)
>
> The horse is made ready for the day of battle,
>   but victory belongs to Yahweh.
>
> (Proverbs 21:31)
>
> No wisdom, no understanding, no counsel,
>   can avail against Yahweh.
>
> (Proverbs 21:30)

But it is also affirmed that one can live with the unknowable and mysterious, for enough is knowable through human experience and reflection, and beyond this enough is known of Yahweh's will and ways, to build confidence that the divine will is for human good.

The vision of divine providence developed in the succession narrative is sufficiently similar to the affirmation of the wise men to suggest that its author was either trained in the court educational establishment or influenced by it. It is even more probable that the author of another literary product of the Solomonic era was a wise man, and this is the author of the Joseph narrative in Genesis.

The Joseph Narrative
Genesis 37, 39–48, 50

In both subject matter and literary style the Joseph narrative forms a distinct literary whole. It is an entertaining, tightly constructed story united from beginning to end by a complex plot whose several parts cannot stand alone but are scenes in a larger drama. The tensions set forth in chapter 37 are not resolved until chapter 50, and the characters undergo organic growth in the course of these chapters. In its length and unity, its rich character development, and its theological vision the Joseph narrative resembles the succession narrative.

The opening scene introduces a family that seems intent on self-destruction (Genesis 37). An overly favored youngest son, the spoiled favorite of a father who loves deeply but with little sensitivity toward his other sons, flaunts his favored position before his brothers, a jealous lot who seek to rid themselves of him and to deceive their father in the process. These are real people whose motives are human and understandable though their actions cannot be condoned, and all of them will undergo profound changes over the years and events that bring Joseph to high position in the Egyptian court.

An almost unbearable tension builds in the two later encounters in which famine brings his brothers to stand in dread before this all-powerful and unpredictable Egyptian official who takes such an unsettling interest in their family. But the tension is broken as the brothers, placed in a situation remarkably like that in chapter 37, indicate that they have changed (Genesis 44–45); they will not this time give up their youngest brother (Benjamin) to escape an unpleasant situation. Joseph, too, has changed. No longer able to toy with them in a cruelly drawn-out test, he reveals his identity, comforts and reassures them, and arranges to bring them, their father, and their families to security in Egypt.

The figure of Joseph, especially as developed in Genesis 40–41, exhibits certain links with wisdom and the court schools. In these chapters the narrative focus moves from the family of Jacob and its tensions to an account of Joseph's rise from the lowest levels to the highest position in the court of Egypt. With his patience and modesty, his tact before superiors, his knack for speaking forcefully when the moment is right, and his ability to back his words with effective action, Joseph is an ideal courtier, a model of the wise and effective official, an ideal illustration of the life style the wise men sought to develop through their teaching and sayings. Indeed, these chapters may reclothe an older didactic tale developed in the court school to demonstrate to aspiring young men the lifestyle designed to produce success. The author of the Joseph narrative, who may himself have been connected with the schools, uses this tale as a transition piece to transform Joseph from a spoiled youth into a man of power, thereby setting the stage for the later confrontations with the brothers.

The theological vision developed in the story provides another link with the teachings of the wise. After their father's death, Joseph's brothers come to him fearful that with Jacob gone he may now seek vengeance. Instead, he reassures them: "Fear not, for am I in the place of God? As for you, you meant evil against me; but God meant it for good, to bring it about that many people should be kept alive, as they are today. So do not fear" (Genesis 50:19–20; see also 45:4–8). Men intend one thing, but the deity intends another (see Proverbs 16:1–2; 21:30–31).

As in the succession narrative, overt mention of the deity is limited in this story, which runs its course on the secular level. Although there are no direct confrontations between the deity and human beings, Joseph's words of reassurance affirm that behind confused and often sordid human motives and actions a larger plan is working for human good. An almost mechanical form of justice is quietly operative here, but there is also a remarkable note of grace. Ruthless attempts by the brothers to rid themselves of a troublesome brat should lead to suffering and death, and, though they do bring about much suffering, many are saved alive. In observing that "you meant evil against me, but God meant if for good," Joseph seems to cite a wise saying to underscore the narrative's theological message.

Only at the conclusion is all this perceived and affirmed, however. The divine action occurs behind the scenes, hidden from the human actors, and it neither annuls nor excuses their actions and intentions. Human beings remain accountable, and destructive forces loosed at the outset roll back over the seemingly accursed family. The narrator here, as in the succession narrative, does not adopt a form of determinism that permits human responsibility to be excused or diminished. Yet he stands within a universe that is ordered for life and wholeness, affirming that his god, who may be hidden at times, is always working in behalf of his creatures, that he orders life according to his will, and that his will is for good.

THE TRAGEDY OF KING SAUL
1 Samuel 9-31

The twofold affirmation that a divine control operates in the course of human history and that it works for good cannot go unchallenged by some whose experience opposes such a statement of belief. For some, life is sheer chaos, or, if ordered, does not appear ordered for good. Such a challenge might well be expected in the varied and cosmopolitan setting of Jerusalem in a period of literary flowering and theological experimentation, and it may possibly be found in the material dealing with King Saul that is embedded in 1 Samuel 9-31.

As the narrative in 1 Samuel is now formed, Saul is presented as a villain, a foil, first for the severe prophet Samuel, then for the heroic David. From Samuel's point of view, Saul personifies the rejection of Yahweh as Israel's only king that some federation circles saw in the request for a human king. Moreover, he is a king who failed, a contrast to the successful David. But beneath this image is another in which Saul seems less an evil man than a tragic hero. It has been suggested that behind the present form of the Saul material stands an older narrative that presents the first Israelite king in a heroic mode and that this material offers the tragic vision as a challenge to the theological affirmation being made at this time by the wise men and in the two narratives already considered.

Saul is first presented as a man of noble birth, impressive physical stature, and great potential (1 Samuel 9:1-2), and this potential appears destined to find realization. Designated by Samuel as future king over Israel (1 Samuel 9:1-10:16), he is publicly proclaimed king after his successful defense of the city of Jabesh-gilead (1 Samuel 11). In this initial success he is like the charismatic judges of an earlier time, acting on sudden impulse as Yahweh's spirit rushes upon him. But he has a flaw that will soon prove fatal.

Trapped between the world of the federation, which is passing, and the world of the monarchy, which is yet to come into full realization, he is asked to protect

Israel from external dangers but is forced to do so using outdated methods. The powers of a king, as these were defined in the ancient Near East, are not to be his, but the task of a king *is* his. He is not, for example, permitted authority over matters religious (1 Samuel 13:8–14; 15:1–35), over which most Near Eastern kings, including David and Solomon, exercised complete control.

The tension between the two worlds appears in chapter 13. Although Saul's troops are deserting him as the Philistines muster their army, he cannot go into battle until the required sacrifices are offered to Israel's god. Since Samuel, who is the proper one to offer them, is late, Saul does it himself, only to be rebuked by Samuel in the name of his god. In chapter 15 the situation is more complex than at first appears. Saul's motives for preserving some booty from the battle against the Amalikites, along with their king, are not clear; but an army long in the field often lives off such booty, and a defeated enemy king who is spared can become a useful ally. But these concerns of royal diplomacy and military policy conflict with the demands of the federation and its god's rules for war. In that ancient context, all defeated persons were destroyed or reserved for the deity, as was all booty. By these rules Saul is a failure but given his task, is success possible?

From this point Saul's charisma rapidly disintegrates into madness. In the unfortunate oath of chapter 14 there is already a hint of trouble to come; with David's appearance in his court and the marriage of this popular young hero to his daughter, the trouble is realized. Obsessed with the need to destroy David, Saul soon drives his supporters and family from him, and his kingdom and personal existence swiftly disintegrate. 1 Samuel 19–22 and 26 offer an intimate portrait of a psychic breakdown that is unique in ancient literature outside the classical Greek tragedies. As Saul is alienated from family and followers, he is alienated from his god as well. Finally all legitimate means of divine-human communication are cut off from him (1 Samuel 28:3–7), and the silence of his god is shattering.

In the end, however, Saul attains grandeur. Confronting the Philistines on the field in one final engagement, he turns for divine guidance before the battle to one of the very mediums he had earlier driven from the land. Learning from the ghost of the now dead Samuel the fate that awaits him on Mount Gilboa, he meets his destiny with open eyes. He is once again about the task to which he was first called: he is fighting Israel's wars. When the battle is lost and his sons are dead, he takes his own life (1 Samuel 31), and in this self-destructive act he regains a control that has for so long eluded him. After his death the men of Jabesh-gilead, the scene of his first successes as king, cremate him and give him an honorable burial with his fallen sons.

In Saul a life of unique potential is destroyed by a union of external circumstances and inner flaws, and therein lies the tragic vision, for at an earlier or later time in history he might have been a success. Had he but part of the power and control that David and Solomon later exercised over all areas of life, he might have succeeded; but because Samuel and his god withhold such authority, because Israel is not yet ready for a king, he is doomed. A sense of divine control is present throughout the narrative—indeed, at some points Saul appears driven by his god to his tragic fate—but who dare assert that the control be for good or that it sustains life?

Tragedy offers a vision, not a system of belief. It offers a particular angle of insight on the human condition that is not generally found in ancient Israelite and early Jewish materials, but it is a vision that Israel will have to confront when history and events seem to shatter all affirmations of divine care and ordering of life for wholeness. This angle of vision seems to come from outside Israel's normal range of experience. In the material dealing with Saul, and especially with his death and burial, there is evidence of an extra-Israelite point of view.

The tragic vision itself, the intense focus on the psychic development and dissolution of a life, and the complex interpersonal relationships (especially the triangle formed by Saul, Jonathan, and David) all set this narrative apart. Here alone is there depicted a successful consultation with a ghost (the use of the word *elohim*, usually translated as "god," in speaking of the dead is also unique). Suicide, cremation of the dead, and desecration of a fallen enemy are not common Hebraic practices but are customarily found in the Aegean cultures represented by the early Greeks and the Hittites. Figures from this cultural area were to be found in the cosmopolitan Jerusalem of David and Solomon, and someone who had contact with them is a likely candidate for author of the early narrative about Saul.

If this tragic account of Saul's life can be isolated in 1 Samuel, it is clear that it was later recast in a form depicting the tragic hero as a villain. By seeking to isolate an early Saul tragedy and set it into the context of this period, we are dealing with hypothesis more than is the case with the other two narratives. But if the proposal is well founded, it offers further illustration of the range of literary and theological activity and experimentation in this golden age of ancient Israelite cultural development, which was all too soon to pass—tradition assigns it but two life spans. For some it would become a vision of a future golden age; for many it set the terms and provided the ingredients for centuries of further development in the traditions of ancient Israel and of Judaism and Christianity as well.

BIBLIOGRAPHIC NOTE

The Succession Narrative

Brueggemann, Walter. "On Trust and Freedom: A Study of Faith in the Succession Narrative." *Interpretation* 26 (1972): 3–19.

Gunn, David M. "David and the Gift of the Kingdom (2 Samuel 2–4, 9–20, 1 Kings 1–2)." *Semeia* 3 (1975): 14–45.

von Rad, Gerhard. "The Beginnings of Historical Writing in Ancient Israel." In *The Problem of the Hexateuch and Other Essays*, pp. 166–204. New York: McGraw-Hill, 1966.

Whybray, R. N. *The Succession Narrative: A Study of II Samuel 9–20 and I Kings 1 and 2.* Studies in Biblical Theology, no. 9. London: SCM Press, 1968.

Wisdom and the Book of Proverbs

Blank, Sheldon H. "Proverbs, Book of." In *The Interpreter's Dictionary of the Bible*, vol. 3, pp. 936–40, Nashville: Abingdon Press, 1962.

————. "Wisdom." In *The Interpreter's Dictionary of the Bible*, vol. 4, pp. 852–61. Nashville: Abingdon Press, 1962.

Brueggemann, Walter. *In Man We Trust: The Neglected Side of Biblical Faith*. Richmond, Va.: John Knox Press, 1972.

Crenshaw, James L. "Wisdom in the OT." In *The Interpreter's Dictionary of the Bible: Supplementary Volume*, pp. 952–56. Nashville: Abingdon Press, 1976.

McKane, William. *Proverbs*. Philadelphia: Westminster Press, 1970.

Scott, R. B. Y. *Proverbs. Ecclesiastes*. Anchor Bible 18. Garden City, N.Y.: Doubleday & Co., 1965.

von Rad, Gerhard. *Wisdom in Israel*. Nashville: Abingdon Press, 1972.

Whybray, R. N. "Proverbs, Book of." In *The Interpreter's Dictionary of the Bible: Supplementary Volume*, pp. 702–4. Nashville: Abingdon Press, 1976.

The Joseph Narrative in Genesis

Coats, George W. *From Canaan to Egypt: Structural and Theological Context for the Joseph Story*. Catholic Biblical Quarterly Monograph Series, no. 4. Washington, D.C.: Catholic Biblical Association of America, 1976.

Humphreys, W. Lee. "Joseph Story, The." In *The Interpreter's Dictionary of the Bible: Supplementary Volume*, pp. 491–93. Nashville: Abingdon Press, 1976.

Redford, Donald B. *A Study of the Biblical Story of Joseph (Genesis 37–50)*. Supplements to Vetus Testamentum 20. Leiden: E. J. Brill, 1970.

von Rad, Gerhard. "The Joseph Narrative and Ancient Wisdom." In *The Problem of the Hexateuch and Other Essays*, pp. 291–300. New York: McGraw-Hill, 1966.

The Tragedy of King Saul

Humphreys, W. Lee "The Tragedy of King Saul: A Study of the Structure of 1 Samuel 9–31." *Journal for the Study of the Old Testament* 6 (1978):18–27.

SECTION 2
FROM DISSOLUTION
TO DESTRUCTION

Jehu, King of Israel (kneeling), from the Black Obelisk

Reproduced by courtesy of the Trustees of the British Museum

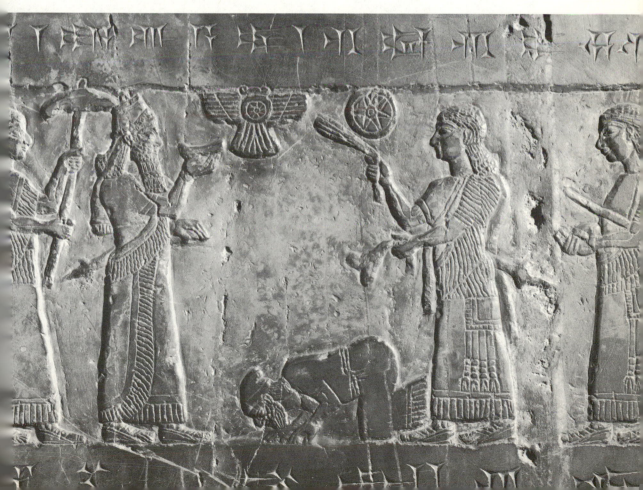

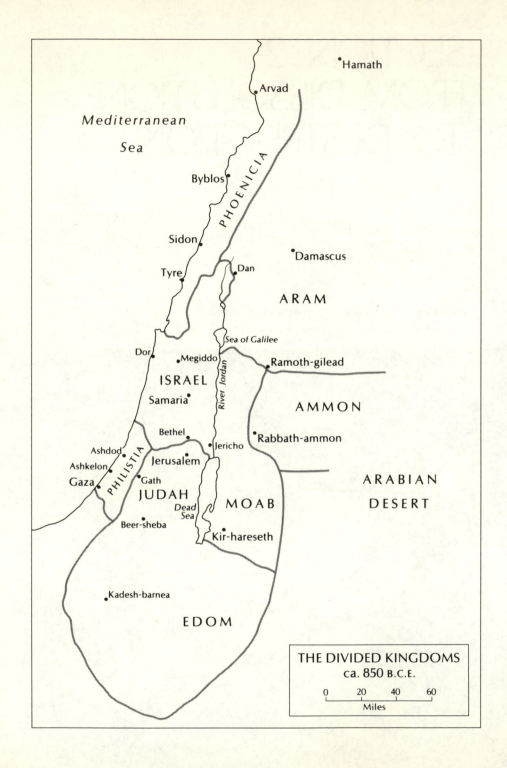

Mediterranean
Sea

Hamath

Arvad

PHOENICIA

Byblos

Sidon

Damascus

Tyre

Dan

ARAM

Sea of Galilee

Dor

Megiddo

Ramoth-gilead

ISRAEL

Samaria

River Jordan

AMMON

Bethel

Jericho

Rabbath-ammon

Ashdod

PHILISTIA

Ashkelon

Jerusalem

ARABIAN

Gaza

Gath

DESERT

JUDAH

Dead
Sea

MOAB

Beer-sheba

Kir-hareseth

Kadesh-barnea

EDOM

THE DIVIDED KINGDOMS
ca. 850 B.C.E.

0   20   40   60
Miles

THE MOSES-SINAI STORY 5
IN NORTHERN ISRAEL

Primary readings: *1 Kings 12–2 Kings 17*
                                   Amos
                                   Hosea

Solomon seized firmly the many lines of allegiance that bound his father's empire together. Although there was little external slippage during his reign (see 1 Kings 11), growing popular dissatisfaction with royal policies threatened to rend the structure asunder, and the pressure was released on Solomon's death. Rehoboam, Solomon's son and successor, was not of his father's stature. When he went to Shechem in 922 B.C.E. to secure the allegiance of the northern tribes but refused to compromise his father's policies in any way, a cry of revolt arose:

> What portion have we in David?
>   We have no inheritance in the son of Jesse.
> To your tents, O Israel!
>   Look now to your own house, David.
>   (1 Kings 12:16)

The old alliance between David and the northern tribes (2 Samuel 5:1–3) was shattered, and the empire fell apart. Although Rehoboam retained the throne in Jerusalem and held the loyalties of the tribes of Judah and part of Benjamin north of the capital, he lacked the will and force to bring back the northern tribes

(1 Kings 12:17–24), and a brief invasion of southern Palestine around 918 B.C.E. by the Egyptian Pharaoh Shishak further diminished his ability to recover the lost territories (1 Kings 14:25–28). Suddenly Israel had become two small nations. The satellite nations were soon independent, and the golden days of empire were past.

The traditions developed in the court of David and Solomon that emphasized Yahweh's promises to the Davidic line, Zion's centrality and inviolability, and divine support for the empire were anathema in the north, and the now separate northern state, which retained the name Israel, turned to Jeroboam to serve as king. A former royal official, then a fugitive from Solomon's power (1 Kings 11:26–40), Jeroboam could not acknowledge the David-Zion traditions any more than the newly independent United States could stamp the face of the British king on its coinage.

Jeroboam found it necessary to establish rival sanctuaries in the cities of Dan and Bethel, near the upper and lower borders of his kingdom, so that his subjects would no longer seek Yahweh in Jerusalem (1 Kings 12:25–33). For his capital he selected the ancient federation center of Shechem. Here, as at the new cultic centers, older traditions and stories rooted in the federation would serve the new nation as alternatives to those that informed Zion and legitimized David's line.

The Elohist Narrative

The Yahwist's epic, which claimed that David's empire was the fulfillment of Yahweh's promise to Abraham, did not find a sympathetic audience among those who had declared their independence from Davidic rule. By the middle of the ninth century B.C.E. a rival account of Israel's origins had been formed, and this is the Pentateuch source that was called E in chapter 3. In time E was incorporated into J, using only E material that differed from J and with J serving as the base. Although E has been preserved in sometimes disjointed fragments—and much was lost in the editorial process—enough remains and can be isolated from J for most scholars to regard it as a united and coherent narrative with its own themes and emphases.

The Covenant at Sinai Because the Elohist narrative is built upon the older federation's story, its range is similar to that covered by the Yahwist. It tells the same basic story, but no prehistory is prefaced to Israel's history; it is not set against a universal backdrop, and Abraham is offered no unconditional promise that anticipates the Davidic empire. Abraham is presented as one whose obedience to his god is absolute, as the events of Genesis 22 demonstrate. Although the other patriarchs appear in this material as well, the bondage in Egypt, the exodus, and the formation of the covenant at Mount Sinai form the heart of the narrative. The climax appears in Exodus 20–24 where, at the foot of the mountain, the covenant between Israel and Yahweh is about to be made.

DIVIDED KINGDOMS of ISRAEL and JUDAH

B.C.E.	Egypt	Judah	Israel	Mesopotamia
900	TWENTY-SECOND DYNASTY (935–725) Shishak (935–914)	Rehoboam (922–915) Abijah (915–913) Asa (913–873)	Jeroboam I (922–901) Nadab (901–900) Baasha (900–877)	
875		Jehoshaphat (873–849)	Elah (877–876) Zimri (876) Omri (876–869) Ahab (869–850)	
850		Jehoram (849–842) Ahaziah (842) Athaliah (842–837) Joash (837–800)	Ahaziah (850–849) Jehoram (849–842) Jehu (842–815)	Shalmaneser III (859–825) Battle of Qarqar (853) Hazael (842–806)
825			Jehoahaz (815–801)	
800		Amaziah (800–783) Uzziah (783–742)	Jehoash (801–786) Jeroboam II (786–746)	
775				
750		Jotham (742–735) Ahaz (735–715)	AMOS HOSEA Zechariah (746–745) Shallum (745) Menahem (745–738) Pekahiah (738–737) Pekah (737–732) Hoshea (732–724)	Tiglath-pileser (745–727) Rezin (740–732) Shalmaneser V (726–722)
725	TWENTY-FOURTH DYNASTY (725–709)		Fall of Israel (722)	Sargon II (722–705)

ELIJAH

ELISHA

ISAIAH

MICAH

A body of legal stipulations is presented that consists of the Ten Commandments (Exodus 20:1–17) followed by an early corpus of law known as the "covenant code" that probably dates from the period of the federation (Exodus 21:1–23:33). The federation's old covenant pattern that stood behind the annual covenant renewal ceremonies is here formative. This covenant is based on voluntary allegiance to Yahweh and is conditioned by stipulations set forth by the deity as the terms of that allegiance. In Exodus 24 the people offer this allegiance to Yahweh alone, and the covenant is sealed.

Story and Law This unit, not the promises made to Abraham, provides the Elohist's focus: absolute obedience to Yahweh and to him alone. The gift and possession of the land depend wholly on continued obedience to the covenant. The Elohist's narrative contains the first extended body of legal material, for it is in relation to the covenant made at Sinai that law became central to Israel's relation with its god. It is a law freely taken because of Yahweh's prior act of deliverance. Yahweh's gift of freedom from Egyptian slavery came first, but a body of law would now define the bond between Israelite and Yahweh.

In the Elohist's narrative Moses is the critical figure from Israel's past. He is not only the human instrument for effecting Yahweh's deliverance but is also the mediator of Yahweh's law and of the covenant itself. He stands between the people and their god; he ascends the mountain, returns with the law, and ratifies the covenant. He becomes the model for the prophetic figure who will stand between deity and people.

The Elohist's narrative seems to date to about 850 B.C.E., a time when the covenant between Yahweh and Israel seemed in danger of extinction, at least in the eyes of men like Elijah and Elisha who were called prophets. This recitation of Israel's story opposed those forces that seemed to be annulling the covenant with Yahweh, upon which these prophets believed Israel's life to depend. In E the Moses-Sinai story is not subsumed by the David-Zion story. The old federation story is recast in its own terms, expanded but not enveloped in other traditions, and there is clear evidence that it lived on among the northern tribes who found in it an identity and potential unity for the new kingdom. The failure of this unity to materialize will form the subject of the rest of this chapter.

Emergence of the Prophets

A prophet named Ahijah who came from the old federation center of Shiloh played an important role in the shattering of the Davidic empire. In an encounter with Jeroboam, who was to become king of the northern state, he pronounced judgment on Solomon for permitting and even encouraging a policy that was broadly tolerant of various religious traditions and deities (1 Kings 11). In the name of his god, Ahijah designated Jeroboam as the future king of the northern part of old Israel, though in time, again in Yahweh's name, he would declare that divine support for Jeroboam's house had come to an end as well (1 Kings 14).

Jeroboam's son Nadab was assassinated by one Baasha, setting in motion a pattern of assassinations, coups, and new dynasties that would punctuate the history of kingship in the north, and it would all end in an orgy of king making and breaking as the state disintegrated just two hundred years after it had come into being. Playing a formative role in this pattern of instability were prophetic figures like Ahijah of Shiloh, among whom there developed a counterforce and a body of traditions by which even kings could be judged and removed.

The Hebrew word translated as "prophet" (*nabi'*) means "one who is called" or "one delegated as a messenger." As early as the period of Saul, bands of prophets had appeared (1 Samuel 10:9–13; 19:18–24) whose erratic behavior and ecstatic utterances seemed to certify that they were possessed by the deity and spoke his word. To some of these early prophetic figures, especially Elijah and Elisha, miracles were ascribed as further certification that they acted through the power of the god. Problems that arise in judging the validity of their claims will be considered later; it suffices to note here that at least some people believed that they spoke Yahweh's words and were under his influence.

Prophets might be sought out even by kings who were faced with a problem or who were experiencing times of personal distress (1 Samuel 9; 1 Kings 14). Although some early prophets may have been little more than visionaries, others would become major forces in Israel's political and religious life, and their words, whether sought or unsought, were not to be treated lightly. Sometimes the prophet appeared alone, others were found in groups, but there was always an air of the mysterious, the numinous, about them which both attracted and repelled. They repelled as does the ill-clad doom-saying preacher on the street corner in today's cities, but they attracted by the fire that burned in their eyes and the commanding thunder in their words. They were like madmen, but the ancients knew that madness was sometimes the result of a human being coming into too close contact with a god.

Elijah   No figure more embodies this air of the mysterious and unpredictable than the greatest of the early group, Elijah the Tishbite. He appears with no introduction or biographical information and seems more a force of nature than a mortal man. He ranges over territory from Phoenicia in the north to a fateful encounter with Yahweh on the sacred mountain in the southern wilderness. King Ahab, the seventh king of Israel (c. 869–850 B.C.E.), regards him with a dread admixed with contempt and terror. With Elijah's appearance, king and prophet come into direct conflict.

In Ahab's Israel we see most fully developed the northern state's potential for limited greatness and prosperity and also for dissolution; for northern Israel occupied the bulk and most productive segments of old Israel, but it also stood in direct contact with the states of Phoenicia and the Arameans to the north and east. If the potential for economic and cultural development was great, so was the danger of political and religious entanglements, alliances, and syntheses. Ahab's queen Jezebel was a Phoenician princess whose marriage no doubt sealed an alliance between the king of Tyre and Ahab's father, an alliance that continued into Ahab's reign and was of vast commercial benefit to both sides. But Jezebel was a strong devotee of the Canaanite Baal, the god of life-giving rain and fertility. By seeking to propagate worship of Baal in her new home she came into direct conflict with Elijah, the equally strong devotee of Yahweh (2 Kings 17–21).

Even the dramatic encounter on Mount Carmel was not decisive in this battle, for soon after Elijah's seeming victory he had to flee for his life into the wilderness. Although he now sought only death, at the sacred mountain he met his god (1 Kings 19). Driven back into battle, he again stood firmly for Yahweh alone against royal authority, and he also attacked all abuses of royal power, including the appropriation of another's land and legalized murder (1 Kings 21). Between Yahweh and Baal, prophet and royalty, sides were clearly drawn, but the issue remained unresolved during Elijah's lifetime. It was only after his mysterious death, and the death of Ahab as well, that Elisha, to whom Elijah's mantle had fallen, became instrumental in bringing down this dynasty. In the name of Yahweh, Elisha designated the military leader Jehu as king. Although the resulting bloodbath (2 Kings 9) did not decide the conflict, in the meeting of Elijah and the royal house of Ahab and Jezebel the terms for the ongoing struggle were fixed.

Samuel, Elijah, and Elisha   Around Elisha there gathered a band of prophets (2 Kings 1–10) who probably recited accounts of the words and deeds of Elijah, of Elisha himself, and of other prophets, named and unnamed, who are encountered in the books of Kings. Among these tales was a loose cycle dealing with Samuel, whom some prophetic circles regarded as the prototype or founder of the line of prophets. Traditions dealing with his birth and upbringing and especially with his conflicts with Saul were treasured because they reflected concern about the abuse of royal power and what the prophets saw as a challenge to Yahweh's absolute sovereignty. The units in 1 Samuel that criticize kingship and set forth its limitation were passed on in these circles (1 Samuel 8; 10:17–27; 12; 13:10–15; 15). The later prophets saw themselves as heirs of the great judges of the federation, of whom Samuel had been the last, and as supporters of the federation's values and ways. Their conflicts with the kings resulted in part from the enmity between these older values and patterns and contemporary political realities.

In the prophetic circles Saul would appear as neither heroic nor tragic but would be perceived as a graphic example of royal wrong-headedness and rebellion against Israel's divine sovereign. His death would be perceived as what one might expect from someone who had rejected the deity's word as communicated through the prophets. Accounts about Samuel and Saul would be recast so as to reflect this point of view and to serve as warnings to future rulers. Segments of the tragic presentation of Saul could have been reformed in this context and the figure of Saul transformed from tragic hero into villain.

The traditions upon which Ahijah, Samuel, Elijah, Elisha, Micaiah (1 Kings 22), and other early prophets founded their understanding of Yahweh and their judgment of Israel and its rulers are not detailed in the accounts of their words and deeds, but they do not appear as wholly unattached to Israel's earlier religious traditions. Elijah's links with the sacred mountain in the wilderness at a critical point in his life suggest that these prophets founded their words upon the story of the exodus, the wilderness meeting between fugitive slaves and their god, and the covenant formed there with its stipulations demanding total allegiance to Yahweh; elements in the Samuel traditions seem rooted in this story as well (1 Samuel 10:17–19; 12:6–25). Hence the old federation story stood at the heart of the prophets' words and deeds as each found therein an ideal identity for the northern state and as each judged its leaders against this ideal. The story's formative role in prophetic preaching becomes more apparent as we turn to the prophets Amos and Hosea who appear toward the end of the history of northern Israel.

Amos and the Reign of Jeroboam II

In the oracles of Amos the Moses-Sinai story becomes the foundation for a searing judgment of northern Israel, its nobility, and its king. Amos was a shepherd from the Judean village of Tekoa south of Jerusalem. Seized by his god (Amos 7:15), he was sent to be a prophet in the northern kingdom during the last decade of the long reign of Jeroboam II (786–746 B.C.E.). For Israel these were years of relatively peaceful relations with neighboring states, a period of rapid commercial, territorial, and economic growth, and a time of religious and cultural change as well. Because many people saw these prosperous years as proof that Yahweh had blessed Israel and supported the state and king, the god was richly praised and served in the cultic establishment, and the bitter condemnations of an outsider were unwelcome. Nevertheless, Amos delivered his message to northern Israel and was expelled by religious authorities because the land could not bear his words (Amos 7:10–17).

These words have been gathered into the Book of Amos, which is found in the collection of the twelve minor prophets. He was the first in a line of men whose words would form separate books, thereby setting them off from earlier prophetic figures. Although often called the "writing prophets," they were primarily speakers who delivered terse oracles of a tightly knit semipoetic structure, speaking in places where audiences would gather, such as at the larger cultic centers or at a city's gate or market.

Generally, others remembered the oracles and brought them together into collections and books bearing the prophet's name. This process of collecting and editing continued for extended periods of time in an attempt to find new relevance in the prophet's words long after his death. But it is this extended process of remembering and collecting that makes the books so difficult for many to read today. There is often no clear pattern in the order in which oracles are given, no chronological or thematic structure. Little if any background information is given about the situation in which the prophet addressed his words. In addition, we have little information about the life setting for individual oracles, and no division is demarked between the prophet's own words and alterations or additions made by those who applied the oracles to later situations.

The Moses-Sinai Story   The foundations for Amos's uncompromising judgment of Israel, its king, and its cult appear clearly in chapter 2. After indicting Israel for crimes of a religious and social nature, he continues in Yahweh's name:

> Yet I [Yahweh] destroyed the Amorite before them,
> > whose height was like the height of the cedars,
> > and who was as strong as the oaks;
>
> Also I brought you up out of the land of Egypt,
> > and led you forty years in the wilderness,
> > to possess the land of the Amorites.
> I raised up some of your sons for prophets,
> > and some of your young men for Nazirites.
> Is it not indeed so, O people of Israel?
>
> > > > > > > > (Amos 2:9–11)

Here the sacred story of the covenant first made in the wilderness at Sinai is freely recalled and presented as the legitimizing basis for Yahweh's strident words of condemnation: "You only have I known of all the families of the earth;/ therefore I will punish you for all your iniquities" (Amos 3:2). In this covenant between Yahweh and his people, total sovereignty lay with the deity. All Israelites, including kings, stood in vassal relationship with their god. Yahweh was king over all, and all were equal in his eyes.

But increased prosperity and growth during this period had resulted in uneven economic distribution and marked social stratification, while the oppression of have-nots by haves had been facilitated by a series of natural disasters that had placed the small farmer in a position of intolerable indebtedness. Although Amos bitterly denounced the oppression of some Israelites by others as a violation of the law that stood at the heart of the covenant (Amos 2:6–8; 4:1–3; 5:10–13; 6:4–7), he interpreted these same disasters as Yahweh's warning to Israel to change its ways (Amos 4:6–11). With increased prosperity, too, had come greater contact with other peoples, which had led to a blending of Yahwism with traditions about the Canaanite Baal. This the prophet declared to be outright apostasy, asserting further that Israel's cultic worship was not only empty but was even a way of avoiding Yahweh's claims (Amos 4:4–5; 5:4–5; 5:21–24).

The Covenant Lawsuit   The situation here is not unlike that in a court of law in which a case of human breach of contract is being heard, and the lawsuit pattern is clearest in Amos 2:6–16. As Amos indicts Israel for crimes against fellow Israelites and for perverting the Yahweh cult (Amos 2:6–8 and 2:12), he acts as an attorney for the deity. In verses 9–11 he summarily reviews the foundations for Israel's existence, the sacred story upon which the covenant is built. In verses 13–16 he proceeds in the name of the god, who is both the aggrieved party and the final judge, to pronounce sentence: Israel shall be utterly destroyed by foreign conquest and exiled from its land (Amos 2:13–16; 3:11 and 3:13–15; 4:2–4; 5:3; 6:7). In this sentence he presents a graphic vision of a nation routed before a conqueror, as though he foresees some form of military action against Israel that will result in total defeat and destruction.

In the last half of the eighth century B.C.E. the Mesopotamian empire of Assyria was expanding under the leadership of a series of able rulers. One area of Assyrian expansion was to the west, into Syria-Palestine and possibly even down into Egypt, though in Amos's days the signs of this expansion were faint. Historians today explain Assyria's expansive empire-building policy in terms of its economic need to control trade routes and sources of material, and in terms of its need either to dominate or to form a buffer zone between its political enemies and itself. Economic and military reasons can be cited to explain Assyrian attempts to control Palestine and thereby gain an avenue into the rich land of Egypt. For Amos, however, such explanations would not have sufficed, for he understood Assyria as the vehicle by which the sentence against Israel would be carried out. He understood the currents of history in theological categories—that is, not in economic, diplomatic, or military terms but as the justified action of a punishing god.

Basic to Israel's understanding of and relation with Yahweh was its experience of this deity in the historical past. Although Yahweh was encountered first and foremost in historical events, history is open-ended and continually breaking forth in forms that are ever new. For the Yahwist, especially in periods of crisis, the question would always be, What is Yahweh doing now? Where is the hand of our god in this? For the Israel of his day, Amos saw the hand of the god in the advance of Assyria.

The Death Sentence   Amos had to pronounce a death sentence on Israel because its actions had made the covenant with Yahweh null and void; but that covenant was Israel's sole support in this world, whether the nation recognized it or not. Yahweh could move nations (Amos 9:7) and stand as judge over the whole earth (Amos 1:3–2:5). Surely, then, he would bring judgment upon those he had singled out as his chosen people when they turned from him (Amos 3:1–2).

The sentence not only announced what Amos perceived to be Yahweh's action in his day but set that action firmly within the framework of Israel's own understanding of the deity. However new and different this action was from that relived in recitation and song in the renewal of the covenant, it was the action of the same deity and it was in line with what Israel knew of its god. In their cultic life the people of Israel looked for a day when Yahweh would appear and finally rout all the enemies of the nation. While Amos agreed that Yahweh would have his day, he declared that Yahweh's own people had become the enemy, and with biting irony he made clear what the day of Yahweh would be like (Amos 5:18–20; 8:9–14).

Amos may have been appalled by his own words. When probably early in his career he envisioned portents of the judgment to come (Amos 7:1–6), he cried out to Yahweh to relent; but in the end Yahweh could not relent (Amos 7:7–9; 8:1–3), and Amos uttered words of doom that were too severe for the land to bear. Accused of treason and heresy, he was driven from the land by the high priest Amaziah, who had charge over the royal sanctuary at Bethel, and was heard from no more. The book that bears his name tells us little else about him because it is not a biography of Amos but a collection of his words believed by the prophet and by those who remembered them to be the word of Yahweh.

Although they are words of total doom, there is at the end a sudden turn and a promise (Amos 9:8b; 9:11–15) that speaks of restoration in which the house of David figures prominently. This is generally thought to reflect the hand of later editors who, in southern Judah, preserved Amos's words after the fall, for in 722 B.C.E. the state of northern Israel was destroyed.

Hosea and the Fall of Northern Israel

Soon after Jeroboam's death in 746 B.C.E. Israel and the other small states in Syria-Palestine were openly confronted by the aggressive Assyrians. Within Israel this brought many dramatic shifts in foreign alliances and even more sudden changes in ruling dynasties, the latter often punctuated by assassinations and coups. As a result of political chaos accompanied by social and economic disorder, Israel simply dissolved (2 Kings 15:8–31; 17:1–6). Although there is no indication that Amos lived to see it, another prophet presided in judgment until the final death agonies. His name was Hosea, and in some ways he provides a striking contrast to Amos.

Unlike Amos, Hosea was a native of northern Israel; and in contrast to the stark oracles of Amos, his words are filled not only with profound sorrow and grief but with a sense of hope and promise that transcends the judgment he must pronounce. This hope does not do away with the judgment or with the sentence of death, but Hosea takes us beyond death to rebirth, beyond dissolution to re-creation.

Above all, Hosea's characterization of Yahweh sets him apart from Amos, his near contemporary. The god of Amos's oracles is stern, almost caustic (Amos 4:1–3; 4:4–5; 3:12), but the god of Hosea's words is a devoted husband, a father whose acts of punishment are also acts of love, and a lover who is deeply wounded by the bride who spurns him. In other instances he speaks of Yahweh as a physician (Hosea 7:1; 11:3; 14:4), as a shepherd totally devoted to his flock (Hosea 13:5–8; 10:11), and as a gardener dedicated to his vineyard (Hosea 9:10; 10:1), and his words reflect the agony of one who must turn on the pride of his creation (Hosea 6:4; 11:1–4; compare 11:8–9 with 12:9).

A Marriage Betrayed   In the ancient Near East, marriages were agreements sealed in contracts or covenants whose stipulations defined the relationship, the obligations of both parties, and the exchange of property. Although love was not of primary concern, it was present in some cases. Hosea, for example, married a woman named Gomer, had children by her, then lost her to other men, only to reclaim her later and attempt to rebuild the marriage. From this tragic personal story he attained deep insight into the shattered relation between Yahweh and Israel, whose crimes he viewed as the betrayal of a love and trust. In this regard chapters 1–3 pose problems for interpreters today. While they offer varied forms of material from different perspectives—a biographical narrative (Hosea 1:1–9), oracles of indictment and sentence (Hosea 2:1–13), words of promise (Hosea 1:10–11; 2:14–23) and an autobiographical account (Hosea 3:1–5)—it is not clear how all these fit together, especially how the events of chapter 1 are related to those of chapter 3. Although some scholars suspect that Hosea 1:10–11 and 2:14–23 contain later additions, it is nevertheless clear that some wrenching personal experience stands behind this material, providing the forms for expressing Yahweh's commitment to and agony over unfaithful Israel.

In addition to his personal experience, Hosea's oracles are informed by the federation's story of deliverance from Egyptian bondage (Hosea 11:1; 13:4), of sustenance in the wilderness (Hosea 9:10; 11:3–4; 13:5), of the covenant first made there (Hosea 6:7, 8:1), and of the gift of the land of Canaan (Hosea 11:2; 13:6). Although the story is the same, the terms of its telling are unique. The wilderness period becomes the first days of a marriage, the days of total fidelity, or, in another view, they become the days of Israel's youth and total trust in the loving divine parent.

But entry into Canaan brought infidelity and rebellion. The bride became an adulteress; the child Israel rejected the parent's love and support for the supposed gifts of the Canaanite deity Baal. Since this violated a covenant that demanded total allegience to Yahweh (Exodus 20:3; Johsua 24:14–20), the confrontation between Yahweh and Baal became the focus of Hosea's message; but this time the defense of Yahweh and assertion of his claims were given a depth and subtlety unmatched by any earlier prophet.

Yahweh and Baal   An uncompromising Yahwist, Hosea was absolute in his demand that sole and total allegiance be given to the deity who had delivered the fugitives from bondage. But the Canaanite Baal was the god of life-giving rains, husband and lord over the earth, linked with a goddess of fertility with whom he mated to produce abundance in crops and in all aspects of life, and his sphere of activity was of life-and-death relevance to those concerned with farming and the tending of herds.

Baal had a story as well in which he engages in mortal combat with a god named Mot ("death") who represents the antithesis of all that he offers. When Mot proves successful in the first stage of combat, Baal is confined to the realm of the dead, and all life on earth ceases. In time Baal is revived by his consort—the female power of fertility found in the earth—and in a second battle he triumphs over Mot. Life returns to the earth, just as each fall the dry summer yields to months of rain and renewed life. Each year at the turn of the seasons this story was reenacted in cultic ceremony with a ritualistic representation of the struggle. Annually the people took part in and reexperienced the renewal of the earth's life. Thus Baal was a deity who lived close to the vital center of the experience of those bound to the land and its produce, and he was ignored only at great risk.

While Baal's story moved to the rhythms of nature and the ever returning cycle of the seasons, Yahweh revealed himself in the history of his people; the tempo of his story was that of linear time, the march of history. Yahweh was a warrior deity who engaged in open combat with the Egyptians to free his people and in combat took the land of Canaan to give to them, but Baal was the god of that land and of its life-giving powers. Whereas Yahweh was at home on a mountain in the wilderness, Baal was in the clouds that brought needed rain and in the dark furrow cut by the farmer's plow. In the world of that time the suggestion that one's allegiance must be wholly confined to one deity was radical and dangerous. On one occasion Yahweh and Baal are said to have fought a battle on Mount Carmel (1 Kings 18), and, in spite of Yahweh's apparent victory, Baal's appeal had remained strong. In Hosea's oracles, however, the battle lines were redrawn.

It has been said that one should select his enemies with care because in conflict with them he will come to resemble them and in one respect this is true of Yahweh's conflict with Baal. In Hosea's oracles Yahweh becomes the giver of gifts ascribed to Baal. Israel, he states, is not only an adulteress but a fool because she does not recognize that it is Yahweh who actually gives the life-sustaining treasures of nature:

And she did not know
    that it was I who gave her
    the grain, the wine, and the oil,
and who lavished upon her silver and gold
    which they used for Baal.
Therefore I will take back
    my grain in its time,
    and my wine in its season;
and I will take away my wool and my flax,
    which were to cover her nakedness.

> (Hosea 2:8–9)

And I will lay waste her vines and her fig trees,
of which she said,
"These are my hire,
which my lovers have given me."

> (Hosea 2:12)

The freer of slaves, the warrior who fights for his people from Sinai, and the conqueror of lands is also the giver of the soil, the rain, and the life in them.

But Yahweh is not Baal. He does not engage in mortal combat and become captive to Death; he is no dying and rising fertility deity; he has no consort who must revive him each year. Yahweh, not Baal, is Israel's rightful lover and husband. In employing the language of love, sex, and marriage throughout his oracles Hosea takes a great risk, for he is using the language and motifs of Baal's own story and of the fertility cult. At the same time, however, he seems confident that the god of exodus, Sinai, and conquest would never be wholly confused or assimilated with Baal.

Indictment and Sentence But Israel did not know Yahweh in the multifaceted way that involves investing the totality of one's being in a living and loving relationship, and this is the essence of Hosea's indictment:

Hear the word of Yahweh, O people of Israel,
    for Yahweh has a controversy
    with the inhabitants of the land.
There is no faithfulness or kindness,
    and no knowledge of God in the land;
there is swearing, lying, killing,
    stealing, and committing adultery;
    they break all bounds and murder follows murder.
Therefore the land mourns,
    and all who dwell in it languish,
and also the beasts of the field,
    and the birds of the air;
    and even the fish of the sea are taken away.

> (Hosea 4:1–3; see also 5:4; 6:3; 6:6; 11:3).

His words are directed most pointedly at Israel's leaders:

> My people are destroyed for lack of knowledge;
>   because you have rejected knowledge,
> I will reject you from being a priest to me.
> And since you have forgotten the law of your God,
>   I will also forget your children.
>
> (Hosea 4:6)

Thus the indictment is issued in the name of Yahweh, sometimes in the legal formula for divorce (Hosea 2:2), and then the people are sentenced.

The means of punishment appear clearer now, for in Hosea's day Assyria was moving ever closer toward Palestine. At a minimum, Assyria sought to make vassals of the small nations and city-states of the area. At most, it sought conquest and total incorporation into its empire structure. After the death of Jeroboam II internal politics became chaotic in northern Israel. Parties formed, some favoring capitulation to Assyrian demands, others favoring resistance and a defensive alliance with Egypt. The infighting elicited murder after murder as king replaced king with no sign of Yahweh's approval or legitimization (Hosea 7:3–7; 8:4). In 732 B.C.E. Damascus, the Aramean city-state to the north of Israel, was ravished by the Assyrian army, while Israel itself was stripped of most of its land and reduced to being the capital city of Samaria. When Samaria fell ten years later, the prophetic sentence had been carried out. Again, what we might today explain in economic, diplomatic, or military terms, the prophet understood in theological terms. This was Yahweh's action, for his people had nullified the covenant and the foundation for their existence was no more.

Beyond Death   At this point Hosea took his greatest risk in declaring that out of the destruction and death and the nullification of the covenant relationship something new would be formed. Just as he had taken his wife back and had sought through discipline to rebuild their marriage (Hosea 3), so Yahweh would build anew from shattered Israel. Assyria had developed a practice of exiling segments of conquered peoples to other parts of the empire for the purpose of breaking geographical, cultural, and religious bonds of national identity and loyalty. Amos had earlier spoken of this as the fate that awaited Israel (Amos 4:2–3; 5:27; 6:7; 7:17), and Hosea likewise looked for an exile representing it as a return to the wilderness (Hosea 2:3) or to Egypt (Hosea 7:16; 8:13; 9:3).

For Hosea, however, the image of the wilderness was double-edged; it was a place of suffering and death but also the location for the bridal days in the old story:

> Therefore, behold, I will allure her,
>   and bring her into the wilderness,

and speak tenderly to her,
And there I will give her her vineyards,

. . .

And there she shall answer as in the days of her youth,
as at the time when she came out of the land of Egypt.

(Hosea 2:16–17)

Although the vision is vague and the immediate future is dark, beyond the death sentence there was to be a new life in relationship with the deity in whose hands was life in all its forms (Hosea 2:14–23). Yahweh was not a god who suffered death at the hands of another to rise again each year. But Yahweh's people would suffer death at his hands, and then the same hands would lift Israel from the ashes of destruction.

Hosea's words, like those of Amos, were preserved and treasured by a few others who took them south to Judah when the northern state fell to Assyria in 722 B.C.E. There they were gradually gathered, ordered, written down, and applied to later generations (note the references to David and his line in Amos 9:11 and Hosea 3:5, as well as the presence of Zion themes in Hosea 1:7). With the collection of Hosea's words came other collections of legends about the earlier prophets. At this time, too, the Elohist's narrative was brought from the ruins of northern Israel and incorporated into that of the Yahwist. In this way the Moses-Sinai story was preserved so that it continued to inform the lives of what remained of the people of Israel.

BIBLIOGRAPHIC NOTE

General Studies on the Prophets

Reference should be made to the studies below in this and the following chapters that deal with individual prophetic figures. Discussions of prophecy, individual prophets and books are also found in the Literary Introductions and Religion and Theology sections of the introductory Bibliographic Note.

Bright, John. *Covenant and Promise: The Prophetic Understanding of the Future in Pre-Exilic Israel*. Philadelphia: Westminster Press, 1976.

Buber, Martin. *The Prophetic Faith*. New York: Harper & Row, 1960. A classic work by a well-known Jewish scholar.

Buss, M. J. "Prophecy in Ancient Israel." In *The Interpreter's Dictionary of the Bible: Supplementary Volume*, pp. 694–97. Nashville: Abingdon Press, 1976.

Clements, Ronald E. *Prophecy and Covenant*. Studies in Biblical Theology, no. 43. London: SCM Press, 1965.

Gottwald, Norman K. *All the Kingdoms of the Earth*. New York: Harper & Row, 1965.

110	Heschel, Abraham J. *The Prophets*. New York: Harper & Row, 1963. One of the finest works on the prophets.

Johnson, A. R. *The Cultic Prophet in Ancient Israel*. Cardiff: University of Wales Press, 1962.

Lindbloom, Johannes. *Prophecy in Ancient Israel*. Philadelphia : Fortress Press, 1963. An excellent introduction to the prophets.

McKane, William. *Prophets and Wise Men*. Studies in Biblical Theology, no. 44. London: SCM Press, 1965.

Napier, B. D. "Prophet, Prophetism." In *The Interpreter's Dictionary of the Bible*, vol. 3, pp. 896–919. Nashville: Abingdon Press, 1962.

Scott, R. B. Y. *The Relevance of the Prophets*. New York: Macmillan Co., 1968.

von Rad, Gerhard. *The Message of the Prophets*. New York: Harper & Row, 1965. A slight reworking of his treatment of prophecy and the prophets in the second volume of his *Old Testament Theology*.

Westermann, Claus. *Basic Forms of Prophetic Speech*. Philadelphia: Westminster Press, 1967.

The Book of Amos

Mays, James L. *Amos*. Philadelphia: Westminster Press, 1969.

Smart, James D. "Amos." In *The Interpreter's Dictionary of the Bible*, vol. 1, pp. 116–21. Nashville: Abingdon Press, 1962.

Terrien, Samuel L. "Amos and Wisdom." In *Israel's Prophetic Heritage*, edited by B. W. Anderson and Walter Harrelson, pp. 108–15. New York: Harper & Row, 1962.

Ward, James M. "Amos." In *The Interpreter's Dictionary of the Bible: Supplementary Volume*, pp. 21–23. Nashville: Abingdon Press, 1976.

———. *Amos and Isaiah: Prophets of the Word of God*. Nashville: Abingdon Press, 1969.

Wolff, Hans Walter. *Joel and Amos*. Philadelphia: Fortress Press, 1977.

The Book of Hosea

Brueggemann, Walter. *Tradition for Crisis: A Study in Hosea*. Richmond, Va.: John Knox Press, 1968.

Mays, James L. *Hosea*. Philadelphia: Westminster Press, 1969.

Smart, James D. "Hosea: Man and Book." In *The Interpreter's Dictionary of the Bible*, vol. 3, pp. 648–53. Nashville: Abingdon Press, 1962.

Ward, James M. "Hosea." In *The Interpreter's Dictionary of the Bible: Supplementary Volume*, pp. 421–22. Nashville: Abingdon Press, 1976.

———. *Hosea: A Theological Commentary*. New York: Harper and Row, 1966.

Wolff, Hans Walter. *Hosea*. Philadelphia: Fortress Press, 1974.

The Elohist

The Elohist is discussed in the Literary Introductions section of the introductory Bibliographic Note.

Fretheim, T. E. "Elohist." In *The Interpreter's Dictionary of the Bible: Supplementary Volume*, pp. 259–63. Nashville: Abingdon Press, 1976.

Wolff, Hans Walter. "The Elohist Fragments in the Pentateuch." In *The Vitality of Old Testament Traditions*, edited by Walter Brueggemann and Hans Walter Wolff, pp. 67–82, Atlanta: John Knox Press, 1975.

6 JUDAH AND THE ASSYRIAN CRISIS

Primary readings: *Isaiah 1–23, 28–39*
Micah
2 Kings 18–20

After his disastrous confrontation at Shechem with representatives of the tribes of northern Israel, Rehoboam fled to Jerusalem where, in spite of his inability to take action against the rebellious tribes (note the role of a prophet in this, 1 Kings 12:17–24), he was able to secure the continuance of Davidic rule over Jerusalem and Judah. In an instant, however, it seemed that the house of David ruled over little more than a small city-state.

In terms of productive land and proximity to trade routes, Judah was now little more than a backwater. In terms of international political clout and economic and military weight, it was negligible. Judah would not experience the constant immediate contact with other states and cultures that characterized northern Israel. Although this resulted in a lower standard of living and a more homogeneous society, it permitted greater political stability, which in turn reinforced the continuance of the David-Zion story.

With the exception of one brief interlude, David's dynasty retained full control over the throne in Jerusalem. Its right to rule seems not to have been questioned, and the traditions supporting it were generally unchallenged until near the end of the nation's existence. The interlude came during the late ninth century B.C.E. when the political turbulence accompanying the fall of Ahab's house spilled from the north into Judah. The queen mother, Athaliah, who was of the family of Ahab, seized control of the state, but after about seven years she was removed and a Davidic heir restored to the throne (2 Kings 11). Thus Judah's political history was unlike that of the unstable northern state. In Judah, royal assassinations reflected intradynastic struggle and always brought another member of David's line to the throne (2 Kings 21:19–26).

The David-Zion story remained the essential religious tradition in Jerusalem and Judah, shaping and governing other forms of story and providing a foundation for national identity and unity. It stood at the heart of the annual cultic celebration of the New Year when the creation and sustenance of the universe, the defeat of chaos and threat to the created order, David's enthronement in Jerusalem and possibly Yahweh's in his temple were all relived and reaffirmed. Although the Moses-Sinai story undoubtedly played some role, the official theology was dominated by the David-Zion story.

That the Yahwist's pattern of harmonizing the two stories became strained is clear on considering two prophets, nearly contemporary with Amos and Hosea in the north, who addressed Judah and its royal house in the last decades of the eighth century B.C.E. On the one hand, Isaiah of Jerusalem was a man of high social position who had easy access to the king and whose words of judgment and hope were informed by the David-Zion story. On the other hand, Micah, a younger contemporary from the rural hamlet of Moresheth, looked bitterly upon the city and ruling dynasty from afar, and had few ties of allegiance with Jerusalem and its king. His story was that of Moses and Sinai unalloyed in its original form by David-Zion traditions.

ISAIAH OF JERUSALEM

No book better reveals the complexity of the process by which a prophet's words are remembered, collected, arranged, enlarged, and supplemented than the Book of Isaiah. Critical scholarship has demonstrated that it contains not only the oracles of the eighth-century B.C.E. Isaiah of Jerusalem but those of an equally great if unnamed prophet of the mid–sixth century B.C.E. whom we now call the Second Isaiah and those of still later prophetic figures as well. The Book of Isaiah is therefore a treasury of prophetic materials that range over many centuries, bringing us a rich tapestry of ancient Israelite and early Jewish religious traditions as they confront successive historical crises.

The words of Isaiah of Jerusalem and accounts about him are found in chapters 1–39, mixed even there with other and later material (see, for example, chapters 24–27 and 33–35). His oracles are complex, containing judgments as harsh and strident as those of Amos as well as hopeful visions of a transformed future that rival segments of Hosea. Isaiah offers elements of condemnation, challenge, and promise that were treasured by later generations as they likewise faced life-and-death decisions.

During his more than four decades as a prophet (742–701 B.C.E.) Isaiah saw Judah come more than once to the edge of destruction and emerge alive but totally subservient to the rising Assyrian imperial power that had engulfed northern Israel. In three distinct historical crises in the life of his people this prophet sought to discern the hand and challenge of his god, and he seems to have changed his position more than once as his words did or did not find a response or as events overran them. In the end he may even have rejected his own story believing his life to have been a failure. In Isaiah we witness a living theology struggling always in new contexts to comprehend the ways of his god with his chosen people. Isaiah was himself remembered by different circles in quite different ways. His legacy was as complex as the man himself.

The Syro-Ephraimite War
Isaiah 1–11, 20

The death trauma of northern Israel in 722 B.C.E. produced shocks that were felt in the surviving Davidic state as well, although the shocks were still remote when Isaiah received his call in 742 B.C.E. (Isaiah 6). While in the temple, possibly during the New Year's festival, he had a vision of Yahweh enthroned and surrounded by his heavenly court and was overcome by terror and a sense of his own human worthlessness. Although direct human contact with the deity can bring death to mortals (Isaiah 6:5; see also 1 Samuel 5:11–12; 2 Samuel 6:6–10), in this case it only brought about a change in Isaiah, who offered his life to the deity (Isaiah 6:6–8) as to a king who commands total allegiance. This same allegiance he would demand time and again from his people on his god's behalf.

Judah shared to a somewhat lesser extent in the prosperity of the period preceding the Assyrian advance. The years of kings Uzziah and Jotham (783–735 B.C.E.) were similar to those of their contemporary, Jeroboam II in Samaria, and the social and religious results were similar as well. In the oracles of chapters 2–5 the prophet is bitterly indicting the people of Judah for their failure to give allegiance to Yahweh alone (Isaiah 2:8–22) and for a breakdown in social justice and mutual concern. A picture emerges of one class oppressing and living off another, of a situation in which justice goes to the highest bidder (Isaiah 3:13–15; 3:16–17; 5:1–7; 5:8–23). The indictments are not unlike those of Amos and are followed by sentences that announce a punishment to come (Isaiah 2:6–22; 3:1–8; 5:5–6). The biting song of the vineyard in chapter 5:1–7, which contains both indictment and sentence, employs a forceful and ironic love song pattern that is characteristic of Isaiah's early utterances.

Yet nowhere in Isaiah's words, in this or any later phase of his career, is reference found to the Moses-Sinai story. Upon what foundation, then, did he base his words of indictment and punishment? That this citizen of Jerusalem grounded his words in the David-Zion story becomes apparent with the inception of the Syro-Ephraimite War (735–734 B.C.E.), a crisis that came at the end of the first phase of his career.

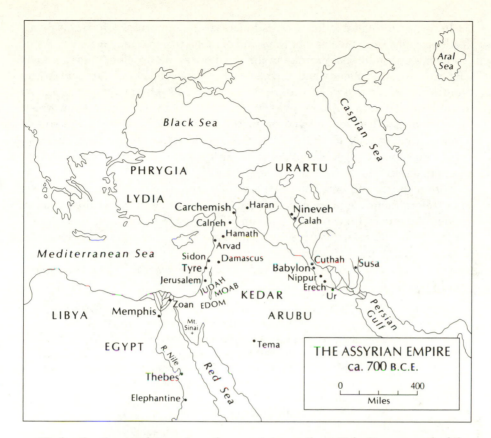

Under the threat of Assyrian advances into northern Palestine, several of the smaller states in that area, which were usually engaged in fighting among themselves, attempted to form a coalition in order to check the invader's movement, though even this alliance was fragile. Under the leadership of the Israelite king of Samaria and the king of Damascus an attempt was made to bring Judah's King Ahaz into the coalition. Failing that, they sought to place a more sympathetic figure on the throne in Jerusalem, for they could not tolerate a potential ally of Assyria to the south if they were to counter Assyrian advances from the north.

In the course of the siege that these two kings brought to Jerusalem, Isaiah confronted King Ahaz with the challenge that he saw implicit in the David-Zion story: place your total and absolute trust in Yahweh and his promises to your royal family and city; believe and you will remain secure on your throne (Isaiah 7). A sign was offered; a child born of a young woman would be named Immanuel. Although this sign remains open to varied interpretations, it seems to have been intended as an encouragement to trust, for the name Immanuel means "God [El] is with us."

In this political and military crisis Isaiah saw an opportunity for Jerusalem's leaders to turn from their earlier ways and demonstrate that they were worthy of Yahweh's unconditional promise to the royal house and to Zion. In giving their attention to other deities and in their lack of concern about rampant social injustice, they were hardly forces for peace and justice, harmony and integrity, though the traditions of Zion spoke of Jerusalem as the very center from which the creator god had formed and ordered this world. Zion was the life source from which harmony and integrity (*shalom*), justice and righteousness (*zedakah*), would flow to all the peoples of the earth, and as such both the city and its king stood under divine protection.

Although city and king had not lived up to their own traditions, in the crisis now before them the prophet found the moment of truth in the literal sense. Underlying the Hebrew word for "truth" (*'emet*) is the verbal root *'aman* (upon which the word "amen" is based) which means in one form "to believe" or "to trust in" and in another form "to be made firm" or "to be established." Isaiah called for trust or belief in Yahweh and his promises by which the city and king would be established for all time:

> It shall not stand,
>   and it shall not come to pass.
> For the head of Syria is Damascus,
>   and the head of Damascus is Rezin.
> And the head of Ephraim is Samaria,
>   and the head of Samaria is the son of Remaliah.
> If you will not believe,
>   surely you shall not be established.
>
> (Isaiah 7:7–9)

As Isaiah perceived it, the radical challenge of the David-Zion story was to place absolute trust in Yahweh, even to the extent of drastically reducing all human initiative. Earlier the Yahwist had developed this element in his presentation of Abraham. Although Abraham appeared first to lack such trust—for he fled to Egypt in the face of famine (Genesis 12:10–20) and attempted to produce an heir by taking the Egyptian handmaid (Genesis 16)—in each case he managed only to muddy the situation. Only in the end was he able to give Yahweh the total allegiance that Isaiah now demanded from his king.

Instead of accepting this challenge, however, Ahaz struck a bargain with the Assyrians (2 Kings 16:10–18), and in the immediate crisis he was successful. Under Assyrian pressure the siege on Jerusalem was lifted, the kings of Samaria and Damascus withdrew, and the city was spared, but the cost was vassalship to Assyria and trust in its king. Ahaz, no doubt, was convinced that he had made the best of a bad choice. He quite likely believed the coalition's chances against Assyria to have been futile. As leader and protector of his people, he had to save them, and from the perspective of hard political reality inactive trust in Yahweh alone would have seemed beside the point. Certainly the king would seek Yahweh's aid and divine blessing on the initiatives taken, but kings themselves had to act.

In Isaiah's eyes, however, Yahweh had been abandoned, and the long-range cost to the state would be great. Yahweh would now bring a punishment that would rid the people of those who demonstrated less than complete trust. Immanuel indeed would now be with them! The sign that had previously supported trust in Yahweh now became a sign of his judgment (Isaiah 7:17). Like Amos earlier, Isaiah warned that the expected day of Yahweh was not to be awaited with hopeful joy (Isaiah 2:12–22). The prophet now looked to a day when Assyria, the support upon which Ahaz relied, would turn on Judah and sweep away all who rejected total trust in Yahweh alone (Isaiah 7:18–25; 10:5–6; 10:28–32).

Just as the promise made to David in 2 Samuel 7 allowed for the possibility of Yahweh's punishment of the king—"with the rod of men, with stripes of the sons of men" (2 Samuel 7:14)—here, too, punishment would be administered through Assyria, the "rod" of Yahweh's anger (Isaiah 10:5–6). But as in 2 Samuel 7, this punishment was to be a winnowing, not an ultimate rejection of the royal line or a denial of the promise. If the instrument of punishment overreached itself, it would be destroyed (Isaiah 10:7–19). The cleansing punishment would be terrible, but the promises made to Zion and its king would remain secure. Yahweh would remain with them as he had remained with Abraham under all circumstances.

Beyond the immediate suffering, however, the prophet offers a vision of a wholly transformed created world, of an order completely integrated and harmonious, ruled by a king whose every act is an act of justice. In this vision human beings and the natural world regain their original pristine and uncorrupted state (Isaiah 9:2–7 and 11:1–9), and in this respect both Isaiah and the Yahwist stand firmly behind the David-Zion story. For the Yahwist, Israel was to be Yahweh's force for blessing and life for all the families of the earth. This tradition informed Isaiah as well as he looked beyond punishment and terror to a new creation by the ultimate sovereign god.

It is possible that Isaiah believed Hezekiah, Ahaz's son and heir, to be the king in whose reign Yahweh would accomplish this restoration. In form and content Isaiah 9:2–7 and 11:1–9 have been compared to oracles issued on the occasion of the birth or ascension to the throne of a crown prince. Isaiah may have delivered them on such an occasion, or they may simply be oracles patterned on that form. In any event they serve, on the one hand, as a final devastating judgment of Ahaz, for promises of peace and security under a new king are not good news to the present king. On the other hand, they offer a vision of hope and promise for the next generation:

Of the increase of his government and of peace
    there will be no end,
upon the throne of David, and over his kingdom,
    to establish it and to uphold it
with justice and with righteousness
    from this time forth and for evermore.
The zeal of Yahweh of hosts will do this.

(Isaiah 9:7)

The wolf shall dwell with the lamb,
    and the leopard shall lie down with the kid,
and the calf and the lion and the fatling together,
    and a little child shall lead them.
The cow and the bear shall feed;
    their young shall lie down together;
    and the lion shall eat straw like the ox.
The sucking child shall play over the hole of the asp,
    and the weaned child shall put his hand on
        the adder's den.
They shall not hurt or destroy
    in all my holy mountain;
for the earth shall be full of the knowledge of Yahweh
    as the waters cover the sea.

(Isaiah 11:6–9)

The Middle Years   At this point the prophet seems to have believed that his work was done, and he waited in sure confidence that Yahweh's word would in time be fulfilled (Isaiah 8:16–18). He had spoken of Yahweh's actions as he perceived them in the life of his people and had made clear the challenge of his story, but, having received no hearing, he waited; he, his children, and his disciples were living reminders of this. Isaiah 6:1–9:7 seems to some scholars to be based on the prophet's first-person account of his actions and words during the Syro-Ephraimite crisis. His career was not yet over, however, for in 711 B.C.E. the Assyrians attacked the city of Ashdod on the southwestern edge of Judah near the Mediterranean coast.

At this time Egypt sought to stem the advancing tide by urging the formation of a coalition of states in Palestine, to which it offered military aid, for the purpose of creating a buffer zone between itself and Assyria. Ahaz's son Hezekiah (715–687 B.C.E.) was now on the throne in Jerusalem and was no doubt under great pressure to join the coalition. Isaiah advised dramatically against it: for many months he walked the streets of Jerusalem naked, as a living symbol of the disgraceful exile that would result should trust be placed in Egyptian promises of aid (Isaiah 20). This sudden reappearance in public some two decades later does not bespeak a change in his policy; it reveals his continued emphasis on the fact that neither human cleverness nor diplomacy but Yahweh alone was the sole support for Judah and Jerusalem, once again reasserting the radical challenge of the David-Zion story.

Egyptian aid for Ashdod did not materialize; the city fell to Assyria. For whatever reason, Judah and Hezekiah did not overcommit themselves to the fated alliance with Egypt, and the Assyrian flood passed by, leaving them largely unharmed. Whether this was because of Isaiah's challenge or the result of a careful assessment of military odds is not clear, but reliance on Egyptian promises of aid was still not forever ruled out as a basis for foreign policy.

The Assyrian Crisis
Isaiah 22, 28-31

In 705 B.C.E. one of Assyria's strongest rulers, Sargon II, died, and for a time it was unclear who his successor would be. In the ensuing turmoil, which approached civil war, it appeared to many vassal states that the Assyrian empire's days were numbered; the time seemed right for a break. Egypt once again seized the opportunity to form an anti-Assyrian coalition in Palestine, offering promises of aid in case of trouble. This time Hezekiah and Judah entered into the alliance fully, even playing an active role in bringing certain reluctant states, such as nearby Ekron, into line, and with this alliance Isaiah's hopes were dashed. His oracles from this third phase of his career, found in chapters 28–31, reveal no diminution of the biting force of his younger days.

In these oracles he reviles the leaders of the state—king, courtiers, priests, and even prophets—as drunkards covered with their own filth (Isaiah 28:7–8) and calls their alliance with Egypt a mad turning from Yahweh, the nation's only firm support. The league with Egypt is a covenant with Mot, the god of death (Isaiah 28:14–22); it is out-and-out rebellion against Yahweh and folly in which everything seems turned upside down (Isaiah 29:13–16; 30:1–2; 30:8–14):

> Woe to those who go down to Egypt for help
>   and rely on horses,
> who trust in chariots because they are many
>   and in horsemen because they are very strong,
> but do not look to the Holy One of Israel
>   or consult with Yahweh!
>
> (Isaiah 31:1)

> The Egyptians are men and not God;
>   and their horses are flesh and not spirit.
> When Yahweh stretches out his hand,
>   the helper will stumble, and he who is helpful will fall,
>   and they will all perish together.
>
> (Isaiah 31:3)

Isaiah damns Egypt as a broken reed that pierces the hand of anyone who leans on it for support (Isaiah 30:3–5; 30:7). Once again he sees the situation as a test by which the people of Judah, and especially their leaders in Jerusalem, can demonstrate their trust in Yahweh and show that they are worthy of their story. Once again the prophet demands the absolute trust and quiet confidence that rests on no human initiative or self-supporting action:

> Therefore thus says Yahweh God,
> "Behold, I am laying in Zion for a foundation
> a stone, a tested stone,
> a precious cornerstone, of a sure foundation:
> 'He who believes will not be in haste.' "
>
> (Isaiah 28:16)

> For thus says Yahweh God, the Holy One of Israel,
> "In returning and rest you shall be saved;
> in quietness and in trust shall be your strength."
>
> (Isaiah 30:15)

But when Sennacherib came to the Assyrian throne, brought the empire under his authority, and in 702–701 B.C.E. turned his attention to the western part of the empire, a desperate, almost giddy wrong-headedness seemed to seize Judah's leaders, who continued to rely on Egyptian promises of aid (Isaiah 29:9–10). Isaiah mocked their last vain attempts to send gifts to Egypt over the dangerous wilderness paths because the main routes were cut off by Assyrian troops (Isaiah 30:6–8). Gifts would not bring Egyptian help because Egypt was worthless and empty, and he therefore named her "Rahab who sits still." As Assyria drew ever closer the prophet declared again that Yahweh would strip the city of all strength, defense, and support until it relied only on him:

> Ho Ariel, Ariel,
> the city where David encamped.
> Add year to year;
> let the feasts run their round.
> Yet I will distress Ariel,
> and there shall be moaning and lamentation,
> and she shall be to me like an Ariel.
> And I will encamp against you round about,
> and will besiege you with towers
> and I will raise siegeworks against you.
> Then deep from the earth you shall speak,
> from low in the dust your words shall come;
> your voice shall come from the ground like
> the voice of a ghost,
> and your speech shall whisper out of the dust.
>
> (Isaiah 29:1–4)

Then, the prophet said, the nation will trust in Yahweh, who will make known his presence as he and no one else delivers his city and people:

But the multitude of your foes shall be like small dust,
    and the multitude of the ruthless like passing chaff.
And in an instant, suddenly,
    you will be visited by Yahweh of hosts
with thunder and with earthquake and great noise,
    with whirlwind and tempest, and the flame of a
      devouring fire.
And the multitude of all the nations that fight
    against Ariel,
    all that fight against her and her stronghold
      and distress her,
    shall be like a dream, a vision of the night.
So shall the multitude of all the nations be
    that fight against Mount Zion.

(Isaiah 29:5–8)

Some scholars have suggested that Hezekiah attempted, in the face of northern Israel's destruction and the apparent internal dissolution of the Assyrian empire, to reconstruct the empire as it had been during the period of Solomon more than two centuries earlier, an age when all things had seemed possible to human initiative and skill. Although there was in Hezekiah's days a reformation of the temple and its cult (2 Kings 18:1–8) which may have been linked with his rejection of Assyrian overlordship, it was all doomed to fail.

In 702–701 B.C.E. Sennacherib's army moved down the Mediterranean coast destroying the members of the coalition. Passing west of Jerusalem, they cut inland destroying a number of Judean settlements to the south between Egypt and Jerusalem. With Egyptian aid thereby blocked they turned their attention to the seat of the Davidic dynasty. The Assyrian king later had the events described on a royal inscription:

> As to Hezekiah, the Jew, he did not submit to my yoke, I laid siege to 46 of his strong cities . . . . I drove out [of them] 200,150 people . . . . Himself I made a prisoner in Jerusalem, his royal residence, like a bird in a cage . . . . Hezekiah himself, whom the terror-inspiring splendor of my lordship had overwhelmed and whose irregular and elite troops which he had brought into Jerusalem, his royal residence, in order to strengthen [it], had deserted him, did send me, later, to Nineveh, my lordly city, together with 30 talents of gold, 800 talents of silver, [other valuable goods], his [own] daughters, concubines, male and female musicians. In order to deliver the tribute and to do obeisance as a slave he sent his personal messenger.*

---

*James B. Pritchard, ed., *Ancient Near Eastern Texts Relating to the Old Testament*, 3d ed., supp. (Princeton: Princeton University Press, 1969), p. 288.

122 Although Judah was devastated, Jerusalem was spared, and some small vestige of independence was preserved only because Hezekiah bought off Sennacherib at a terrible cost. The dream of a renewal of the golden age evaporated.

Again, as in the days of Ahaz, the Davidic ruler resorted to human means of deliverance. Although the citizens of Jerusalem were spared the torture and death that usually awaited those who threw off Assyrian authority, in Isaiah's eyes they had sold their souls to save their lives. Isaiah 22 may contain the prophet's final words. The scene is striking: the joyful city with its citizens shouting from the rooftops, exultant in their sudden deliverance; the prophet turning away to weep bitterly over the destruction of his people:

> In that day Yahweh God of hosts
> 	called to weeping and mourning,
> 	to baldness and girding with sackcloth;
> and behold, joy and gladness,
> 	slaying of oxen and killing of sheep,
> 	eating flesh and drinking wine.
> 	"Let us eat and drink, for tomorrow we die."
>
> Yahweh of hosts has revealed himself in my ears:
> 	"Surely this iniquity will not be forgiven you
> 	till you die,"
> 	says Yahweh God of hosts.
>
> (Isaiah 22:12–14)

In these final lines the prophet seems to reject his own traditions. Here death is the final word; the promises held out to David and Zion have been nullified and made void by the city and its king.

Let us now return to the conclusion of Isaiah's call in chapter 6:

> Then I said, "How long, O Yahweh?"
> 	and he said:
> 	"Until cities lie waste without inhabitant,
> 	and houses without men,
> 	and the land is utterly desolate,
> 	and Yahweh removes men far away,
> 	and the forsaken places are many in the midst
> 		of the land.
> 	And though a tenth remain in it,
> 	it will be burned again,
> 	like a terebinth or an oak,
> 	whose stump remains standing
> 		when it is felled."
>
> (Isaiah 6:11–13)

Three times Isaiah had called to his people in his god's name; three times he had interpreted political and military crises as Yahweh's summons; and at least twice his call had been rejected. He in turn had rejected one generation of leadership and placed his hopes on its successor, but Hezekiah had ultimately proved no better than his predecessor. Where now could Isaiah turn? It was as if his oracles of warning and promise, punishment and rebirth, had only made the people more committed to their own resources. He alone can see what has happened, and in the end he alone weeps as he turns from the story that had informed his life as Yahweh's prophet. This is the true tragedy of the Assyrian crisis.

The Isaiah of Legend

But chapters 36 and 37 of the Book of Isaiah offer an account of Sennacherib's siege against Jerusalem that differs from both the material presented in Sennacherib's inscription and from our own reconstruction of the third phase of Isaiah's career. (This third narrative is repeated in 2 Kings 18:13–19:37, with the striking addition of 2 Kings 18:14–16.) It would appear then that we have three different windows onto the events of 701 B.C.E., and the problems of reconstructing what actually took place only multiply with the sources available.

In Isaiah 36–37 we are told that when negotiations were being conducted for Jerusalem's capitulation Hezekiah placed absolute confidence in Yahweh (note the thrust of the Assyrian official's speech in 36:4–10 and 36:13–20), and Yahweh miraculously drove the invader from Jerusalem's walls (Isaiah 37:36–38). What Isaiah had so often demanded was finally given: complete and absolute trust in Yahweh. No mention is made of a huge payment or of the prophet's tears. How are we to square this account with that of Sennacherib? Which, if either, is correct? How do we explain the variance?

For some scholars the solution lies simply in accepting one or another account of the events as substantially correct and then fitting Isaiah's oracles into this account as fully as possible. But others have proposed that Isaiah 36–37 offers two different campaigns of Sennacherib telescoped into one. In the first campaign Sennacherib was triumphant, as his own account suggests and as the material in 2 Kings 18:14–16 (missing from Isaiah) implies. On this occasion Hezekiah paid the Assyrians a staggering sum for continued existence even in humiliation and defeat, and it is in this context that the oracles of Isaiah are to be understood.

Then a decade or so later Sennacherib again campaigned against Judah and Jerusalem which were once again, at Egyptian urging, considering the withdrawal of their loyalty as vassals. In this second encounter, which is recounted in Isaiah 36–37, something occurred to cause the sudden withdrawal of the Assyrian army, and the Assyrians, for understandable reasons, did not choose to record their defeat. But there is no clear evidence of a second Assyrian march into Palestine late in the reign of Sennacherib, and the more we learn about his last years, the less room there is to be found for a campaign in this region.

It is also possible that both Sennacherib's account and that in Isaiah 36–37 are exaggerated. In essence this interpretation suggests that Hezekiah did capitulate and pay a large sum to the Assyrians and that the details of this event, as well as the figure for the number of people taken (200,150), were exaggerated in Assyrian records. In short, the Assyrians recorded this as one more in a succession of victories, for they had accomplished their goals: Judah and Jerusalem were once again loyal and had learned a lesson.

At the same time, however, the citizens of Jerusalem had escaped the fate of many who rebelled against Assyrian authority. In the inscription previously noted, Sennacherib tells what happened to the people of Ekron who did not submit to him: "I assaulted Ekron and killed the officials and patricians who had committed the crime and hung their bodies on poles surrounding the city. The common citizens who were guilty of minor crimes I considered prisoners of war."* In what one scholar has called their policy of "calculated frightfulness," other Assyrian rulers provided graphic descriptions of impalement, flaying, flailing, burning alive, and other brutalities to serve as an example and warning to other vassals.

For the people of Jerusalem, survival and continuance in their homeland were seen as a cause for rejoicing. Few among the city's population would know the price paid; in the immediate circumstances few would care; and on this basis would grow the legendary account of Yahweh's deliverance of the city. Had tradition not long affirmed, and Isaiah repeatedly reaffirmed, that Yahweh would protect his inviolable city of Zion? Was not such a theme at the heart of songs heard each year in the temple in Jerusalem? (See Psalms 2, 110, 46, 48.) From this perspective, the events of 701 B.C.E. reconfirmed the David-Zion story and dramatically certified its promises.

It is ironic that Isaiah was caught up into this popular legend from which the David-Zion story received new life because it is a form that the Isaiah of the oracles would have denounced as a sure path to death. It must be emphasized, however, that the David-Zion story as Isaiah presented it demanded a response of passive confidence and absolute trust in Yahweh alone and placed no value on human initiative. To most of his fellow countrymen this negation of human action would quite likely have seemed radically overdrawn. Why must human initiative and cleverness stand as counter to Yahweh's will and support? Cannot Yahweh help those who help themselves?

At all events, the miraculous character of the deliverance was accentuated as the legend dealing with the crisis was retold over the decades. In time the legend found its way into the collected body of material about Isaiah as well as into the history found in the Book of Kings, and on this popular level the David-Zion story would be reconfirmed as the locus for the identity of the people of Judah and as the foundation for their relation with their god.

---

*Pritchard, *Ancient Near Eastern Texts*, p. 288.

A contemporary of Isaiah, the prophet Micah was his opposite in almost every way. Isaiah was a cosmopolitan figure from the city of Jerusalem. Micah was a peasant from the hamlet of Moresheth located southwest of the capital. This area bore the initial brunt of the Assyrian march against Judah, and it was such outlying territory that suffered most from the foreign policy formed in the capital. Isaiah loved Jerusalem and its traditions and to the end of his life remained committed to his vision of what the city could be. Micah bore a fierce hatred of the city on the hill with all its elegance and alien corruption, speaking of it with a blunt clarity that would be recalled years later (see Jeremiah 26:18):

> Hear this, you heads of the house of Jacob
>> and rulers of the house of Israel,
> who abhor justice
>> and pervert all equity,
> who build Zion with blood
>> and Jerusalem with wrong.
> Its heads give judgment for a bribe,
>> its priests teach for hire,
>> its prophets divine for money;
> yet they lean upon Yahweh and say,
> "Is not Yahweh in the midst of us?
>> No evil shall come upon us."
> Therefore because of you
>> Zion shall be plowed as a field;
> Jerusalem shall become a heap of ruins,
>> and the mountain of the house a wooded height.
>
>> (Micah 3:9–12)

This oracle reflects nothing of Yahweh's unconditional promise to the Davidic dynasty and to Zion. Indeed, Micah's citation of the words of Jerusalem's citizens is a polemical perversion of their story, and here lies his greatest difference from Isaiah. That Micah builds his indictment and sentence upon the Moses-Sinai story is clearest in a unit exhibiting the classical form of a summons to trial in a covenant lawsuit.

> Hear what Yahweh says:
>> Arise, plead your case before the mountains,
>> and let the hills hear your voice.
> Hear, you mountains, the controversy of Yahweh,
>> and you enduring foundations of the earth;
> for Yahweh has a controversy with his people,
>> and he will contend with Israel.
>
>> (Micah 6:1–2)

He goes on to speak of a conditional covenant built upon the old story of the federation:

> O my people, what have I done to you?
>   In what have I wearied you? Answer me!
> For I brought you up from the land of Egypt,
>   and redeemed you from the house of bondage;
>   I sent before you Moses, Aaron, and Miriam.
> O my people, remember what Balak king of Moab devised,
>   and what Balaam the son of Beor answered him,
>   and what happened from Shittim to Gilgal,
>   that you may know the saving acts of Yahweh.
>
> (Micah 6:3–5)

In his words the federation's story lived on in Judah as it had in the kingdom of northern Israel. He even uses the designation "Jacob and Israel" for the Judean state, for his perspective is that of the ancient tradition in which there is but one Israel in covenant with Yahweh. The breaking of this covenant could result only in death, and announcement of the death sentence could not be silenced (Micah 2:6).

Whether Micah envisioned any renewal or restoration beyond the destruction is a moot point. Most scholars regard the material in Micah 4:1–5:15 and 7:8–20 as later expansions of his words, at points reflecting the strong influence of the Davidic traditions. To what extent there is a core reflecting Micah's own vision is unanswerable in view of this expansion. In their present form, his collected oracles are incorporated into the more normative traditions of the Davidic house: the Moses-Zion story is encompassed in the controlling vision of the David-Zion story.

Here it is important to recall that soon after the fall of Samaria in 722 B.C.E. and probably in the days of Hezekiah, the Elohist narrative was combined with the Yahwist epic in such a way that the Yahwist's structure remained dominant. Although Elohistic material was woven into the basic framework of J only where it offered something distinct, it had the effect of submerging the controlling vision of E, in this way producing an expanded form of the Yahwist's epic. (It is possible that at this stage the Joseph story, too, made its way into J, still further expanding the older epic.) In compiling a new edition of J, the reign of Hezekiah seems again to follow the model of Solomon's period when the original Yahwist epic was created.

Preserving segments of the Elohist's epic in J and enveloping the oracles of Micah in the David-Zion story (note also Amos 9:11–15 and Hosea 2:18–19) temporarily stilled tensions between the two stories as the thrust of the Moses-Sinai story and its conditional covenant was blunted. Within the next century, however, the tension between the two stories and their different understanding of Yahweh's covenant would break forth again in a direct conflict whose issue would determine the fate of the nation.

Isaiah of Jerusalem

> Blank, Sheldon H. *Prophetic Faith in Isaiah*. New York: Harper & Row, 1958. A discussion of the prophet and the legends that grew about him.

> Childs, Brevard S. *Isaiah and the Assyrian Crisis*. Studies in Biblical Theology, no. 3. London: SCM Press, 1967.

> Kaiser, Otto. *Isaiah 1–12*. Philadelphia: Westminster Press, 1972.

> ———. *Isaiah 13–39*. Philadelphia: Westminster Press, 1974.

> North, Christopher R. "Isaiah." In *The Interpreter's Dictionary of the Bible*, vol. 2, pp. 731–44. Nashville: Abingdon Press, 1962.

> Ward, James M. *Amos and Isaiah: Prophets of the Word of God*. Nashville: Abingdon Press, 1969.

> ———. "Isaiah." In *The Interpreter's Dictionary of the Bible: Supplementary Volume*, pp. 456–61. Nashville: Abingdon Press, 1976.

> Whedbee, William. *Isaiah and Wisdom*. Nashville: Abingdon Press, 1971.

The Book of Micah

> Leslie, E. A. "Micah." In *The Interpreter's Dictionary of the Bible*, vol. 3, pp. 369–72. Nashville: Abingdon Press, 1962.

> Mays, James L. *Micah*. Philadelphia: Westminster Press, 1976.

KINGDOM of JUDAH (725–587 B.C.E.)

B.C.E.	Egypt	Judah				Assyria
725	TWENTY-FOURTH DYNASTY (725–709)	Ahaz (735–715)		ISAIAH		Sargon II (721–705)
	TWENTY-FIFTH DYNASTY (716–663)	Hezekiah (715–687)				
700				MICAH		Sennacherib (704–681)
	Tirhakah (685–664)	Manasseh (687–642)				Esarhaddon (680–669)
675						Ashurbanipal (668–627)
	TWENTY-SIXTH DYNASTY (664–610)					
650						
		Amon (642–640) Josiah (640–609)				
625				ZEPHANIAH		
				NAHUM		Fall of Nineveh (612)
600	Neco (610–594)	Jehoahaz (609) Jehoiakim (609–598)		HABAKKUK	JEREMIAH	
		Jehoiakin (598) Zedekiah (597–587)	First Captivity (598) EZEKIEL Fall of Jerusalem (587)			
575						

THE SECOND CRISIS

7

Primary readings: *Jeremiah*

Nahum

Habakkuk

Zephaniah

Obadiah

From Manasseh to Josiah

In Judah and Jerusalem political and religious tensions increased for several decades after the time of Isaiah and Micah. There was a tension between the David-Zion story found in the oracles of Isaiah and the popular development of this tradition complex found in Isaiah 36–37. Between the David-Zion and Moses-Sinai stories there was a submerged tension that events would eventually bring to the surface and strain to the breaking point. These events climaxed in the destruction of Jerusalem in 587 B.C.E., bringing the historical existence of Israel as a nation to an end.

In the remainder of his reign King Hezekiah did not break his vassal ties with Assyria, nor did his son Manasseh, a pragmatic ruler with a realistic understanding of Judah's restricted political position on the international scene. Manasseh's reign (687–642 B.C.E.), the longest of any member of the house of David, was marked by relative peace and limited prosperity, but it also exhibited a religious pluralism that earned the scorn and condemnation of those who produced the books of Kings (2 Kings 21:1–16). There can be little doubt that the popular form of the David-Zion story gave support to his rule. Anyone who

129

opposed the royal policy, especially anyone informed by the Moses-Sinai story and its unbending demand for allegiance to Yahweh alone, would have been driven underground or martyred (2 Kings 21:16).

That there were such figures is attested by the sudden emergence of two forms of the Moses-Sinai story at the end of the seventh century B.C.E.. One form is found in the oracles and life of the prophet Jeremiah. The other informed a broad review of Israel's history from just before the taking of the land of Canaan through Nebuchadnezzar's final destruction of Israel in 587 B.C.E. This is the so-called deuteronomistic history comprising the books of Deuteronomy through 2 Kings (excluding Ruth). This chapter will center on the prophet Jeremiah. The deuteronomistic history will be the subject of the Epilogue to Part I because it attempts to review and assess the theological significance of the history of ancient Israel.

Above all, the year 627 B.C.E. was crucial both for Near Eastern history and for the development of ancient Israelite religious traditions. In that year Ashurbanipal, the last strong Assyrian king, died, but even before his death the Assyrian empire had overextended itself, and without a strong ruler it began to dissolve. In 614 B.C.E. the religious center of Ashur fell; the political capital of Nineveh was lost two years later; finally Assyria fell before the combined attack of Babylonians from southern Mesopotamia and Median tribes from the northeast. The fall of Nineveh brought rejoicing to the smaller states in Palestine because it seemed to hold out the possibility of independence. The brief Book of Nahum, which probably originated just before this event, anticipates Assyria's death with bitter relish.

Around 627 B.C.E., too, King Josiah of Judah undertook a series of religious and political reforms that brought about a reemergence of the Moses-Sinai story in Jerusalem and a declaration of Judah's independence from Assyria. Josiah had succeeded the brief reign of Manasseh's son Amon, who had followed his father's policies and had died in a palace coup; popular pressure had placed Josiah on the throne, and the conspirators had been executed (2 Kings 21:19–26). Josiah was a minor at the time of his enthronement and little is known of the first years of his reign, but it is clear that basic changes were taking place that would climax in the reform undertaken under the impetus of the Moses-Sinai story. Of this more will be said in the next chapter, for Josiah's reform is closely linked with the Book of Deuteronomy.

Also ascribed to this period are the words of a prophet named Zephaniah in whom we see the David-Zion story preserved and continuing to inform prophetic judgment and promise. Although denouncing the crimes of Manasseh and speaking of Yahweh's punishment for a perversion of the Yahweh cult, he nevertheless offered hope to those who adhered to Yahweh through this period of tribulation. In their attention to Zion and to Yahweh's destruction of its enemies the oracles of Zephaniah recall those of Isaiah of Jerusalem, whose disciple he may have been.

Finally, in 627 B.C.E. Yahweh called Jeremiah to be his messenger. During this prophet's fifty-year career the dissolution of the Assyrian empire was succeeded by the rise of the Neo-Babylonian empire in which the reforms of Josiah were abandoned, the king lost his life, and Judah and Jerusalem became unwilling vassals to a new power. The two stories of old Israel came into final dramatic conflict, and within a few decades the life of the state had come to an end. It was in this historical crisis that Jeremiah sought to find the hand of his god.

THE ORACLES OF JEREMIAH

Jeremiah's career can be divided into three periods to which his oracles are assigned: the Josiah years (Jeremiah 1:4–6:30), the reigns of kings Jehoiakim and Jehoiakin (Jeremiah 7:1–20:18) and the period of Zedekiah (Jeremiah 21:1–25:14). These divisions are only approximate, however, for, like other prophetic books, the Book of Jeremiah contains a mixture of materials, including later oracles added by those who preserved, collected, and edited his words. Oracles against other nations in Jeremiah 46–51 cannot all be attributed to the prophet himself and cannot always be securely dated. There are, in addition, two distinct blocks of material that require separate consideration—the so-called "laments" of Jeremiah and the Baruch biography. The former are distributed throughout Jeremiah 10–20; the latter is found in chapters 26–45.

The Josiah Years　When first encountered, Jeremiah seems an unlikely figure for the task confronting him. He was called to be a prophet even before his birth (Jeremiah 1:5), and he spoke in the city of Jerusalem, rebuking its kings and princes, priests and prophets (Jeremiah 1:18). A small, isolated figure standing against the entire religious and political structure of the state, he had begun as a youth and outsider (Jeremiah 1:6) from the small rural village of Anathoth to the north of Jerusalem. He was of priestly descent but of a line that was probably traceable to Abithar, the priest from Shiloh in David's day, whom Solomon had later had exiled from Jerusalem for political reasons (1 Kings 2:26–27).

Like Amos and Micah, Jeremiah's roots were set in the rural countryside that often bore the brunt of political and economic policies devised in Jerusalem. With such ancestry and roots, he stood outside the mainstream of Judah's power circles and life and had little love for the royal city or its temple priesthood and cult. Yet in Jerusalem he would denounce the royal city's corruption and announce its coming destruction, and it was a task that would almost destroy him.

Jeremiah's early oracles echo the tones and themes of the older prophets of northern Israel, especially the sensitive strains of Hosea. Like them, he builds on the story of slaves delivered from Egyptian bondage who entered into a covenant relationship with Yahweh at Sinai. But the covenant stipulations have now been violated and the relationship is fractured:

> They did not say, "Where is Yahweh
> > who brought us up from the land of Egypt,
> who led us in the wilderness,
> > in a land of deserts and pits,
> in a land of drought and deep darkness,
> > in a land that none passes through,
> > where no man dwells."
> And I brought you into a plentiful land
> > to enjoy its fruits and its good things.
>
> > (Jeremiah 2:6–7)

As in Hosea's oracles, the wilderness wandering is seen as a period fraught with danger but also as the bridal days of love between Yahweh and Israel (Jeremiah 2:2–3). The falling apart of this relationship came as they entered Canaan and is again described as harlotry and adultery (Jeremiah 2:11; 2:13; 2:20; 2:23–25; 2:27–28; 2:33; 3:19–20). Divorce seems the only recourse (Jeremiah 3:1–5).

The context for the oracles is that of the covenant lawsuit, with indictments pronounced for crimes against fellow Israelites and especially for failure to give devotion to Yahweh alone. The sentence is destruction (Jeremiah 1:13–14; 4:5–31; 5:15–17). Early visions underscore the urgency Jeremiah attributed to this. What to others would appear as everyday sights—the shoot of an almond tree or a cooking pot tipped on the fire—were in Jeremiah's eyes urgent signs of Yahweh's imminent judgment (Jeremiah 1:11–16). The first omen is constructed on the similarity between the Hebrew words for "almond" (shaqed) and "watching" (shoqed). The second suggests the means by which Yahweh will carry out his sentence: an enemy will come rolling out of the north, the traditional line of march into southern Palestine for an army from Mesopotamia.

Jeremiah's reaction to King Josiah's reforms, entailing the removal of overtly non-Yahwistic elements from the temple in Jerusalem and possibly some attention to social abuses in the nation, is not given. But the reforms were curtailed in any case when Josiah was cut down in the military ferment accompanying the collapse of Assyria (2 Kings 23:29–30). In the ensuing years Jehoiakim, Josiah's son and successor, abandoned his father's policy, and Jeremiah's words would become more severe as his tone increasingly echoed that of Amos and Micah.

Kings Jehoiakim and Jehoiakin　The failure of Josiah's reform not only curtailed the drive for independence from foreign domination but seemed to many to be a judgment by history against the Moses-Sinai story. After Pharaoh Neco killed Josiah and placed Jehoiakim on the throne, a brief period of Egyptian control of southern Palestine was followed by forced recognition of Babylonian authority. Babylon had been instrumental in bringing about the fall of Assyria, and under Nebuchadnezzer II it took over the old Assyrian empire. By checking Egyptian advances into the area, Babylon's authority soon reached from the Persian Gulf to the Nile. But submitting to this new authority was difficult for Judah. To Jeremiah the reign of Jehoiakim (609–598 B.C.E.) seemed to combine the worst of Manasseh's religious and social policies with a foolish political attempt to throw off the Babylonian yoke. Support for the latter policy was found in a revival of the David-Zion tradition in its popular form which encouraged a belief that Yahweh would once again defend his city and its king against all foes.

In a sermon delivered in the temple, Jeremiah declared that relying on the promises of this tradition in the face of overt social oppression and apostasy from Yahweh was suicidal (Jeremiah 7). How, he asked scornfully, can people who murder, commit adultery, swear falsely, burn incense to Baal, and go after other gods imagine themselves to be safe merely by entering the temple of Yahweh? A mere magiclike recitation of the words "this is the temple of Yahweh, temple of Yahweh, temple of Yahweh" cannot atone for crimes or ensure protection. For having "turned Yahweh's temple into a den of thieves," Yahweh will make it into a ruin like the ruin at Shiloh, the old federation center that had been destroyed centuries earlier in conflict with the Philistines.

Behind the recitation that Jeremiah parodies lay a confidence and belief in Yahweh's promises to Zion and the Davidic line that constituted the official theology of the royal establishment and the state, and to mock it was to risk not only blasphemy or heresy but treason as well. In fact, this sermon delivered in the royal and religious center for the state brought charges of treason against Jeremiah, who was placed on trial for his life. Jeremiah 7 contains the sermon; the reaction to it is found in Jeremiah 26:

> The priests and the prophets and all the people heard Jeremiah speaking these words in the house of Yahweh. . . . Then the priests and the prophets and all the people laid hold of him, saying, "You shall die! Why have you prophesied in the name of Yahweh, saying, 'This house shall be like Shiloh, and this city shall be desolate, without inhabitant'?" And all the people gathered about Jeremiah in the house of Yahweh.
>
> (Jeremiah 26:7–9)

Brought before the officials of the state, Jeremiah's defense—that he simply spoke the word of Yahweh (Jeremiah 26:12–15)—raised monumental problems. While it was acknowledged that Yahweh did speak through the voice of human beings called by him, how could one determine whether the claim to be Yahweh's messenger was valid? Were there any external signs, any tests that could be applied, to show that a particular set of claims was true? Could the genuine prophet be clearly distinguished from someone who sought to deceive or was himself deluded? The answer is that there were no reliable tests. Jeremiah could merely state his claim and then place himself at the mercy of the court. It was the prophet's call that certified him as one who spoke for the deity, but the call was an intensely personal experience that left no external marks for others to see.

That no miracles are offered is striking in comparison with legends about

134 Elijah, Elisha, and even Isaiah of Jerusalem (Isaiah 38–39). But even then the dramatic miracles performed by Elijah on Mount Carmel had carried little weight; he was soon in flight in the wilderness and seemingly alone. The issue was therefore as follows: if Jeremiah was a prophet, he could not be held guilty for delivering the words of the deity; but his words were so alien to what the people believed of Yahweh that they could not be sure of the prophet's authenticity.

In this case a precedent was recalled and Jeremiah was given the benefit of the doubt. Had not an earlier prophet named Micah said similar things about Jerusalem and the temple without being put to death? Some seemed to recollect that his words had even been heeded (Jeremiah 29:19), although to complete the picture the account of Jeremiah's trial ends with a notice about a prophet named Uriah who spoke "in words like those of Jeremiah" but for whom royal justice had resulted in pursuit, capture, and execution (Jeremiah 26:20–23). A final note stating that "the hand of Ahikam, the son of Shaphan, was with Jeremiah so that he was not given over to the people to be put to death" suggests that Jeremiah was not totally without recourse, for Ahikam was a high-level official of the state.

Still, Uriah's execution and the near death of Jeremiah indicate something of the religious and political tensions of these years, and these tensions increased until Jeremiah was driven underground. In time he could only dictate his words for another to proclaim (Jeremiah 36), but his indictments remained unabated in their severity and his words continued to pronounce divine sentence upon his people.

A prophetic colleague of Jeremiah provides another perspective on these critical years of Jehoiakim's reign. Along with several basic indictments and sentences of Judah and Jerusalem in the classical manner, Habakkuk raises an issue that will loom large for decades to come. Addressing his god, he asks:

> Thou who art of purer eyes than to behold evil
> and canst not look on wrong,
> why dost thou look on faithless men,
> and art silent when the wicked swallow up
> the man more righteous than he?
>
> (Habakkuk 1:13)

Habakkuk's answer to the question of divine justice and rule is to wait, even in the face of unmerited suffering, with unmoved confidence in Yahweh's ways. A hymn attached to Habakkuk 3 reinforces this confidence in Yahweh's power to save his own, but that the question was even raised is expressive of the agony that some suffered in these years. "The righteous shall live by his faith" (Habakkuk 2:4), he declares, but in these days that same faith often brought one to the edge of death.

The Period of Zedekiah Jehoiakim's policy of withholding allegiance to Babylon brought Nebuchadnezzar's army to Jerusalem in 598 B.C.E. After a siege of some months the city was taken; many prisoners were exiled (Jehoiakim had died but his son Jehoiakin was among the exiles); and tribute was taken together with the treasures of the temple. The city and temple were not destroyed, however, and retained a semiindependent status. Zedekiah, an uncle of Jehoiakin, was placed on the throne of Jerusalem as a Babylonian puppet, but this did not blunt the force of the independence movement or of the traditions that gave it support.

It was soon being said even in Babylon, that since Yahweh had meted out punishment against his city and people, now was the time for restoration; he would soon secure the release of the captives from exile, and they and the temple's treasures would return home (see Jeremiah 29). This pattern is remarkably like that found in the oracles of Isaiah more than a century earlier. Punishment did not indicate that Yahweh had withdrawn his loving support. Israel had only been winnowed and refined. Both in exile and in Jerusalem people eagerly awaited their god.

Because the former king, Jehoiakin, remained alive in exile, Zedekiah may have lacked the power, even if he had the will, to oppose the anti-Babylonian freedom forces within the government. Certainly he could not change the prevailing theology that informed them, and compounding the pressure was an Egyptian initiative that promised military aid for withholding allegiance from Babylon. Apparently, Egyptian failures to live up to their past commitments had had no effect. For his part, however, Jeremiah denounced all dreams of restoration and freedom from the yoke of Babylon. To the exiles he wrote that they must expect no immediate return (Jeremiah 29); to those at home he said that those now in control of the state were rotten figs compared with those lost in 598 B.C.E. (Jeremiah 24). There was nothing to do but submit to Yahweh's will and bow before the yoke of Nebuchadnezzar.

As the independence movement gained momentum, fed by promises of Egyptian aid and informed by the David-Zion story, Jeremiah's advice again sounded like treason. Babylon's army returned; Egyptian aid failed; and during a brief respite in the Babylonian siege on the city the prophet was arrested for crimes against the state (Jeremiah 37:11–15), thrown into a cistern to die, and rescued only in the nick of time (Jeremiah 38:1–13). Yet during even these last days his words to the hapless Zedekiah remained unchanged (Jeremiah 37:16–21; 38:14–28).

In time he was jailed again (Jeremiah 32:1–5), and he remained in jail until the city fell. Chapters 39 and 50 of the Book of Jeremiah (see also 2 Kings 24:18–25:30) describe the destruction. Jeremiah was allowed to stay on amid the ruins, but the life of the nation Israel had come to an end. The land was reorganized into a part of the Babylonian provincial structure and governed by an Israelite named Gedeliah who was backed by Babylonian authority. In the confused aftermath of these events, Gedeliah was assassinated by a few remaining fanatical nationalists, and Jeremiah was taken to Egypt against his will by people who feared and fled Babylonian reprisals. There in the original land of bondage he ended his days in exile and obscurity.

There is bitter irony in our last view of Jeremiah in chapter 44. He has been forced to go down to Egypt, to the land from which Yahweh had delivered Israel in its birth. Yahweh's people could not live freely on the land he had given them; the life of fugitives in the land of slavery now seemed preferable to them. Even in Egypt he rebukes his people for giving up their allegiance to Yahweh, but they now turn on him and, in a reversal of prophetic logic, claim that it was their allegiance to Yahweh alone that had brought this wrath of the other gods upon them:

> Then the men who knew that their wives had offered incense to other gods, and all the women who stood by, a great assembly, all the people who dwelt in Pathros in the land of Egypt, answered Jeremiah: "As for the word which you have spoken in the name of Yahweh, we will not listen to you. But we will do everything that we have vowed, burn incense to the queen of heaven, and pour out libations to her as we did, both we and our fathers, our kings and our princes, in the cities of Judah and in the streets of Jerusalem; for then we had plenty of food, and prospered, and saw no evil. But since we left off burning incense to the queen of heaven and pouring out libations to her, we have lacked everything and have been consumed by the sword and by famine."
>
> (Jeremiah 44:15–18)

The facts are no longer a matter of dispute, only their meaning. The prophet's task had been to interpret theologically the crisis faced by his nation, to point to the hand of Yahweh in the historical experience of his people, but now this means of interpreting history is turned against Yahweh and prophet alike. Their experience suggests to the fugitives that the foundations of life are now to be found elsewhere than in Yahweh. Thus the people of Israel, who had first met Yahweh and heard his word in Egypt, now reject him and his word in this same land of bondage.

Although Jeremiah's life seems to end in failure and mockery, there is more to be said about him and the book that contains his oracles. We must still give attention to his laments, the cries of agony that reveal the human cost of the prophetic task, and to a semibiographical account of his last years. Jeremiah also offers a striking vision of a new covenant to replace the old one, and this will be considered in the Prologue to Part 2 of this study, for in it are found the first signs of the birth of Judaism from the ashes and ruins of old Israel.

The Laments of Jeremiah

In ancient Israel one aspect of the prophet's role was to present the petitions of the people to their god (see Jeremiah 21:2; 42:2–3), to represent each to the other, because he was in special contact with the deity. Indeed, Yahweh more than once warned Jeremiah to cease praying for his people because they were no longer Yahweh's people and he no longer their god (Jeremiah 7:16; 14:11). In his own person, however, Jeremiah gave vivid expression to the agony and suffering of his people as the sentence he pronounced became fact. After the capture of Jerusalem in 598 B.C.E. his cry of anguish came from the heart of a true son of Israel who loved and was one with his nation:

> My grief is beyond healing,
>   my heart is sick within me.
> For the wound of the daughter of my people
>   is my heart wounded.
> I mourn, and dismay has taken hold on me.
> O that my head were waters,
>   and my eyes a fountain of tears,
> that I might weep day and night
>   for the slain of the daughter of my people.
>   (Jeremiah 8:18–9:1)

Given a chance to leave them for a better life in Babylon after 587, he refused and remained amid the nation's ruins (Jeremiah 40:1–6). By the people, however, he was seen as a heretic and traitor. Because Yahweh's word was put in his mouth at his call (Jeremiah 1:9–10), he embodied both the creative and destructive words of the deity. In his words and action the prophet represented both the people and the god each to the other; but when the two were so wholly out of phase, when their fractured relationship seemed beyond repair, he was himself nearly crushed between them. Forced to give form and flesh to the words of indictment and sentence, he destroyed the foundation for his own existence as well.

When the sentence that Jeremiah pronounced was not immediately forthcoming, he was mocked by his people and felt betrayed by his god. Isolated and alone, torn to the depth of his physical and psychic being, attacked by his own family, he expressed his agony in a series of unique laments, which, though they come close to a form of blasphemy, may have preserved his sanity. The laments are found in Jeremiah 11:18–23; 12:1–5; 15:10–11; 15:15–20; 17:14–18; 18:18–23; and 20:7–11. Although they cannot be cited in full here, they are worth repeated readings because they speak with a bluntness that is not characteristic of most religious discourse.

Cries from the depths of a chaotic abyss, the laments accuse Yahweh of supporting evil (compare Habakkuk 1:13), of seduction and betrayal, of setting up his prophet and making a fool of him.

> Why is my pain unceasing,
>   my wound incurable,
>   refusing to be healed?

Wilt thou be to me like a deceitful brook,
    like waters that fail?

                   (Jeremiah 15:16)

O Yahweh, thou hast deceived me,
    and I was deceived;
thou art stronger than I,
    and thou hast prevailed.
I have become a laughingstock all the day;
    everyone mocks me.
For whenever I speak, I cry out,
    I shout, "Violence and destruction!"
For the word of Yahweh has become for me
    a reproach and derision all day long.

                   (Jeremiah 20:7–8)

At points he calls for the violent destruction of the very people for whom he has elsewhere wept (Jeremiah 8:18–9:1):

Therefore deliver up their children to famine;
    give them over to the power of the sword,
let their wives become childless and widowed.
May their men meet death by pestilence,
    their youths be slain by the sword in battle.
May a cry be heard from their houses,
    when thou bringest the marauder suddenly upon them!
For they have dug a pit to take me,
    and laid snares for my feet.

                 (Jeremiah 18:21–22)

Always he protests his innocence and his devotion to his task:

In thy forbearance take me not away;
    know that for thy sake I bear reproach.
Thy words were found, and I ate them,
    and thy words became to me a joy
    and the delight of my heart;
for I am called by thy name,
    O Yahweh, God of hosts.
I did not sit in the company of merrymakers,
    nor did I rejoice;
I sat alone, because thy hand was upon me,
    for thou hadst filled me with indignation.

                 (Jeremiah 15:15–17)

If I say, "I will not mention him
    or speak any more in his name,"
there is in my heart as it were a burning fire

> shut up in my bones,
>   and I am weary with holding it in, and I cannot.
>
>   (Jeremiah 20:9)

In some instances the deity does not respond; in others he gives the prophet renewed support (Jeremiah 11:21–23; 20:11). Most remarkable are two instances of seeming rebuke which are also implied renewals of his call as described in Jeremiah 1:4–10:

> If you have raced with men on foot, and they have
>   wearied you,
>   how will you compete with horses?
> And if in a safe land you fall down,
>   how will you do in the jungle of the Jordan?
>
>   (Jeremiah 12:5)

> If you return, I will restore you,
>   and you shall stand before me.
> If you utter what is precious, and not what is
>   worthless,
>   you shall be as my mouth.
> They shall turn to you,
>   but you shall not turn to them.
> And I will make you to this people
>   a fortified wall of bronze;
> they will fight against you,
>   but they shall not prevail over you,
> for I am with you
>   to save and deliver you,
>   says Yahweh.
>
>   (Jeremiah 15:19–20)

Reinforced and enlivened, Jeremiah returned to his task because he could not do otherwise (Jeremiah 20:9). As a youth he had turned in fear from his call; as a prophet he had several times turned in terror from his task, only to have it renewed. Thus for all their harshness, Jeremiah's laments express his ever deepening trust in and reliance on his god, for his depth of feeling reveals the depth of his relationship with the deity as well. Although other prophets suffered agonies and doubts (see Amos 7:2, 5; Isaiah 22:4; 6:11), theirs did not reach the depth of Jeremiah's terror, for no other prophet had a career that encompassed more than a half-century of constant activity. Even Isaiah of Jerusalem had two decades elapse between the phases of his prophetic activity.

Those who preserved the words of the prophets showed little interest in these figures as human beings, concerning themselves more with Yahweh's word. Therefore, little that we today seek in the way of psychological insight or even of simple biographical information is to be found in the prophetic books. With

Jeremiah, however, the situation is otherwise, and we value the laments even more for what they tell us about the man who filled the role of Yahweh's prophet. It can be suggested, too, that these laments reflect not so much a change in the interests of the ancient editors as an enlargement of their conception of the prophetic office itself, of the prophet as the vehicle of Yahweh's word.

The Baruch Biography

This expanded conception of the prophet's role finds expression in another distinct body of material in the Book of Jeremiah. While other prophetic books offer sparse biographical or autobiographical material about the lives of the prophets (see Amos 7:7–10; Hosea 1 and 3; Isaiah 7 and 36–39), the Book of Jeremiah presents in chapters 26–45 extensive biographical units that are generally ascribed to Baruch, Jeremiah's loyal companion and scribe. Clearly, this material was produced by someone who knew the prophet well. It was Baruch, for example, to whom Jeremiah dictated many of his oracles when he could no longer appear in public, and it was Baruch who read these in the temple before the people, courtiers, and finally the king, only to find himself driven underground as well (Jeremiah 36). The concluding unit in chapter 45 indicates that Baruch remained loyal, continued to share the life of his friend, and has given us this record of the prophet's last years.

On close inspection, however, Baruch's narrative does not form what we would today call a formal biography. No information is given about the subject's birth or upbringing, and nothing is said of his death. The narrative begins with his career as prophet already under way, and it ends with Jeremiah seemingly a failure in Egypt. What is reported here is his continued suffering and rejection by the leaders and citizens of Jerusalem as his harsh words increasingly appear to them as heretical and treasonous. What Baruch offers, in fact, is a narrative about the fate of Yahweh's word in the final years in the life of old Israel.

In these chapters we encounter a deepening understanding of the relationship between the prophet and the divine word he carries to his people. Yahweh's word is no longer identified only with certain words of the prophet but is revealed in his actions and emotions, in his total being. Baruch offers a vision of the divine word as alive, as taking human form in the life of his friend. In this most critical period in the life of Israel he demonstrates not a new concern for the prophet as human being but a new conception of the nature of the prophetic task. Although the word of Yahweh remains central, his word is now seen in the form of a human life.

Baruch tells of the word's imprisonment, trial, and sufferings, climaxing in Egypt, the land of slavery, where Yahweh's word is totally rejected and the Moses-Sinai story is turned on its head and denied. The word finally seems to exist in but one man who is a failure and captive in an alien land. Yahweh's word of summons, which had centuries ago called Israel into existence out of

Egyptian bondage and had been experienced again and again in the retelling, was now returned against its will to Egypt and there abandoned. The break between god and people was complete, but the word was not stilled. It had predated the life of Jeremiah, and it would live on in exile after his life came to an end. For a time, Baruch suggests, it lived in the form of Jeremiah, and the self-revealing notice in Jeremiah 45 suggests that it would continue to live with those who preserved Jeremiah's oracles.

The brief unit that concludes the biographical material breaks the narrative's chronological flow by redirecting attention from Jeremiah to Baruch, for in a time of great tension and danger the loyal scribe sought from Yahweh, through Jeremiah, an indication of what might be in store for him, who had also suffered long. The divine response is blunt: "Behold, what I have built I am breaking down, and what I have planted I am plucking up—that is, the whole land. And do you seek great things for yourself? Seek them not; for, behold, I am bringing evil upon all flesh, says Yahweh; but I will give you your life as a prize of war in all places to which you may go" (Jeremiah 45:4–5).

From the death struggle that is to come, Baruch will take away only his life; all else will be lost—possessions, family, home and land, city and nation, religion and story. The foundations for his identity as an Israelite, will be gone. Stripped of all but life itself he will, however, survive. But with human life there is memory, and among people like Baruch, stark exiles from old Israel and Jerusalem, memory would survive of Yahweh's word as expressed in the oracles and life of Jeremiah. For this remnant —stripped, isolated, and scared—would be reborn in varied forms as earliest Judaism, and Jeremiah's words were an informing force in that rebirth.

Stories in Conflict

Before we turn to the rise of Judaism, attention must be given to what may well have been the most direct confrontation between the two stories of ancient Israel, both of which had their roots in the formative stages of Israel's history. The Moses-Sinai story, first found in the creedlike recitals of the federation, was re-presented and relived again and again in the cultic renewal of the covenant. This covenant defined the relation between deity and people and had been conditioned from the outset by a body of stipulations. The David-Zion story had roots in pre-Israelite Jerusalem (Jebus). As adapted in the time of David and Solomon, it spoke of Yahweh's unconditional promise to uphold and support the city, its people, and the Davidic line and affirmed Jerusalem to be the creative center of the cosmos. In Jerusalem this story was reexperienced annually in the cultic celebration of the New Year, the re-creation of an ordered universe, and the enthronement of the king and of Yahweh himself in his temple on Zion.

Both stories opened the Israelites to ever new aspects of their relationship with their god and provided profound means for reflecting upon and expressing their experience with Yahweh. Both gave overarching shape to later recitals of Israel's history, and both informed the prophets' words of indictment, sentence, and promise. But the David-Zion story was centered in Judah and especially in the royal city of Jerusalem; in rural areas of Judah and in northern Israel the Moses-Sinai story was predominant; and in the course of Jeremiah's long career the two stories came into full and dramatic conflict. This is most apparent in the confrontation between two Yahweh prophets, Jeremiah and Hananiah, in August of 594 B.C.E. as related in Jeremiah 27–28.

Earlier that year Jeremiah had placed on his shoulders a wooden yoke symbolizing the worldwide authority that Yahweh had granted Nebuchadnezzar and to which he wished all to submit, and this yoke Jeremiah had worn before the royal officials of Judah and a number of foreign envoys who were then in Jerusalem to plan a rebellion against Babylon. At this time Hananiah appeared as a prophet announcing in Yahweh's name that in two years his god would break the Babylonian yoke and return the exiles of 598 B.C.E. to Jerusalem. In a symbolic action of his own, he broke the wooden yoke from the shoulders of Jeremiah, who reappeared wearing an iron yoke shortly thereafter. In Yahweh's name Jeremiah reaffirmed his earlier words and sentenced Hananiah to death.

Jeremiah's words of indictment and sentence were informed by the Moses-Sinai story: Nebuchadnezzar was to be the instrument of Yahweh's death sentence, and all the faithful Yahwist could do was submit to it. Although the story on which Hananiah based his announcement is not made clear in this account (which is plainly told from Jeremiah's perspective), it is most likely to have been the David-Zion story as remembered in its popular form: Yahweh would protect his city and its king, as historical precedent had demonstrated, and could be trusted to uphold his promise on the basis of this story. Like the great Isaiah, Hananiah called for a strength of conviction that ran counter to any objective assessment of the military situation facing Judah. In his view, however, even in league with the other small city-states and nations in Palestine, Judah was no match for Babylonian arms. Only absolute confidence in Yahweh and his promises would enable Judah to stand against such superior force.

Although both men claimed prophetic authority to speak the word of Yahweh and though both had roots in old and valued traditions, there were no sure tests by which such claims could be certified by others. Not that attempts to formulate criteria were not forthcoming. In Jeremiah 28:8–10, for example, Jeremiah himself offers a guide through precedent, though in matters of this sort precedent tends to be ambiguous. Deuteronomy 18:15–22 offers guidelines that are tied exclusively to the outcome; that is, any prophet who claims to speak in Yahweh's name should be assessed on the basis of whether his words come true.

In the present case, however, this test fails as well, for both men spoke in Yahweh's name and to wait and see how events worked out would have been to court disaster. The prophetic word challenges the hearer in the present, in the face of all its possibilities, uncertainties, and ambiguities. It carries the force of the imperative: you cannot wait; the decision must be made *now*. The criteria offered in Deuteronomy serve later generations who wish to survey the past and decide who the prophets of Yahweh were; but hindsight is a luxury of historians, not the prerogative of rulers and politicians.

Pressed for an immediate decision, the leaders endorsed Hananiah's course, placing their trust and confidence in the David-Zion story in spite of the defeat and disgrace suffered in 598 B.C.E. Perhaps they were too committed to this course of action to change; certainly, the option Jeremiah offered Zedekiah (Jeremiah 37:16–17; 38:14–23) could not have appealed to that leader. But it is also possible that they truly believed Yahweh would not let them be utterly destroyed, even when all human initiative and effort had seemed to fail. If so, what Isaiah had so vainly sought was finally given, and with the fall of Jerusalem in 587 B.C.E. history had judged between the prophets and their stories. Later generations preserved the oracles of Jeremiah, who was recognized as a true prophet of Yahweh. There is no Book of Hananiah, and he is now called a false prophet. The David-Zion story was shattered in the form in which it had lived for so long because it seemed to bring only destruction and death.

Jerusalem, all by which it had defined itself and by which it had lived, was now shattered. All structures, institutions, persons, and places that the David-Zion story had invested with vital significance lay in ruins. The living and life-giving symbols were dead. In Psalm 89, which may have arisen during this crisis, we have a hymn that begins with a recollection of the all-pervading authority of the divine creator and sustainer (Psalm 89:1–18), then recounts the unconditional promises made to David and his line (Psalm 89:19–37), and then suddenly becomes a lament (Psalm 89:40–51):

> Thou hast breached all his walls;
>   thou hast laid his strongholds in ruins.
>   . . .
> Thou hast removed the scepter from his hand,
>   and cast his throne to the ground.
>   . . .
> How long, O Yahweh? Wilt thou hide thyself forever?
>   How long will thy wrath burn like a fire?
>   . . .
> Yahweh, where is they steadfast love of old,
>   which by thy faithfulness thou didst swear to David?
>   (Psalm 89:40, 44, 46, 49)

In this second crisis in the history of Jerusalem, the ancient nation of Israel died, but Jeremiah's words were preserved as those of Yahweh to inform future generations who would build anew out of the ashes of the old. Their story forms the subject of the second part of this book.

BIBLIOGRAPHIC NOTE

The Book of Jeremiah

Berridge, John M. *Prophet, People, and the Word of Yahweh: An Examination of Form and Content in the Proclamation of the Prophet Jeremiah.* Zurich : EVZ Verlang, 1970.

Blank, Sheldon H. *Jeremiah: Man and Prophet.* Cincinnati: Hebrew Union College Press, 1961.

Bright, John. *Jeremiah.* Anchor Bible 21. Garden City, N.Y.: Doubleday & Co., 1965.

Holladay, W. L. "Jeremiah the Prophet." In *The Interpreter's Dictionary of the Bible: Supplementary Volume,* pp. 470–72. Nashville: Abingdon Press, 1976.

Muilenburg, James *Jeremiah the Prophet."* In *The Interpreter's Dictionary of the Bible,* vol. 2, pp. 823–25. Nashville: Abingdon Press, 1962.

Nicholson, E. W. *Preaching to the Exiles: A Study of the Prose Traditions in the Book of Jeremiah.* Oxford: Basil Blackwell, 1970.

The Books of Habakkuk, Nahum, Obadiah, and Zephaniah

Leslie, E. A. "Habakkuk." In *The Interpreter's Dictionary of the Bible,* vol. 2, pp. 503–5. Nashville: Abingdon Press, 1962.

———. "Nahum, Book of." In *The Interpreter's Dictionary of the Bible,* vol. 3, pp. 498–99. Nashville: Abingdon Press, 1962.

———. "Zephaniah, Book of." In *The Interpreter's Dictionary of the Bible,* vol. 4, pp. 951–53. Nashville: Abingdon Press, 1962.

Muilenburg, James "Obadiah, Book of." In *The Interpreter's Dictionary of the Bible,* vol. 3, pp. 518–19. Nashville: Abingdon Press, 1962.

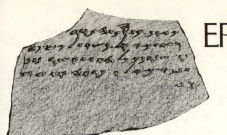

EPILOGUE TO PART 1

THE DEUTERONOMISTIC HISTORY

A Search for Roots

Throughout the ancient Near East in the middle of the first millenium B.C.E. there was a turning to the distant past, to first roots and origins as these were ideally imagined or remembered, in the subconscious hope of finding there directions and meanings against the present tug of largely incomprehensible forces for disintegration. The shape of the ancient Near East as it had been for more than two thousand years was changing. The overarching political structure, with power centers in Egypt and Mesopotamia and the buffer state of Syria-Palestine in between, would soon dissolve. Nebuchadnezzar's short-lived Neo-Babylonian empire would be the last vestige of the old order. First under Persians from the mountains of Armenia and southern Russia, later under Greeks and Romans from the Mediterranean basin, different political configurations would emerge; new power centers would be established; and new peoples, languages, stories, and ways of viewing life would enter the Near East.

Into his royal center at Nineveh, Ashurbanipal, the last great king of the Neo-Assyrian empire, gathered a vast library of materials from all periods but especially from the most ancient period in Mesopotamian history, perhaps reflecting a hope that these ancient sources would provide guidance for the ambiguous present. Egypt likewise experienced a rebirth of older patterns in art, literature, religious practice and theology, and in its language as well. In Judah and Jerusalem some would turn back to Moses, attempting to redeem the crisis of 587 B.C.E. by placing it in the theological framework of the old federation story of Israel's origins, for only in this way could Israel's tragic end be understood as the harsh but just action of its god Yahweh.

In Moses, who had led Israel from Egyptian slavery, who had mediated the covenant on Mount Sinai, and whose death before the promise of land had been fulfilled had given an effective symbol to Israel's tragically unfulfilled promise, they found a mirror in which to view their own experience. This group found its charter in the Book of Deuteronomy, which received its final form at their hands. From this base they reviewed Israel's history from the entrance into Canaan—the point at which, according to Hosea and Jeremiah, Israel had begun to go wrong—to the exile in Babylon after 587 B.C.E. They produced an extended theological survey of Israel's history that now comprises the books of Joshua through 2 Kings. Their work is called the deuteronomistic history because its basis for judgment is found in Deuteronomy.

In 2 Kings 22 we are told that in the course of repair work on the temple in Jerusalem a book of law was discovered which, when read to King Josiah, evoked a dramatic reaction. This book is now believed to be some form of Deuteronomy, perhaps only the legal sections of chapters 12–26 though it is likely to contained some of the hortatory material in earlier and later chapters as well. This rich corpus of law and instruction may have been brought to Judah by fugitives from the fall of northern Israel along with the Elohist narrative and prophetic collections of oracles and legends, for it included older collections that had been formed and reformed in that state for a time. It is now believed that this deuteronomistic legacy may have existed secretly in the south during Manasseh's reign, only to reappear as a guiding force in the course of Josiah's reforms. Its discovery, in any case, was a recovery of Israel's roots.

Centralizing all legitimate worship of Yahweh in the temple of Jerusalem and closing all other places of worship and sacrifice in the land, for these were viewed as especially susceptible to corruption by non-Yahwistic practices and deities, was a critical element of Josiah's reform. (The centralization is prescribed in Deuteronomy 12; compare 2 Kings 23.) Although from the earliest federation days there had always been a central sanctuary that served as a focus for Yahweh worship, many other cultic places had been permitted and even staffed by priests throughout Israel. Now, however, sacrifices would be offered to Yahweh alone and only in Jerusalem, and only there would a legitimate clergy be found. (There may have been an earlier, abortive attempt to centralize worship in Jerusalem during the period of Hezekiah [2 Kings 18:19–25] when the deuteronomistic and other northern traditions first arrived in the south.) Broadly, then, the Josiah reform can be seen as an attempt to return to Yahweh alone, for, as the covenant based in the Moses-Sinai story makes clear, Yahweh tolerates no rivals. In this return the demands of earlier prophets found a response.

Deuteronomy contains both historical narrative and law, often interwoven into brief sermonlike units demonstrating that fidelity to the law brings life and peace while disobedience brings death. In form, the book as a whole (excluding chapters 32–34 which deal with Moses' final word and death) resembles that of the earliest covenant of the federation period. It begins with a survey of past relations between Yahweh and his people (Deuteronomy 1–11), then recalls the covenant stipulations in the collections of laws (Deuteronomy 12–26). This is followed by a series of blessings and curses aimed at enforcing the covenant (Deuteronomy 27–28), and finally the business is put into writing (Deuteronomy 31:24–29). This is the old covenant form, clearly conditional in thrust, that is founded in the Moses-Sinai story. In the course of Josiah's reform this story found support even in the royal circles of Jerusalem.

Founded in Deuteronomy, the deuteronomistic history of Joshua through 2 Kings utilizes varied sources, some with little reworking. Several of these are quite old, among them the liturgically structured Joshua 1, 3–6, the tragedy of King Saul, the succession narrative, and the prophetic complexes dealing with Samuel, Elijah, and Elisha. We turn now to the Book of Deuteronomy and the historical review based in it, for it provides a summing up and search for meaning in the failure of the nation Israel.

Prophet, King, and Levite

Because Deuteronomy appeared as a voice from the past addressing the present and future, it must be understood primarily in the context of Judah's last days and the fall of the nation. The material constantly looks ahead to the time when the land would be settled, when the cry would go out for a king, and to the days of prophets. Although the sermon is given on the eastern edge of the Jordan in the plains of Moab, the book looks ahead to the fully developed state of Israel. It is a projection into the seemingly more secure past of later issues, problems, and doubts.

Deuteronomy offers regulations for the cultic year, for the administrative officials in the central sanctuary, for the conduct of worship and sacrifice, for the administration of justice in the state, for the political, economic, social, and military structures that will shape the nation, and for those who will have to make these structures serve the people. Some of the laws are ancient, others reflect later situations, and it is often difficult to separate the two, for law must be able to preserve old forms and values and still adapt to new situations. Essentially, Deuteronomy reflects an older, rural-based legal system (compare Exodus

21–23) that has been recast to fit urban patterns. The situation of the farmer has been expanded to include that of the merchant and even the king.

Law must give expression to a society's ideals and visions while at the same time providing for their confrontation with reality. In Deuteronomy reality breaks through in the allowance for kingship, which to some in Israel was the source of all corruption (see 1 Samuel 8, for example). But the kingship found here is a limited one, for when the ruler takes the throne "he shall write for himself a copy of this law, from that which is in charge of the Levitical priests; and it shall be with him, and he shall read it in all the days of his life" (Deuteronomy 17:18–20). Although this king is limited by a constitution rather than by the prophet's word, prophetic rebuke of the abuse of royal authority was no doubt a formative factor in the limitation.

Deuteronomy recognizes that prophets will appear as bearers of Yahweh's word, but the multiplication of prophetic claims and counterclaims, especially in the decades prior to 587 B.C.E., is also reflected in the regulations requiring a suspension of overready belief. Although some common Near Eastern forms of ascertaining the divine will and intent are outlawed (Deuteronomy 18:9–14), rules are set forth for determining the true prophet. As previously noted, these can be used only by those who enjoy the luxury of hindsight (Deuteronomy 18:15–22). While they offer little help in the immediacy of the prophetic imperative, they can guide those who later attempt to hear the prophetic word from the past.

Those who are called Levites seem to have been a part of the group that came out of Egyptian slavery and later dispersed throughout Israel, preserving the old Moses-Sinai story and administering the worship of Yahweh in local places. Because they served in shrines that were closed by Josiah's reform, they were allowed to serve in the temple of Jerusalem. The likeliest members of the deuteronomistic group, the Levites preserved and reformed the law through the centuries, and the sermonlike units of Deuteronomy may reflect their preaching. Provision is made for their support (Deuteronomy 18:1–8), and they are placed in charge of the book of law. It was in these Levitical circles, in alliance with certain court officials in Josiah's reign, that the "rediscovered" Mosaic traditions in the form of Deuteronomy provided an informing direction for the reform.

In the service of this reform, too, a broad historical survey of Israel's past was put forth in a first edition of the deuteronomistic history and includes the material in the Book of Joshua through 2 Kings 23:25. Here Israel's history in any period is assessed according to the degree to which its leaders were faithful to the covenant with Yahweh and its stipulations. Paramount is the question of whether total allegiance had been given to Yahweh and to him alone.

To the authors of the deuteronomistic history, Yahweh was clearly to be seen in past events, and a succession of prophets had directed attention to their theological significance. From Moses through Joshua (Joshua 23), Samuel (1

Samuel 12), Nathan (2 Samuel 12), Ahijah (1 Kings 12:29–40; 14), and various unnamed prophets (1 Kings 13) to Elijah, Elisha, and Isaiah of Jerusalem, Yahweh had warned Israel that any violation of the covenant stipulations would bring punishment and the risk of death. Throughout the deuteronomistic history, prophets make clear the challenge of Yahweh's actions in set speeches and occasional death-scene testimonies (Deuteronomy 29–34; 1 Samuel 12), and the history demonstrates that these speeches had set forth the actual course of events. Israel had prospered when it was loyal to the covenant and had suffered when it was disloyal.

This pattern is revealed in the framework that was used to bind together the once separate stories about the federation's tribes and judges in the Book of Judges:

> And the people of Israel did what was evil in the sight of Yahweh,
> forgetting Yahweh their God, and serving the Baals and the Asheroth.
> Therefore the anger of Yahweh was kindled against Israel, and he sold
> them into the hand of [here appears the name of some oppressor].
> But the people cried to Yahweh, and Yahweh raised up a deliverer for
> the people of Israel.
>
> (Judges 3:7–9; see also 3:12; 4:1–2)

Even earlier than this the pattern had been the same, as the Achen affair of Joshua 7 demonstrates. In many later instances people who disregard the prophetic warning are punished, but there is always a divine relenting before death and total destruction. In Isaiah's case, as legend preserved the events of 701 B.C.E., the people and king listened, obeyed, and were delivered. By contrast, the kingdom of northern Israel was finally destroyed because its chaotic situation had made reform impossible (2 Kings 17).

The warning offered to Judah and Jerusalem by this shattering event is set forth in 2 Kings 17, where it is followed by the positive example of Isaiah and Hezekiah and then by the negative example of Manasseh. In this way the history is brought down to Josiah's reform, which is not only demanded by the redis-covered law book and the preaching of Moses and the prophets but supported by all history. Loyalty to Yahweh and his stipulations brings life and security, gifts of the god who first called Israel into being from Egyptian slavery. Disloyalty will result only in death.

Back to the Wilderness

There was also a political aspect to Josiah's reform. Assyria was passing from the world stage. When the vassals in Palestine withdrew their allegiance and Assyria was unable to respond, for a brief period Judah was free. But the dream that Israel might return to the golden days of Solomon (2 Kings 23:15–20) fell apart when Josiah, judged the best king by all the deuteronomistic historians, was killed by the Egyptian pharaoh in 609 B.C.E. At the end of Assyria's life the Egyptians aided their former enemy to prevent another power from moving into Syria-Palestine (2 Kings 23:29–30). But the aid came too late, and a brief period of Egyptian control of Palestine was cut short by King Nebuchadnezzar of Babylon.

Josiah's son Jehoahaz, whom the Egyptians had set on the throne in Jerusalem, was replaced by Jehoiakim, control of Israel was again in foreign hands, and the reformers were shaken to their theological foundations. The very history in which they had sought support and guidance seemed now to have judged them. With their hopes dashed and their ideal king dead, many reacted by rejecting the Moses-Sinai story in favor of the David-Zion story, which regained its preeminence in royal circles. A memory of this experience would stand behind the final rejection of Jeremiah's words by the fugitives in Egypt (Jeremiah 44).

The reform had not been enough; the evil that had arisen during the reign of Manasseh had been too great to allow more than a brief respite before the coming divine wrath—in such terms the deuteronomistic circle comprehended the failure of the reform and the death of Josiah (2 Kings 22:14–20). Not long after 587 B.C.E. surviving members of the older group who were now in exile issued a second edition of the deuteronomistic history, not to support a reform but to comprehend the tragedy and to justify Yahweh. Jeremiah is not found in this history, although the Book of Jeremiah contains material that is in both style and theological perspective very similar to some of its units. Since both deal with Yahweh and the death of Israel, it may be that segments of the Jeremiah material were preserved within deuteronomistic circles and that they were meant to be read together.

Both state that Yahweh dealt the death blow through Nebuchadnezzar because Israel in its last decades had returned to the policies of Manasseh (2 Kings 24:1–9; 24:18–20). The oracles of Jeremiah flesh out these summary statements: Israel's death was the work of Yahweh, and he was justified in doing it because, as their historical review clearly demonstrated, Israel's own actions had repeatedly nullified the covenant upon which her life depended. But the fugitives in exile and those who remained amid the ruins in the land that was no longer theirs needed not only to comprehend the reason for the tragedy but to live in the present and future. It was not enough to state that Yahweh's actions had been justified. How could they face a future without a nation?

The deuteronomistic history ends with a faint note of hope. Its final words tell of a still living member of David's line, the exiled King Jehoiakin, who, having scarcely occupied the throne, had been exiled in the captivity of 598 B.C.E. and imprisoned in Babylon. Years after the death of Nebuchadnezzar we are told that under a new king, Jehoiakin's status changed.

And in the thirty-seventh year of the exile of Jehoiakin king of Judah, in the twelfth month, on the twenty-seventh day of the month, Evil-merodach,

king of Babylon, in the year that he began to reign, graciously freed
Jehoiakin, king of Judah, from prison; and he spoke kindly to him, and gave
him a seat above the seats of the kings who were with him in Babylon. So
Jehoiakin put off his prison garments. And every day of his life he dined
regularly at the king's table; and for his allowance, a regular allowance was
given him by the king, every day a portion, as long as he lived.

(2 Kings 25:27–30)

The notice is brief and prosaic, but for a new generation of deuteronomistic
historians writing from exile it provided a spark that could ignite hope for the
future, and from such a spark those who now had nothing but their lives would
shape a new religion. In attempting to comprehend what had been, the deuteronomistic historians in exile looked mostly to the past; but at the end they turn
to a glimpse of what the future might be. Life could be sustained in exile. Others
would take up the task of rebuilding, and it is with them that the second part of
this book will deal.

BIBLIOGRAPHIC NOTE

For a discussion of the books of Joshua, Judges, 1 and 2 Samuel, and 1 and 2 Kings,
consult the works listed in the Bibliographic Notes to the Prologue to Part 1 and
chapter 1.

Clements, Ronald E. *God's Chosen People: A Theological Interpretation of the Book of Deuteronomy.* London: SCM Press, 1968.

Cross, Frank Moore. "The Themes of the Book of Kings and the Structure of the Deuteronomistic History." In *Canaanite Myth and Hebrew Epic,* pp. 274–90. Cambridge, Mass.: Harvard University Press, 1973.

Freedman, David Noel. "Deuteronomic History, The." In *The Interpreter's Dictionary of the Bible: Supplementary Volume,* pp. 226–28. Nashville: Abingdon Press, 1976.

Lohfink, N. "Deuteronomy." In *The Interpreter's Dictionary of the Bible: Supplementary Volume,* pp. 229–32. Nashville: Abingdon Press, 1976.

Nicholson, E. W. *Deuteronomy and Tradition.* Philadelphia: Fortress Press, 1967.

von Rad, Gerhard. *Deuteronomy.* Philadelphia: Westminster Press, 1966.

———. "Deuteronomy." In *The Interpreter's Dictionary of the Bible,* vol. 1, pp. 831–38. Nashville: Abingdon Press, 1962.

———. *Studies in Deuteronomy.* Studies in Biblical Theology, no. 9. London: SCM Press, 1953.

Weinfeld, Moshe. *Deuteronomy and the Deuteronomic School.* Oxford: Clarendon Press, 1972.

Wolff, Hans Walter. "The Kerygma of the Deuteronomic Work." In *The Vitality of Old Testament Traditions,* edited by Walter Brueggemann and Hans Walter Wolff, pp. 83–100. Atlanta: John Knox Press, 1975.

Old Testament lands photographed from space

Photograph courtesy of NASA

PART 2
THE RISE
OF JUDAISM

King Darius, founder of Persepolis, fights a demon in the form of a lion

Morath/Magnum

A section of stairway, Audience Hall at Persepolis

Elbers/Alpha

Near Qumran, overlooking Dead Sea and cliffs in which the Dead Sea Scrolls were discovered

Religious News Service

Excavation of the Essene colony of Qumran

Benbassat/Leo de Wys

Air view of the Essene settlement at Qumran

By courtesy of the Israel Department
of Antiquities and Museums

Steps of a cistern at Qumran

By courtesy of the Israel Department
of Antiquities and Museums

Rock caves near Qumran

Benbassat/Leo de Wys

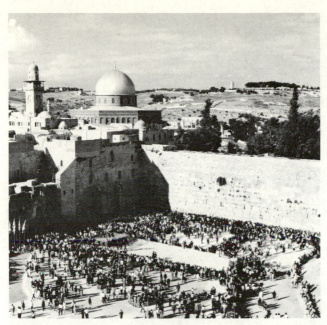

Masada
Courtesy of the Consulate
General of Israel

Wailing Wall, Jerusalem
Braun/FPG

**Nineteenth century photograph of
people praying at the Wailing Wall**
The Bettmann Archive

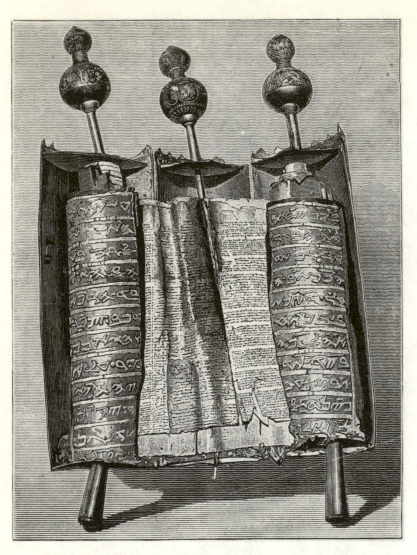

Ancient scroll of the Pentateuch, said to have been written by Eleazar, son of Aaron

The Bettmann Archive

PROLOGUE TO PART 2

Primary readings: *Psalm 137*
                        Lamentations
                        Jeremiah 30–32

With Nebuchadnezzar's destruction of Jerusalem and the deportation of many of the city's leading citizens, ancient Israel died and its survivors passed through several stages of grief—from shock and denial through anger and bargaining with fate and finally to acceptance and rebuilding. Although life would never again be the same, slowly it could be shaped anew as pieces of the past were recovered, new structures discovered, and the death gradually absorbed into the survivors' story and life. Among those who survived the tragedy of 587 B.C.E.—exiles in Babylon and fugitives in Egypt as well as those remaining amid the ruins of a land now a part of the Babylonian provincial system—all these stages of grief were observable.

THE CRISIS

Psalm 137 is one of the earliest responses to Israel's death by those in exile in Babylon:

> By the waters of Babylon
> there we sat down and wept

when we remembered Zion.
On the willows there
    we hung up our lyres.
For there our captors
    required of us songs,
    and our tormenters, mirth, saying,
    "Sing us one of the songs of Zion!"

How shall we sing Yahweh's song
    in a foreign land?

> (Psalm 137:1–4)

"How shall we sing Yahweh's song in a foreign land?" To sense the agony that lies behind these words, to comprehend the fear in that question, is to begin to understand the extent of the crisis. Denial and bitter anger also find expression in this lament:

If I forget you, O Jerusalem,
    let my right hand wither!

> (Psalm 137:5)

O daughter of Babylon, you devastator!
    Happy shall he be who requites you
    with what you have done to us!
Happy shall he be who takes your little ones
    and dashes them against the rock!

> (Psalm 137:8–9)

The destruction was complete; all spheres of life were shattered. Indeed, since in old Israel all social, legal, economic, and political institutions and structures were god-given, divinely certified and sustained, the crisis called the power, if not the very existence of Yahweh into question. How could Yahweh allow this to happen? How could he permit what he had built to be so utterly devastated?

Mount Zion lay in ruins; the inviolable city of promise had been ravished. The temple, the focus of so much pride and trust (see Jeremiah 7:4), had been stripped of its treasures and set afire, its vessels and furnishings now stood before the god Marduk in his temple in Babylon. Of the royal line of David only a dim spark remained in the imprisoned Jehoiakin. The chosen people were slain or fugitives amid strange nations or aliens in their own land now incorporated into an alien empire. The joyful songs of the New Year's festival were now haunting echoes of a dead past. The David-Zion story with its eternal promises was an obscene mockery.

Even the Moses-Sinai story offered little comfort at first. Perhaps Yahweh was angry, but what could human beings have done to provoke such total retribution? The crisis was theological, because Israel's land had been a gift from

Yahweh, and the oldest form of Israel's story emphasized this with great force: the formation of the nation was Yahweh's work, the conquest his action, and Israel his chosen. Where now was the god who had willfully toyed with the divine pharaoh of Egypt? What now of the saving events of which they sang in the festivals of covenant renewal and celebration? When the sacred words, songs, and actions came now to mind the pain was unbearable. Albert Camus speaks of such hopelessness in describing other exiles in *The Plague*: "Thus, they too came to know the incorrigible sorrow of all prisoners and exiles, which is to live in company with a memory which serves no purpose."*

The survivors of a death die in part as well, for a self-defining relationship and role are taken away. A wife who loses her husband, for example, is no longer a wife as before. To retain the old role for too long as if nothing has changed is pathological. In this way the survivors of the fall of Israel lost an essential part of their existence. Like Baruch (Jeremiah 45), they had life, nothing more; they could no longer be Israelites when there was no nation Israel. Certainly, old Jerusalem could no longer be an enlivening force in spite of many vows to the contrary (see Psalm 137:5–6).

By all the canons of the Near East at that time, Yahweh was either impotent, uncaring, or dead, or he had joined forces with Marduk of Babylon, with whom the future seemed to lie, especially for those exiled in Babylon. Moreover, Babylon offered rich alternatives; its myths, stories, rituals, and songs telling of Marduk and his city were alluring to those whose own experience strongly certified all claims about Marduk's powers. The exiles were now in Marduk's land, and for those who remained in Palestine the land belonged to Yahweh no longer. All lands were foreign now, and how could one sing of Yahweh, god of Israel, or tell of his mighty acts in ritual and story, in a foreign land?

Many exiles adopted the social, cultural, and religious ways of Babylon and in time those of its Persian successor. Like the lost tribes of northern Israel, these exiles either vanished from sight or remained only as names in surviving business or trade documents. For those who took this path, anger and denial gave way to acceptance and to a gradual building of new lives and identities. Although it took several generations, to many it must have been the only sane course available.

For others, too, the cry of lament would yield in time, to alternative ways of coping, and with them we will be concerned in our study of the rise of Judaism. Even for them, however, the cries of rage and fear served a purpose, for only in this way could the changed situation be accepted and dealt with. If the anger could not always be directed at the god himself, it could be centered on hated Babylon; or if this was dangerous, it could be transferred to people like the Edomites:

---

*Albert Camus, *The Plague* (New York: Random House, Modern Library, 1946), p. 66.

> Remember, O Yahweh, against the Edomites
> the day of Jerusalem,
> how they said, "Raze it, raze it!
> Down to its foundations!"
> O daughter of Babylon, you devastator!
> Happy shall he be who requites you
> with what you have done to us!
> Happy shall he be who takes your little ones
> and dashes them against the rock!
>
> (Psalm 137:7–9)

Former neighbors of Israel with whom relations had never been warm, the Edomites were eager to rejoice over Israel's fall and to seize what they could of the shattered remains. Tradition linked Esau and Jacob, Edom and Israel, as brothers, and they hated each other bitterly (Genesis 25 and 27, and compare the words of Obadiah). But anger is a necessary part of grief, and it must find expression.

In the Book of Lamentations, too, grief is exhibited in several of its characteristic stages. Five carefully constructed poems offer expressions of agony, fear, questioning, confession, and a hopeful turning to the future. These laments, which later traditions would ascribe to the prophet Jeremiah, were written soon after the destruction of 587 B.C.E., probably by one or more of those who remained in Palestine, for they contain no hint of the situation of Babylonian exiles or Egyptian fugitives. A full range of emotions is expressed, and the grief seems unbounded. Yet the artistic structure of the poems reveals considerable control and mastery; the limiting of the seemingly unlimited is an important aspect of the outpouring of grief. In the bitterest wail, in the halting song of lament, in the funeral dirge, in the cry of confession of the individual and community, grief is both expressed and controlled, both defined and placed in perspective.

The poems take the rigidly structured form of alphabetic acrostics. In chapters 1 and 2 the first word of the first line of each three-part stanza begins with a successive letter of the Hebrew alphabet (this is lost, of course, in translation). In the third chapter each line of the twenty-two stanzas begins with the next letter. Chapter 4 is the simplest of the acrostics, with twenty-two lines each beginning with the successive letter. Chapter 5 has twenty-two lines, the number of letters in the Hebrew alphabet. This form is found elsewhere in Near Eastern and Hebrew literature (compare, for example, Psalm 119 and Proverbs 31:10–31) and requires a measure of virtuosity.

Through the rigid form the sufferings and chaos of the last years of Judah and Jerusalem are depicted in graphic terms and with brutal realism. Hopes for Yahweh's intervention and deliverance, the fundamental importance of now destroyed symbols and institutions, strike the reader with stark immediacy:

My eyes are spent with weeping;
    my soul is in tumult;
my heart is poured out in grief
    because of the destruction of the daughter of my people,
because infants and babes faint
    in the streets of the city.
They cry to their mothers,
    "Where is bread and wine?"
as they faint like wounded men
    in the streets of the city,
as their life is poured out
    on their mothers' bosom.

                  (Lamentations 2:11–12)

Arise, cry out in the night,
    at the beginning of the watches!
Pour out your heart like water
    before the presence of Yahweh!
Lift your hands to him for the lives of your children,
    who faint for hunger
    at the head of every street.

                  (Lamentations 2:19)

Women are ravished in Zion,
    virgins in the towns of Judah.
Princes are hung up by their hands;
    no respect is shown the elders.

                  (Lamentations 5:11–12)

Sometimes an observer describes the fallen city; sometimes it is the personified "daughter" or "virgin daughter" of Zion or Jerusalem or Judah or "my people" who speaks. In the fourth song the description reaches a crescendo:

The tongue of the nursling cleaves
    to the roof of its mouth for thirst;
the children beg for food,
    but no one gives to them.
Those who feasted on dainties
    perish in the streets;
those who were brought up in purple
    lie on ash heaps.

                  (Lamentations 4:4–5)

Now their visage is blacker than soot,
    they are not recognized in the streets;
their skin has shriveled upon their bones,
    it has become as dry as wood.

                  (Lamentations 4:8)

In these desolate cries, the lamenters first turn to their god in an appeal for him to take notice:

> O Yahweh, behold my affliction,
>   for the enemy has triumphed!
>
> (Lamentations 1:9)

> Look, O Yahweh, and see!
>   With whom hast thou dealt thus?
> Should women eat their offspring,
>   the children of their tender care?
> Should priest and prophet be slain
>   at the sanctuary of Yahweh?
>
> (Lamentations 2:20)

Then the appeal becomes confession:

> Yahweh is in the right,
>   for I have rebelled against his word;
> but hear, all you peoples,
>   and behold all my suffering.
>
> (Lamentations 1:18)

A frame of reference has been found for comprehending what had happened. The prophets who had indicted and sentenced Yahweh's people for violating the covenant allegiance had provided one context. Although they were seldom heeded in their own days, some survivors remembered their words, and it was in exile that an impetus arose for the formation of the prophetic books as we now have them. It was too late for warnings, but understanding could lead to acceptance. Remembered prophetic indictments and sentences set in the context of the covenant lawsuit, along with poems of lament, provided the material for very basic liturgical expressions of agony and grief that would lead to confession. And with confession and the adoption of a framework within which the tragic destruction might be comprehended, it became apparent that all links with Yahweh were not severed.

With confession would come expectations that could be built into hope, anticipation, and even confidence. The destruction had been brought about by the people of Yahweh in their turning from their god, but in the act of confession they turned back to the god in whom they had once placed their trust and who had sustained them. The third poem in Lamentations exhibits a level of confidence that is striking in view of what had gone before.

> For Yahweh will not cast off forever,
>   but, though he cause grief, he will have compassion
>   according to the abundance of his steadfast love;

for he does not willingly afflict
　　or grieve the sons of men.
　　　　　　(Lamentations 3:31–33)

Let us test and examine our ways,
　　and return to Yahweh!
Let us lift up our hearts and hands
　　to God in heaven:
"We have transgressed and rebelled,
　　and thou hast not forgiven."
　　　　　　(Lamentations 3:40–42)

I called on thy name, O Yahweh,
　　from the depths of the pit;
thou didst hear my plea. . . .
Thou didst come near when I called on thee;
　　thou didst say, "Do not fear!"
　　　　　　(Lamentations 3:55–57)

Although there remained many questions to be asked and answers to be sought, this *was* a beginning. By providing a structure for delimiting and binding the terror, the lament brought initial comprehension and acceptance. It was not enough to know that Judah and Jerusalem had brought the destruction upon themselves and that Yahweh was just, but knowing that provided the strength to seek new structures, forms, songs, and stories and to set the foundations for a new identity for both individuals and communities.

As some among the exiles, fugitives, and aliens turned to face their future they found in the ruins of old Israel shattered symbols and traditions that might be taken up, reformed, and reshaped into something new in a world different from any they had known before. The survivors of old Israel would forever remain scattered, rebuilding their identities as individuals and communities against and in interaction with rich but alien settings in Babylon and Egypt or dispersed throughout the known world as well as in a Palestine that would remain an outpost in one or another foreign empire. Life was preserved, and with that came a recognition that new songs could be sung, new stories could be told and lived, new theological formulations and structures and institutions could take shape even in foreign lands. The cry of terror would become the cry of birth as well.

A sense of both discontinuity and continuity arises as we survey the attempts to come to terms with the crisis of 587 b.c.e. Prophetic words of promise and challenge, collections of legal materials, the old federation's story, pieces of the David-Zion story, and other literary and theological forms will be taken up, remolded, reformed, and at times joined with materials that seem new and foreign. In prophetic vision, on the level of theological speculation, and on the plane of everyday life, the grief process that began in Psalm 137 and Lamenta-

168 tions would lead to the birth of a new religion. Since it is new, Judaism is distinguished from older Israelite traditions though it claimed to be the heir of old Israel. This claim is in part theological or confessional. Christianity and Islam make such a claim for themselves as well. In Judaism's case, however, the claim finds historical verification, for we shall discover it to be firmly rooted in Israelite soil.

JEREMIAH AND A NEW COVENANT

As a creative process, grief has two parts. First there is the facing of death and a comprehension that leads to acceptance and attempts at understanding. Second, having faced the past realistically, one can turn to the future, to the building of new roles and relationships, to the creation of a fresh identity and another life. In the words of Jeremiah both stages are found. Presiding over the last days of his nation he had stood firmly within the Moses-Sinai story: Yahweh had destroyed Israel, and he had done so for reasons that they could acknowledge, their god was not dead, impotent, or unjust. Jeremiah's oracles were now recalled and collected by those in exile, not because he had predicted the fall but because he had made sense of it, setting it in a theological perspective that allowed them to look directly into the face of the tragedy.

But Jeremiah addressed the future as well. At the time of the final siege of Jerusalem when Jeremiah was in prison charged with treason, he redeemed by purchase a tract of family land at Anathoth (Jeremiah 32). While this was no time for land speculation in Judah, even if ancient law demanded that all possible means be explored for holding on to family land (see Leviticus 25: 25–28), the purchase was made with all the legal formalities. The account of this transaction is placed unchronologically after chapters 30–31 to dramatize the assertions that the death of old Israel was not the end of Yahweh's work. Like Hosea before him, Jeremiah saw redemption growing out of destruction.

The word put into his mouth at his call empowered Jeremiah not only to "pluck up and to break down, to destroy and to overthrow" but also "to build and to plant" (Jeremiah 1:10). In chapters 30–31 this latter thrust is most apparent, and this unit is justly called the Book of Consolation. Although individual units within these chapters come from several periods of the prophet's career, some possibly from the very early years, the collection as a whole, followed by the certifying account of the land sale, is a product of the survivors—some say of Baruch—who sought not only comprehension of what had happened but indications of what was yet to come. In these oracles, which address the fallen state of northern Israel as well as Judah, the same prophet who in word and flesh had given form to Yahweh's wrath now embodies divine compassion, grief, and expectations for his people. Before the tragic fall these words of restoration *through* punishment would have provided cold comfort for they in no way annulled the death sentence, but perspective on a prophet's words makes all the difference. To tell a living nation that a small part of them will survive is hardly good news, though the same announcement after the fall might appear as a source of comfort and hope.

The Book of Consolation climaxes in the proclamation of a new covenant:

> Behold the days are coming, says Yahweh, when I will make a new covenant with the house of Israel and the house of Judah, not like the covenant which I made with their fathers when I took them by the hand to bring them out of the land of Egypt, my covenant which they broke, says Yahweh. But this is the covenant which I will make with the house of Israel after those days, says Yahweh: I will put my law within them, and I will write it upon their hearts; and I will be their God, and they shall be my people. And no longer shall each man teach his neighbor and each his brother, saying, "Know Yahweh," for they shall all know me, from the least of them to the greatest, says Yahweh; for I will forgive their iniquity, and I will remember their sin no more.

> (Jeremiah 31:31–34)

It must be underscored that this covenant is *new*, and as such its announcement would not be unqualified good news to those who had found life under the old. But the old covenant was void; the new one would be written on the heart of each individual. The relationship with Yahweh that had been formed through reexperience of the sacred story in ritual and song and that had led to acceptance of the law is now internalized, set at the center of each individual's existence like an instinct, for the heart was then the vital locus of the human being.

Although the discontinuity between old and new is sharp, the form is that of Israel's earliest allegiance to Yahweh. The law remains at the covenant's center, as does the old formula "I will be their God, and they shall be my people" (Jeremiah 31:33; compare Hosea 1:9 and Exodus 6:7). An ingathering of the scattered fugitives and exiles and a rebuilding of a nation are all announced, though in general terms and in a manner directed as much to the individual as to the community. This turning to the future through the use of old forms to present a radically new reality is found in greater extent, specificity, and intensity in the words of two other prophets, Ezekiel and the prophet of Isaiah 40–55.

BIBLIOGRAPHIC NOTE

The Book of Lamentations

> Gordis, Robert. *The Songs of Songs and Lamentations*. New York: KTAV Publishing House, 1974.

> Gottwald, Norman K. "Lamentations, Book of." In *The Interpreter's Dictionary of the Bible*, vol. 3, pp. 61–62. Nashville: Abingdon Press, 1962.

> Hillers, Delbert R. *Lamentations*. Garden City, N.Y.: Doubleday & Co., 1972.

For works on the Book of Jeremiah, see the Bibliographic Note to chapter 7.

SECTION 1
THE BABYLONIAN
AND PERSIAN PERIODS

Ruins of Persepolis, Iran
Reichstein/FPG

NEO-BABYLONIAN EMPIRE

B.C.E.		
625	Nabopolassar (626–605)	
600	Nebuchadnezzar (605–562)	First captivity of Jerusalem (598)
575		Fall of Jerusalem (587) Exile
550	Amel-marduk (562–560) Neriglissar (560–556) Nabonidus (556–539)	
525	Cyrus takes Babylon (539)	

THE PROPHETS AND
A NEW NATION

8

Primary readings: *Ezekiel*
                        Isaiah 40–66
                        Haggai; Zechariah 1–8

EZEKIEL: PROPHET IN EXILE

The transition from old Israel to early Judaism also governed the life and ministry of the prophet Ezekiel, a younger contemporary of Jeremiah, who presided over the death of Israel from exile in Babylon. Among the first to be deported in 598 B.C.E., he began his ministry after his call in 593, and his last oracle is set in 571. The extensive details in his vision of the temple in chapters 8–11 have led some to believe that he exercised his early ministry in Jerusalem, but this sort of detailed attention to affairs in the homeland is characteristic of exiles in any age. While many of his finely tuned theological discourses reveal a mind steeped not only in the traditions of his own people but in those of the larger Near Eastern world as well, his heritage was rooted in Israel's temple, and its forms of worship infused his every word. He was, in fact, of priestly descent.

Unlike the oracles of Jeremiah, Ezekiel's words often appear cold and analytical. A sensitive reading, however, can cut beneath their intricate surface to feelings so intense as sometimes to appear bizarre, repulsive, and even unbalanced. Indeed, the term "baroque" has been applied to many units of the book, yet these units are constructed with artistry and precision, complex symbolism,

174　　　and rich detail. In the visions of chapters 1–3, for example, which utilize both Israelite and foreign motifs, the prophet is very careful to avoid suggesting that what he experienced was anything more than "the appearance of the likeness of the glory of Yahweh," in this way holding himself thrice removed from the deity whom no mortal dare approach.

The book as a whole is structured into three distinct parts: chapters 1–24 contain oracles against Jerusalem and Judah and are dated before 587 B.C.E.; chapters 25–32 contain oracles against foreign nations; and chapters 33–48 contain oracles of restoration that reflect his message after the fall. In the following pages, however, this structure will be simplified to only two categories—before and after the fall.

Before the Fall

Like Jeremiah and others before him, Ezekiel understood the coming destruction in terms of the covenant lawsuit and the Moses-Sinai story. Within this frame of reference, however, his presentation is unique, for the cultic sphere is here expanded to typify the full essence of Israel's relation with Yahweh. It is here, the prophet declares, that Israel's alienation from her god is most fully seen and from here that it extends to every other area of life. The intrusion into Yahweh's temple of varied foreign practices and deities—for example, Tammuz of Mesopotamia or a solar deity of Egyptian origin—resulted in the departure of the "glory of Yahweh" from his cult and sacred city (Ezekiel 10–11).

Great theological care is exercised in these chapters, as in the roughly contemporary deuteronomistic concern, to make clear that the "word of Yahweh" dwelt in the temple in Jerusalem and not Yahweh himself, who is beyond the highest heavens (see the dedicatory prayer of Solomon in 1 Kings 8 and Deuteronomy 12:10–14; 12:20–21). Designating Yahweh's presence as his "word" or his "glory" indicates a recognition that the categories of human thought serve merely as pointers toward a divine sphere that may be perceived in oblique glimpses but can never be fully grasped. We are far removed here from the older traditions preserved, for example, in the Yahwist's narrative in which Yahweh meets, walks, and talks with mortals.

In Ezekiel's view, the corruption of Israel's cultic life reflected a still deeper corruption that had penetrated all areas of Israel's existence and would soon bring about a total rupture of the covenant relationship, and to demonstrate that this is true he offers extended surveys of Israel's past history with Yahweh in the form of elaborate allegories. Although he remains well within the Moses-Sinai tradition, his vision of Israel's impending death leads him to radicalize the story. Whereas Hosea and Jeremiah could see the period of deliverance and wilderness wandering as an ideal time in Israel's relation with her deity (Jeremiah 2:2–3; Hosea 2:15), Ezekiel regards even the bridal days as a time of rebellion. Israel's beginnings were darkened by the same cloud that darkens his own days. In his vision, there has been no golden age of total devotion.

Chapter 20 presents four phases of Israel's history, in each of which Yahweh's saving appearance is rejected, leading to divine wrath and then forgiveness:

> But they rebelled against me and would not listen to me; they did not every man cast away the detestable things their eyes feasted on, nor did they forsake the idols of Egypt. Then I thought I would pour out my wrath upon them and spend my anger against them in the midst of the land of Egypt. But I acted for the sake of my name, that it should not be profaned in the sight of the nations among whom they dwelt, in whose sight I made myself known to them in bringing them out of the land of Egypt. So I brought them out of the land of Egypt and brought them into the wilderness. I gave them my statutes and showed them my ordinances, by whose observance man shall live. Moreover I gave them my sabbaths, as a sign between me and them, that they might know that I Yahweh sanctify them. But the house of Israel rebelled against me in the wilderness; they did not walk in my statutes but rejected my ordinances, by whose observance man shall live, and my sabbaths they greatly profaned.
>
> (Ezekiel 20:8–13)

To Ezekiel this recital leads only in a circle that is about to close for a fourth time in his own day, and the vision leads him to some remarkable observations—among them, that Yahweh was driven to offer Israel "statutes that were not good and ordinances by which they could not have life; and I defiled them through their very gifts in making them offer by fire all their first-born, that I might horrify them; 1 did it that they might know that I am Yahweh" (Ezekiel 20:25–26).

Equally striking are two extended allegories dealing with the history of the monarchy. In chapter 16 Jerusalem is introduced with the statement that "your origin and your birth are of the land of the Canaanites; your father was an Amorite, and your mother a Hittite" (Ezekiel 16:3)—a reflection, perhaps, of the pre-Israelite history of Jerusalem. Even more stunning, however, is the manner in which the allegory is developed.

The city is said to have been abandoned at birth, without even an initial washing, and left in the open country to die. Yahweh, who found the child "weltering in your blood," adopted and nurtured her and in time took her as his bride. But the bride became a whore, and the description of her life climaxes in the statement that here sister Samaria "has not committed half your sins" (Ezekiel 16:51). In chapter 23 the two cities are again presented as two women named Oholah and Oholibah, both of whom became harlots during their youth in Egypt but who were preserved by Yahweh in spite of it. But the life of the sisters is once again presented as unchanged, and Jerusalem is once again judged the worse offender.

The relationship with Yahweh is finally terminated because the city and its people never acknowledge the foundation of their life. Death is the only sen-

176 tence, and it is announced not only in words but in strange actions described in chapters 4, 5, 12, and 24. Although the prophet appears to be mad, it is the insanity of the times and the terror of Yahweh's deeds that are reflected. Before the coming horror, the usual patterns that sustain life must be suspended. Even grief over the death of his beloved wife must be restrained. The word of his god infuses Ezekiel's total being, and his every action becomes the living word of Yahweh (Ezekiel 24:15–24).

After the Fall

Just as word arrives of the fall of Jerusalem (Ezekiel 33:21–22), there is an unexpected reversal in Ezekiel's oracles in which judgment becomes promise and the prophet offers hope for a future that must just then have seemed bleak indeed to those in exile. What more devastating news could there be for exiles than that the homeland, so loved and longed for, was no more. A careful reading of the prophet's words in chapters 1–24 should temper our surprise, however, for in its present form the Book of Ezekiel mediates the transition from judgment to promise through a collection of oracles that are directed against other nations, especially those that find delight in Israel's fall. Even in the oracles of doom a concern for the ongoing life of the exiles is clear. Now that the city has fallen this concern must present itself in new forms, for now the radical break with the old structures of life in Israel is complete.

In chapters 14 and 18 the prophet directs his attention not to the community—only the bare rudiments of new communal structures were emerging in the alien setting—but to the suffering individuals for whom he is responsible as Yahweh's "watchman" (Ezekiel 33:1–9). (This image added a new dimension to the prophetic office, with the prophet bearing an almost pastoral responsibility to implore individuals to turn to their god.) Although Yahweh's wrath falls on the nation as a whole and although all suffer (compare Jeremiah 45), not all members can be judged equally guilty. Is this fair? In the face of what must have seemed overwhelming evidence to the contrary, Ezekiel says yes.

At the time, an old saying was being bandied about: "The fathers have eaten sour grapes, and the children's teeth are set on edge" (Ezekiel 18:2; see also Jeremiah 31:27–30, and contrast Exodus 20:5), but this is now refuted in an extended and exacting argument. Yahweh, the prophet says, will judge each individual life according to its own particular quality but not on the basis of a rigid ledger of debits and credits. At any point one may turn from wickedness or righteousness and reverse whatever governing pattern has been established to that point. Yahweh's ways, Ezekiel claims, are not only just but ever open to human initiative and change. This attribution of individual responsibility is underscored in chapter 14 by the statement that even if Noah, Daniel, and Job—legendary figures well known for their intense piety—should plead for others, they alone would reap the rewards of their righteousness (compare this with the older vision expressed in Genesis 18:22–33), for merit is nonnegotiable and cannot be transferred to others.

Ezekiel's answer to the problem of individual suffering and divine justice would not satisfy all who survived the death of old Israel, and the issue would arise again. However, the older point of view reflected in the deuteronomistic history (2 Kings 23:26–27, for example) and in the popular saying cited above was not adequate either. It is to Ezekiel's credit that he raised the issue clearly in the immediate context of deep human tragedy.

In spite of the detached coolness and almost legalistic circumlocution of these chapters, they confront a basic human dilemma with pastoral concern. At the end of chapter 18 the reasonable tone becomes an impassioned appeal:

> Therefore I will judge you, O house of Israel, everyone according to his ways, says Yahweh God. Repent and turn from all your transgressions, lest iniquity be your ruin. Cast away from you all the transgressions . . . and get yourselves a new heart and a new spirit! Why will you die, O house of Israel? For I have no pleasure in the death of anyone, says Yahweh God; so turn, and live.
>
> (Ezekiel 18:30–32)

The cry of a god who has not given up his people even in exile is the essential fact that breaks through the theological speculation in these chapters.

Finally, in a vision the prophet sees a valley full of dry bones representing old Israel, which suddenly come together into new living forms (Ezekiel 37). This is a promise of a renewed community, not of an individual's resurrection after death. Chapters 33–39 describe a new nation, a full historical entity with essential structures, institutions, and officials, and here again we find a juxtaposition of old and new, of continuity in the face of radical dislocations.

The homeland will once again be free from foreign control; it will be redistributed and refreshed. Political structures will take new shape; cult and temple will be reestablished; Israel and Judah will be reunited; and over all shall rule a king of the Davidic line. Past experience of monarchy has left its mark, however, and Ezekiel offers a king whose authority and office are subsumed under the obligations of the covenant, in line with the political theory of Deuteronomy 17:14–20. In all this the old Moses-Sinai story provides not only a basis for judgment but the foundation for a vision of a restored Israel.

Ezekiel 40–48 presents a detailed picture of this restoration in units that some judge to have come from persons later than the prophet. While the complexity of these chapters may reflect reworking by those who found their hopes sustained in Ezekiel's words, their core comes from the prophet himself, and in them the promise set forth in chapters 33–39 finds concrete development. Here we may have the expression of those who claimed to have received renewed heart from their god: "A new heart I will give you, and a new spirit I will put within you.

And I will take out of your flesh the heart of stone and give you a heart of flesh" (Ezekiel 36:26, compare Jeremiah 31:31–34). But it is above all the temple that is restored, for in the new Jerusalem as in the old the temple is at the heart of this prophet's vision:

> Afterward he brought me to the gate facing east, and behold, the glory of the God of Israel came from the east; and the sound of his coming was like the sound of many waters; and the earth shone with his glory. And the vision I saw was like the vision which I had seen when he came to destroy the city, and like the vision which I had seen by the river Chebar; and I fell upon my face. As the glory of Yahweh entered the temple by the gate facing east, the Spirit lifted me up, and brought me into the inner court; and behold, the glory of Yahweh filled the temple.
>
> (Ezekiel 43:1–5)

THE SECOND ISAIAH

The oracles of Ezekiel and Jeremiah span two ages; those of the next prophet are wholly of the era that is bursting into bloom even as he speaks. He may, like Jeremiah and Ezekiel, be of priestly background, for his words have the form of priestly oracles of deliverance and hymnic proclamations of Yahweh's authority. He may have lived in Jerusalem before the fall, but this, too, is speculation for no biographical information about him exists. His name is not even known; critical scholarship has come to call him Deutero- or Second Isaiah. Yet in some ways he is the greatest of the prophets, drawing together in his oracles the full range of traditions from old Israel.

In the Second Isaiah, continuity with the past only underscores a radical discontinuity. Here is a prophet who, with words excerpted from ancient recitals of Yahweh's saving action in the exodus, calls upon his fellow exiles in the name of their god to turn in full trust to the future that awaits them:

> Thus says Yahweh,
> who makes a way in the sea,
> a path in the mighty waters,
> who brings forth chariot and horse,
> army and warrior;
> they lie down, they cannot rise,
> they are extinguished, quenched like a wick:
> Remember not the former things,
> nor consider the things of old.
> Behold, I am doing a new thing.
>
> (Isaiah 43:16–19)

Above all others he teaches Israel's heirs to sing new songs to Yahweh in the land of exile.

The oracles of this prophet are found in chapters 40–55 of the Book of Isaiah, which reveals better than any other book the prophetic tradition's ongoing character of remembrance and reapplication to new settings. Although the Second Isaiah's followers may trace their spiritual heritage to the Isaiah of Jerusalem, the new prophet faces a totally different situation. In form and content, chapters 40–55 stand apart from what has come before. Assyria is gone, as are Judah and Jerusalem, and the time is now the middle of the sixth century B.C.E. Scholarly recognition of the distinct character of chapters 40–55 enables us to acknowledge this unnamed prophet's contribution to the survival of his people as well as to Western religious tradition.

New Exodus and New Zion

The opening words of chapter 40—"Comfort, comfort my people!" (Isaiah 40:1)—emphasize the dramatic change that has taken place. The indictments and sentences pronounced by the old prophets had been true; Israel's death had come at the hand of her god because of covenant violations: "She has received from Yahweh's hand double for all her sins" (Isaiah 40:2; the double punishment probably reflects a legal form designating payment in full). But all that is past, and the Moses-Sinai story now becomes the basis not for judgment but for a vision of a new Israel.

Created out of the pieces of the Assyrian empire by Nabopolassar and especially by his son Nebuchadnezzar, the Neo-Babylonian empire began to disintegrate at the latter's death in 562 B.C.E.. A swift succession of kings led to Nabonidus whose seventeen-year reign brought about internal strife and removal of the royal establishment from Babylon to the city of Tima far into the Arabian desert. Although the reasons behind this ruler's quixotic policies are not clear, they were instrumental in bringing down the empire. But this is likely to have occurred in any case because in the mid–sixth century B.C.E. the Persians began a march across the Near East under the leadership of Cyrus. As early as 547, when the Kingdom of Lydia fell, Babylon's position had become untenable. In 539 the city was handed over to Cyrus by Babylonians who saw him as a savior because their own king had abandoned them. According to an inscription drawn up at the time, Marduk, the god of Babylon, took Cyrus's hand, thereby legitimizing his rule. A new era in the history of the Near East had begun.

The historical advent of Cyrus sparked the oracles of the Second Isaiah, whose dates are generally assigned to the final years of Babylon—that is, about 550–540 B.C.E.—for there is no indication that he actually witnessed Cyrus's entry into the city. Like the prophets before him, he interprets this new crisis theologically, viewing Cyrus as Yahweh's instrument. Yahweh is leading Cyrus from victory to victory, he says, in order to shatter the power of Babylon so that Israel might be released. This announcement is expressed in terms both impressive and shocking to former Israelites:

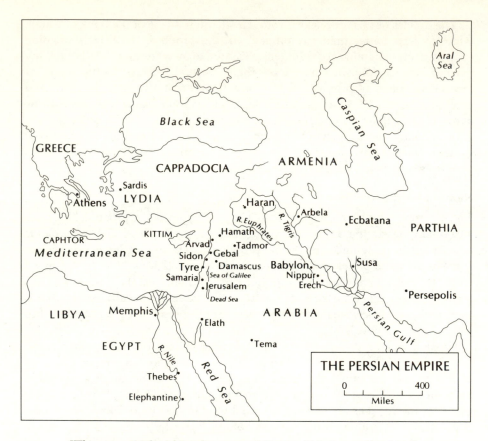

THE PERSIAN EMPIRE

0   400
Miles

> [Thus says Yahweh], who says of Cyrus, "He is my shepherd,
>   and he shall fulfill my purpose."
> Thus says Yahweh to his anointed, to Cyrus,
>   whose right hand I have grasped,
> to subdue nations before him
>   and ungird the loins of kings,
> to open doors before him
>   that gates may not be closed. . . .
>   (Isaiah 44:28–45:1; see also 41:25 and 45:3–4)

Such terms were reserved for the kings of David's line and were not used of gentiles, even of gentiles who might rule the world.

Like Ezekiel and Jeremiah, the Second Isaiah also looks for the rebuilding of a nation Israel. The exiles' return from Babylon to the land of promise will be a new exodus, and the command goes out to build a royal highway for the return through the wilderness (Isaiah 40:3–5). This time, however, the march will not be marked by struggle and deprivation:

> I will open rivers on the barge heights,
> > and fountains in the midst of the valleys;
> I will make the wilderness a pool of water,
> > and the dry land springs of water.
>
> > (Isaiah 41:18)

From all ends of the earth the children of Israel shall return home (Isaiah 43:1–8); from the bondage of exile they shall be released (Isaiah 49:8–13). In the heart of the old federation story the prophet finds a typology for the announcement of a promise for today and tomorrow. The notes are familiar, but the song is new (Isaiah 42:10).

The highway through the wilderness seems to be patterned on the grand processional road over which the gods of Mesopotamia came as they entered Babylon each New Year. They came to join Marduk, the god of Babylon, in a festival that reaffirmed his authority over heaven and earth. In like manner, on the highway cut through the wilderness "the glory of Yahweh shall be revealed, and all flesh shall see it together" (Isaiah 40:5), for Yahweh himself would return to Zion (Isaiah 40:9–11), which would then be rebuilt to stand at the head of all nations as Yahweh's inviolable abode (Isaiah 49:14–23; 52:1–2; 52:7–12). Like the promises made to Abraham and David, the promise of a new Zion is firm and forever (Isaiah 51:1–3). We may also recall here Isaiah of Jerusalem's vision of a restoration of the created universe in its pristine state as Yahweh's peaceable kingdom (Isaiah 9 and 11).

The Second Isaiah unites elements from the David-Zion story with the Moses-Sinai complex to form a new vision, which places him in line with the Yahwist. Old Israel's death had been understood in terms of the Moses-Sinai story, but the future is now depicted in motifs drawn from each: a new exodus will climax in a new Zion. The promise that seemed shattered is as firm as that made to Noah after the flood:

> For this is like the days of Noah to me:
> > as I swore that the waters of Noah
> > shall no more go over the earth,
> so I have sworn that I will not be angry with you
> > and will not rebuke you.
> For the mountains may depart
> > and the hills be removed.
> but my steadfast love shall not depart from you
> > and my covenant of peace shall not be removed,
> > says Yahweh, who has compassion on you.
>
> O afflicted one, storm-tossed, and not comforted,
> > behold, I will set your stones in antimony,
> > and lay your foundations with sapphires.

In righteousness you shall be established;
you shall be far from oppression,
for you shall not fear;
and from terror, for it shall not come near you.

(Isaiah 54:9–14)

It must be noted, however, that no mention is made of restoring the Davidic royal line. The promise that in earlier days had been addressed to David and his dynasty is now made to the people as a whole. The Second Isaiah's only reference to the Davidic promise is spoken to all exiles:

Ho, everyone who thirsts,
come to the waters;

Incline your ear, and come to me;
hear, that your soul may live;
and I will make with you an everlasting covenant,
my steadfast, sure love for David.

(Isaiah 55:1–3)

And the central theme of the David-Zion story is dramatically refocused.

This vision of a new exodus and new Zion provides the exiles with themes for constructing new identities, and this is the thrust of Isaiah 43:16–19: "Remember not the former things," for the verb "to remember" in Hebrew carried a special nuance. Israel *remembered* both ancient stories in a cultic setting that allowed the events presented to be reexperienced through a combination of word and action, myth and ritual. In this way the stories had remained the formative center of both the nation and the individual Israelite. But now the nation was dead and the cultic center in ruins. The Second Isaiah therefore seeks to recast the old stories to offer a new focus for individual hope and trust. For those in exile, to build upon Yahweh's past acts would be a failure to recognize the finality of the events of 587 B.C.E. It is rather upon a future that Yahweh has already set in motion—"Now it springs forth, do you not perceive it?"—that a new life with Yahweh could be based.

Yahweh and Marduk

The Second Isaiah's vision is attractive, but it flies in the face of experience. Upon what possible basis might the exile risk investing his life in it? As we have seen, the question of allegiance was immediate and pressing for those exiled in Babylon, and by all reasonable criteria Marduk of Babylon seemed to have an irrefutable claim because he was triumphant; the future lay with him in his city. For many exiled sons and daughters of Israel, cultural and political assimilation was the only course of action. How, then, could one accept the visions of this prophet as anything but madness, the dreams of one who cannot face facts?

The Second Isaiah is compelled to take on the Babylonian deities with a range of weapons, harsh mockery among them. The triumphal procession of the gods over the sacred highway in the New Year's festival is turned into a humiliating procession into captivity (Isaiah 46:1–2; compare 40:3–6). Moreover, the gods of Babylon are said to be mere hunks of wood and stone overlaid with metal (Isaiah 41:6–7; 40:18–20; 44:9–20); how stupid are those who bow down before them (compare Jeremiah 2:27). In a deliberate misunderstanding of the nature and function of images in the Near East, the idols and their makers/worshipers are ridiculed:

> To whom will you liken me and make me equal,
> and compare me, that we may be alike?
> Those who lavish gold from the purse,
> and weigh out silver in the scales,
> hire a goldsmith, and he makes it into a god;
> then they fall down and worship!
> They lift it upon their shoulders, they carry it,
> they set it in its place, and it stands there;
> it cannot move from its place.
> If one cries to it, it does not answer
> or save him from his trouble.
>
> (Isaiah 46:5–7)

In a second line of attack the Babylonian gods are challenged to confront Yahweh and match his ability not only to cause events in history but to make them known beforehand. Here the Second Isaiah aligns himself with the older prophets and emphasizes a formative theme found in the deuteronomistic history as well: Yahweh not only acts in history but announces through prophets what he is going to do. In the language of the court of law the gods are summoned:

> Set forth your case, says Yahweh;
> bring your proofs, says the King of Jacob.
> Let them bring them, and tell us
> what is to happen.
> Tell us the former things, what they are,
> that we may consider them,
> that we may know their outcome;
> or declare to us the things to come.
> Tell us what is to come hereafter,
> that we may know that you are gods;
> do good, or do harm,
> that we may be dismayed and terrified.
> Behold, you are nothing,
> and your work is nought,
> an abomination is he who chooses you.
>
> (Isaiah 41:21–24; see also 45:20–21)

184   It was Yahweh who brought success to Cyrus, just as it was Yahweh who gave success to Nebuchadnezzar and who used Sennacherib of Assyria as his punishing rod (Jeremiah 27:6–7; Isaiah 10:5–6), and in all this Yahweh made his acts clear beforehand through the words of his prophets.

In contrast to this harsh attack, a deep compassion characterizes the deity's appeals to the exiles:

> But Zion said, "Yahweh has forsaken me,
>   my Lord has forgotten me."
> Can a woman forget her sucking child,
>   that she should have no compassion on the son of her womb?
> Even these may forget,
>   yet I will not forget you.
>   (Isaiah 49:14–15; see also 40:10–11, 27–31;
>   41:14–15; 44:1–5)

The fact that old Israel had deserved punishment did not nullify the compassion of her god (Isaiah 42:14–17). Throughout these units strong announcements of Yahweh's authority and action are blended with a compelling appeal to trust him.

The most profound counter, however, lay in the prophet's presentation of Yahweh as creator. The theme is not new, of course; the Yahwist had presented it at the outset of his theological history, and it was an essential ingredient in the old David-Zion story as well. But on Marduk's home ground this motif found new relevance, for the Babylonians claimed that Marduk was creator and sustainer and that all owed him allegiance both in heaven and on earth. The foundation for his authority was found in a creation story relived in the cult each spring.

This story told of Marduk's successful engagement in battle with a monster named Tiamat, who represented the primordial force for death and chaos that continually threatens life and order. In the first month of each year the gods came to Babylon, and in the course of a fourteen-day ceremony the created universe was renewed as Marduk defeated Tiamat once again. The priests of Babylon fashioned this story into a document called the *Enuma Elish*, which may be described as the Magna Carta for Marduk and the city of Babylon.

To this concept the Second Isaiah presents a challenge in hymnic refrains that are interlaced throughout his songs and oracles:

> Thus says Yahweh, God,
>   who created the heavens and stretched them out,
>   who spread forth the earth and what comes from it,
> who gives breath to the people upon it
>   and spirit to those who walk upon it.
>   (Isaiah 42:5, see also 40:28; 44:24–27; 45:12 and 45:18)

In this way Marduk is met on his own ground. As in the David-Zion story of old Jerusalem, it is the creator deity whose claims are set out, and it is as creator that his authority is certified:

> For thus says Yahweh,
>   who created the heavens (he is God!),
> who formed the earth and made it
>   (he established it;
> he did not create it a chaos,
>   he formed it to be inhabited!):
> "I am Yahweh, and there is no other.
> I did not speak in secret,
>   in a land of darkness;
> I did not say to the offspring of Jacob,
>   'Seek me in chaos.'
> I Yahweh speak the truth,
>   I declare what is right."
>
> (Isaiah 45:18–19)

As creator of the universe, Yahweh can claim authority over all nations; he can move kingdoms and destroy empires:

> I made the earth,
>   and created man upon it;
> it was my hands that stretched out the heavens,
>   and I commanded all their host.
> I have aroused him [Cyrus] in righteousness,
>   and I will make straight all his ways;
> he shall build my city
>   and set my exiles free,
> not for price or reward,
>   says Yahweh of hosts.
>
> (Isaiah 45:12–13)

All land is Yahweh's land; there is no foreign place in which his songs cannot be sung.

In the words of the Second Isaiah, creation is both the establishing and ordering of the universe and the rebuilding of the nation Israel. The new exodus and Zion are further instances of Yahweh's creative work:

> Thus says Yahweh, your redeemer,
>   who formed you from the womb:
> I am Yahweh, who made all things,
>   who stretched out the heavens alone,
>   who spread out the earth—Who was with me?

who confirms the word of his servant,
    and performs the counsel of his messengers;
who says of Jerusalem, "She shall be inhabited,"
    and of the cities of Judah, "They shall be built,
    and I will raise up their ruins";
who says to the deep, "Be dry,
    I will dry up your rivers;"
who says of Cyrus, "He is my shepherd,
    and he shall fulfill all my purpose;"
saying of Jerusalem, "She shall be built,"
    and of the temple, "Your foundation shall be laid."

(Isaiah 44:24; 44:26–28)

Although the prophet's immediate task is to bring comfort, restore hope, and enliven frightened exiles in an alien land, a clear and impressive theological structure stands behind the several themes that we have isolated. In the eyes of the Second Isaiah, only Yahweh is god, for none is like him in any way (Isaiah 40:18–26; 41:24; 41:29; 45:5; 45:22; 46:9). Here is the first conscious expression of what can justifiably be called monotheism in the Hebraic tradition:

Thus says Yahweh, the King of Israel
    and his Redeemer, Yahweh of hosts:
"I am the first and I am the last;
    besides me there is no god.
Who is like me? Let him proclaim it,
    let him declare and set it forth before me.
Who has announced from of old the things to come?
    Let them tell us what is yet to be.
Fear not, nor be afraid;
    have I not told you from of old and declared it?
And you are my witnesses!
Is there a God besides me?
    There is no Rock; I know not any."

(Isaiah 44:6–8)

Certainly the seeds of monotheism had been present much earlier in Israel, but it was in direct life-and-death confrontation with Marduk that they bore fruit. Among defeated exiles whose god seemed dead the assertion is made that Yahweh is the only god; he alone orders and shapes the universe and the lives of all men and women in it. In confrontation with Yahweh, other gods can do nothing and therefore are nothing.

If Yahweh is creator, then the range of his concern and action is universal —another link between the prophet of the exile and the Yahwist. Already in Ezekiel the assertion was found that Yahweh will restore Israel to "show my greatness and my holiness and make myself known in the eyes of many nations. Then they will know that I am Yahweh" (Ezekiel 38:23), that is, the restoration of Israel from a few scattered exiles and fugitives will bring all nations to acknowledge him. The Second Isaiah's message is nationalistic insofar as it is a new nation-state that is to be reconstructed in Palestine, but that event will be a witness to all nations to Yahweh's supreme authority (Isaiah 43:8–13). That a universal perspective envelops the nationalistic is most impressively developed in four distinct songs.

The Servant of Yahweh

Critical analysis of Isaiah 40–55 has isolated four units that share a common theme—Isaiah 42:1–4, 49:1–6, 50:4–9, and 52:13–53:12—each of which deals with a figure called the servant of Yahweh. Volumes have been devoted to the critical issues revolving about these units, but the most salient questions concern the servant's identity, the nature of his mission, and the cause and meaning of his suffering. With few exceptions, scholars today agree that these four songs come from the same hand as the rest of Isaiah 40–55.

In Isaiah 42:1–4 the speaker is Yahweh, who designates the servant as "my chosen, in whom my soul delights." Endowed with Yahweh's spirit the servant will quietly establish justice throughout the earth. The element of force is not present in his activity which will be like that of gently flowing water.

In Isaiah 49:1–6 the servant himself addresses all the nations, claiming that his god designated him for his role before his birth. Nurtured by Yahweh, he continues to find strength and support in him even though his efforts appear to have been fruitless. His mission is described as directed first to Israel—"to bring Jacob back to him, and that Israel might be gathered to him"—but this mission is then vastly expanded:

> It is too light a thing that you should be my servant
> > to raise up the tribes of Jacob
> > and to restore the preserved of Israel;
> I will give you as a light to the nations,
> > that my salvation may reach to the end of the earth.
>
> > > > (Isaiah 49:6)

Here nationalism is caught up in universalism, and it must also be noted that Yahweh is to be glorified through his servant's activity (Isaiah 49:3). In Isaiah 50:4–5 echoes of Jeremiah's laments are heard in a description of suffering that is answered by assurance of Yahweh's continued aid. With this to strengthen him, the servant is able to challenge in legal terms many who would deny him.

Before turning to the fourth song we should ask who this servant is. Some have sought an answer in Israel's past—Moses, Jeremiah, the Second Isaiah, one of the Davidic line. Others have looked for a future figure—a second Moses or someone of the prophetic line; Christian tradition views Jesus as such a figure. Others suggest that the reference is not to an individual but to a group since singular forms are often used for collectives in Hebraic literature. Indeed, the second song (in what some believe to be an interpretative gloss added to the text later) identifies the servant as Israel: "And he said to me, 'You are my servant, Israel, in whom I will be glorified'" (Isaiah 49:3). Israel is called Yahweh's servant elsewhere in chapters 40–55 (Isaiah 41:8; 42:19; 44:1–2; 44:21; 45:4; 48:20), and other terms used of the servant in the three songs are applied to Israel as well.

But the servant's mission is said to be directed to Israel. Can Israel have a mission to herself? Some believe that only a part of old Israel is intended: the segment that has been through the refining fire of exile and is now renewed by the prophet's words has a mission to the larger remnants of the nation. This interpretation corresponds to the prophet's message: he has been called to revitalize the exiles with his announcement of Yahweh's new action; these exiles will serve to restore the larger Israel; and by this means vivid testimony of Yahweh's authority will shine forth to all the world. Although none of these solutions is entirely satisfactory, it is reasonably clear that the servant's mission is universal in thrust, and in this respect Israel is to hold a unique place in Yahweh's work.

The fourth and longest song (Isaiah 52:13–53:12) raises a number of problems ranging from textual questions to uncertainty about its several speakers. Yahweh seems to speak first, designating as his servant one who, in spite of suffering and disfiguring disgrace, will gain the awe of nations and rulers. It is probably these rulers who next speak, acknowledging that he in no way appears as favored: "He was despised and rejected by men, a man of sorrows"; he passively accepts his fate "like a lamb that is led to the slaughter, and like a sheep that before its shearers is dumb." Although the servant dies and receives a dishonorable burial, interlaced with the description of his sufferings is an assertion that his agony makes others whole:

> But he was wounded for our transgressions,
>   he was bruised for our iniquities;
> upon him was the chastisement that made us whole,
>   and with his stripes we are healed.
> All we like sheep have gone astray,
>   and Yahweh has laid on him the iniquity of us all.
>
> (Isaiah 53:5–6)

A final divine response speaks of a future glorification of the servant in which he will take part and emphasizes once again that "he bore the sin of many and made intercession for the transgressors."

When this song is brought into conjunction with the other three, problems of interpretation abound. Although it is here made clear that the servant's suffering is unmerited, nowhere is this said of Israel or even of that part of old Israel in exile in Babylon. In this song, too, the language does not suggest that a group is the subject. Although most interpreters link the fourth song with the other three, it moves well beyond them in length and in its depiction of the servant's suffering, yet it also has links with them. Here we will speculate about the authorship of the fourth song, for speculation it must be.

In the tense days of Nabonidus, when factions were sharply divided within Babylon and as Cyrus loomed on the horizon, the Second Isaiah's words would have been regarded as treasonous. Although we know little about Babylon in its last days, we do know that years earlier, between 598 and 587 B.C.E., some prophets among those taken to Babylon in the first exile had announced that the empire would soon be overthrown and that the exiles would return home (Jeremiah 29). Jeremiah disagreed and predicted that these prophets would be executed by Babylonian authorities. If the Second Isaiah met this fate in the last days of the Neo-Babylonian empire—and this is speculation—his sudden and probably horrible death would have had a great impact on his followers. How could this have happened to the one who had announced Yahweh's salvation? How could he, who above all others had preserved confidence in the god's ultimate care for his people, die on the brink of the realization of his visions?

In such a case his disciples might adopt a motif from the first three songs and reapply it to their master in a fourth song of their own composition. In the three earlier songs the Second Isaiah probably speaks of the faithful in exile as the servant. In the fourth song this image is recast in an attempt to comprehend his martyrdom: it is for them that he suffered and died, the final act of purification. In attaining this new way to comprehend suffering as well as in gaining insight into the value of human life and death, a profound contribution was made not only to the exiles of that time but to all the varied religious traditions of the Western world.

PROMISE AND FULFILLMENT

Restoration of Jerusalem

In 539 B.C.E. Babylon fell to the army of Cyrus, and it seemed that the promise held forth by the Second Isaiah was soon to be fulfilled. In the following year Cyrus issued a decree enabling exiles to return to their homeland (Ezra 1:1–4; 6:2–12), providing for the return of the sacred vessels that had been taken from Yahweh's temple, and offering funds for its rebuilding. This edict mirrors a policy of governance in marked contrast to that of the Babylonians or earlier Assyrians. Cyrus did not seek to extinguish all traces of national identity and attachment to a land through deportation. Self-rule and internal cultural and religious freedom were encouraged. Loyalty was based not on terror but on self-interest. Stability was fostered under Persian rule, and this made allegiance worth the price.

A few years after the edict was issued, some exiles decided to return under the leadership of Sheshbazzar, a descendant of David, whom the Persians

PERSIAN EMPIRE

B.C.E.		
550	Cyrus (550–530)	SECOND ISAIAH
		Cyrus takes Babylon (539)
		Cyrus's edict (538)
525	Cambyses (530–522)	Zerubbabel
	Darius I (522–486)	
		HAGGAI & ZECHARIAH
		Temple built (520–515)
500		
	Xerxes I (486–465)	
475		
	Artaxerxes I (465–424)	JOEL
		MALACHI
450		
		Nehemiah comes to Jerusalem (445)
		EZRA
425		
	Xerxes II (423)	
	Darius II (423–404)	
400	Artaxerxes II (404–358)	
375		
	Artaxerxes III (358–338)	
350		
	Arses (338–336)	
	Darius III (336–331)	
325		

appointed governor over the former territory of Judah. Under Sheshbazzar work began on the temple in Jerusalem, but then there is a gap in our knowledge. The event so anxiously awaited was finally taking place, but little is said about it in the materials preserved. It did not become an event to be remembered in the full sense of that term because its actuality ill matched the hopes that had been aroused by the prophets.

Although more than one group may have made the journey back to Palestine, most exiles seem to have remained in Babylon. The prospect of returning to a land last seen in ruins and of returning to a very uncertain future could not have appealed to those second- and third-generation exiles who found life in Mesopotamia more than tolerable under evenhanded Persian authority. Because two or three generations had passed in exile, Palestine was for many Jews a memory rather than an experienced part of their lives. While they might cherish their distant roots, the risk of relocating and of reordering their lives around them was too great.

Those who did return did not enter an empty land, for it had remained in the hands of "some of the poorest of the land" (Jeremiah 52:16) who had not been taken into exile. Many of these would have settled into abandoned homes and farms over the decades so that newcomers with old land claims and a sense of superiority as the refined and purified servants of Yahweh would not have found a warm welcome. Moreover, Jerusalem and its outskirts were under the political control of officials in the city of Samaria to the north and were part of a large province that took in most of Syria-Palestine. Such officials would not hesitate to check any developments in an older, rival center of power. All in all, it must have seemed to those who had returned a time not of triumph but of attending to land claims, building homes, planting crops, and eking out a subsistence—in short, a time for rebuilding life from its roots up.

The Third Isaiah Chapters 56–66 of the Book of Isaiah, which contain oracles of one or more disciples of the Second Isaiah, reflect this situation. The setting is once again Palestine, not Babylon, and the time is roughly 535–520 B.C.E. While these oracles do exhibit an expectant tone, it is no longer the advent of Cyrus or a new exodus that is anticipated. Indeed, the new exodus had been too much like the old, and the new Zion that was taking shape was inauspicious. In Jerusalem social abuses and cultic irregularities rivaling those of the bad old days (Isaiah 59:1–8) elicited a rebuke whose force at times approached that of the preexilic prophets (see Isaiah 57:1–13).

Beyond rebuke, however, the task was twofold: to sustain and to enflame, and in part this was a pastoral task. Those who had invested so much in the return only to be discouraged by the conditions encountered there needed to be sustained:

> The Spirit of Yahweh God is upon me
> because Yahweh has anointed me

> to bring good tidings to the afflicted;
>> he has sent me to bind up the brokenhearted,
> to proclaim liberty to the captives,
>> and the opening of the prison to those who are bound.

(Isaiah 61:1)

In addition, the flame of hope had to be fed. Trust that their god would act was fading in the course of mundane and empty days that gave little sign of any divine presence. There was no stirring among nations to acknowledge Yahweh's authority; little glory shone from Zion to attract them (compare Isaiah 40:15; 43:9; 49:6). If this was the best that Yahweh could do, perhaps others were right and he was a second-rate deity (Isaiah 59:1). Those whose oracles are found in chapters 56–66 had somehow to distinguish Yahweh's hand in a setting that seemed to have nothing to do with "the high and lofty One who inhabits eternity, whose name is Holy" (Isaiah 57:15). They had to bridge a gap between the god in the heavens and men and women of "contrite and humble spirit" (Isaiah 57:11).

Those whom we designate as the Third Isaiah are often judged inferior to the earlier prophets, and while they do attain an impressive vision and force at some points, on the whole they fall short of sustained greatness. Great men and women are in part produced by great crises. It is the difficult task of others to make sense of the everyday and petty, to find therein as well, where so much of life is lived, the challenge and hand of their god:

> Behold, the hand of Yahweh is not shortened,
>> that it cannot save,
> or his ear dull, that it cannot hear.

(Isaiah 59:1)

Haggai and Zechariah

In 530 B.C.E. Cyrus died and was succeeded by his son Cambyses, who matched him neither as a military leader nor as ruler of an empire. In 522 B.C.E. Cambyses died, perhaps by his own hand, as he returned from an attempt to suppress dissent in Egypt. It would take two years or more for Darius, a Persian general, to secure the throne. From Palestine, hundreds of miles from the capital in Susa, it must have seemed that the Persian empire was disintegrating; perhaps the long awaited moment had finally arrived.

Two prophets suggested that this was the case: Haggai, who spoke for about four months in 520 B.C.E., and Zechariah, whose activity lasted from 520 to 518 B.C.E. Sure that the long anticipated moment had come, each addressed himself to the task of preparing the community in Jerusalem for a divine restoration of Israel. First, the temple and a proper cult had to be established. Second, action must be initiated to establish an independent state of Israel. With some effort the first task was accomplished because it was within the limits permitted by Cyrus's own edict; the second task, however, proved abortive.

Haggai described the period as one of small things, of people struggling to survive while in the process losing their direction, values, and identity. They sought to build homes for themselves, for example, but neglected the home of Yahweh (Haggai 1:3–11). Crop failure because of drought was interpreted as the deity's attempt to rouse his people from their stupor. The summons went out to build the temple, and if the result was not on the scale of the first temple (Haggai 2:1–9), it was at least completed by 515 B.C.E. The high priest Joshua took charge of the cult, and a full round of service was resumed.

For Haggai and Zechariah, however, rebuilding the temple was only one part of a larger national renewal that focused on a man named Zerubbabel, about whom little is known beyond the fact that he was of Davidic descent and had been appointed by the Persians to succeed Sheshbazzar as governor of Judah. But even this leaves uncertainty about the extent of his authority, especially in relation to the authorities in Samaria. The oracles of Haggai and Zechariah suggest that hopes formed around Zerubbabel for the rebirth of an independent Israel ruled once again by a Davidic king and that this was to be Yahweh's work, effected by the fall of the Persian empire: "Speak to Zerubbabel, governor of Judah, saying, I am about to shake the heavens and the earth, and to overthrow the throne of kingdoms. . . . On that day, says Yahweh of hosts, I will take you, O Zerubbabel, my servant, the son of Shealtiel, says Yahweh, and make you like a signet ring; for I have chosen you, says Yahweh of hosts" (Haggai 2:20–23; see also Zechariah 3:8; 4:14; and 6:9–14, which many suggest originally referred to Zerubbabel).

In anticipating the total restoration of Israel, Haggai and Zechariah stand in the line of both the First and Second Isaiah. But unlike the latter, they hope for a Davidic king, and the locus for these hopes was the David-Zion story. A new and righteous king would rule again in Zion (compare Isaiah 9 and 11), climaxing in an inpouring to Jerusalem of all nations to seek Yahweh, whom they would acknowledge as god of all the earth:

Thus says Yahweh of hosts: Peoples shall yet come, even the inhabitants of many cities; the inhabitants of one city shall go to another saying, "Let us go at once to entreat the favor of Yahweh, and to seek Yahweh of hosts; I am going." Many peoples and strong nations shall come to seek Yahweh of hosts in Jerusalem and to entreat the favor of Yahweh. Thus says Yahweh of hosts: In those days ten men from the nations of every tongue shall take hold of the robe of a Jew saying, "Let us go with you, for we have heard that God is with you."

(Zechariah 8:20–23)

But it was not to be. The Persian empire was shaken but did not dissolve. Darius seized the throne, Zerubbabel simply vanished. Whether he was removed by Persian authority as the leader or symbol of an independence movement or whether the movement was never even noticed by the Persians is not known. Although the temple had been restored, Jerusalem and Judah remained under Persian rule, and little is known about events in southern Palestine for the next few decades. This failure undoubtedly accounts for the paucity of information about Zerubbabel, just as earlier dashed hopes may explain the lack of information about the return from exile. Dwelling on shattered dreams provides little substance for building anew.

In one respect this failure was a historical judgment on the great exilic prophets as well as on Haggai and Zechariah, for reality fell far short of a full national renewal of Israel, and we know of no further movement toward national independence for the next three centuries or more. From this point onward, moreover, prophecy either waned or was transformed. But the legacy of the prophets of the exile was not a nationalistic dead end. The rebuilt temple would become a focal point for many Jews in centuries to come; new and rich modes would be developed for speaking and singing of Yahweh; hopes and promises were later recast to sustain and enrich generations of Jews and Christians alike. Most fundamental of all, life continued in relation with Yahweh, and the foundations were set for a new religious community.

BIBLIOGRAPHIC NOTE

The Exile

    Ackroyd, Peter R. *Exile and Restoration: A Study of Hebrew Thought in the Sixth Century B.C.E.* Philadelphia :Westminster Press, 1968.

    Raitt, Thomas M. *A Theology of Exile*. Philadelphia: Fortress Press, 1977.

The Book of Ezekiel

    Eichrodt, Walther. *Ezekiel*. Philadelphia: Westminster Press, 1970.

    Howie, C. G. "Ezekiel." In *The Interpreter's Dictionary of the Bible*, vol. 2, pp. 203–13. Nashville: Abingdon Press, 1962.

    Zimmerli, W. "Ezekiel." In *The Interpreter's Dictionary of the Bible: Supplementary Volume*, pp. 314–317. Nashville: Abingdon Press, 1976.

The Second and Third Isaiah

    McKenzie, John L. *Second Isaiah*. Garden City, N.Y.: Doubleday & Co., 1968.

    Muilenburg, James. "Introduction and Exegesis to Isaiah 40–66." In *The Interpreter's Bible*, vol. 5, pp. 381–773. Nashville: Abingdon Press, 1956.

    North, Christopher R. "Isaiah." In *The Interpreter's Dictionary of the Bible*, vol. 2, pp. 731–44. Nashville: Abingdon Press, 1962.

    ————. *Isaiah 40–55*. New York: Macmillan Co., 1964.

_____. "Servant of the Lord, The." In *The Interpreter's Dictionary of the Bible*, vol. 4, pp. 292–94. Nashville: Abingdon Press, 1962.

_____. *The Suffering Servant in Deutero-Isaiah*. New York: Oxford University Press, 1956.

Smart, James D. *History and Theology in Second Isaiah: A Commentary on Isaiah 35, 40–66*. Philadelphia: Westminster Press, 1965.

Stuhlmueller, Carroll. *Creative Redemption in Deutero-Isaiah*. Rome: Biblical Institute Press, 1970.

Ward, James M. "Isaiah." In *The Interpreter's Dictionary of the Bible: Supplementary Volume*, pp. 456–61. Nashville: Abingdon Press, 1976.

Westermann, Claus. *Isaiah 40–66*. Philadelphia: Westminster Press, 1969.

Haggai and Zechariah

Hanson, Paul D. "Zechariah, Book of." In *The Interpreter's Dictionary of the Bible: Supplementary Volume*, pp. 982–83. Nashville: Abingdon Press, 1976.

Neil, W. "Haggai." In *The Interpreter's Dictionary of the Bible*, vol. 2, pp. 509–11. Nashville: Abingdon Press, 1962.

_____. "Zechariah, Book of." In *The Interpreter's Dictionary of the Bible*, vol. 4, pp. 943–47. Nashville: Abingdon Press, 1962.

9 THEOLOGICAL ISSUES CONFRONTING EARLY JUDAISM

Primary readings: *Job*
                           Proverbs 1–9
                           Ecclesiastes

In confronting the crisis of 587 B.C.E. the prophets Jeremiah, Ezekiel, the Second Isaiah, Haggai, and Zechariah stood as conscious heirs of old Israel's religious traditions. Shattered as these traditions were, they nevertheless provided symbols, themes, and forms for comprehending the tragedy and for offering a vision of restoration. In the books of Job and Ecclesiastes and in other literature designated as "wisdom," however, there is no reference whatsoever to any of the motifs, themes, or symbols found in ancient Israel's stories and songs. Although the authors of these materials were all Jews and heirs of old Israel struggling with fundamental religious questions, there are no allusions here to the patriarchs, the exodus, the forty years in the wilderness, to Sinai and the covenant, to the land of promise, or even to such leaders as Moses and Joshua. No mention is made of any of the themes linked with Zion/Jerusalem and with the house of David. There is, in fact, very little that can be called distinctively Israelite in these works.

Nevertheless, these works, too, must be regarded as attempts to respond to the theological crisis of 587 B.C.E. They cannot be fully accounted for, as many have attempted, simply by designating them as "wisdom" and suggesting that the wise men were uninterested in the basic themes of Israel's stories. For these authors the past was dead and could not be revived, and their very silence introduces an important new chapter in the history of ancient Israel and early Judaism.

THE BOOK OF JOB

Structure

While the Second Isaiah often receives highest praise within strictly Jewish and Christian confines, within larger circles the Book of Job is ranked among the greatest works of Western literature. The book is a poetic meditation on a well-known old folk tale about a man who is the essence of righteousness and piety. Ezekiel at one point alludes to Job along with Noah and Daniel as a man of this sort (Ezekiel 14:20), and his story must have been common coin in the world of the exiles, some of whom no doubt saw their own experiences reflected in Job's seemingly undeserved sufferings. A stark form of this popular tale is attached to the poem as both prologue (Job 1 and 2) and epilogue (Job 42:7–17). In a series of brief scenes alternating between heaven and earth the prosperous and devout Job loses his possessions, family, and health because of a divine wager, yet he refuses to curse his god. The claims of the Satan—the term is not a proper name but the title of a member of the heavenly court who serves as an advocate—are refuted, Job does not break, and in the end he is restored to a state even surpassing his initial one.

In its depiction of an apparently unmotivated divine attack and in the hero's unbending fidelity to his god—"Yahweh gave, and Yahweh has taken away; blessed be the name of Yahweh"—the tale may well be of Mesopotamian origin, for the Mesopotamians often depicted their deities as acting on impulse in ways that exceed human comprehension. In the Mesopotamian view, moreover, this potentially tragic divine order did not release human beings from their obligation to remain obedient servants of the gods.

From this springboard the author of Job devises a complex poetic composition. The poem opens with a moving lament in which Job curses the day of his birth. Then in three cycles he is addressed by and answers each of three friends. The third cycle appears disrupted at the end, and several reconstructions have been attempted. The conclusion of the third cycle introduces a poem on wisdom (Job 28) which many consider to be an insertion by a later hand. At the end of the third cycle, in any event, the central issue remains unresolved, and Job places his case in the hands of the deity. This is done by means of an elaborate three-part oath in which he reviews his once happy state (Job 29), contrasts it with his present situation (Job 30), then asserts his integrity through a form of

198 negative confession (Job 31). The frame of reference is that of the law court, for in the ancient world, when human insight failed to resolve a legal claim, the accused took an oath of innocence and the matter was turned over to the gods.

At this point, when traditional legal patterns demand that only the deity answer, a young man named Elihu breaks in (Job 32–37), taking up themes from the earlier dialogue with some new emphases. He also provides a brief comic interlude (note his long-winded introduction of himself) in a situation filled with terror, for Job has just set his challenge directly in the lap of the god. Many regard the Elihu interlude as secondary, but it does prepare the stage for Yahweh's answer to Job from the whirlwind. This is presented in two parts (Job 38:1–39:30 and 40:6–41:34) punctuated by Job's submission (Job 40:1–5 and 42:1–6).

It is often suggested that segments of Yahweh's second response (especially that dealing with the crocodile in Job 41:10–34) were added to the poem at a later time, as were the Elihu speech and Job 28. Although the folk tale is much older, the poem has been dated from the mid- to late sixth century B.C.E. Reflections of Jeremiah's laments in chapter 3, as well as the absence of any consideration of suffering in the terms delineated in the fourth servant song of the Second Isaiah (Isaiah 52:13–53:12), suggest a date between these prophets; about 550 B.C.E. cannot be far wrong.

Theodicy and Piety

Although the Job of the poem is not the Job of the folk tale—from chapter 3 onward he is hardly a patient and loyal devotee of his god (compare James 5:11)—the broad issue is set in the folk tale. On the one hand, there is the problem of theodicy: Do the gods order this universe in a way that men and women can recognize as fair? On the other hand, there is the issue of the range and limits, cost and intensity, of one man's loyalty to his deity. The two issues are intimately linked as aspects of the interaction of a god and his creature.

The folk tale emphasizes that human beings must remain subservient and devoted to gods in all situations. Any appearance of divine injustice or irrationality simply reflects a fundamental limitation of comprehension within the human creature himself. To cry out against or to question such gods is to overstep the boundaries of the human situation and to transgress the structure of the universe. It is best for a person to pursue the daily round of service to the gods, mindlessly if necessary, and to accept good and bad as they come.

This solution, however, is rejected in all three cycles of dialogue. Job does cry out against and even curse his god. He is injured, he is outraged, and he will not submerge his agony in a debasement of his humanity. Human beings are not cowering dogs, and a fundamental injustice in the divine governance of this world cannot be allowed to turn men into something less than they are. But what are mortals in the deity's eyes? Can they be what Job knows or at least hopes he is?

Part 2 / The Rise of Judaism

The friends who seek to bring Job true comfort and not some mind-deadening panacea must not be judged as unfeeling or crass even when they seem finally to attack him. For comforters must help the afflicted to place his suffering in some larger perspective that will sustain or reconstruct life; they must restore order to an existence that has become chaotic. In this regard it must be noted that Job insists not only on asserting his relative innocence but on radically redefining the context of his situation. The recent tendency to regard him as a figure of tragic heroism should not obscure what others have regarded as his dangerous potential for blasphemy. He poses a fundamental threat to the identity of his three friends, for in confronting him they risk their lives. They do not lightly dismiss him, thereby preserving their beliefs intact and unchallenged; time and again they face his assaults upon them and their world.

In the sometimes oblique give-and-take of the dialogue, the issues are defined and a radical individualizing occurs. Job is one individual, a unique life, and he will not permit his sufferings to be accounted for in relation to a sinful community, whether of his own immediate family or as extended through ancestors. If Job's suffering is his, so must be the crime. This is a view that found acceptance in old Israel—we need only recall the deity's response to Baruch's "What about me?" (Jeremiah 45) or the reason given by the deuteronomistic historian for the sudden death of Josiah in his prime (2 Kings 23:26–27)—but Job breaks from this perspective. Ezekiel's assertions of the distribution of divine justice in direct accord with individual human worth (Ezekiel 14 and 18) are also rejected in spite of the numerous variations presented by Job's friends.

The individual human life is here defined within the brackets of individual birth and death. Within these limits a person exists; within them meaning must be found and justice demonstrated. Although Job toys for a moment with the hope of some existence beyond death, this escape will not serve (Job 14; the problematic text of Job 19:25–27 makes its thrust difficult to interpret), for death offers no solution to the basic issue of a renewed or transformed relation with his god (Job 10:18–22).

Throughout the poem Job affirms his integrity and innocence. If the course of human events is under divine guidance, then the god is not just. But he never questions the deity's absolute sovereignty. His god is a real opponent; before him mortals are but grass or fleeting sparks (Job 14:1–6); and the contest is ultimately one-sided. He must fall before his divine opponent, yet this too is unjust:

> God will not turn back his anger;
>> beneath him bowed the helpers of Rahab.
> How can I then answer him,
>> choosing my words with him?
> Though I am innocent, I cannot answer him;
>> I must appeal for mercy to my accuser.
> If I summoned him and he answered me,

I would not believe that he was listening to my voice.
For he crushes me with a tempest,
   and multiplies my wounds without cause;
he will not let me get my breath,
   but fills me with bitterness.
If it is a contest of strength, behold him!
   If it is a matter of justice, who can summon him?
Though I am innocent, my own mouth would condemn me;
   though I am blameless, he would prove me perverse.
I am blameless; I regard not myself;
   I loathe my life.
It is all one; therefore I say,
   he destroys both the blameless and the wicked.
When disaster brings sudden death,
   he mocks at the calamity of the innocent.
The earth is given into the hand of the wicked;
   he covers the faces of its judges—
     if it is not he, who then is it?

(Job 9:13–24)

Only in the laments of Jeremiah is so blunt a charge leveled against the deity.

The dialogue ends with the issue undecided. Job utters his oath of innocence, concluding with a formal self-imposed curse:

Oh, that I had one to hear me!
   (Here is my signature! Let the Almighty answer me!)
Oh, that I had the indictment written by my adversary!
Surely I would carry it on my shoulder;
   I would bind it on me as a crown;
I would give him an account of all my steps;
   like a prince I would approach him.

If my land has cried out against me,
   and its furrows have wept together;
if I have eaten its yield without payment,
   and caused the death of its owners;
let thorns grow instead of wheat,
   and foul weeds instead of barley.

(Job 31:35–40)

The God's Answer

More than once Job calls attention to the radical gulf separating the deity from humankind and dreams of some sort of mediator who might bring them together (Job 7:17–21; 9:1–12; 9:15–16):

For he is not a man, as I am, that I might answer him,
   that we should come to trial together.

> There is no umpire between us,
>> who might lay his hand upon us both,
> Let him take his rod away from me,
>> and let not dread of him terrify me.
> Then I would speak without fear of him,
>> for I am not so in myself.
>
> (Job 9:32–35)

In fact, Job and his god are brought together, and the mediator is none other than Yahweh himself. This time it is the deity, not Job, who redefines the framework within which the basic issue of a renewed or transformed relationship between man and god will be confronted.

In a forceful if brutal series of rhetorical questions the deity marshals all creation to his side, and Job is overwhelmed. He realizes in a quite new way what he himself had said earlier—that human beings *are* insignificant before the creator of the universe. This disjunction between deity and mortal climaxes in the second divine speech in which Behemoth and Leviathan, cosmic chaotic monsters before which human beings have always stood in dread, are presented as mere playthings in the deity's hands. It cannot be overemphasized that in this divine self-revelation there is absolutely no mention of any of the great themes of Israel's old stories. The god is presented solely as creator of the universe, as the one who set chaos within its limits.

Diverse evaluations have been made of this divine speech. For a few it is the response of a divine bully beating his subject into submission. For others it is a forceful statement of the deity's grandeur, a declaration of his independence from all human structures and dogmatic systems—even those that define the god as just—which have but limited usefulness in the unbounded diversity and force of nature. Even Job's oath and his demand that the deity enter the court and indict him force the god into a frame too small to hold him.

Others find the god's answer to be no answer at all but only a seductive dodge of the issue. Still others find the rhetorical questions a certification of a just and rational pattern in life even if this cannot be fully perceived by human beings. Finally, the divine answer is for some an act of acceptance by the deity in which contact is made between Job and his god.

Although there are elements of truth in all these evaluations, we suggest giving attention to the first lines of the epilogue, in which the poet, in linking his own work with the old folk tale, may offer some clue to his intention: "After Yahweh had spoken these words to Job, Yahweh said to Eliphaz the Temanite: 'My wrath is kindled against you and against your two friends; *for you have not spoken of me what is right, as my servant Job has*'" (Job 42:7, italics added). While it is possible that the italicized reference is only to Job's final words in 42:1–6, it is more likely to encompass the totality of what he has had to say. Why are the friends who had appeared as the deity's defenders now rebuked? Even more striking is the assertion that Job speaks "what is right" (or in another possible translation, "spoke as he ought"). How is it possible that he whose words have reached a pitch of blasphemy can now be affirmed?

A solution may be found in observing how Job and his friends speak as well as in what they say. Although the friends say a great deal about the deity, they never say anything *to* him; their words are always couched in the third person. Job, however, turns repeatedly from the friends to confront the deity directly (see Job 9–10, for example); and since he alone addresses Yahweh, he alone is open to a divine reply. Only in his manner of speech is there potential for a direct relationship. In a sense, the friends set their theological systems and statements of belief in the way of any direct encounter with the god they defend. The author seems to say that a relationship cannot be sustained when one party closes himself off, even in a shell of dogma, but relationships are possible, even when founded in outrage, where there is direct communication.

Perhaps this is what the author wishes finally to give his fellow exiles. Although there is only silence here about Israel's historical situation, it is asserted that a relation between individuals and the god is possible if the complex systems of belief and dogma that individuals construct are not permitted to limit the deity's sovereignty. Whatever new songs and stories the heirs of old Israel will now form are to be recognized as imaginations of the human heart and not a substitute for the deity whose freedom is absolute.

The poem of Job may have served the exiles as a dramaturgic substitute for the cultic reliving of the sacred stories of old Israel, presented perhaps during their coming together on those painful days when the old stories had previously been relived. Then, perhaps, the strength was found to ask questions that seemed too dreadful to ask but that had been forced on them by all they had lived through and still faced. In bringing such questions together and giving them a new form, the drama began to shape a new community. Through honest confrontation with hard questions the exiles turn from the god of old Israel to a god who touches their life anew.

PHILOSOPHICAL WISDOM

The author of the Book of Job was a highly educated man of wide-ranging interests who not only drew his imagery, motifs, and themes from the varied literature of the Near East but also addressed questions concerning the world's pattern as each individual perceives it. That he avoided the fundamental themes of the stories of ancient Israel seems, within the context of the times, to reflect a negative judgment on this heritage. Although his work eludes strict classification, he did draw upon wisdom material in the exemplum of the ideal pious man and in the vast listing of natural phenomena in Job 38–39, and it is therefore possible that he was trained in a wisdom school.

To review, the earliest aphoristically expressed wisdom was an attempt to locate order in, and to exercise a measure of control over, the world by putting experience into words and by drawing comparisons and contrasts between differing things, actions, or persons. In society's smaller and simpler forms men and women who are especially adept at expressing this *predidactic wisdom* are venerated as sages, but the expression occurs on only a limited scale with a very restricted range of experience taken into account.

In time this initial form of expression may be expanded in one or two directions. On the one hand, more wide-ranging and systematic attempts to order the natural world may be developed in the form of onomastica—i.e., long protoscientific lists of varied phenomena such as trees, animals, or occupations (see 1 Kings 4:33)—which are used to teach about the world's variety. On the other hand, the earlier sayings may be used for purposes of advice, admonition, and instruction. In this *didactic wisdom* new emphasis and use are given to older sayings, and new sayings are formed, although the concern remains primarily practical. Protoscientific lists, instructions, and admonitions were developed, collected, and utilized for the most part in urban centers and especially in the royal court. Solomon's name, for example, is identified with this type of wisdom material and even with some collections of songs, such as the Song of Songs in the Hebrew Bible.

Precisely when further developments took place in Israelite and Jewish tradition is not clear, but their results may be seen in the Book of Job, in the poem of Job 28, in the initial chapters of Proverbs, and in the Book of Ecclesiastes. These works reflect a tradition of *postdidactic* or *philosophical wisdom* which sought to identify the essential patterns of the universe and to explore their availability to human comprehension. Because this is Hebraic material the questions are generally cast in terms of the relationship between man and the deity, who is sometimes but not always designated as Yahweh, the god of Israel.

The crisis of 587 B.C.E. must have served as a watershed for wisdom circles as well, for the destruction of the nation and ensuing exile raised questions about order and justice in creation with a new urgency, and the judgment on older traditions encouraged a search for new forms in which to ask questions and seek answers. The direct exposure of the exiles to the varied literary traditions of the larger world provided new possibilities for those prepared to accept them. Thus the author of Job made use of an old tale, probably of Mesopotamian origin; and, as the Book of Job makes clear, the results of new inquiry sometimes opposed the assertions of divine order and justice that lay behind most older Israelite tradition as well as the practical advice of the wise teacher.

Wisdom's Call and Character

The first nine chapters of Proverbs offer units that are longer and more fully developed than the brief sayings in the following chapters. This need not

204   indicate that this material postdates chapters 10–31, for some of it may predate
the exile. What distinguishes chapters 1–9 from the remainder of the book is the
highly appealing personification of a figure called Wisdom (*hokmah* in Hebrew)
and her counterpart named Folly, both of whom directly address the reader with
great charm. In seductive tones that suggest the appeals of ancient Near Eastern
fertility cults and their goddesses, Lady Wisdom summons young men, offering
them life and lasting happiness:

> Does not wisdom call,
>   does not understanding raise her voice?
> On the heights beside the way,
>   in the paths she takes her stand;
>
> "To you, O men, I call,
>   and my cry is to the sons of men."
>
> (Proverbs 8:1–4)
>
> "Take my instruction instead of silver,
>   and knowledge rather than choice gold;
> for wisdom is better than jewels,
>   and all that you may desire cannot compare with her."
>
> (Proverbs 8:10–11)
>
> "I have counsel and sound wisdom,
>   I have insight, I have strength.
> By me kings reign,
>   and rulers decree what is just;
> by me princes rule,
>   and nobles govern the earth.
> I love those who love me,
>   and those who seek me diligently find me.
> Riches and honor are with me,
>   enduring wealth and prosperity.
> My fruit is better than gold, even fine gold,
>   and my yield than choice silver."
>
> (Proverbs 8:14–19; see also 9:1–6,
and contrast Folly's call in 9:13–18)

She offers advice, truth, and understanding that will bring authority, respect,
enduring wealth, and long life.

In other instances a teacher appears in the role of a father who addresses
the student as his son, forcefully recommending Wisdom and what she offers in
admonitions not unlike those of older teachers:

> Hear, O sons, a father's instruction,
>   and be attentive, that you may gain insight;

for I give you good precepts:
do not forsake my teaching.
When I was a son with my father,
tender, the only one in the sight of my mother,
he taught me, and said to me,
"Let your heart hold fast my words;
keep my commandments, and live;
do not forget, and do not turn away
from the words of my mouth.
Get wisdom; get insight.
Do not forsake her, and she will keep you;
love her, and she will guard you.
The beginning of wisdom is this: Get wisdom,
and whatever you get, get insight.
Prize her highly, and she will exalt you;
she will honor you if you embrace her.
She will place on your head a fair garland;
she will bestow on you a beautiful crown."

(Proverbs 4:1–9)

In Proverbs 8:22–31 Lady Wisdom claims to be the first of Yahweh's creative acts and to have been present before the earth itself was formed. Indeed, she may herself have played a formative role in the creation of the universe—possibly, for the meaning of the term often translated as "workman" in verse 30 is disputed. If she is a goddess created by Yahweh to exist alongside him, little in old Israelite tradition has prepared us for her appearance. That she may be a poetic personification of the deity's creative and sustaining power as it is manifest in the patterns of the cosmos seems the more likely option within the broad setting of early Hebraic tradition.

Within the wider context of the Near Eastern and Mediterranean world, however, a goddess of this sort would readily have been accepted, and there is evidence that Yahweh and a possibly female counterpart as well were worshiped within a Jewish military colony at Elephantine, Egypt, during the early centuries of exile. If the author of Proverbs 8:22–31 intended no more than a poetic description of Yahweh's wisdom revealed in creation, the unit takes a line that is highly susceptible to misunderstanding in this wider setting.

Whichever option is accepted, it must be emphasized that in this hymn wisdom is part of the creative process itself. Wisdom is here Yahweh as he is made available to the world and perceived by human experience. Lady Wisdom did play an active role in the creation, for it is stated elsewhere that Yahweh "by wisdom founded the earth, by understanding he established the heavens" (Proverbs 3:19). Here, then, as in Job 38–41, the created natural order is the sphere in which Yahweh is best encountered.

Although others in the ancient world comprehended their gods primarily within the natural world, the early prophets had inveighed against these gods because their cults had been viewed as a fundamental threat to ancient Yahwism. Yet Israel knew that Yahweh, too, used and was revealed by nature's forces (Hosea). Psalm 19, for example, states that "the heavens are telling the glory of God;/and the firmament proclaims his handiwork." But the psalm moves on quickly to speak about Yahweh's ordinances and commandments, which were set within the Moses-Sinai story, rooted in a prior experience of the deity on the historical level of exodus and conquest. In the oracles of the Second Isaiah, however, the order of priorities has shifted, for here it is Yahweh the creator of heaven and earth whose promises can be trusted to bring about a new exodus and rebuild Zion. In the Book of Job, both in Yahweh's speeches and in the dialogue, the created order is the sphere in which the deity is encountered and comprehended; other traditions are ignored.

Thus, in the period following the death of Israel, there was a new orientation toward creation themes and myths, and the world of nature became a primary locus of divine revelation. But the image of El/Yahweh as creator stood at the heart of the David-Zion story, certifying its promises. We therefore witness here a shift in primary emphasis not without precedent in old Israel, but there are limits within this new orientation as well. These are presented in a poetic unit inserted into the Book of Job and now composing chapter 28.

The unit begins as a song praising the capacity of human beings to master, control, and utilize nature (Job 28:1–11). Human knowledge and technical power seem unlimited:

> He [the human being] cuts out channels in the rocks,
> and his eye sees every precious thing.
> He binds up the streams so that they do not trickle,
> and the thing that is hid he brings forth to light.
>
> (Job 28:10–11)

But immediately the question is posed: "Where shall wisdom be found? And where is the place of understanding?" (Job 28:12). For all their abilities, human beings cannot plumb the wisdom of Yahweh; even Death hears but rumors of it. The deity alone beholds wisdom in full:

> God understands the way to it,
> and he knows its place.
> For he looks to the ends of the earth,
> and sees everything under the heavens.
> When he gave to the wind its weight,
> and meted out the waters by measure;
> when he made a decree for the rain,
> and a way for the lightning of the thunder;
> then he saw it and declared it;
> he established it, and searched it out.
>
> (Job 28:23–27)

The order in the created universe reflects the wisdom of Yahweh but also certifies the limitations on human wisdom. The divine speeches in Job are cast in just these terms; they may reveal an ordered cosmos, but first and foremost they are assertions of divine freedom from human control and comprehension. For humankind, recognition of the deity's sovereignty is wisdom enough:

> And he said to man,
> "Behold, the fear of Yahweh, that is wisdom;
> and to depart from evil is understanding."
>
> (Job 28:28)

Nature both reveals and conceals the creator, just as it both supports and destroys human life.

KOHELET

Human limitations and nature's opacity are nowhere better expressed than in the work of a man called Kohelet (probably "assembler") in Hebrew and "the preacher" in Western tradition, though he is more a teacher than a preacher. His book is Ecclesiastes (a rough Greek translation of his title), which later Jewish tradition, taking a clue from the author's literary stance in 1:12–2:26, assigned to Solomon, some calling it the product of his jaded old age. Although we do not know the author's name, he is described in the epilogue (Ecclesiastes 12:9–14) as a teacher and artful composer of wise sayings. He appears to be in the line of the older wise teachers who taught the art of successful and happy living to youths whose families could afford his fees.

Vanity of Vanities

Kohelet's instructions on how to live have value insofar as they may generally be said to work, but no structure can be built upon them that permits a sense of harmony with the cosmos and its creator. Further, there is no communication whatsoever with the author's god because his understanding of the deity will not permit it. In Kohelet's view, we live our lives in a world of circular movement, and to think that we have found something new is merely a sign of our finiteness, for we neither remember well enough nor observe broadly enough to know whether anything is new. While there is a creator god and there is order in his creation, neither can be known in a way that will lay a foundation for lasting confidence, for wisdom is limited and ultimately empty as well. Hence Ecclesiastes ends with a bittersweet charge to the young, a moving allegory on old age (Ecclesiastes 11:9–12:9), and the observation, "Vanity of vanities, says the Preacher, all is vanity."

Ecclesiastes does not progress from stated premises to reasoned conclusions but meditates on a basic theme that took shape in Kohelet's own mind. Although advice on how to live is scattered throughout the work, the predominant

208 theme consists of observations on the limitations of human knowledge, a stark denial that the created universe is either just or rational, and an assertion of the radical separation of human beings from their creator. It seems to have been a daybook—a collection of largely private jottings about daily observations—and was probably made public by student admirers after Kohelet's death. These are the reflections of an old man who has lived long and fully but who now sees it all passing from him. Although he is sensitive to human suffering, his own pain is of the sort found in everyday life, and it appears to have led in his case to weary acceptance and analysis rather than to sustained outrage.

Circularity of Nature   The circularity of nature is mirrored in the opening and closing words of the book: "Vanity of vanities; vanity of vanities! All is vanity" (Ecclesiastes 1:2; 12:8). The word we translate as "vanity" is the Hebrew *hebel* denoting a fog or mist, something having no definable form or quality, something that cannot be grasped. This thematic word is interlaced throughout the work and reinforced by other repeated phrases such as "a striving after [or feeding on] the wind" so that Kohelet's conclusion is kept ever before the reader: all is emptiness.

Considering the cycles of nature (Ecclesiastes 1:4–7), Kohelet finds only a wearisome mechanical repetition going nowhere and revealing little. Then comes a devastating phrase: "There is nothing new under the sun." In the context of old Israelite tradition it was precisely the totally new and unexpected, Yahweh's breaking into human history in ever new ways, that formed the essence of the old stories and songs and the words of the prophets. Israel's challenge was to comprehend Yahweh's new acts, a challenge most keenly felt by the prophets. But in Kohelet's thoughts there is no reference to the events, persons, or themes of the old stories. Indeed, there is very little that clearly identifies the book as Israelite or Jewish. Although it is written in Hebrew, the deity is not called Yahweh or given any other name or title. He is called "God" or, in an attempt to gain even greater abstraction and distance, "the God." Quite likely the name Yahweh carried so much traditional content that it was unsuited to Kohelet's needs.

Human Activity   When observation of nature yields little, Kohelet plunges into life, steeping his mind in wisdom (Ecclesiastes 1:13–18), pursuing pleasure, and building a paradisiacal setting for his enjoyments (Ecclesiastes 2:1–11). Here he assumes the guise of Solomon, whose legendary wisdom and wealth (1 Kings 10) would equip him like no other to pursue the experiment. But neither wisdom nor pleasure has lasting value; he seeks some ultimate enduring truth which he does not find. It is true, he says, that wisdom is better than folly, but only in degree, not in kind, for both the wise and the foolish die, and wisdom exacts its own price (Ecclesiastes 1:18; 2:12–15). He therefore concludes: "Nothing better for a man than that he should eat and drink, and find enjoyment in his toil. This also, I saw, is from the hand of God. . . . For to the man who pleases him God gives wisdom and knowledge and joy; but to the sinner he gives the work of gathering and heaping, only to give to one who pleases God. This also is vanity and a striving after wind" (Ecclesiastes 2:24–26). But even this conclusion is inconclusive. Kohelet knows that the pleasurable moments in life must not be missed because they offer a brief respite from angst. That they will not last, however, becomes an obsession toward the end of the book (Ecclesiastes 11:9–12:9).

The final segment of chapter 2 employs what appears to be conventional religious language: "the one who pleases God," "the sinner," "the God," but in Kohelet's usage this language is stripped to its basics. Sin is not here an act of disobedience or rebellion. At this level, sin is folly or blindness (the fundamental meaning of the Hebrew *hata* is "to miss the mark or path"). It is, for example, to fail to enjoy the fruit of one's toil when such enjoyment is possible or to overvalue work and its rewards. To please god is to recognize and follow life's set path, to take things as they come and not to place values on them that they cannot carry. Even his use of "the God" strips that term of all personal or relational quality. It denotes the sustaining force that orders the cosmos, not one to whom lament, thanksgiving, or petition is offered. The god is not even addressed in anger, for the gulf between deity and creature is here absolute. Mortals cannot cross it, and the deity does not.

Human Finitude The third chapter commences with a hymn affirming that every act or event has its fitting place in the scheme of things. There are, to be sure, patterns undergirding the created universe, but the question is whether human beings can perceive them and order their lives about them. The wise teachers would say yes: the good can be known and acted upon, and rewards will come to those who do so.

Kohelet agrees that humans may attain limited knowledge but believes that the limits finally undercut any essential meaning found in life. The god who "has made everything beautiful in its time" has also "put eternity [others would translate the term as "forgetfulness"] in man's mind, yet so that he cannot find out what the God has done from the beginning to the end" (Ecclesiastes 3:11). At the vital core of the human being is a limiting factor that is both a curse and a salvation: a curse because it is a limitation; a salvation because its anaesthetizing effect preserves sanity. Limited awareness allows us to live within human confines without knowing that there are limitations. We need not look into the bottomless pit every moment of our lives; we can direct our attention closer to the everyday:

> Go, eat your bread with enjoyment, and drink your wine with a merry
> heart, for God has already approved what you do. Let your garments be
> always white; let not oil be lacking on your head. Enjoy life with the wife
> whom you love, all the days of your vain life which he has given you under

the sun, because that is your portion in life and in your toil at which you toil under the sun. Whatever your hand finds to do, do it with all your might; for there is no work or thought or knowledge or wisdom in Sheol, to which you are going.

(Ecclesiastes 9:7–10)

Here there is gusto in the call to live meaningfully in the face of emptiness, but the recognition of emptiness leads elsewhere to a tone of depression (Ecclesiastes 7:1–4; 6:1–6) that is most pronounced when Kohelet faces the fact of death (Ecclesiastes 3:19–22; 12:1–7). In chapter 9:4 he cites what appears to be a popular saying: "But he who is joined with the living has hope,/for a living dog is better than a dead lion." To this Kohelet assents but adds his own ironic twist:

> For the living know that they will die,
>   but the dead know nothing,
>   and they have no more reward.
> (Ecclesiastes 9:5)

Not only do the dead not know that they will die, "but the memory of them is lost. Their love and their hate have already perished, and they have no more forever any share in all that is done under the sun" (Ecclesiastes 9:5–6). For the Israelite and early Jew, immortality lay in offspring or in works that would live on in the memory of others, but Kohelet regards these possibilities as no more reliable than human beings are trustworthy (Ecclesiastes 1:11; 6:1–6; 7:15–18).

The several works considered in this chapter exhibit a fundamental recasting of basic issues. As previously noted, there is little that is distinctly Israelite in them. The author of Job, the wise men, and Kohelet all draw heavily on the thought patterns and literary forms of the contemporary Near East in their search for ways to comprehend the new. The realm of nature and creation mythology are now predominant, and the individual—the single life between birth and death—is the center of concern. Kohelet has no sacred community about him, and Job likewise is isolated and alone. Even when he receives a divine answer to his challenge, it is as a reply to one man facing his god, and the response is a radical statement of divine freedom.

BIBLIOGRAPHIC NOTE

The Book of Job

> Dhorme, Edouard P. *A Commentary on the Book of Job*. London: Thomas Nelson & Sons, 1967. A reissue of an old but useful depth study of Job.
>
> Gordis, Robert, *The Book of God and Man: A Study of Job*. Chicago: University of Chicago Press, 1965.

Pope, Marvin H. *Job*. Garden City, N.Y.: Doubleday & Co., 1973.

———. "Job, Book of." In *The Interpreter's Dictionary of the Bible*, vol. 2, pp. 911–25. Nashville: Abingdon Press, 1962.

Terrien, Samuel L. "Introduction and Exegesis to Job." In *The Interpreter's Bible*, vol. 4, pp. 877–1198. Nashville: Abingdon Press, 1954. An excellent introduction.

———. *Job: Poet of Existence*. Indianapolis: Bobbs-Merrill, 1958.

Zuckerman, B. "Job, Book of." In *The Interpreter's Dictionary of the Bible: Supplementary Volume*, pp. 479–81. Nashville: Abingdon Press, 1976.

Proverbs 1–9

McKane, William. *Proverbs*. Philadelphia: Westminster Press, 1970.

Scott, R. B. Y. *Proverbs. Ecclesiastes*. Anchor Bible 18. Garden City, N.Y.: Doubleday & Co., 1965.

von Rad, Gerhard. *Wisdom in Israel*. Nashville: Abingdon Press, 1972.

Whybray, R. N. *Wisdom in Proverbs: The Concept of Wisdom in Proverbs 1–9*. Studies in Biblical Theology, no. 45. London: SCM Press, 1965.

The Book of Ecclesiastes

Blank, Sheldon H. "Ecclesiastes." In *The Interpreter's Dictionary of the Bible*, vol. 2, pp. 7–13. Nashville: Abingdon Press, 1962.

Gordis, Robert. *Koheleth: The Man and His World*. New York: Jewish Theological Seminary of America Press, 1951. A very useful introduction and translation.

Priest, J. F. "Ecclesiastes." In *The Interpreter's Dictionary of the Bible: Supplementary Volume*, pp. 249–50. Nashville: Abingdon Press, 1976.

Scott, R. B. Y. *Proverbs. Ecclesiastes*. Anchor Bible 18. Garden City, N.Y.: Doubleday & Co., 1965.

Wright, Addison G. "The Riddle of the Sphinx: The Structure of the Book of Qoheleth." In *Studies in Ancient Israelite Wisdom*, edited by James L. Crenshaw, pp. 245–66. New York: KTAV Publishing House, 1976.

10 WILDERNESS AND TEMPLE

Primary readings: *Genesis 1–11 and 17; Exodus 19, 25–31, 35–40*
Leviticus 17–26; Deuteronomy 34
Joel; Malachi
1 and 2 Chronicles; Ezra, Nehemiah

The first five books of the Old Testament are today regarded as a separate unit which Jews call the Torah. Although popular tradition has long ascribed this unit to Moses, he was not the author of the material in its present form, which took shape in the course of a long and extremely complex process. At the heart of the Torah is an ancient story that first appeared in creedlike recitations in Deuteronomy 26 and Joshua 24. In its oldest form—that used by the Yahwist—it climaxed in the taking of the land of promise as recounted in Joshua.

But the Torah does not include the Book of Joshua. Although everything else is there—creation and a prehistory, the patriarchs and their treasured promise, Egyptian bondage and release, wilderness wanderings, encampment at Sinai, and departure for the promised land—the promise remains unfulfilled at the end of the Book of Deuteronomy. Except for some land east of the River Jordan, the promised land is not entered. Somehow, when these first five books were set apart and given their special designation, the Book of Joshua was set at the head of the so-called Former Prophets, which range through 2 Kings and comprise what we have called the deuteronomistic history.

From the Torah's vision, then, it would seem that fulfillment of Yahweh's promise was yet to come, and it is clear that the old Moses-Sinai story has here undergone a radical transformation. This recasting of the ancient story was the work of Jewish circles in exile and in diaspora whom scholars now designate as priests (P) because of their clear interest in establishing and regulating the cult. It was still another response to the crisis of 587 B.C.E.

PRIESTLY CIRCLES

On the basis of literary style, vocabulary, content, and theological perspective, scholars now believe the first five books of the Old Testament to be a combination of four once-distinct strata. Three of these have already been considered in relation to Israel's religious traditions: the Yahwist (J), the Elohist (E), and Deuteronomy (D). The fourth is P, an outgrowth of the exile and early postexilic years. The priests in Babylonian exile and the eastern diaspora reveal interests similar to those found in the last chapters of Ezekiel. Much of P (that is, most of the latter part of Exodus and all of Leviticus) consists of collections of laws dealing with the establishment of the Yahweh cult, its personnel, and its proper execution. Because P is also interlaced with lengthy genealogies—those long lists of "begats" and names and ages that epitomize for many the extreme tedium in reading parts of the Bible—and exhibits a rather flat narrative style, it is regarded as dull even by many scholars.

That much of P makes for uninteresting reading today, however, should not obscure the daring vision and reorientation of older traditions that these priests offered the Jews of their day. For those who must live in exile they presented a new life style that would provide them a distinct identity as Jews and that would therefore become formative for later Judaism. Like the prophets of the exile, they asserted that Yahweh's authority and action must still define the lives of his people, for Yahweh had not abandoned them and had yet to perform his greatest works. The priests also sought typological roots in the past for their vision of the future. If that future seems less immediate in P than in the prophets' words, this simply reflects the continuing experience of life in an alien setting and a concern for the daily lives of those so situated.

Yahweh as Creator

Like the Yahwist, the priests begin their narrative with an account of creation (which now stands first in Genesis 1:1–2:4 and is quite distinct from that of J). Carefully constructed on a seven-day pattern with repetitive key phrases, a cosmic perspective, and a solemn tone, it is liturgical in character, a recitation for formal occasions of public reading and worship. It may once have been a separate document, the first fruit of priestly activity in exile, for when set against the *Enuma Elish*, the Babylonian account certifying Marduk to be the creator of heaven and earth, it has a marked polemical thrust. In building his announcement of Yahweh's new action for his people, the Second Isaiah set Yahweh in direct opposition to Marduk on the basis of creation themes. Genesis 1:1–2:4 arises from the same setting and, on close reading, also stands in an antagonistic relationship to the *Enuma Elish*, both recalling the Babylonian epic and turning Marduk's own story against him.

In the beginning there is watery chaos from which an ordered universe will be produced (the first two verses of Genesis do not offer a statement of creation out of nothing). But in Genesis this watery chaos—called *tehom*, a term akin to Tiamat, the name of the monstrous deity of the chaotic salt waters in the *Enuma Elish*—is an inert thing, not a living creature. In Genesis, creation is a separation and ordering of inert chaos, and the created universe is not an assembly of deities with assigned stations and functions.

Light drives back darkness; the waters divide and dry land appears; vegetation is formed; the heavenly bodies are fixed in their courses to mark times and seasons; varied forms of animal life are created. Each is affirmed as the god's handiwork, but he alone is divine; all else is mere creation. Climaxing creation is the formation of human beings in the "image of God," and these beings are charged to "be fruitful and multiply, and fill the earth and subdue it; and have dominion over the fish of the sea and over the birds of the air and over every living thing that moves upon the earth" (Genesis 1:28).

Both Genesis and the *Enuma Elish* begin with a watery chaos from which the created universe is formed, the stages of creation take place in roughly the same order, and human beings stand at the end. In Genesis, however, Yahweh is the creator: the god of defeated Israel, not the god of triumphant Babylon. And all other Mesopotamian deities, linked as they are to aspects of the world of nature, are reduced to mere things; for Yahweh alone is divine, the universe is not. In Genesis, moreover, human beings are formed in the deity's image to rule and subdue the created world. In the Babylonian account they are said to have been created as an afterthought merely to relieve the many gods of heavy toil.

The assertion that human beings are to subdue and rule all creation carries a force of meaning that is lost in most translations, a force that approaches "rape and pillage," and this may be the intent here. For the priests dare to assert to confused, defeated, and hopeless exiles that they are charged by their god the creator to use, enjoy, and govern nature, although this is the very force that their Babylonian captors worshiped and served. A whole world-view is overturned; the supernatural is stripped from the world of nature; Marduk is met on his own ground and is set aside. Surely the exiles would recognize that the deity who could bring order to chaotic waters was not powerless before the historical chaos that seemed to govern the lives of his people.

An Unfinished Story   The defeat of chaos is also the thrust of the flood narrative that follows the account of creation. In an account found in the Babylonian epic of Gilgamesh, the flood seems an unreasoned act that terrifies the gods themselves who were so frightened by the deluge that they ascended to heaven and cowered like dogs. In Genesis, however, the flood is the instrument of a righteous deity, is easily overcome by him (Genesis 6–9), and creation is renewed (Genesis 9:1–7).

The priests' narrative is then punctuated by a series of genealogical lists (Genesis 5:1–32; 10:1–32; 11:10–32, and so on) and its structure defined by a number of god-initiated relationships that have the form of unconditional covenants. The first covenant concludes with the act of creation, certified by the evaluation: "And behold, it was very good" (Genesis 1:31), and the day of Sabbath rest is instituted (Genesis 2:1–4). The second covenant is found in the assurance given to Noah and his sons that the human race will not again be handed over to chaos. Humanity is provided further sustenance in being allowed to eat meat (Genesis 9:3; compare Genesis 1:29). In the third covenant Abraham is singled out from all humanity and is told, "I will make my covenant between me and you, and will multiply you exceedingly" (Genesis 17:2). From this point, all male offspring of Abraham are to bear the sign of this relationship on their flesh in the form of circumcision.

In the fourth covenant the deity reveals himself by the name Yahweh, first to Moses and then to his people at Sinai (see the encounter between Yahweh and Moses in Exodus 6), and in the context of this final covenant the vast bulk of the priestly material is to be found, much of it no doubt reaching well back into the life of old Israel. Details regarding the establishment of the cult, the construction of its apparatus, instructions for distinguishing the several levels of temple personnel, regulations for the conduct of day-to-day and special services, taboos, rites of purification, and much more are here brought together in larger and smaller collections and put into definitive form. Much of the incidental lore was probably passed down orally from father to son as the latter was trained to take his place in the specialized world of the cult. Certain large collections, such as the so-called Holiness Code in Leviticus 17–26, represent intermediate stages in the process and are likewise brought into the larger priestly work. All are given the form of laws set forth to Moses by Yahweh and delivered by Moses to the Israelites encamped at the foot of Mount Sinai.

Set amid an unfinished narrative about the formation of Israel, this vast body of cultic lore seems at once irrelevant and a powerful affirmation. On the one hand, these laws cannot be observed in the wilderness, on alien soil, in exile; the temple in Jerusalem is necessary for their execution. On the other hand, their very preservation in such detail affirms that the temple in Jerusalem will once again be the point of meeting between Yahweh and his people.

The necessity of writing down and defining this formerly fluid lore was in all likelihood the result of the radical dislocation of 587 B.C.E. and the destruction of the temple. Whereas a stable nation could assume a steady succession of generations and preservation of the heritage, the nation's death and exile had made such preservation uncertain at a time when for some the need was greater than ever. For death and exile did not relegate this lore to a dead past; it would be needed when Israel once again lived in her own land and served her god in cultic worship. In short, these vast collections of law are a testimony to the priests' certainty that Yahweh's promise was still valid, and their addition to the ancient story not only alters its character but reaffirms the claim made when the ending was cut off.

A Life Style for the Wilderness

While most of the legal material in the priestly document deals with the homeland, its cult, and its temple, other regulations do not. These are linked with the covenant relationships established, first, between Yahweh and all humanity, then with Noah and his sons, and finally with Abraham and his seed. Linked to the six days of creation in Genesis 1, for example, was a seventh day when the god rested from his work (Genesis 2:1–4), setting an example for human beings to follow. Men and women at all social levels, from slave to monarch, are to refrain from labor on this day of Sabbath, which is to be set apart for prayer and praise, for studying the Torah, and, not least, for enjoying the good things the creator has provided. It is a day for reaffirming and strengthening ties with the deity. In time, among communities of Jews in diaspora, a special place would be established for study, prayer, and praise. This was the synagogue, and it would become the focus of Jewish life on the Sabbath.

After the flood Noah was given permission to eat meat as well as vegetables (Genesis 9:1–7), but there were restrictions on the manner in which animal flesh may be eaten. Above all, the life blood must not be in it, and additional dietary regulations concerning what may or may not be eaten and how food is to be prepared are found elsewhere in the Torah (Leviticus 11 and 17, for example). Finally, bound with the deity's promise to Abraham is an external sign of the relationship formed between the patriarch and his god. Each male in Abraham's line is to be circumcised to identify him as Yahweh's man (Genesis 17).

Two distinct characteristics are observable in these regulations. First, they do not require the temple for their observance; they may be enacted anywhere at any time by anyone who would bind his life to Yahweh. Second, they define a set of practices that are not followed by the gentile world at large. In the light of these factors, the regulations provide the basis for a style of life whose customs place the Jew to a degree outside the cultural mainstream. By distinguishing those who observe them, these customs do not permit the setting of deep roots into alien soil.

On the day of Sabbath rest, for example, normal activity did not cease in the world at large. Circumcision was not a practice that many observed in the Persian and later Greek worlds. Finally, in the Near East of antiquity, little social or business intercourse was conducted without recourse to the dining table. Contracts were concluded, marriages formed, land exchanged, friendships made and sustained over meals because partaking of another's fare was a sign of respect and trust. But such everyday intercourse was prevented if the kind of food one ate and the manner in which it was prepared were restricted in ways not characteristic of the outside world.

In each case ancient practices have been recast. Although we do not know the historical origin of the Sabbath, its observance is part of the Decalogue (Exodus 20:8–10) and Deuteronomy 5:12–14; note the different motive offered in each instance), and Amos condemns perfunctory observance in Amos 8:5–6. But observing the Sabbath in old Israel would not set one apart; it was a means of nurturing a relationship with the deity but not of distinguishing an individual from the immediate environment. Again, circumcision seems to be based in puberty rites; in older and less complex societies sexual maturity also signaled social maturity: a man married and became a full and accountable member of his community. But when circumcision becomes the norm for all male infants born into a Jewish family, it is no longer a rite of passage but a badge of identity as a Yahwist (this recasting seems to be reflected in the strange story in Exodus 4:24–26). Finally, the roots of the dietary laws are varied, complex, and obscure, reflecting among other things cultic taboos and hygienic needs, but in the context of diaspora they, too, identify one as a Yahwist.

In the priests' narrative the chosen people are last seen as pilgrims moving through alien land toward a goal to be fulfilled in another time and place, and this is the vision, drawn from the ancient story of their past, that the priests now hold out to the scattered sons and daughters of old Israel. They, too, are exiles encamped for a time in an alien land, and they, too, must focus their hopes on the promise ahead. Like the Israelites in the Sinai wilderness, they must avoid setting roots in the land through which they pass, for diaspora is not to become their permanent condition, and regulations must be adopted to facilitate this. They must resist assimilation into the world into which they are now dispersed because hope and heart and fundamental identity lay in the future.

Thus, the priestly document not only affirms Yahweh's continuing authority and action in the lives of his people but offers them a pattern for life that will ensure them a distinct identity. Although not everyone would accept this pattern, for many Jews the total vision offered a way to define their lives and to live with hope. It was therefore to have a profound effect on the further development of Judaism.

NEHEMIAH AND EZRA IN JERUSALEM

Since the destruction of Jerusalem this text has focused for the most part on the exiles in Babylon and on the larger eastern diaspora because in this setting occurred most of the creative attempts to confront that crisis. But life in the homeland was not dormant during this period. Nehemiah and Ezra had links with the priestly circles, and their work exhibits the first evidence of the profound impact of that vision on the homeland.

Very little is known about events in and around Jerusalem from the time the temple was completed in 515 B.C.E. until Nehemiah's arrival in 445, a period in which scholars generally place the books of Joel and Malachi. In essence, these books reveal a continuing struggle for survival and show that, in the aftermath of the dashed nationalistic hopes of Haggai and Zechariah, little had changed. Although the temple had been built, the rebukes found in segments of Haggai and Isaiah 56–66 were still appropriate, and hope for a fundamental change had waned. Little more was done to rebuild Jerusalem, probably because of tensions with officials in Samaria to the north. Both Joel and Malachi, the last in a long line of prophets, displayed a marked interest in the temple and its cultic worship; both looked to a future day of judgment and of blessing (Joel 3; Malachi 2:17–3:5); and to both men, present reality fell far short of future expectations.

A report of such present realities reached Nehemiah in the Persian court of Artaxerxes I in Susa (Nehemiah 1:1–3), where he was the king's cupbearer, an office with more authority than its title suggests and one permitting personal access to the king. Shocked by the state of affairs in the homeland, he obtained royal permission to go there as governor of Judah for a limited term. That he was in Jerusalem as an official of the king of Persia must be emphasized because, although much in his and Ezra's programs has a strongly separatist character, there is no hint in either of a nationalistic movement. They sought only a reformed Jewish province within the Persian empire, not the rebirth of a nation. All traces of that ideal had vanished with Zerubbabel, and many decades would elapse before it reappeared.

In a secret nocturnal excursion Nehemiah took stock of the situation in Jerusalem as soon as he arrived; then, against both internal and external opposition, he set about rebuilding the city's walls. This aroused concern among Sanballat, the governor of Samaria, Tobia the Ammonite, and Gershem, a leader of some Arab tribes, because a walled city was generally an independent city, and these men had vested interests in preventing the appearance of a rival power center in southern Syria-Palestine. Nevertheless, the walls went up with remarkable speed. But Nehemiah was less successful in reordering the community's internal life. In Palestine as well as in parts of diaspora, Jews and gentiles were intermingling freely, and Nehemiah sought to prevent this by breaking up all marriages between Jews and foreigners and by means of other rules set for community life and worship (Nehemiah 10:28–39 and 13:3–27). This program had only limited success, however.

Nehemiah's political difficulties and his plans for meeting them are detailed in his memoirs (Nehemiah 1:1–7:5). Other documents arising from the political struggles of this period are to be found in the books of Ezra and Nehemiah, where they are presented, however, in a telescoped and disordered way, making any reconstruction of details difficult. In the material's present form, Ezra seems to precede Nehemiah, with their careers in no way overlapping. Because this poses a number of historical problems, however, we here place Nehemiah in Jerusalem first, with Ezra appearing during his second term as governor.

At the end of his twelve-year term as governor, then, Nehemiah returned to Jerusalem to be reappointed for a second term. It is possible that Ezra came with him, also bearing Persian authority—his title can best be translated as "secretary for Jewish affairs"—and armed with a document that would succeed in ordering life in Jerusalem and the territory of Judah. Scholars generally agree that this was either the priestly document or the Torah in essentially its final form, for either the priests themselves or their heirs wove into P the combined Yahwist, Elohist, and Deuteronomy to form the Pentateuch as it is now shaped.

A public reading of segments of this material enabled Ezra to reorder community life around the vision of the priests (Nehemiah 9); that he was himself of priestly descent and also carried Persian authority was no doubt instrumental in his success. In this way Jerusalem was brought within the Torah's vision for Judaism and became the spiritual center for many Jews both at home and abroad. The Torah served well to define a distinct community within the relatively tolerant Persian empire. Nationalistic elements were muted within the priests' vision since a renewed nation Israel was envisaged only in terms of a vague and distant future. Claims of this sort, set in a story of the distant past and leading to no revolutionary outbreaks, the Persians could tolerate or ignore.

Of Nehemiah we know little and of Ezra even less, which is surprising in view of the second-Moses role he would come to have in Jewish tradition. Like Moses, he appears more as a part of the ongoing tradition than as a distinct historical personage. That there was an Ezra cannot be doubted, but the details of his career are lost. Under both Nehemiah and Ezra, however, the restoration of Jerusalem was completed, and a hierocracy was created—that is, a community centered about a cult and governed by priests along with officials appointed to represent a distant king. The vision of the Torah combined with political authority derived from the larger world led to the formation of a unique community in and about Jerusalem.

THE CHRONICLER'S HISTORY

The books of 1 and 2 Chronicles, together with those of Ezra and Nehemiah, comprise a unified account of Israel's history from Adam to Jerusalem near the end of the fifth century B.C.E. when the reformation brought about by Nehemiah and Ezra was completed. The account seeks to demonstrate that the hierocratic situation in effect at that time was the climax toward which Israel's story had been moving from the first. Although much of the chronicler's work parallels the deuteronomistic history (Joshua through 2 Kings), which seems to have served as one of its sources, his interests and certain of his fundamental presuppositions differ markedly from those informing the deuteronomistic corpus.

220 As presented by the chronicler, Israel's history falls into several unequal parts. 1 Chronicles offers a genealogical outline from Adam to David with chapters 10–29 devoted wholly to King David, whose personal faults, which are all too clear in 1 and 2 Samuel and 1 Kings, are studiously ignored. Instead, David is hallowed as the founder of the temple cult in Jerusalem, although he did not actually build the temple. The first nine chapters of 2 Chronicles are devoted to Solomon's execution of his father's plans. The remainder of this book is concerned with the history of Judah from Solomon's death through the exile and edict of Cyrus. Special attention is given to kings Jehoshaphat, Hezekiah, and Josiah, for each had played a notable role in the temple's history. Cyrus's decree permitting the exiles to return and the city to be rebuilt is repeated in the first chapter of Ezra, and the account continues through Ezra's own work in Jerusalem. To this the Book of Nehemiah is appended.

This history centers on the temple, its cult, priests, and ranks of supporting clergy and demonstrates that the fates of individual kings and the nation are directly related to their support or rejection of the temple. Little is said of the kingdom of northern Israel because, since the days of its first king, Jeroboam I, it had established rival centers of worship. Likewise little is said of Israelite cults and patterns of worship before the establishment of the temple.

In this history the chronicler finds a rigid doctrine of starkly individualistic reward and punishment. No member of the Davidic dynasty ruled or lived longer than King Manasseh, for example, and no king was judged to be more corrupt; on this point the deuteronomistic history and the Chronicles agree. Why should one so evil enjoy such a long and untroubled life? Although both histories agree that Josiah, his son and successor, was the finest king since David, he had died in battle in the middle of his life's work.

The deuteronomistic history does not answer directly but implies that Josiah suffered for his father's sins: "The fathers have eaten sour grapes, and the children's teeth are set on edge." But the chronicler will not accept this; in his view, each individual reaps what he has sown. In 2 Chronicle 33:10–13 Manasseh's long life and reign are attributed to his recognition of Yahweh while in captivity in Babylon:

> Yahweh spoke to Manasseh and to his people, but they gave no heed. Therefore Yahweh brought upon them the commanders of the army of the king of Assyria, who took Manasseh with hooks and bound him with fetters of bronze and brought him to Babylon. And when he was in distress he entreated the favor of Yahweh his God, and he humbled himself greatly before the God of his fathers. He prayed to him, and God received his entreaty and heard his supplication and brought him again to Jerusalem into his kingdom. Then Manasseh knew that Yahweh was God.

No mention is made of this event in 2 Kings. Assyrian records indicate that Manasseh was a vassal of Assyria; and while we cannot prove that he was not taken to Babylon and there had a conversion experience, the event fits too neatly into a preconception of divine retribution. Indeed, this is but one example of what several critics have described as the chronicler's shoddy historical method. Although we should not apply modern standards to ancient writers who had methods and concerns of their own, a suspicion remains that the chronicler's facts are not only selected and tailored but perhaps even constructed to fit theory. This is especially apparent in a comparison of two widely separated units dealing with King David. In 2 Samuel 24 it is Yahweh who sets out to punish David; in 1 Chronicles 21 Satan is responsible for the fate of Israel and her king. To the chronicler, the ideal king and temple planner just could not be punished by his god.

Once his intent and bias are clearly discerned, the chronicler provides us with useful items of historical interest. His construction of events during Josiah's reform, whose beginning he dates several years before the discovery of the book of the law, is probably nearer the truth than the account in 2 Kings. He is our only source for the history of Jerusalem and Judah during the period of exile and early diaspora, having preserved a number of documents purported to be from this later period, even if they are out of historical order and show some reconstruction along theological and Yahwistic lines (2 Chronicles 36:22–23 and Ezra 1–6).

But the chronicler's work exhibits a static quality, a willingness to accept the present situation as ideal and in no need of change. The dynamic open-endedness of the deuteronomistic history and the prophetic challenge and promise of the old sacred story are absent. To the chronicler it appears that Persia will rule the world forever; there is no sense that Yahweh has climactic works yet to be revealed. The work commends political quietism, acceptance of Persian rule, and recognition of the authority of the high priest in Jerusalem.

In less than a century, however, the Persian empire was shattered by the army of Alexander of Macedon. The world situation once again changed in fundamental ways, and Judaism faced new challenges in its attempts to discern and respond to the ways of its god in history. Before considering the profound impact of Alexander's conquests on early Judaism we must give attention to other attempts to come to terms with diaspora. The way of the priests was but one avenue, and only when it is seen in conjunction with other attempts to form a lifestyle can the creative variety of Judaism in the Persian world be appreciated.

BIBLIOGRAPHIC NOTE

The Priestly Document

Brueggemann, Walter. "The Kerygma of the Priestly Writer." In *The Vitality of Old Testament Traditions*, edited by Walter Brueggemann and Hans Walter Wolff, pp. 101–13. Atlanta: John Knox Press, 1975.

222   Cross, Frank Moore. "The Priestly Work." In *Canaanite Myth and Hebrew Epic: Essays in the History and the Religion of Israel*, pp. 293–325. Cambridge, Mass.: Harvard University Press, 1973.

Levine, B. A. "Priestly Writers." In *The Interpreter's Dictionary of the Bible: Supplementary Volume*, pp. 683–87. Nashville: Abingdon Press, 1976.

McEvenue, Sean E. *The Narrative Style of the Priestly Writer*. Rome: Biblical Institute Press, 1971.

Noth, Martin. *Leviticus*. Philadelphia: Westminster Press, 1975.

———. *Numbers*. Philadelphia: Westminster Press, 1968.

von Rad, Gerhard. *Genesis*. Philadelphia: Westminster Press, 1972.

Westermann, Claus. *Creation*. Philadelphia: Fortress Press, 1974.

1 and 2 Chronicles, Ezra, and Nehemiah

Freedman, David Noel. "The Purpose of the Chronicler." *Catholic Biblical Quarterly* 23 (1961): pp. 436–42.

Myers, Jacob M. *I Chronicles*. Garden City, N.Y.: Doubleday & Co., 1965.

———. *II Chronicles*. Garden City, N.Y.: Doubleday & Co., 1965.

———. *Ezra. Nehemiah*. Garden City, N.Y.: Doubleday & Co., 1965.

Pfeiffer, Robert H. "Chronicles I and II." In *The Interpreter's Dictionary of the Bible*, vol. 1, pp. 572–80. Nashville: Abingdon Press, 1962.

———. "Ezra and Nehemiah, Books of." In *The Interpreter's Dictionary of the Bible*, vol. 2, pp. 214–19. Nashville: Abingdon Press, 1962.

Talmon, S. "Ezra and Nehemiah: Books and Men." In *The Interpreter's Dictionary of the Bible: Supplementary Volume*, pp. 317–28. Nashville: Abingdon Press, 1976.

JUDAISM ENGAGING A GENTILE WORLD   11

Primary readings: Ruth; Jonah
                       Esther
                       Daniel 1–6

During the Persian period (539–333 B.C.E.) a vital shift occurred in the attitude of many of the heirs to old Israel. In describing it, the word *diaspora* replaces the word *exile*. Exile denotes a temporary state of affairs or at least the hope that it will be temporary. Exiles root their loyalties, hopes, and identity not in the alien place but in the homeland and await the day when their separation will be overcome. Diaspora, however, denotes a condition that is accepted, if not desired, as lasting a long time; it implies that the present situation and place of residence are now home. In Jeremiah's words to the Babylonian exiles of 598 B.C.E.: "Build houses and live in them; plant gardens and eat their produce. Take wives and have sons and daughters; take wives for your sons and give your daughters in marriage. . . . But seek the welfare of the city where I have sent you into exile, and pray to Yahweh on its behalf, for in its welfare you will find your welfare" (Jeremiah 29:5–7).

For the prophets, to whom exile was only a stage in Yahweh's greater plan for his people, the old Israelite religious traditions still possessed great potential. But as exile became diaspora the old symbols and stories lost their vitality for some; for others they seemed to have died with old Israel. Thus the author of Job, the wise men, and Kohelet made no reference to the thematic traditions of old Israel but broke new ground in seeking answers to fundamental religious questions.

There were others, now scattered across the face of the Near East, who adapted to diaspora through complete assimilation into the new context, which, after two or three generations, was not really new at all. One became Persian, Egyptian, Greek, or Syrian by accepting the language, customs, dress, values, loyalties, and, above all, the religion of the place into which events had thrust one. Many Jews in diaspora took this way by inaction and inertia if not with forethought and intention. Because it is the very nature of this way to obliterate the traces of those who take it, at best only a few characteristic names would distinguish them from the world into which they had merged. Most just vanished. Still others sought a way that would enable them to live in their new world fully and deeply while still remaining Jewish. This chapter will consider several tales that came out of diaspora that reveal a remarkable openness to the alien world at large and to possibilities for rich lives in that context.

The Books of Ruth and Jonah

Two brief but delightful tales that emerged in the years of early diaspora express a great openness to the foreign world into which Judaism had been thrust. The Book of Jonah presents a legend about a prophet who is briefly mentioned in 2 Kings 14:25. Commissioned by his god to "go to Nineveh, that great city, and cry against it; for their wickedness has come up before me" (Jonah 1:2), he flees in the opposite direction, taking a ship destined for Tarshish at the edge of the known world. But his god hunts him down, and, after three days in the belly of a great fish, he is cast upon the shore from which he set out and is once again commissioned by Yahweh. Knowing that escape is futile, Jonah carries out his task and is stunned when the people of Nineveh—from king to slave and even livestock—don sackcloth and repent, causing the deity to forgive them. Jonah then leaves the city in a huff to await the outcome, and as he waits he is taught a lesson in compassion by his god.

The Book of Jonah reveals an openness toward pagans, both the sailors of chapter 1 and the citizens of Nineveh, for while they appear simple and even childlike in their awe and devotion, they retain a receptivity to the deity that Jonah's sophistication prevents. As presented here, the people of Nineveh are a far cry from the brutal Assyrians of the last two centuries of Israel's life, and they are also different from the pagans encountered in the prophetic attacks on other nations (compare, for example the Book of Nahum). Compared with these well intended if naive folk, Jonah appears a fool. His priorities are out of order; he is less devoted to his god than to his own idea of how his god should behave. One can become angry because his god is "a gracious God and merciful, slow to anger, and abounding in steadfast love, and repentest of evil" (Jonah 4:2) only if

one's own reputation is given highest priority, but of such cloth a fool is cut
(Jonah 4:6–11).

This tale makes a declaration of divine freedom as clear as that found in the Book of Job. Jonah's god is not restricted by his prophet's image of him or by an oracle of doom (Jonah 3:1–4); he can change his mind (Jonah 3:10) even if this embarrasses his messenger. It has been suggested that Jonah spoofs a type of narrow-minded prophet of the Persian period, one who might, for example, vigorously support the exclusive policies of Nehemiah and Ezra. The tale is a warning that such small people have small gods.

In contrast, the Book of Ruth offers no villains. Set in the days of the federation and rooted in material passed down from that period, it is a story of devotion that far exceeds the minimum required in a difficult situation. Even Orpah in chapter 1 and the unnamed kinsman in chapter 4 meet the basic requirements of loyalty and would not be condemned for their actions, but Boaz and especially Ruth go far beyond normal expectations in their devotion to Naomi's welfare and their obligation to the deceased.

In this respect it is striking that Ruth is a Moabite and not a native of Israel; an alien, she becomes an Israelite—"Your people shall be my people, and your God my God" (Ruth 1:16). She is both devoted and clever; acting in her mother-in-law's behalf, she endangers herself and her reputation but triggers a series of events that climax in her marriage to Boaz and the birth of a male heir for Naomi and the dead man. An openness to gentiles similar to that in the Book of Jonah is found here where national identity is clearly secondary to religious allegiance and devotion to kinfolk, and the links at the end of the book that bring Ruth into David's family line reinforce this openness (Ruth 4:17–22).

The Tale of Esther and Mordecai

The Book of Esther has received mixed reviews over the centuries because of its supposedly nationalistic thrust and lack of overt religious content. Martin Luther said that it did "Judaize too greatly and have much pagan impropriety." For others, however, its association with the boisterous festival of Purim has ensured its ongoing popularity. The tale stands as the festal legend for Purim, which celebrates the triumph of the Jews of the eastern diaspora over hostile pagans seeking their total destruction. Yet this nationalistic thrust (confined mostly to chapters 8 and 9) stands in marked contrast to the tale's inner character, which is essentially one of court intrigue and conflict, of rivalry between courtiers, and of the acquisition, use, and abuse of power.

The tale opens with a short piece (chapter 1) that may once have been a separate unit. The Persian king Ahasuerus (Xerxes I) holds a royal feast for all in his realm, high and low alike, and the scene is set with an extended description of the trappings and manners of the court. In the course of this feast the king summons his consort Vashti demanding that she appear in the royal crown to display her beauty to the assembled notables, but she refuses. (Later tradition said that she refused because she was to wear only her crown.) Suddenly the empire is in confusion; word of the queen's disobedience to her husband would surely provoke all women in the realm to follow suit. To prevent this the royal advisers meet in formal session, and, utilizing all the bureaucratic machinery of the empire, issue royal edicts to all corners of the earth, in all the languages of the empire, commanding that "every man be lord in his own house" (Esther 1:22). This opening vignette makes a place in the royal court for Esther, who becomes queen by winning a competition to fill the vacuum created by Vashti's departure.

Although the reader is told that Esther is Jewish, the king and court are not so informed because her uncle Mordecai, a courtier who had once uncovered a plot to assassinate the king, has so instructed her. There is nothing about her to indicate that she is Jewish: nothing in the manner of her daily life, dress, diet, practices, language, or bearing that would give her away; nor does her Jewishness hamper her full and effective engagement with the Persian world. Even the names Esther and Mordecai are based on the names of the Babylonian deities Ishtar and Marduk. Of course, Mordecai is known by his fellow officials to be Jewish. While his refusal to bow before Haman, who had been made second in rank in the empire, is somehow linked with his Jewishness, the link is not clear (Esther 3:4). The refusal can best be understood in terms of personal rivalry and the courtier's sensitivity to the trappings of rank and position.

As the tale unfolds, bare events are related with a factual objectivity that leaves it to the reader to perceive the ironies, reversals, and coincidences that play upon the central figures. We are not told in detail, for example, of Haman's feelings as he spends the better part of a day leading Mordecai about in honor, giving homage that he had designed for himself to the person he had come to have hanged, for all this is related in only one verse (Esther 6:11). Likewise, a series of seemingly unrelated happenings—a pair of intimate dinners hosted by the queen for the king and his most trusted official; royal insomnia; Haman's bitterness at another chance encounter with Mordecai; Haman's upsetting his own timetable in his haste to destroy Mordecai—all are skillfully used by Esther and Mordecai to defeat their enemy and take his place.

In all this, however, their own success and the salvation of their fellow Jews coincide completely with the welfare of the king. For just as Haman represents his plot to destroy Mordecai and the Jews in terms of financial benefit to the king (Esther 7:3–4), so the note in Esther 10:1 suggests that Mordecai uses his new powers at the end to advance the royal fortunes as well as to save his people. Personal success, loyalty to fellow Jews, and service to the king come together in this tale. Esther and Mordecai are fully Persian as well as Jewish, and it is as clever and effective courtiers that they demonstrate that they are loyal Jews.

Although the tale was no doubt told and retold in the communities of the eastern diaspora in the later Persian and early Hellenistic periods largely because of its entertainment value, underlying the entertainment is a distinct definition of Jewishness. It affirms for Jews of the diaspora the possibility of living rich and creative lives in the new setting while still remaining devoted and loyal members of the community of Jews. The openness to the foreign world is akin to that in Ruth and Jonah and even in the Joseph narrative in Genesis. There is nothing about Jewishness as here defined that interferes with engagement with that world in any way. Little is found here of the priests' vision or life style.

Neither is there much that can be called overtly religious, let alone specifically Jewish. The fast that Esther calls for in chapter 3 reflects the most universal of religious practices, for example, and this is the only book in the Hebrew Bible in which the deity is not mentioned directly. While there may be an oblique reference in the notice of the "other place" (Esther 4:14) and a suggestion of divine guidance and protection throughout, the hand of the god is here hidden and does not break into the regular flow of events.

Esther's story is told on the level of human intentions, human actions, and human history and in this respect is heir to the Joseph and succession narratives of the empire of David and Solomon. The lack of reference to the traditions of ancient Israel is the more striking since this story finds the people once again endangered in a foreign land. Surely we might expect an appeal for help to the god who had delivered his people from the pharaoh of Egypt. Although this lack of religious element would be set aright as additions were made by later hands, the additions reflect the religious sensitivities of a later period.

No doubt a primary factor in the tale's preservation is that it provides a quasi-historical foundation for the popular festival of Purim. The origins of Purim are now obscure, though it may derive from the New Year's celebrations in Persian times, a festival enjoyed by Jews as well. If the tale was thus used to legitimize a festival whose roots lay elsewhere, its central thrust was blunted by later additions; for chapter 9, with its account of Jewish victories and details about the celebration of Purim, was added to bind the older tale to the festival but its tone is in marked contrast to that of the older tale. In Esther 9 the line between pagan and Jew is sharply drawn, their hostility is underscored, the festival becomes a celebration of Jewish triumphs, and King Ahasuerus, always somewhat slow-witted and malleable, becomes absurd as he allows the slaughter of one large segment of his people to spare another segment. This later use of the tale probably occurred when external forces were placing stress on pagan-Jewish interrelationships and when creative and rewarding interaction with the diaspora environment was becoming more difficult for Jews.

The Tales of Daniel 1-6

Although the first six chapters of the Book of Daniel are set in the last years of the Babylonian empire and the early Persian period, critical study places the author or authors in the second century B.C.E. While it is recognized that while the book's final form, and especially the visions that make up its second half, come from the second century, the tales originated in an earlier setting in which pagan-Jewish tensions had not yet reached the critical phase depicted in the visions. Thus the tales must be approached on two levels: first, in relation to the context in which they took shape; second, in relation to the later period of persecution in which they continued to be informing, though with different emphases (the second matter will be considered in chapter 12).

Like the tale of Esther and Mordecai, the adventures of Daniel and his three friends in Daniel 1–6 are set within royal courts of lavish oriental splendor, where power and wealth depend upon the favor of the king and intrigue is ever present. As a whole, the tales divide into two groups. One group deals with conflicts in which one courtier or group seeks to undo another (Daniel 3 and 6); in the other a seemingly impossible task is set before the hero, whose fate hinges on his ability to deal with it (Daniel 1, 2, 4, and 5; note as well the story of Joseph in Egypt in Genesis 40–41). In the first group the hero is finally able to outmaneuver his rivals and take their place; in the second the hero succeeds when all others fail and receives due recognition and reward.

Daniel 1 introduces the rest of the tales by detailing the scene and describing the heroes as men of remarkable physical appearance (very important in the ancient world), learning, and skill. The first tale describes a court contest in which Daniel and his companions, in spite of their simple diet, surpass all the others in training for court service notwithstanding that the others have all the resources of the royal establishment at hand (compare Esther, who does not refuse full use of the beauty preparations available in the Persian harem).

A second contest follows in Daniel 2. Like pharaoh before him, Nebuchadnezzar has a troubling dream. Summoning his courtiers skilled in dream interpretation—and no ancient court would be without them—he poses his challenge: Tell me my dream and its interpretation. If you are successful your rewards will be great; if you fail you will be torn limb from limb. In Daniel 4, which takes the form of a royal decree relating past events, the king at least describes his dream. In both instances, however, the corps of pagan magicians, enchanters, sorcerers, and Chaldeans fails, and in each case Daniel dramatically succeeds not only in saving his own neck and those of his rivals but in receiving honor, riches, and power as well.

In chapters 3 and 6 rival factions are pitted against one another for royal favor, each seeking to eliminate the other. In each case the pagan courtiers persuade the king to issue an irrevocable decree (note this motif in Esther as well) by which they can entrap their opponents and ensure their death. But Daniel and his companions escape, much to the king's relief, and displace their rivals, who, in chapter 6, suffer the fate they had set for the hero. Daniel 5 is again a court contest, now set at a feast. This time Daniel reads and interprets the strange writing on the wall when all others are stumped. He is again lavishly rewarded and promoted, even though his interpretation of the divine message announces the king's downfall and is accompanied by a stern lecture on the ruler's evil ways.

While the Daniel tales and the tale dealing with Esther and Mordecai are of the same general type, tensions with the pagan world and the line between things Jewish and non-Jewish are here more sharply drawn. In Daniel 1, for example, the heroes reject the rich fare of the court training establishment out of loyalty to their god and their religious heritage. In chapter 6 Belshazzar rewards Daniel in spite of a stern lecture and dire sentence. In chapters 2 and 4 the meaning of the king's dream is made known to Daniel by the "God in heaven who reveals mysteries," and Nebuchadnezzar honors both the courtier and his god—chapter 4 is, in fact, a decree to that effect. In chapters 3 and 6 the plot hinges on the courtiers' Jewishness in the sense that their heritage sets them apart and provides a handle by which their enemies can attempt to entrap them. Practices linked with their religious identity not only distinguish but endanger them and have the potential to blunt any effective life in the royal setting.

This sharply distinguishes Daniel from Esther and Mordecai, who would not rebuke the king so openly because there is nothing in Esther's Jewishness that sets her apart and identifies her as a Jew. Esther and Mordecai are completely assimilated into their pagan setting. In the tales of Daniel, however, the food eaten or rejected, certain acts of devotion, certain prohibitions, and an openly expressed relationship with a particular deity—all define what it means to be a Jew. Indeed, Daniel seems to be moving toward the style of Judaism that is defined by the Torah.

In the tales of Daniel, too, the deity is the central character. Although there is not a single direct reference to him in the Book of Esther, the divine presence is everywhere in Daniel, both as the focus of the plots and as the focus of the courtiers' loyalty—the latter being of critical importance because it lies behind the rejection of royal food, the refusal to pay homage to the king's image or to offer prayers to the ruler, and is the source of Daniel's ability to interpret dreams and cryptic messages.

In the tale of Esther and Mordecai, loyalties to king and to one's fellow Jews do not conflict, but in Daniel a choice is forced: in certain situations one cannot be both Jew and Babylonian or Persian. In chapter 3 this view climaxes in the words of Daniel's three friends to King Nebuchadnezzar: "Shadrach, Meshach, and Abednego answered the king, 'O Nebuchadnezzar, we have no need to answer you in this matter. If it be so, our God whom we serve is able to deliver us out of your hand, O king. But if not, be it known to you, O king, that we will not serve your gods or worship the golden image which you have set up' " (Daniel 3:16–18).

The friends are saved by their god as Daniel is saved from the den of lions. In all six tales, in fact, the courtiers appear only in relation to the god and are necessarily more passive than Esther or Mordecai because they rely on divine support and a miracle, not on their own wits. Along with the notice of elevation and reward for the courtiers, attention is directed to the honor paid the god as well (Daniel 2:46–47; 3:28–29; 4:1–37; 6:25–27). Belshazzar alone withholds royal acknowledgment of the deity's authority, and Belshazzar is killed the very night Daniel announces his fate.

With the exception of Belshazzar, the pagan kings are presented not as evil but as foolish, trapped by their own words and blinded by their position but responsive to divine displays of power and discipline. This is not the image of pagan kings offered by later Judaism, even in the visions of the second part of the Book of Daniel. In general, Daniel 1–6 affirms the life style of Esther and Mordecai but with variations and a sense of much greater hazard, for the courtier still moves within the context of the pagan world, which still partly provides the terms for his success. Although tensions between loyalties do not lead to an ultimate break, the possibility arises in Daniel 3:18; and while one wonders why it does not arise in chapter 5 as well, rich and creative life in interaction with the pagan setting is still affirmed.

But this is possible only with the aid of the deity; miracles are needed. In the final analysis, it is loyalty to his god that enables Daniel to overcome all dangers in the foreign context. Even if this loyalty contributes to the dangers, allegiance to one's god has precedence over all others, and loyalty to the deity means observing the practices and prohibitions that set the Jew apart. This observance may have been regarded as necessary to avoid complete assimilation and loss of identity. For Esther's Jewishness was largely generic, but Daniel's is defined by acts of devotion and by certain practices akin to those envisioned by the priestly circles. In time, historical changes in the Near East and eastern Mediterranean world would subject this style of Judaism to the severest of tests.

BIBLIOGRAPHIC NOTE

The Book of Jonah

    Fretheim, T. E. *The Message of Jonah*. Minneapolis: Augsburg, 1977.

    Landes, George. "Jonah, Book of." In *The Interpreter's Dictionary of the Bible: Supplementary Volume*, pp. 488–91. Nashville: Abingdon Press, 1976.

    ———. "The Kerygma of the Book of Jonah." *Interpretation* 21 (1967): 3–31.

    Neil. W. "Jonah, Book of." In *The Interpreter's Dictionary of the Bible*, vol. 2, pp. 964–67. Nashville: Abingdon Press, 1962.

The Book of Ruth

    Campbell, Edward F. *Ruth*. Garden City, N.Y.: Doubleday & Co., 1975.

    Hals, Ronald M. "Ruth, Book of." In *The Interpreter's Dictionary of the Bible: Supplementary Volume*, pp. 758–59. Nashville: Abingdon Press, 1976.

_____. *The Theology of the Book of Ruth*. Philadelphia: Fortress Press, 1969.

Harvey, D. "Ruth, Book of." In *The Interpreter's Dictionary of the Bible*, vol. 4, pp. 131–34. Nashville: Abingdon Press, 1962.

The Book of Esther

Humphreys, W. Lee. "Esther, Book of." In *The Interpreter's Dictionary of the Bible: Supplementary Volume*, pp. 279–81. Nashville: Abingdon Press, 1976.

_____. "A Life Style for Diaspora: A Study of the Tales of Esther and Daniel." *Journal of Biblical Literature* 92 (1973): 211–23.

Moore, Carey A. *Esther*. Garden City, N.Y.: Doubleday & Co., 1971.

The Book of Daniel

Frost, S. B. "Daniel." In *The Interpreter's Dictionary of the Bible*, vol. 1, pp. 761–68. Nashville: Abingdon Press, 1962.

Hartman, Louis F., and Di Lella, Alexander A. *The Book of Daniel*. Garden City, N.Y.: Doubleday & Co., 1978.

Porteous, Norman W. *Daniel*. Philadelphia: Westminster Press, 1965.

SECTION 2
THE CHALLENGE
OF HELLENISM

Model of Herodian Temple, Jerusalem

Lessing/Magnum

APOCALYPTIC VISION AND EMERGING NATIONALISM

12

Primary readings: 1 and 2 Maccabees*
Isaiah 24–27
Zechariah 9–14
Daniel 7–12

From this point onward we will focus for the most part on Jerusalem and the Jews in southern Palestine. In part this shift from the eastern diaspora represents a shift in the center of Jewish concerns; in part it reflects the sources at our disposal, for the next few centuries offer limited data concerning the further development of Jewish communities outside Palestine, especially in the east. Although these diaspora communities continued to represent the majority of Jews, for many in the diaspora Jerusalem either remained or became the center of interest and authority.

UNDER PTOLEMAIC AND SELEUCID RULE

During the last third of the fourth century B.C.E. rapid and sweeping changes altered the basic composition of the Near East and eastern Mediterranean world. Until this time Persian authority had extended from upper India through Egypt.

---

* These books are found in the Old Testament of Roman Catholics but in the Apocrypha, not in the canonical Bibles of Protestants and Jews.

Although Persian expansion into Greece had been checked on several occasions, this still left most of the east united under Persian rule and largely at peace. Most Jews lived under a unified political structure, which facilitated their communication among different communities. In the decade that followed 333 B.C.E., however, all this changed, for in that year Alexander the Great began a campaign of conquest from Macedonia in upper Greece that would not end until the Persian empire fell and the world came under Greek rule.

It did not come under a single and unified leadership, however, for on Alexander's death in 323 B.C.E. conflicts broke out among his closest followers, and three independent, often mutually hostile, kingdoms were formed. The smallest and weakest kingdom, which remained in the hands of kings in Macedonia, Alexander's home, included Greece and parts of western Anatolia with claims on Cyprus and Crete, but the bulk of the territories fell to two generals in Alexander's army. Most of ancient Mesopotamia, from eastern Anatolia to the Persian Gulf, with conquests further east, fell to General Seleucus and formed the Seleucid empire. Syria-Palestine and Egypt went to General Ptolemy and constituted the Ptolemaic empire. The line dividing these large power blocks fell somewhere in northern Syria at first, but once again the Syria-Palestine corridor became a disputed buffer between rival kingdoms, and not only was Jerusalem caught between rival nations as it had been centuries earlier with Assyria or Babylon and Egypt but Judaism as a whole was now split between hostile powers. An ill-defined but generally hostile border separated Jews of the eastern diaspora from those in Palestine and Egypt. No longer would news and persons flow between east and west as in the days of Nehemiah and Ezra and earlier.

While tensions between Jews and gentiles were not unknown within the Persian empire, there was a broad official tolerance and even encouragement of local traditions, customs, and religious practices. Not only was Judaism permitted but the treasures of the state were sometimes available to foster its development, and the varied styles of Judaism were permitted to take shape amid a unified political structure that ensured worldwide peace and stability. Following Alexander's death the eastern Mediterranean and Near East continued to be composed of various cultural and religious groups, but to these a new force was added. Across the east Alexander had left Greek outposts to govern and manage trade, and these Greek communities remained distinct from the natives, sometimes as separate cities with their characteristic gymnasiums and theaters, sometimes as enclaves within a city, but never adopting the natives' language, dress, manners, or gods. In these outposts far from the homeland Greek culture and religion were perpetuated, for the Greeks harbored a consciousness of marked cultural superiority.

There was, to be sure, an unconscious mixture of things Greek and native, but the heirs of the Hellenic tradition were not absorbed into the newly taken

NEAR EAST under the GREEKS

B.C.E.		
350		
	Alexander the Great (336–323)	
325	PTOLEMIES	SELEUCIDS
	Ptolemy I Lagi (323–285)	
		Seleucus I (312–280)
300		
	Ptolemy II Philadelphus (285–246)	
275		Antiochus I (280–261)
		Antiochus II (261–246)
250		
	Ptolemy III Euergetes (246–221)	Seleucus II (246–226)
225		Seleucus III (226–223)
	Ptolemy IV Philopator (221–203)	Antiochus III (223–187)
	Ptolemy V Ephiphanes (203–181)	
200	Seleucids take Palestine (200–198)	
		Seleucus IV (187–175)
175	Ptolemy VI Philometor (181–146)	Antiochus IV Epiphanes (175–163)
	Desecration of the Temple (167)	Antiochus V (163–162)
150		Demetrius I (162–150)

territories. There was no missionary thrust among them, no planned attempt to win the world to Hellenism, but because Hellenism was the culture of the new rulers it exuded a strong attraction for others. For those who saw reflected in Greek successes on the battlefield evidence of Greek superiority in every area of life, alignment was clearly the path to follow. For the Jews, and especially those who sought to define Judaism within the Torah patterns, Hellenism offered a compelling rival.

From the end of the fourth century to about 200 B.C.E. most of Palestine was under Ptolemaic rule, and though this line of kings did not directly interfere with the continued development and practice of Judaism, Hellenism would nevertheless have a marked impact on it. Within Greek Alexandria in northern Egypt a large and important Jewish community formed that was to become one center for the penetration of Judaism by Greek traditions. Beginning around the middle of the third century B.C.E., the Torah, then the prophets, and finally other writings were translated into Greek. The Septuagint, as this translation is now called, reflects an important stage in the formation of a limited and fixed Bible. On other levels as well, Jewish communities in and around Alexandria became the locus of developments reflecting strong Greek influence, but the Jews were not forced under the Ptolemaic rulers to take up Greek ways or to reject their heritage. This was to change suddenly in the first third of the second century B.C.E.

ANTIOCHUS IV AND THE MACCABEES

In 200–198 B.C.E. the Seleucid king Antiochus III took Syria-Palestine from Ptolemaic hands, and within three decades a crisis developed. The Seleucid empire was always the largest of the three that grew out of Alexander's conquest. Composed of the widest collection of distinct national and cultural groups, some for long periods only nominally under Greek or earlier Persian rule, it was ever in danger of collapse from overextension. The forces for disintegration climaxed in the early decades of the second century B.C.E. when renewed emphasis on native cultural and religious traditions became linked with movements toward national independence.

The third Seleucid to rule over Palestine and Jerusalem bore the brunt of this. His name was Antiochus IV Epiphanes, and he has come down in history as a consummate villain. Intensely devoted to his Greek heritage and easily given to extremes, he was a harsh man, not about to underestimate himself or his authority, and he was in a very difficult situation. Recognizing the links between cultural and religious distinctness and movements for national independence, he determined to thwart all attempts to foster local cultural and religious traditions by imposing Greek practices, ideals, and values on all his subjects.

Because his empire seemed about to fragment in many places at once,

Antiochus could not tolerate any move toward independence in Palestine, which would probably be supported by the Ptolemies to the south; hence he sought to impose Hellenism on the Jews in and around Jerusalem. Since this meant outlawing anything that set the Jews apart, Torah Judaism suddenly fell outside the law. This was not a case of slow Hellenistic infiltration into Judaism; it was a case of Torah Jew or Greek.

Possession of the Torah was prohibited, as were circumcision, observance of the Sabbath, and the dietary laws. Jews were forced to eat the flesh of pigs in open rejection of their tradition and to acknowledge a pagan god in an act of public worship. In time a statue of Zeus was erected in the temple of Jerusalem, and the Yahweh cult was desecrated by the offering of a pig upon its altar. The line between Jew and Greek was sharply drawn, and the power of a world empire stood against Torah Judaism.

The Hasidim and Martyrdom

Judaism in Palestine was already fractured. Even before Antiochus, many Jews had been attracted to appealing modes of Greek thought, artistic expression, and customs. Especially among cosmopolitan and upper-class Jews with large land holdings or widespread commercial interests, some engagement with Hellenism was necessary. Because one might even wish to conceal Jewishness, Greek names were taken alongside, or in place of, Jewish names even by the high priests (Daniel 1:6–7; Esther 2:7). A surgical procedure was developed that allowed one to hide circumcision from view when participating naked (in the Greek way) in the gymnasium games. In time, Seleucid support was even sought and bought by successive claimants to the position of high priest, resulting in an unedifying spectacle of priestly coups, assassinations, and bribes.

It is easy today to condemn this Hellenistic segment within Judaism as compromising, worldly, and weak, but Hellenistic tradition had much to offer Jews. It would influence even those who first resisted it, and it could be argued from Jewish tradition that the demands of self-preservation and the survival of family and friends took precedence over matters of diet or Sabbath. Many, no doubt, acceded to the demands of Antiochus only to save their lives, for life was the ultimate gift of god and it was sacred. But there were also some who opposed any form of compromise, demanding that Torah Judaism be affirmed and maintained in all its aspects.

These persons are called Hasidim, a term related to the Hebrew *hesed*, which means "loyalty" or "faithfulness," and they were loyal to their god and Judaism as they believed these must be defined. The Torah was the gift and command of this god and was not to be rejected even in the face of death. Martyrdom now became a distinct possibility (Daniel 3:16–18). The Torah Jew must now choose between religious identity and political allegiance, for the line between the two, so long blurred, was again harshly etched by the actions of Antiochus IV.

In this period such figures as the old man Eleazar and the mother and her seven sons (2 Maccabees 6–7) opted for a horrid death rather than reject any part of their heritage.

It must be emphasized, however, that in addition to being a conflict between Jew and gentile, this conflict reflected a split within Judaism as well. The emergence of the Hasidim clearly defined two levels of Jewishness. On one level a person was Jewish by birth, but on another level Jewishness became a matter of total commitment to what the Hasidim believed to be definitive for a Jewish life style. This called for a personal decision that transcended the facts of birth, it called upon some to face death, others to hide in caves in the hills, and others it drove to arms.

The Maccabees

In time, active resistance broke out. In 167 B.C.E. a man of priestly descent named Mattathias refused to offer an unclean sacrifice to a pagan deity. He and his sons attacked the king's officers in their hometown of Modein and even slew a Jew who complied with the demand. Thus began a guerrilla action that turned into a war for freedom. Mattathias was succeeded by his third son Judas, who was also called "the Maccabee," meaning "the hammer," and the Maccabean uprising succeeded against what must have been overwhelming odds. What had begun as a guerrilla action against Seleucid forces resulted in the taking of Jerusalem from foreign hands, the restoration of the temple cult, and the liberation of parts of Palestine. The restoration of the cult is said to have taken place in 164 B.C.E., three years to the day after its desecration by Antiochus, and the event has been celebrated ever since in the joyous eight-day festival of Hanukkah.

After the death of Judas, his brothers continued the struggle, in time ruling a new state as the founders of a royal line that bears their family name, the Hasmonean dynasty. The story of this struggle for independence is told in two forms in the books of 1 and 2 Maccabees, both of which provide lively accounts of this critical period in the history of Judaism. 1 Maccabees takes the side of the resistance and covers the period from about 175 B.C.E., the year that Antiochus became king, to 134 and the death of Simon, the last of the sons of Mattathias. Scholars believe that most of the book was written around 140 B.C.E. (chapters 14–16 being a later extension of the history to 134), quite soon after the events it narrates.

2 Maccabees, written in the first century B.C.E. and covering from about 176 to 161, is an edited abridgment of a history in five books, which has not survived, by one Jason of Cyrene. While the author of 1 Maccabees views the struggle as under divine guidance, in his narrative the course of events occurs more on the human level. In 2 Maccabees the hand of the deity is more overt, appearing in the form of miracles and visions that depict the future. 2 Maccabees also has a more overt theological thrust. Themes first developed in Judaism in the second and first centuries B.C.E.—for example, resurrection of the body (2 Maccabees

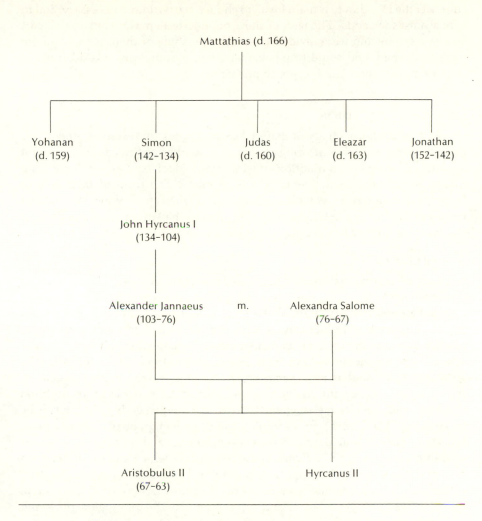

THE MACCABEES and HASMONEANS (167–63 B.C.E.)

Mattathias (d. 166)

Yohanan (d. 159)   Simon (142–134)   Judas (d. 160)   Eleazar (d. 163)   Jonathan (152–142)

John Hyrcanus I (134–104)

Alexander Jannaeus (103–76)   m.   Alexandra Salome (76–67)

Aristobulus II (67–63)   Hyrcanus II

7:11; 14:46) and the creation of the universe out of nothing (2 Maccabees 7:28)—find expression here as well.

The further story of the Hasmonean dynasty and the extent to which it remained on the path charted by its founders will be considered in the next chapter. Here we must examine a form of literary and religious expression that experienced its first flowering under the persecutions of Antiochus IV. This material presents a new and distinct theological vision of the will and ways of the deity. For we must ask, What gave to those who resisted Antiochus the determination, courage, and strength to do so? What vision of their god could empower the Hasidim to remain loyal, to choose martyrdom if necessary, and to fight against such odds? The Jews in and around Jerusalem were but a small part of a vast empire and were divided internally, yet some of them resisted all the power that the world could bring against them. A source for this determined courage may be found in the apocalyptic vision.

THE APOCALYPTIC VISION

Daniel 7–12 contains a body of material that intrigues some, repels others, and puzzles everyone. While it brings together a number of threads from ancient Israelite and early Jewish tradition and draws on wider Near Eastern themes and motifs as well, the result seems bizarre to many. The form of this body of literary expression and theological speculation is called apocalyptic. We will first note several of its characteristics and then discuss the latter part of the Book of Daniel in the context of the crisis provoked by Antiochus IV.

General Characteristics

A series of cryptic visions in Daniel 7–12 is seen by one Daniel, who, as presented in chapters 1–6, was a Jew of high rank in the royal courts of several Babylonian and Persian kings of the sixth century b.c.e. Because the visions are so complex that Daniel cannot fully comprehend them, an interpreter is provided, in the form of an angel named Gabriel (Daniel 7:15–16; 8:15–17), and other angels are mentioned by name as well (for example, Michael in Daniel 10:12–13; 12:1). This is a culmination of the long development of such intermediaries between the divine and the human. In early Israelite tradition nameless and faceless messengers had appeared representing the deity (see Genesis 19:1; 22:11; 28:12, for example), and these had gradually become more prevalent, distinct, and identified with specific names and functions.

Daniel's visions are filled with baroque symbols which can be understood only by those with special insight. Strange hybrid beasts composed of the parts of different creatures recall the monsters of older Near Eastern mythic tradition. As these creatures grow out of and replace one another, strange actions and sometimes even stranger fates are ascribed to them. Much attention is given to numbers and to the determination of times and dates in this material; certain periods of time take on distinct qualities and are marked by definite beginnings and endings. An ancient Near Eastern and especially Persian influence seems apparent in this as well.

Throughout this panorama of strange symbols, motifs, and images an outline of history is presented that offers a preview of the future to a worthy figure of the past, in this instance Daniel. Critical study of the Book of Daniel, however, agrees in setting the author of these visions in the period of Antiochus IV, for, as the historical survey draws closer to this period, precise details are given that are lacking in the more general and less accurate review of the earlier periods. While the author is sure that good will ultimately triumph, when his vision moves to Antiochus' last years, he is looking into the uncertainty of the future: Antiochus is not yet dead, and his death as envisioned in Daniel 11:40–45 will not, in fact, be met in this way.

Nevertheless, by attributing his visions to a notable figure from the past (here Daniel; other apocalyptic visions are attributed to Adam, Enoch, Noah, Abraham, and Ezra), the author gives the impression that the whole of world history has been predicted from the beginning and that the end will follow true to the pattern. The visions are granted and sealed, to be revealed to the elect only at the proper time (Daniel 12:9). Addressed to those suffering under the persecutions of Antiochus, they call for steadfast trust and provide a foundation for that trust. The apocalyptic vision, then, offers a view of a predicted past and a fixed future in which the triumph of the deity is assured. From beginning to end, all has been determined by a deity whose control over the historical process is absolute. The use of symbols and cryptic numbers, as well as the attribution of the visions to a past figure, may in part reflect the author's need to remain anonymous in order to avoid running afoul of local authorities.

Vision, Prophecy, and Wisdom

In the English translations of the Hebrew Bible—following the pattern of the Septuagint—the Book of Daniel is placed immediately after that of Ezekiel, though in the Hebrew Bible itself it is placed with a mixed collection called Writings, which is made up of Psalms, Proverbs, Job, Esther, and Lamentations, among other works. Said to be an outgrowth of the earlier prophetic tradition, the apocalyptic material is certainly its heir and at least its semilegitimate offspring. Several prophets had had visionary experiences—Ezekiel's involved powerful symbols and baroque constructions, Zechariah is said to have had night visions requiring an interpreter—and early examples of apocalyptic materials are also embedded in the prophetic collections.

Chapters 9–14 of the Book of Zechariah and chapters 24–27 of Isaiah, for example, contain many of the motifs, themes, and forms developed in the apocalyptic vision, but these units are difficult to date because very little is known about the internal situation in Palestine from Nehemiah and Ezra until the days of the Maccabees, and it is in this time frame that they are to be set. For these earlier materials we do not have documents like 1 and 2 Maccabees which provide a historical setting for Daniel 7–12. But in Daniel 9:1–27 the author of the visions acts as an executor for the prophetic heritage, reinterpreting the statements in Jeremiah 25:11–12 and 29:10 that Yahweh's punishment of his people by means of forced submission to Babylon would last seventy years. This reinterpretation was necessary because foreign, if not Babylonian, oppression was still a fact centuries later.

Like prophecy, the apocalyptic vision looks to the future and finds the hand of the deity revealed in the course of human history. Events on the human stage reflect not only human intention and realization but a divine will, and both the prophet and the visionary claim to reveal the god's word. But in this attitude toward history they also differ substantially. For the prophet's roots are in either the Moses-Sinai or David-Zion story of ancient Israel, and he interprets the current situation of his people in their light. The apocalyptic vision is more universal in focus; it ranges over centuries, and there is little reference in it to either story. Changes in the essential configuration of the world, the rise and fall of whole empires, are at the heart of this material, and the changes occur with a fixity and determination that are not to be found in the prophetic material.

On the one hand, the apocalyptic visions are more elaborately constructed than the shorter, more pointed words of a prophetic oracle, giving the impression of conscious literary craft (though the distinction becomes less sharp as one moves toward such figures as Ezekiel and Zechariah). On the other hand, the deity's actions in history are less dynamic and open-ended in the apocalyptic vision. In the prophet's oracle, human history is determined by a series of unpredicted interactions between god and people, and the future is more or less uncertain, not only because the god can change his mind but because human initiative and intention play an essential role. Indeed, it is precisely because Israel is off course that the prophetic word is provoked. In the apocalyptic vision, however, history unfolds as a divinely written script, compelling in its very fixity: "And the king shall do according to his will; he shall exalt himself and magnify himself above every god, and shall speak astonishing things against the God of gods. He shall prosper till the indignation is accomplished; *for what is determined shall be done*" (Daniel 11:36; italics added).

The apocalyptic vision moves from creation to re-creation, revealing a pattern rooted in ancient creation myths in which a divinely ordered universe comes increasingly under the sway of a revived chaos. But at exactly the point at which chaos seems finally to triumph, the creator god will destroy it once and for all precisely as the monster of chaos was destroyed in the first act of creation. Then a new order, a new heaven and earth, will come into being. The very fixity of this outline undergirds the assurance that the god will triumph.

Most important in understanding the appeal of these visions is their assertion that the persecutions of Antiochus constitute the climax that precedes the divine shattering of evil. The people of this time stand on the brink of history's fulfillment, for the curtain is about to rise on the final act; at any moment the deity will break into the course of events and destroy the forces of evil permanently. The apocalyptic vision calls believers to a state of red alert to be ready for the climax of the whole course of human history and to stand fast in spite of surface appearances, for the deity's triumph is not apparent in any realistic assessment of the situation; the vision seeks to reveal the true flow of events that is not apparent at first glance.

The wise man of old had sought to comprehend the deeper meaning of events; only the fool misread the moment or was led astray by surface appearances. Likewise, the apocalyptic vision tells the reader that the seeming triumph of evil is not a sign that the god has lost control but is only a part of the overall divine plan and that it is according to this reality that life should be ordered. One cannot change the patterns of history but can only seek them out, formulate them, and build a life in accord with them. A passive quality in the apocalyptic vision calls not for action but for allegiance, for the events on earth are merely microcosmic reflections of the real battle that is being waged in the transcendant sphere of the divine. Creation and destruction, order and chaos, good and evil are ultimately forces that are larger than life and beyond human ken.

Vision, Torah, and Story

The Antiochus crisis most endangered the Torah style of Judaism, and it is to this particular construction of the Jewish heritage that the apocalyptic vision summons believers to be loyal even in the face of death. The strength to do this is provided by a vision of an all-controlling deity who is not impotent in the face of the chaotic forces unleashed by Antiochus IV because even this crisis is part of a plan fixed at the beginning of time and clear to anyone who can crack the code.

Torah Judaism as formulated in the priestly document offers a life style set within an open-ended story of promise for an indefinite future perhaps many generations away; it tells the Jew to live as a pilgrim, in but not of the world. The apocalyptic vision is also empowered by a promise, but the promise is here seen as reaching fulfillment; indeed, among some Jews in the Palestine of 167–165 B.C.E. it meant the rebirth of the old nation Isreal. The apocalyptic vision therefore gives the Torah vision strong reinforcement. By asking Jews to become part of a small select group defined by a life style and a vision and to stand fast therein in spite of the hostile forces arrayed against them, it gives the Torah vision a sense of life-and-death immediacy.

Finally, while the destruction and expected rebirth of old Israel were comprehended within the conditional promise of the Moses-Sinai story as it had been reformed in priestly circles, the details of what would be reborn appeared in the garb of motifs drawn from the David-Zion story. Although the crisis of 587 B.C.E. would seem to have shattered this story's unconditional promises beyond repair, aspects of it had already reappeared in the hope set forth by the Second Isaiah and even more in the challenges of Haggai and Zechariah. In the apocalyptic vision, the nation Israel would one day be free and independent again and sustained by Yahweh, whom all peoples would then recognize as sole creator, sustainer, and lord of history. Jerusalem would once again be his temple home; the house of David would rule anew from its heights; and Yahweh would renew the fight against the forces of chaos. Like the wars of old, this would be a holy war, and, like the conflict recalled in the New Year's festival (see especially Psalms 46 and 48, 2, and 110), it would shake the foundations of the earth.

It is above all in the finality of this vision of the future that the old David-Zion story is mostly to be seen. In the apocalyptic vision, threads of prophecy, wisdom, Torah, and the two stories of old Israel all come together, blended into a unique way of comprehending the deity's dealings with humankind. Although this vision goes beyond all the older traditions in drawing upon resources outside those of the ancient Israelites and early Jews, it is at heart a continuation and recasting of the old material in the face of a present filled alike with danger and with promise.

Daniel 7–12

The author of Daniel 7–12 addresses himself to the crisis of 167–165 B.C.E., finding a foundation for his visions in the all-controlling deity of the tales of Daniel 1–6 and a model for all who face present persecution in the loyalty of the heroes of these older stories. He does not, however, iron out all the tensions produced by adding the visions to the older tales and inserting them into a new setting. With the partial exception of Belshazzar, for example, the rulers depicted in Daniel 1–6 are not in the image of Antiochus IV. No Torah Jew expected Antiochus suddenly to see the evil of his ways and to address hymns of praise to the god of Daniel; no Hasid could ever have served in his court, and none would have taken rewards from him for faithful service. In spite of this, the tales do issue a clear call for loyalty to Israel's god and heritage, and they depict a deity who will stand by his saints (as the faithful elect style themselves):

> And the kingdom and the dominion
>> and the greatness of the kingdoms under the whole heaven
>> shall be given to the people of the saints of the Most High;
>> their kingdom shall be an everlasting kingdom,
>> and all dominions shall serve and obey them.
>
> (Daniel 7:27)

Here are echoes of the unconditional promise made to the house of David in prophetic oracle and cultic hymn.

That we today find historical inaccuracy in segments of the visions, and errors both in the earlier period especially (there was no empire of the Medes, and Belshazzar was never king) and when the future is the subject (Antiochus did not meet the fate set for him in Daniel 11:40–45), should not blunt either the appeal made or the affirmation behind it. The god of Israel sets forth a design of world history that he will bring to fruition very soon. Trust in him is the source of true security; even the Maccabees are described in Daniel 11:34 as only "a little help." As in the vision of Isaiah of Jerusalem centuries earlier, there is no blending or confusion here of human and divine support; the basis for life and security is clearly seen to lie with the divine.

Finally, Daniel 7–12 introduces a number of themes and motifs that will receive rich and varied development in the centuries that follow. Here we shall note only one striking new claim that first appears in Daniel 12:

> At that time shall arise Michael, the great prince who has charge of your people. And there shall be a time of trouble, such as never has been since there was a nation till that time; but at that time your people shall be delivered, every one whose name shall be found written in the book. And many of those who sleep in the dust of the earth shall awake, some to everlasting life, and some to shame and everlasting contempt. And those who are wise shall shine like the brightness of the firmament; and those who turn many to righteousness, like the stars for ever and ever
>
> (Daniel 12:1–4).

How difficult it must have been to comprehend the martyrdom of those who accepted death rather than betray their heritage. How could one comprehend the death of those who took up the challenge of the apocalyptic vision in the very last days, who came so near the fulfillment of the promise only to die when in sight of the goal and because of their loyalty.

In ancient Israelite and early Jewish thought, human life had been defined within the brackets of life and death: death was the end of existence, and any life that followed was but a dim shadow of the former state as one's shade entered the netherworld. But now one of the brackets was removed, and one's relationship with the deity need never end. One's mortal sufferings could be seen as lasting for only a moment in the face of eternity and one's mortal happiness as a mere reflection of the glories that lay ahead.

The vision of a life and a reward after death may have been adopted from external sources, as forms of such speculation and belief had taken shape in Persian and especially in Greek circles. Although the details would take time to develop and varied patterns would eventually emerge, it was the crisis that gave birth to the apocalyptic vision that also allowed this belief to take root in Judaism, and the belief would radically change the whole perception of what it meant to be human. We shall meet this concept again as we see how Judaism continued to confront the challenge of Hellenism and to develop the apocalyptic vision over the course of the next two centuries.

Hellenistic Period: Historical and Literary Background

Discussion and documents are also found in the histories and literary introductions in the introductory Bibliographic Note.

Bickerman, Elias. *From Ezra to the Last of the Maccabees*. New York: Schocken Books, 1962. A brief but useful introduction.

Charles, R. H. *Apocrypha and Pseudepigrapha of the Old Testament*. New York: Oxford University Press, 1913. An old but still standard critical edition of the material.

Foerster, Werner. *From the Exile to Christ: A Historical Introduction to Palestinian Judaism*. Philadelphia: Fortress Press, 1964.

Gowan, Donald E. *Bridge between the Testaments: A Reappraisal of Judaism from the Exile to the Birth of Christianity*. Pittsburgh: Pickwick Press, 1976.

Hengel, Martin. *Judaism and Hellenism*. Philadelphia: Fortress Press, 1974.

Metzger, Bruce. *An Introduction to the Apocrypha*. New York: Oxford University Press, 1957.

Orlinsky, Harry M. "Maccabees, Maccabean Revolt." In *The Interpreter's Dictionary of the Bible*, vol. 3, pp. 197–201. Nashville: Abingdon Press, 1962.

Pfeiffer, Robert H. *History of New Testament Times: With an Introduction to the Apocrypha*. New York: Harper & Brothers, 1949. Long a standard work.

Rost, Leonhard. *Judaism outside the Hebrew Canon: An Introduction to the Documents*. Nashville: Abingdon Press, 1976.

Russell, D. S. *Between the Testaments*. London: SCM Press, 1960.

Schalit, Abraham, ed. *The Hellenistic Age: Political History of Jewish Palestine from 332 B.C.E. to 67 B.C.E.* New Brunswick, N.J.: Rutgers University Press, 1972.

Tcherikover, Victor. *Hellenistic Civilization and the Jews*. New York: Atheneum, 1970.

Apocalyptic Material

Funk, Robert W. *Journal for Theology and the Church, No. 6: Apocalypticism*. New York: Herder & Herder, 1969.

Hanson, Paul D. "Apocalypse, Genre," and "Apocalypticism." In *The Interpreter's Dictionary of the Bible: Supplementary Volume*, pp. 27–34. Nashville: Abingdon Press, 1976.

———. "Apocalyptic Reexamined." *Interpretation* 25 (1971): 454–79.

———. *The Dawn of Apocalyptic: The Historical and Sociological Roots of Jewish Apocalyptic Eschatology*. Philadelphia: Fortress Press, 1975.

Hartman, Louis F., and Di Lella, Alexander A. *The Book of Daniel*. Garden City, N.Y.: Doubleday & Co., 1978.

Mowinckel, Sigmund. *He That Cometh*. Nashville: Abingdon Press, 1956. A classic.

Porteous, Norman W. *Daniel*. Philadelphia: Westminster Press, 1965.

Rist, M. "Apocalypticism." In *The Interpreter's Dictionary of the Bible*, vol. 1, pp. 157–61. Nashville: Abingdon Press, 1962.

Russell, D. S. *The Method and Message of Jewish Apocalyptic*. Philadelphia: Westminster Press, 1964. An excellent study.

1 and 2 Maccabees

Brownlee, W. H. "Maccabees, Books of." In *The Interpreter's Dictionary of the Bible*, vol. 3, pp. 201–15. Nashville: Abingdon Press, 1962.

Goldstein, Jonathan A. *I Maccabees*. Garden City, N.Y.: Doubleday & Co., 1976. An extended introduction to 1 and 2 Maccabees with translation and commentary on 1 Maccabees.

13 THE ESSENES OF QUMRAN

Primary reading: *Theodor H. Gaster*, The Dead Sea Scriptures in English Translation (*Garden City, N.Y.: Doubleday & Co., 1976*).

Judas the Maccabee and his brothers Jonathan and Simon, who took up leadership when he died, not only won independence for their people but established the Hasmoneans as rulers over the new nation. Terms of peace were reached with the Seleucids, and under John Hyrcanus I (134–104 B.C.E.), the first ruler of the second generation of Hasmoneans, the territory of Israel was expanded. John also assumed the position of high priest in the temple in Jerusalem—outraging some Jews because the legitimacy of Hasmonean claims to that position was severely clouded—and the dual position enlarged the power that he passed on to his sons, Aristobulus I (104–103 B.C.E.) and Alexander Jannaeus (103–76 B.C.E.).

On his death, Alexander Jannaeus was succeeded by his wife Alexandra Salome (76–67 B.C.E.), who in turn passed authority on to her son Aristobulus II. In 63 B.C.E., however, another son, Hyrcanus II, who had earlier been designated high priest, seized the throne as a figurehead for Rome, for in the previous year Roman forces had made Syria a part of their eastwardly expanding empire, and a year later the Roman general Pompey entered and took Jerusalem. The independent state formed by the Maccabees fell, and the area was once again under foreign governance.

Hasmonean rule had lasted for about a century; Roman rule in southern Palestine would endure for almost 130 years before segments of the Jewish population in Palestine, again informed in part by apocalyptic visions, rebelled in 66–70 C.E. This rebellion also reflected divisions within Judaism as much as differences between Jews and Romans; Jews appeared on both sides of the conflict. Divisions between Jews and gentiles, as well as tensions within Judaism that broke into open conflict in the days of Antiochus IV remained over the next two centuries and more. On the one hand, the Torah style of Jewishness firmly restricted contact with non-Jews; to many of the Torah Jews, the Hasmoneans and later Roman sympathizers seemed more like Hellenistic princes than loyal Jews, especially as the realities of survival forced even them into actions having little to do with the ideal kingdom of their god. On the other hand, to Jews whose understanding of Judaism did not forbid intercourse with the world at large the politics and convictions of those who sparked the warfare appeared limited, inflexible, and foolish.

The divisions within Palestinian Judaism from about 150 B.C.E. to 66 C.E. were not always clear-cut, and because source material is both limited and difficult to interpret, to attempt to define them almost two thousand years later is inevitably to produce a picture that is sketchy at some points and hypothetical at others. Although the best way to capture the Judaic variety of this period is to analyze the life and development of certain Jewish groups, sometimes called sects, not all Jews in southern Palestine were associated with one or another sect, and to center attention on Jewish communities in Palestine is to consider only a part of Judaism. Even less is known of the Jews in the eastern diaspora, though they then constituted the vast majority of Jews in the world. This chapter will focus on a sect called the Essenes; the next chapter will consider other major sects; we shall then consider the impact of the revolt of 66–70 C.E. on the life of each sect and on Judaism as a whole.

THE ESSENE COMMUNITY

Until thirty years ago little was known about the Essenes. Josephus, a Jewish historian who lived in the second half of the first century C.E., provides a brief description of them, and even briefer remarks are to be found in the works of the Roman Pliny the Elder and the Jewish Philo of Alexandria. In the late winter of 1946 or early spring of 1947, however, a Bedouin youth discovered the first of what would become known as the Dead Sea Scrolls in a cave on the cliffs near the northwest corner of the Dead Sea. Although the period of initial discovery and purchase coincided with the tensions and open conflict accompanying the birth of modern Israel, the scrolls made their way into the market and proved to be of great value both to the Bedouin who found them and to the scholars who in time acquired them.

The eleven scrolls fall into two groups. The first group consists of copies,

252   ranging from tiny fragments to almost complete scrolls, of all but one of the
books now found in the Old Testament; only the Book of Esther is not represented. The second group preserves previously unknown materials. On exca-
vating the caves, as well as a nearby ruin known as Khirbet Qumran and some
adjacent remains and a cemetery, archaeologists uncovered evidence that, when
combined with the information provided by the scrolls, evokes a picture of a
small band of Jews founded in the Torah who literally lived out the Moses-Sinai
story with a fervor enflamed by apocalyptic hopes. Most scholars today identify
this community with one branch of the sect called Essenes.

Origin and Shape of the Community

The origin of the Essenes is obscure. Some have suggested that they were heirs
of the Hasidim who had resisted the persecutions of Antiochus IV to win the
freedom to follow the religious practices set forth in the Torah. Although
political independence was but a means to that end, so extreme was this period
of persecution that Judas the Maccabee himself had set the Torah aside in ruling
that Jews could take up arms in self-defense even on the Sabbath. But the
victorious Hasmoneans had then further accommodated their pattern of life to
the exigencies of governing a small nation in a world of continuing flux, so that
to Torah Hasidim the later Hasmonean policies and life style must have seemed
a betrayal of the very cause for which they had fought.

The founder of the Qumran community may have been a priest who was
driven from the Jerusalem temple and persecuted, perhaps because he opposed
Hasmonean takeover of the high priesthood. In any case, their documents make
it clear that the people of Qumran rejected the temple cult and its priesthood,
found its calendar to be irregular, and depicted a "wicked priest" as the most
hated villain in Essene writings, characterizing him and his cohorts as the "sons
of Absalom," as disloyal to their heritage as David's son had been to his father.
Historians have attempted to link such symbolic designations with individuals
during the reign of the Hasmoneans or later, but the descriptions are so cryptic
and the particulars so few that no one reconstruction carries conviction over the
others.

On the basis of coins found in the Qumran ruins, the period of John Hyrcanus I (134–104 B.C.E.) seems the most probable date for the founding of the
community, but it is also possible that the sect existed for a time before a part of
it established camp at the edge of the wilderness. Developing a theme found in
Amos 5:27, the material speaks at points of an exile or sojourn in the "land of
Damascus," which may refer to the life at Qumran, cut off and lived in an alien
setting, though it might also refer to a period of forced withdrawal after these
people came into conflict with the ruling powers of the state and temple. It is
clear, in any event, that the Essenes considered themselves to be outside the
power structure that governed Palestinian Judaism at this time. Their power lay

in their vision of their god and the certainty that he had set them apart for his own purposes.

Thus they lived totally apart from others, Jews and gentiles alike. Their monastery was located on a terrace beneath the steep cliffs that run parallel to the shore of the Dead Sea. The area is hot, humid, and as forbidding as the nearby sea with its life-destroying salinity. Rainfall is sparse; what water exists comes from the Wadi Qumran, a deep ravine that cuts through the cliffs to the west and through which water flows for a small part of the year. Only south of the monastery is there any sort of greenery, supported by a spring now called Ain Feshkha. In every way the edge of the wilderness, the area is only a short distance south of the place where, according to tradition, Joshua led the Israelites across the Jordan River into the land of promise.

Excavations at Qumran have uncovered the remains of a refectory, storerooms, a scriptorium in which scrolls were probably copied, a potter's shop, a tannery, and a complex water system running from the Wadi Qumran to a series of pools and channels that interlace the ruins. To the south, near the Ain Feshkha spring, are the remains of farm buildings, stock pens, and various industrial complexes, all of which indicate either a communal use or that they were designed to supply the community with basic necessities. Archaeologists have uncovered no private dwellings; evidence indicates that some of the caves were occupied, while other community members seem to have lived in tents or simple huts around the central complex.

On entering the community, all possessions were relinquished. Members were assigned a clearly defined rank, and one worked at tasks assigned according to individual skill, intelligence, and the needs of the brotherhood. All aspects of life were regulated, authority was sharply defined and strict, and any violation of the rules brought punishments that ranged from reduction in food allotment through demotion in rank to temporary or permanent expulsion—the latter being regarded as tantamount to death, for the Essenes set themselves against all others as the people of the promise, the elect, and to be cut off from the community was to be cut off from the source of life.

Relations with the outside world were restricted to those few leaders of the community who could make such limited contacts as were needed; others were wholly cut off. To enter the brotherhood one underwent a two-year period as a novice, in the course of which full participation in community life was restricted, and one was trained and thoroughly examined in the group's rules and beliefs. This period also provided a way to withdraw from the preparatory program and reenter the world, for full participation in the life of the brotherhood at Qumran demanded total commitment.

This pattern of life is described in one of the documents found in the caves and has been called the "Manual of Discipline" because it constitutes the rule for what appears to have been a monastic community. This manual indicates that celibacy was the rule in the Qumran community, and, indeed, the cemetery reveals a preponderance of male skeletal remains; the few graves containing the remains of women and children are in annexed parts of the cemetery and may belong to persons who lived on the community's outskirts. Although Jewish law neither demands nor recommends celibacy, this brotherhood lived in a state of constant preparedness for a climactic holy war against the forces of evil and chaos, and this meant that all who fought must be ritually pure, which involved sexual abstinence (see 1 Samuel 21:4 and 2 Samuel 11:11).

Finally, many years before the discovery of the Dead Sea Scrolls there was found in a repository for used and worn scrolls and books in an Egyptian synagogue a document that came to be called the "Zadokite Document." Only with the discovery of the Qumran materials, and especially the "Manual of Discipline," did it become clear that this, too, was an Essene writing. Although it resembles the manual in many ways, the rule of life that it sets forth is not for a camp in the wilderness but for urban groups, which suggests that the Essenes were not limited to the group at Qumran. Urban Essenes lived in the world, where they could marry, have families, pursue occupations, and interact to a degree with life around them, though they, too, followed a pattern of life that defined them as Essenes.

At Qumran, then, we have an essentially monastic community encamped in the wilderness, living the Torah life style, and infused with apocalyptic immediacy. Because in their own eyes the promise so long delayed was about to be fulfilled, they set down minimal roots and were ready at any moment of the day or night for the advent of their god and his final confrontation with the forces of evil and chaos.

The Essene Bible and Hymn Scroll

Some of the most tantalizing references to events and figures in the history of the sect are found in a series of commentaries on older Israelite and early Jewish materials, especially on the books of the prophets. Preserved fragments of commentaries on Isaiah, Hosea, Micah, Habakkuk, and selected psalms are called *pesherim*, from the Hebrew verb *pashar*, which means "to solve a puzzle, to interpret a vision or dream." A related term is *raz*, which denotes the working out of a puzzle or riddle. This terminology suggests that, to the Essenes, the traditions of the past were puzzles or riddles whose deepest meanings were to be disclosed only to teachers whose special insight and knowledge enabled them to penetrate the material's surface to its basic level of meaning.

The *pesherim* cite a line from the prophetic tradition and follow it with several lines of interpretation. Such commentaries may have served as material for private study, or they may have been read at gatherings of the brotherhood—at meals, for example. The following commentary on Habakkuk 1:13, the most extensively preserved of the *pesherim*, illustrates their style:

Why dost thou look [idly] upon traitors, and keep silent when the wicked confounds him that is more righteous than he? This refers to the "house of Absalom" and their cronies who kept silent when charges were leveled against the teacher who was expounding the Law aright, and who did not come to his aid against the man of lies when the latter rejected the Torah in the midst of their entire congregation.*

Clearly, the Essenes regarded the prophets' sayings as words from their god addressed directly to them and their particular situation. The words had two distinct levels of meaning. On the surface or literal level the prophet spoke as an intermediary between the god and the people of his day, bringing theological meaning to their particular historical situation. On the second level, however, the deity addressed those Essenes who had the insight to see depths of meaning not apparent even to the prophet. To the modern reader it is striking that this deeper meaning has no clear link with the literal sense of the words. Of the commentary on Habakkuk 2:1–2, for example, it is said:

God told Habakkuk to write down the things that were to come upon the latter age, but He did not inform him when that moment would come to fulfillment. As to the phrase, that *he who runs may read*, this refers to the teacher who expounds the Law aright, for God has made him au courant with all the deeper implications of the words of His servants the prophets.

The full import of Habakkuk's words was known only to the "teacher of righteousness," whom some identify as the community's founder, and to the teachers who followed in his path.

This method of interpretation permitted words, phrases, clauses, and whole sentences to be excerpted from both the historical context in which they had been spoken and the grammatical context in which they now stood, a method that was greatly to influence Judaism and early Christianity by providing a new way of bringing the past to bear on the present. In the passage cited above, for example, the phrase that "he who runs may read" was entirely removed from its original context. In the setting of Habakkuk's message it meant that the divine response to the prophet's question about human suffering was to be posted in characters so large that even those who ran by would not miss it—that is, it was to be presented as boldly and clearly as possible. To the Essenes, however, a play on the Hebrew verb meaning "to run" as well as "to be conversant with" (a double meaning also found in the French *au courant*) provided a basis for undergirding the teacher's authority. Elsewhere Genesis 41:40 is cited in support of the teacher even though in the Joseph narrative it clearly concerns the authority given to Joseph by pharaoh.

---

*This and all other extracts in this chapter are from Theodor H. Gaster, *The Dead Sea Scriptures in English Translation* (Garden City, N.Y.: Doubleday & Co., 1976).

At the deepest level this manner of interpretation aimed at reapplying the older tradition directly to the Essene situation, for this small isolated brotherhood dared to assert that they were the ultimate focus of all the deity's words to his people throughout the whole course of their history. Thus interpreted, the Bible pervaded their daily lives. They were literally a "Bible people," not only in terms of the titles and orders of their brotherhood but in the sense that they were to read, hear, discuss, and meditate on the Bible at meals, in daily conversation, and even in the privacy of their own thoughts. Idle conversation was strictly prohibited. Every moment of every day was to be filled with their Bible, and one who could interpret the meaning of the tradition was to be readily available.

Also among the Dead Sea Scrolls is an extended collection of Essene hymns composed in part of direct and indirect citations from and allusions to older materials, providing a montage of interlocking references to the Bible. Some form of worship that centered in the reading of scripture accompanied by prayer and praise must have been part of the regular rhythm of life at Qumran. This worship would involve no regular pattern of sacrifice, since the Essenes, like most of diaspora Judaism, were cut off from the temple. They were not separated from it by physical distance, however; they had cut themselves off because the temple had fallen into corrupt hands, and they looked for the day when it could be recleansed as in the days of Judas the Maccabee. Hence they gave much thought and concern to the ideal temple and its cult but took no part in its present life.

Beyond this, evidence of the community's worship life is limited. Clearly the Sabbath was observed with great care; no work of any sort was permitted. A laving ceremony may have been a part of the individual's entrance into the full life of the brotherhood, and archaeologists have found some evidence of what may have been a cultic meal celebrated by community members.

The Sons of Light and Darkness

In a literal reenactment of the Torah, the Essenes lived as a camp in the wilderness in a continual state of readiness for a war in which the deity and his forces of heaven would forever destroy the power of evil and chaos, the promise of the Torah vision would be realized, and the kingdom of Israel would be reborn. The men at Qumran believed that this war would come about very soon and that they were to play a formative part in the new creation. What for many Jews had become a vague hope for the distant future was for these men a vital expectation giving form and reason to their lives.

Nowhere is this clearer than in one of the most striking of the scrolls found in 1947, which has been given the title "The War of the Sons of Light against the Sons of Darkness." The war scroll is an exact battle plan for the struggles that would bring the kingdom of their god to realization. Details about troop deployment, the kinds of arms to be used, the course of engagements, and much more are set out in a form based on contemporary Roman military patterns.

Here above all we can see how the apocalyptic vision first set forth in the days of the Maccabees informed the hopes and lives of the Essenes.

In a segment of the "Manual of Discipline" there is preserved a brief expression of the theological foundations of the apocalyptic vision, describing the powers that govern the world both for good and for ill and the situation and obligations of the faithful in the face of these powers. The unit begins with a statement that this teaching would bring others to an "inner vision"—that is, to a distinct and special insight that belonged to the Essenes alone. Then follows the rigidly deterministic assertion that the god of Israel not only controls the course of human history but had fixed it in its course from the beginning: "All that is and ever was comes from a God of knowledge. Before things came into existence He determined the plan for them; and when they fill their appointed roles, it is in accordance with His glorious design that they discharge their functions. Nothing can be changed."

The deity sent two spirits, one of truth and one of perversity, to direct human beings for an allotted period of time. That both are the deity's creations is emphasized to prevent an apparent dualism from compromising the creator god's absolute authority. Here we encounter some of the tension that informs the radical monotheism of the apocalyptic vision, for evil is here not simply the result of human perversity; sin and suffering are the work of powers that transcend the human sphere. The vividly described Angel of Darkness, elsewhere called Belial, is such a superhuman force:

All who practice perversity are under the domination of the Angel
of Darkness and walk in the ways of darkness. Through the Angel of
Darkness, however, even those who practice righteousness are made liable
to error. All their sin and their iniquities, all their guilt and their deeds of
transgression are the result of his domination: and this, by God's
inscrutable design, will continue until the time appointed by Him.
Moreover, all men's afflictions and all their moments of tribulation are due
to this being's malevolent sway. All of the spirits that attend upon him are
bent on causing the sons of light to stumble.

Human beings, however, must choose between the two forces warring for control of the world:

Thus far, the spirits of truth and perversity have been struggling in the
heart of man. Men have walked both in wisdom and folly. If a man casts his
portion with truth, he does righteously and hates perversity; if he casts it
with perversity, he does wickedly and abominates truth. For God has
apportioned them in equal measure until the final age, until "He makes all
things new." He foreknows the effect of their works in every epoch of the
world, and He has made men heirs to them that they might know good and
evil. But [when the time] of Inquisition [comes], He will determine the fate
of every living being in accordance with which of the [two spirits he has
chosen to follow].

Here lies a further tension that is inherent in a number of theological systems. It apparently results from the need to affirm human responsibility for decisions as well as divine control over the course of history—that is, what we do makes a difference even in a larger context that we do not control. The tension is more apparent in a system of abstract thought than in an expression of belief that grows out of the struggle to bring sense to human experience. For the Essene vision was not abstract speculation; it was the fruit of a bitter struggle to survive as loyal followers of their god. In 66 C.E. a war did break out between segments of Palestinian Judaism and Rome, and its outcome would decide the fate of the Qumran community and its vision. Before examining its impact on the Qumran brotherhood, however, we must consider other sectarian groups that were formative in the life of Palestinian Judaism during this period.

BIBLIOGRAPHIC NOTE

Betz, O. "Dead Sea Scrolls." In *The Interpreter's Dictionary of the Bible*, vol. 1, pp. 790–802. Nashville: Abingdon Press, 1962.

————. "Essenes." In *The Interpreter's Dictionary of the Bible: Supplementary Volume*, pp. 277–79. Nashville: Abingdon Press, 1976.

Cross, Frank Moore. *The Ancient Library of Qumran and Modern Biblical Studies*. Garden City, N.Y.: Doubleday & Co., 1961. A basic introduction to the scrolls and their significance for Bible study.

————. "The Early History of the Apocalyptic Community at Qumran." In *Canaanite Myth and Hebrew Epic*, pp. 326–42. Cambridge, Mass.: Harvard University Press, 1973.

de Vaux, Roland. *Archaeology and the Dead Sea Scrolls*. London: Oxford University Press, 1973. A report by the excavator of Qumran.

Dupont-Sommer, A. *The Essene Writings from Qumran*. New York: Meridian Books, 1961. Introduction to the scrolls and a fresh translation.

Farmer, W. R. "Essenes." In *The Interpreter's Dictionary of the Bible*, vol. 2, pp. 143–49. Nashville: Abingdon Press, 1962.

Ringgren, Helmer. *The Faith of Qumran*. Philadelphia: Fortress Press, 1961. Excellent.

Vermes, Geza. "Dead Sea Scrolls." In *The Interpreter's Dictionary of the Bible: Supplementary Volume*, pp. 210–19. Nashville, Abingdon Press, 1976.

————. *The Dead Sea Scrolls in English*. Baltimore: Penguin Books, 1962.

SADDUCEES, SAMARITANS, ZEALOTS, AND PHARISEES

14

Primary readings*: *Tobit*

Judith

Additions to the Book of Esther

The Wisdom of Solomon

Ecclesiasticus

The Letter of Baruch

The Letter of Jeremiah

The Prayer of Azariah and the Song of the Three Young Men

Susanna

Bel and the Dragon

The Prayer of Manasseh

Introduction

Between 150 B.C.E. and 66 C.E. political lines shifted once again in the Near Eastern and Mediterranean world. The Ptolemaic and Seleucid empires were absorbed by Roman authority, which stopped in Mesopotamia; the eastern portions of the older Seleucid empire came under Parthian control, which posed the major threat to Roman rule in the east; and eastern diaspora Jewish communities were again cut off from one another and from the homeland by hostile borders.

The Romans built their eastwardly expanding empire around an evolving blend of local self-rule, partial local autonomy, and direct rule by Roman appointees, and the extent to which individual Jews were part of the scattered communities in which they lived varied with local conditions and the degree of tolerance on both sides. Some Jews attained positions of great prominence in government and commerce, a few even holding vast estates. Others who con-

---

*All these readings are found in the Roman Catholic Old Testament and in the Apocrypha of Protestants and Jews.

JUDEA under the ROMANS

B.C.E.	Roman Emperors	Procurators of Judea	
50			Pompey takes Jerusalem (63)
25	Augustus (30 B.C.E.–14 C.E.)		Herod the Great (King of Judea) (37–4)
1 B.C.E.			Herod Antipas (Tetrarch of Galilee) (4 B.C.E.–39 C.E.)
1 C.E.		Coponius (6–9)	Archelaus (Ethnarch of Judea) (4 B.C.E.–6 C.E.)
	Tiberius (14–37)	Ambibulus (9–12)	
		Annius Rufinus (12–15)	
		Valerius Gratus (15–26)	
25		Pontius Pilate (26–36)	
	Gaius Caligula (37–41)	Marcellus (36–37) Marullus (37–41)	Herod Agrippa I (King of Judea) (41–44)
	Claudius (41–54)	Cuspius Fadus (44–46) Tiberius Alexander (46–48) Ventidius Cumanus (48–52)	
50		M. Antonius Felix (52–60)	
	Nero (54–68)	Porcius Festus (60–62) Albinus (62–64)	
	Galba (68–69) Otho (69) Vitellius (69)	Gessius Florus (64–66)	Jewish Revolt (66–72) Fall of Jerusalem (70)
75	Vespasian (69–79)		Masada (72)
	Titus (79–81) Domitian (81–96)		Academy at Jabneh
	Nerva (96–98)		
100	Trajan (98–117)		
	Hadrian (117–135)		
125			Bar Kokhba War (132–135)

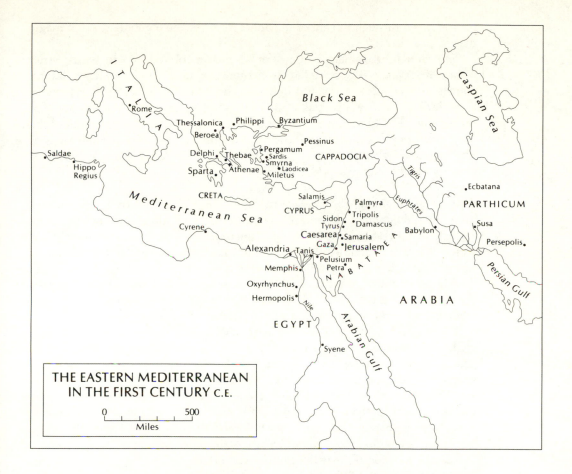

THE EASTERN MEDITERRANEAN
IN THE FIRST CENTURY C.E.

0   500
Miles

structed their religious identity around the Torah and the synagogue were cut off from the world's mainstream and power structures. Those who continued to suffer because they were different must have longed intensely for the homeland, which to others must have represented little more than a faint hope for the future. Varied reflections of the diaspora Judaism of this period can be found in two documents: the tale of Tobit and the Wisdom of Solomon—the former originating in the eastern diaspora; the latter, from Alexandria in Egypt.

Tobit   Tobit is an exiled Jew living in Assyria who observes the Torah punctiliously in spite of the dangers that this poses. Nevertheless he is blinded in an accident. Far to the east lives Sara, the daughter of another exiled Jew. Sara is unable to keep a husband beyond the wedding night because each groom is attacked by a demon before the marriage is consummated. The fates of the two families become entwined as Tobit's son Tobias weds Sara and Tobit's blindness is cured through the aid of the angel Raphael and a goodly dose of magic that he provides.

This delightful romantic tale offers a picture of Judaism in which strict Torah observance is admixed with elements of magic and popular folklore. Angels appear with names and defined roles as in the apocalyptic visions of Daniel; demons play a part as well, although their influence can be thwarted through magic. Throughout the tale abides a firm conviction that the god of the Jews will uphold and deliver those who do not forsake him in their time of distress. Loyalty to the heritage as defined in the Torah is the sole source of security and life in this world.

Wisdom of Solomon   Some decades later than Tobit, and from the western rather than the eastern diaspora, came the Wisdom of Solomon, which takes the form of an address by King Solomon to the pagan rulers of the earth, though it is aimed at Jews and gentiles alike. To the Jew it affirms the care and protection of a sovereign deity; to the gentile it presents this deity and the way of Judaism as the highest truth. A number of Hellenistic philosophical and religious themes are here blended with a basic Hebraism that uncovers new aspects of the latter while bringing the former within a Jewish frame of reference.

The author, a member of the large Jewish population of Alexandria, a Hellenistic cultural center, is more a popularizer than an original thinker. His goal is to bolster fellow Jews who find their heritage and life style outdated or a source of shame or persecution and at the same time to recommend Judaism as worthy of gentile esteem. In chapters 1–6, for example, he seeks to demonstrate that the god of the Jews is the source of justice, without which there is no true wisdom (compare the description of Solomon's wisdom in 1 Kings 3), and he goes on to show that the deity always cares for those who remain loyal to him. While acknowledging that the faithful sometimes suffer, he affirms that this must be borne and will pass (chapters 7–9). It is his god alone who sustains his people, and his review of Israel's history demonstrates this as well as the ignoble fate that ultimately overtakes the nonbeliever (chapters 10–19).

The author draws on Platonic, Neo-Platonic, Stoic, and other Hellenistic systems to support his arguments. In the Wisdom of Solomon 8:7 he presents the four cardinal virtues of classical Greek thought:

> And if any one loves righteousness,
> her labors are virtues;
> for she teaches self-control and prudence,
> justice and courage;
> nothing is more profitable for men than these.

Elsewhere he speaks of a preexistent soul (Wisdom of Solomon 8:19–20) that is imprisoned in the physical body (Wisdom of Solomon 9:15). This concept is based on a Greek distinction between the material and immaterial, as is the emphasis placed on the cultivation of the latter at the expense of the former.

Indeed, it is the deity's assurance of a blessed immortality not bound to a bodily existence (compare Daniel 12:2) that finally allows the author to overcome the problem of suffering in a way not available, for example, to the author of Job:

> But the souls of the righteous are in the hand of God,
>   and no torment will ever touch them.
> In the eyes of the foolish they seemed to have died,
>   and their departure was thought to be an affliction,
> and their going from us to be their destruction;
>   but they are at peace.
> For though in the sight of men they were punished,
>   their hope is full of immortality.
> Having been disciplined a little, they will receive
>   great good,
> because God tested them and found them worthy of himself;
> Like gold in the furnace he tried them,
>   and like a sacrificial burnt offering he accepted them.
> In the time of their visitation they will shine forth,
>   and will run like sparks through the stubble.
> They will govern nations and rule over peoples,
>   and the Lord will reign over them for ever.
>
>   (Wisdom of Solomon 3:1–8)

The author asserts further that at times his god even brings someone to an early death so that he can avoid physical bondage and suffering.

Chapters 13–15 attack pagan idols in a manner that recalls not only the Second Isaiah but also a number of contemporary gentile attacks on older forms of religious belief and practice. Finally, in the Wisdom of Solomon 2:24 the serpent of Genesis 3 is presented as the Devil and the source of all evil and death in the created world.

Although these two documents make it clear that the widely dispersed Jewish communities were significant in the development of Jewish tradition between 150 B.C.E. and 66 C.E., sectarian groups centered in Palestine exercised the strongest formative influence on the style of Judaism that would characterize the Common Era.

THE SADDUCEES

To the Romans, the Sadducees were the natural indigenous leaders of Palestinian Judaism. For the most part members of the social upper crust, what we would today call the "establishment," they were the group best able to accommodate their lives to, and even thrive under, foreign rule in Palestine. That they were Jewish—and notwithstanding that both contemporary and later critics have

264　denied this—did not prevent them from forming strong ties with non-Jews. In one sense they were the most Palestinian oriented of all the sects, not in seeking an independent state of Israel but in focusing their religious identity on the temple and its cult, which had the effect of restricting their existence to the city and its surrounding areas.

The Sadducees claimed to be the heirs of David's priest Zadok—the word *Sadducee* seems, in fact, to be a Greek form based on the name Zadok—and therefore the legitimate overseers of the Jerusalem temple, a claim that bound them to the Hasmoneans. The Essenes, however, not only contested this but claimed to represent the true priesthood themselves. To the Essenes, who refused to have anything to do with a temple profaned by unholy hands, the Sadducees were to be included among the Sons of Darkness. As we have seen, the Qumran community may have originated in a dispute over the legitimacy of those who governed the life of the temple; but, in terms of genuine power, Sadducee claims carried the day.

Temple and Torah

While not all priests were Sadducees, the two overlapped. The daily and weekly round of sacrifice and other forms of worship, punctuated by the great yearly festivals, constituted their religious life, and as long as foreign rulers did not greatly interfere with the routine of temple service the Sadducees could live with them. The Torah was recognized as a body of legal material regulating the operation of the temple and its cult, and the Sadducees read the Torah literally, taking account only of what was plainly stated there. No method of interpretation allowed for a second or deeper level of meaning, and no authority was granted to a vast body of oral tradition that was growing about the Torah, interpreting and applying it to ever changing circumstances and conditions.

Most of the restrictive practices and customs that set one apart and required the purity prerequisite for sacred contact the Sadducees reserved for priests during the performance of their duties. To Jews pursuing their day-to-day lives they not only allowed but encouraged a full measure of freedom to interact with the world at large, believing that Jewish life need not fundamentally prohibit life in and of the world. Indeed, the survival of Judaism as they defined it demanded an easy rapprochement with the Roman world. The secular powers were not perceived as an opposing force but as the guarantors of a context for a rich full life.

With respect to particularities of belief, the Sadducees were conservative, acknowledging little that was new, of foreign influence, or of folk derivation. They denied that there was a resurrection, judgment, or effective life after death, and they rejected the confluence of themes that compose the apocalyptic vision—divine determinism, the action of angels or demons, and the imminent end of the age. For them, the apocalyptic vision characterized circles that stood against the world in which they were at home; moreover, there was little in the

Torah, when taken literally, that supported this vision.

It is true, of course, that an established upper class and those allied with it generally find the status quo congenial; they seldom feel the need to overturn it, and those who might desire to do so are anathemas. Among the Sadducees, then, the open-ended dynamic of the ancient sacred story as now formed in the Torah was lost. Their vision was nearer that of the author of the Chronicles, and the Torah became only a guide for conduct in a world that was in no need of present or future change.

The Wisdom of Jesus ben Sirach

In their easy interaction with the larger world, their upper-class orientation and tastes, and their conservatism the Sadducees stood in a line with the wise men of old. This is clear in considering the work of Jesus ben Sirach, whose teachings in the book called Ecclesiasticus characterize him as an early or proto-Sadducee. Jesus ben Sirach was a professional teacher in the pattern of Kohelet and other postexilic wise men. In what he called his "house of study" in Jerusalem he instructed middle- and upper-class youth in the art of successful, happy, and full living, basing his words on a religious and ethical foundation. Around 190 B.C.E. his teachings were put into writing, and in 132 B.C.E. they were translated into Greek by his grandson, as the book's prologue informs us.

Like the wise teachers before him, ben Sirach believed that this world is the handiwork of a divine creator who orders it for human good. Its patterns and structures can be perceived with sufficient clarity for men and women to live their lives in harmony with them; and to do so is to live in harmony with the deity's will, for observance of the rules of life is divine service. A life of moderation, carefully chosen companions and spouse, obedience to one's superiors, hard work, and devotion to family characterize the style of life recommended in his writings, and in them wisdom and Torah finally come together.

The older wise men had spoken little of Torah, but ben Sirach presents in Ecclesiasticus 24 a lovely hymn, developing themes already encountered in segments of Proverbs 1–9, in which wisdom offers herself and the gifts of life and prosperity in the manner of an ancient fertility goddess. Here wisdom again approaches full and independent status as a separate divine being who was formative in the creation of the world:

> Wisdom will praise herself,
>> and will glory in the midst of her people.
> In the assembly of the Most High she will open her mouth,
>> and in the presence of his host she will glory:
> "I came forth from the mouth of the Most High,
>> and covered the earth like a mist.
> I dwelt in high places,
>> and my throne was in a pillar of cloud."

(Ecclesiasticus 24:1–4)

Wisdom then claims special ties with Israel, and these focus on the temple and the sacred city:

> Then the Creator of all things gave me a commandment,
>   and the one who created me assigned a place for my tent.
> And he said, "Make your dwelling in Jacob,
>   and in Israel receive your inheritance."
> From eternity, in the beginning, he created me,
>   and for eternity I shall not cease to exist.
> In the holy tabernacle I ministered before him,
>   and so I was established in Zion.
>
>   (Ecclesiasticus 24:8–10)

There she thrived like a lush fruit tree, her rich gifts offered to others in a summons that recalls the figure in Proverbs 8 and 9:

> Come to me, you who desire me,
>   and eat your fill of my produce.
> For the remembrance of me is sweeter than honey,
>   and my inheritance sweeter than the honeycomb.
> Those who eat me will hunger for more,
>   and those who drink me will thirst for more.
> Whoever obeys me will not be put to shame,
>   and those who work with my help will not sin.
>
>   (Ecclesiasticus 24:19–22)

The concluding lines, however, are stunning:

> All this is the book of the covenant of the Most High God,
>   the law which Moses commanded us
>   as an inheritance for the congregation of Jacob.
>
>   (Ecclesiasticus 24:33)

The Torah is no longer the story of the deity's dealings with his people; it has become a guidebook of rules for devout and successful living. The narratives are now merely illustrations of the lessons offered by teachers of law and wisdom. The sacred story is no longer an experience relived each year or the basis for critique of the state of Israel's political structure. To Jesus ben Sirach the Torah is a book of eternal truths. The great review of Israel's past heroes—the "let us now praise famous men" of Ecclesiasticus 44–50—serves only as a model of faith, not as the locus of ever new experiences of the deity. The dynamic and open-ended vitality of Israel's historical self-understanding is here blunted. As in the world view of the author of the Chronicles, all is stable and fixed and the future but a continuation of the present.

Jesus ben Sirach's review climaxes with an extended hymn in praise of the high priest Simon, the greatest and last of Israel's heroes. For this wise teacher the priesthood and the regular pattern of temple service form the heart of Israel's life. The revelation of divine will is timeless, as regular and static as the eternal round of the cultic year. It is in the priest's temple service and in the instruction of the wise teacher that the god's will is known and realized. The imperative of each unique historical moment—an imperative that rang through the prophet's oracle and the apocalyptic vision—is lost.

This static, upper-class, priestly orientation well illustrates the tone and temper of the Sadducees. In temple service was the human being's response to the deity, and in attunement to the eternal orders of the universe as revealed in the Torah and the words of the wise was the way of life. But history would intervene in the lives of the Sadducees with a force that could not be ignored, and they would find their way judged by events in the history of their people.

SAMARITANS, ZEALOTS, AND CHRISTIANS

Samaritans

At the conclusion of his historical review Jesus ben Sirach inserts a brief bitter notice:

> With two nations my soul is vexed,
>   and the third is no nation:
> Those who live on Mount Seir,
>   and the Philistines,
>   and the foolish people that dwell in Shechem.
>
>   (Ecclesiasticus 50:25–26)

Those on Mount Seir were the Edomites, long hated by Israelites as rivals for control of the area to the south and east of the Dead Sea and as ravishers of Judah and Jerusalem after Nebuchadnezzar's destruction of the city in 587 B.C.E. (recall Psalm 137:7). The Philistines, of course, had been an early threat to Israel's life. That which "is no nation" refers to the Samaritans—not to the people of Samaria, the old capital of northern Israel, but to those who now lived at the oldest federation center at Shechem.

Although their origins are hidden from us now, scholarship has attempted to isolate the source of the fundamental split between the Samaritans and other Jews. The division may have arisen from conflicts between groups in and around Samaria and those who returned to rebuild Jerusalem's temple and walls in the sixth and fifth centuries B.C.E. It may also lay in antagonisms between the people of Jerusalem and the mixed population into which the Assyrians brought foreigners after conquering the northern kingdom in 722 B.C.E. (2 Kings 17:24–41). Indeed, the tensions between northern and southern Israel go back to conflicts within the earliest federation. These conflicts and those in the days of Nehemiah, however, were political, involving questions of who would govern Syria-

Palestine. The account in 2 Kings 17 reads, in fact, like a later anti-Samaritan polemic read back into history.

On their first clear appearance in history the Samaritans lived in Shechem. On Mount Gerizim, just outside the city, they built a temple, for they firmly believed that the deity had chosen Shechem, not Jerusalem, for his dwelling place and that they represented the only legitimate cult and priesthood. Of course, neither the Sadducees nor most Jews accepted this claim. Since Josiah's reform in the seventh century B.C.E. the weight of tradition, practice, and vested interest had combined to override the legitimacy of such claims by any group outside Jerusalem, and to assert otherwise was to fly in the face of a basic tenet of Judaism. For this reason many people even denied the Samaritans a Jewish identity; they were linked with the events described in 2 Kings 17 and traced from foreign stock.

Yet the Samaritans, like the Sadducees, found the locus of ultimate sacred authority in the Torah, which provided the pattern for their cultic and personal lives, ordered their temple service, and, when their temple was destroyed, as it had been by John Hyrcanus in 128 B.C.E. and again later by the Roman Emperor Hadrian, the Torah provided a structure within which they could rebuild and preserve their identity. Except for the temple on Mount Gerizim, the Samaritans stood well within the range of Judaism, and to suggest that they were the bastard offspring of segments of old northern Israel and pagans tells us more about how fellow Jews perceived them than about their true origins. By the time of Jesus of Nazareth no more pejorative term could be found than "Samaritan," and no figures were less likely to capture the sympathy of the Jewish community in southern Palestine (see, for example, Luke 10:29–33).

Isolated from the mainstream of Judaism, the Samaritans continued to exist with little change. Even today small groups are found near Tel Aviv and Nablus, the modern city beside the mound that was ancient Shechem. Their temple stands now on Mount Gerizim, and they continue to follow the customs and laws of their forefathers.

Zealots

In spite of fundamental differences between them, the Sadducees and Samaritans composed the conservative wing of Judaism in this period, but no links existed between these groups and the Zealots. Indeed, although there were individuals termed "zealots" or "zealous," especially during the first century of the Common Era, it is not clear that, except for a very brief period, there ever was a sect called Zealots. Those who would include the Zealots with other sects note that Josephus described them along with the Sadducees, Pharisees, and Essenes in the late first century C.E. What defined a Zealot was an intense desire for an independent state of Israel and a determination to act toward that goal. This often entailed waging a form of guerrilla war against Rome and doing everything possible to exacerbate tensions between the occupying forces and native Jews.

Beyond the desire for independence, however, it is difficult to discern any theological vision that motivated Zealots. They do not appear to have been sustained by an apocalyptic vision of their god's control and action in history, nor do they seem to have had a unified program or distinct style of life. If on the surface they seemed to want the same thing as the Essenes, they did not withdraw from the world to live as the elect awaiting the action of their god but withdrew only to wage war with the enemy. At best they were heirs of the Maccabees; some may, in fact, have been little more than bandits or highwaymen attacking Romans and wealthy Jewish "sympathizers" under the guise of an independence movement. They are nevertheless important in the history of the Jews because in time they sparked a war with Rome that would profoundly affect the future course of Judaism.

Christians

To attempt an adequate treatment of the earliest Christian groups would require a second volume. Here we must simply note that early Christianity emerged from Judaism during this critical era and that early Christians took much of their Israelite and early Jewish heritage into their Bible as their Old Testament. Jesus (a Greek form of the Hebrew name Joshua) was a Jew, as was Paul, who boasted of his training as a Pharisee. The earliest Christian community was centered in and around Jerusalem in the middle decades of the first century c.e. The title Messiah given to Jesus of Nazareth, as well as many of the motifs used in the story of his passion, death, and resurrection, were drawn from Jewish tradition (note especially the use made of Psalm 22; Isaiah 52:13–53:12; and Zechariah 9:9 in the Gospels). In Christian circles these older traditions, and especially the oracles of the prophets, were interpreted in a manner akin to that of the Essenes as clearly pointing ahead to Jesus.

In designating Jesus as Messiah, however, the early Christians were not using that title in its normal connotation. Even for Jews it meant more than one anointed with oil and set apart in the manner of a king or priest; it denoted a royal figure who would be instrumental in the apocalyptic last days in restoring the kingdom of Israel and the universal rule of her god. Taken up into the apocalyptic vision, the title acquired a rich set of nuances, but these did not include a scandalous crucifixion for the provocation of civil unrest. It is striking that in the Gospels, when Jesus is clearly identified as Messiah by his followers, the term is redefined in terms of his death and resurrection (Matthew 16:13–23; Mark 8:27–33; and Luke 9:18–27). It seems that the image of the suffering servant in Isaiah 52:13–53:12 was used to modify the import of the designation, which goes well beyond anything in the Jewish tradition of that time.

As the early Christians moved away from their Jewish roots, finding a more

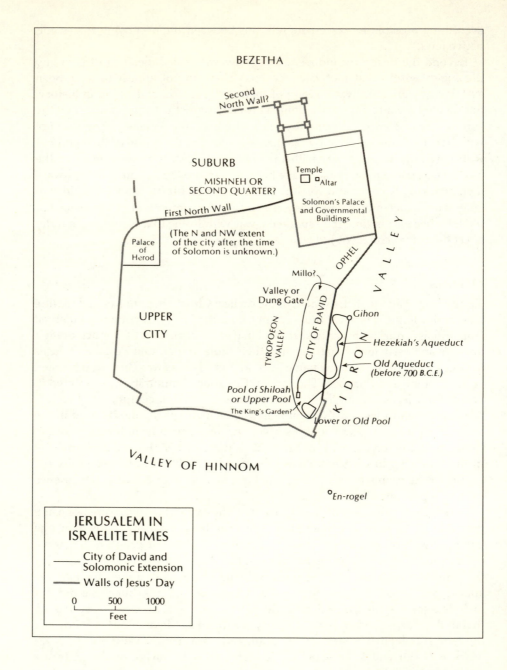

BEZETHA

Second
North Wall?

SUBURB

MISHNEH OR
SECOND QUARTER?

First North Wall

Temple
☐ ▫ Altar

Solomon's Palace
and Governmental
Buildings

(The N and NW extent
of the city after the time
of Solomon is unknown.)

Palace
of
Herod

Millo?

OPHEL

Valley or
Dung Gate

Gihon

UPPER

CITY

CITY OF DAVID

TYROPOEON
VALLEY

KIDRON VALLEY

Hezekiah's Aqueduct

Old Aqueduct
(before 700 B.C.E.)

Pool of Shiloah
or Upper Pool

The King's Garden?

Lower or Old Pool

VALLEY OF HINNOM

°En-rogel

JERUSALEM IN
ISRAELITE TIMES

——— City of David and
Solomonic Extension

——— Walls of Jesus' Day

0   500   1000

Feet

sympathetic hearing in the gentile world, they used new designations to describe their experience and comprehension of the man Jesus. For to call Jesus the Messiah when speaking to a non-Jew was to convey very little, but to speak of the Son of God was to meet the Roman world on more familiar ground. But this discussion exceeds the range of the present study. Here we simply note the fact that within the matrix of Judaism in the first decades of the Common Era, Christians were slowly defining themselves as well.

THE PHARISEES BEFORE 66 C.E.

The term *Pharisee* probably comes from the Hebrew word *parash*, which means "to be separate, distinct, or cut off." Whether the Pharisees adopted this term themselves or whether others first applied it to them in mockery, they clearly were a people who separated themselves from other Jews and gentiles alike. Today, however, the term connotes hypocrisy and a greater devotion to external appearances than to essential internal matters. This connotation is the result of their depiction in the New Testament, where they are frequently termed "hypocrites," a "brood of vipers," and the like. In the Gospels they generally appear as opponents of Jesus, who often develops his teachings against them.

But the New Testament's witness to the nature of Pharisaism is more complex than first appears, for at several points in their Bible the early Christians seem to be allied with them, especially against the Sadducees (Luke 13:31; Acts 5:34–39; 23:6–9; and 26:5). Essentially the New Testament reflects the fact that in the late first century C.E., when the Gospels were shaped, the Pharisees defined Judaism and stood as primary rivals to Christianity.

The Hasmoneans, Herod, and Hillel

The origins of this sect are obscure as well. It is often suggested that the Pharisees, like the Essenes, were heirs of the Hasidim, the loyal Torah Jews in the days of Antiochus IV, and that they struggled against the course pursued by the Hasmoneans, believing that these rulers had aborted the cause for which their ancestors had fought and suffered. For the war against Antiochus and Seleucid rule had not been just a war for political independence; it had been a necessary means toward creating an environment in which Jews could live as they saw fit.

The Jewish historian Josephus makes it clear that the Pharisees, unlike the Essenes, continued the political struggle to gain control of the instruments of state in order to ensure the observance of Torah Judaism. During the reign of the Hasmonean king Alexander Jannaeus (103–76 B.C.E.) a great many Pharisees were crucified or forced into exile. On the accession of his wife Alexandra Salome, however, they found a sympathetic figure as head of state; and when the instruments of power came within their grasp, they in turn executed or drove away many of their opponents. But Alexandra's reign was brief, and the struggles between her sons for the throne brought the Romans to the scene in 63 B.C.E. The situation against the Pharisees reached its nadir under Herod the Great, a Jew of disputed heritage and legitimacy, whom the Romans established as a puppet ruler over Judah.

At the same time, however, the Herod years (37–4 B.C.E.) witnessed the careers of Hillel and Shammai, two of the most revered of all Pharisaic rabbis. Although little is known about either man, there is reason to believe that, by redefining its nature, Hillel set Pharisaism on a radical new course. He may have recognized that the Pharisees would not survive their political losses under Herod. Unable to effect their vision of Judaism by controlling the machinery of state, they would therefore have to take a different path.

A Table Fellowship When we cut beneath the New Testament's generally hostile tone toward the Pharisees, they no longer seem intent on obtaining and using political power. In the first decades of the Common Era they appear as a group seeking to define itself as a sect, not by physically withdrawing from the world but in a mode of conducting their daily lives. This detachment was to be achieved chiefly in the area of diet—that is, in terms of what could or could not be eaten, with whom one could eat, how food was to be prepared, how tithed, and so on. We have already seen that in the Near East little political, social, economic, or cultural interaction took place without the sharing of food. Hence if the number of those with whom one could dine were radically restricted, interaction was limited to a circle that observed the same regulations.

In Exodus 19:6, when the fugitive slaves first come to Mount Sinai, the deity tells them, "You shall be to me a kingdom of priests and a holy nation." To be priests means to be set apart for more direct contact with the deity; one must stand back from the everyday, the mundane. For the Pharisees in the second stage of their development, this priestly ideal was to be binding not only on a few priests and not only for a limited period of formal divine service; all Jews were to be as priests for every moment of their lives.

To achieve this ideal they found that the Torah regulations required further refinement, definition, and application to new situations. A method of interpreting the Torah and a growing body of oral tradition had been developing gradually over the generations, and for centuries this material had been passed on orally in the form of teachings by masters or rabbis, of whom Hillel and Shammai were the greatest, to followers who might in time become rabbis themselves. This growing body of oral law remained fluid, reflecting different schools of interpretation, and would eventually attain written form, first in the Mishnah and then in the Talmud. In this detailed application of Torah to daily life, the course taken by Shammai and his disciples was generally more conservative than that taken by Hillel and his followers.

In their own way the Pharisees took their stand in the Torah as developed in priestly circles during the earlier exile and diaspora, as if to say that they, too, in view of the alien forces ruling the homeland, were aliens. In adopting the style of a table fellowship sect they strove to be in but not of this world. No longer would they try to seize the world's instruments of power to implement what they believed to be a divinely ordained pattern of life. They became a purified seed out of whom a larger community might grow. They were now to compel by example rather than by force.

A System of Belief The New Testament makes it clear that the Pharisaic belief in a judgment, resurrection, and effective life after death not only distinguished the Pharisees from the Sadducees but aligned them with the early Christians (see Matthew 22:23–33; Mark 12:18–27; Luke 20:27–70; Acts 4:1–2 and 23:6–9). Josephus, too, distinguishes the two sects in telling us that the Pharisees "attribute everything to Fate and to God; they hold that to act rightly or otherwise rests indeed for the most part with men, but that in each action Fate cooperates." While asserting that the deity does exercise direct control over human history, the Pharisees nevertheless wished human freedom and individual responsibility to be preserved. They did not allow assertions of divine control to become totally deterministic, nor did they reach the point of the predictive clarity found in portions of the apocalyptic vision.

To suggest that they were defined by certain shared dogmas, however, is deceptive. There is little to indicate that holding a body of beliefs was necessary for identification as a Pharisee. There is no document, including the Torah, that contains a terse statement of belief or confession. The Pharisees were sustained by a vision of a deity who acted in human history, who upheld and yet judged his people, whose promises were still alive and valid as affirmed in the Torah, and whose words of judgment and promise were renewed in the prophets' oracles, but none of this took the form of a codified system to which all must subscribe. One became a Pharisee not by believing in a certain way but by following a certain style of daily life.

The Israelites and early Jews never permitted a rigid separation of belief and action. Belief entailed action, knowing involved relationships; one's beliefs were determined and made manifest by what one did. Yet at Qumran an annual review of the brotherhood examined both how each member believed as well as how he lived, and at the heart of the "Manual of Discipline" is a precise doctrinal statement which, though intended to enliven and inform a style of life, sets out a dogmatic system to which all Essenes had to subscribe. There is evidence of nothing like this in Pharisaic circles.

The story of the sectarian groups within Palestinian Judaism will be continued in the next chapter. As a whole, these groups represented but a small, if significant, part of Judaism within Palestine. Not only did all Jews not identify with one or another sect; what it meant to belong to one group or another varied—while entrance into the Qumran brotherhood entailed a period of formal training and probably a formal initiation, for example, economic and social status may have been significant factors for many Sadducees—and each sect undoubtedly had admirers who stood in loose assocation with it as well.

ADDITIONAL WRITINGS

Judaism both within and beyond the sects remained a rich and varied phenomenon as evidenced by a number of further Jewish writings from this period. Several of these works reflect the influence of the Pharisees, and some scholars have ascribed them directly to members of that sect.

The Book of Judith offers a fictitious tale that is set in the distant past and plagued with factual inaccuracies. Judith, the widow of a man of some wealth and herself a striking beauty, is a Jewish woman (which is what her name means) who is a model of Torah piety and heroic self-sacrifice. Through careful observance of the Torah, total trust in her god, and clever deception of the somewhat stupid enemy leader she overcomes a foreign threat to the Jews in southern Palestine, though it is clear throughout the tale that the deity effects the deliverance of these people through her. The tale renews a call to remain firm in one's heritage and to trust one's god even in the face of death. It could have served as an incentive to resistance and even to direct action in the days of the Antiochus persecutions. It could also have strengthened the resolve of the Pharisees in the period when they suffered under the Hasmoneans and Herod.

In her heroic willingness to risk her life for her people, Judith stands even ahead of Queen Esther, for on learning of the danger confronting her people Judith rebukes the men of her city whose faith seems to flag, while Esther must be rebuked by Mordecai (Esther 4:4–14). Scrupulous observance of the Torah (although the bag used to carry her special food returns with a most unclean item in it), prayer, and confession of confidence in the deity (Judith 8:9–27; 9:1–14), the active presence of the deity and references to him even on the lips of gentiles (Judith 5:1–24)—all characterize the later tale.

But the tale of Esther and Mordecai would later be modified. Additions to the Book of Esther altered both the presentation of the central figures and the book's overt theological thrust, bringing it more in line with the Book of Judith. In one case (Additions to Esther 15:1–16) the drama was heightened. Prayers by both the heroine and hero bring them into line with Torah Judaism, or at least present them unhappy with demands imposed on them by the pagan setting. In short, they become more kosher. Esther asks her god:

> But save us by thy hand, and help me, who am alone and have no helper but thee, O Lord. Thou hast knowledge of all things; and thou knowest that I hate the splendor of the wicked and abhor the bed of the uncircumcised and of any alien. Thou knowest my necessity—that I abhor the sign of my proud position, which is upon my head on the days when I appear in public. I abhor it like a monstrous rag, and I do not wear it on the days

when I am at leisure. And thy servant has not eaten at Haman's table, and I have not honored the king's feast or drunk the wine of the libations. Thy servant has had no joy since the day that I was brought here until now, except in thee, O Lord God of Abraham. O God, whose might is over all, hear the voice of the despairing, and save us from the hands of evildoers. And save me from my fear!

(Additions to Esther 14:14–19)

It is impossible to imagine these words from the queen Esther of the older tale. The edicts issued by Haman and Mordecai add both verisimilitude and an antigentile thrust (note especially the Additions to Esther 10:10; 11:7). Mordecai's dream and its interpretation (which, in the Additions to Esther, bracket the older book) underscore the guiding hand of the deity throughout the course of events. As in the apocalyptic vision, all has been set out beforehand, and the ordained course is followed.

But development did not stop here, for material found in the work of Josephus and in later collections of Jewish lore attempts to explain how Esther managed to eat only kosher food, how she avoided the pagan's marriage bed, and why Mordecai refused to bow down to Haman. The length to which these explanations go—suggesting that an angel took her form in the king's bed, for example, or that she was daily sent food from Mordecai's home or from Jerusalem—suggest how far some Jewish circles had come from the life style depicted in the original tale. But the earlier form of the book was preserved as well, indicating that not everyone found it offensive.

Additions were also made to the Book of Daniel. The Prayer of Azariah and the Song of the Three Young Men emphasize the piety of Daniel's companions as they are saved from the furnace, for in the earlier book the pagan king had praised the deity and the three companions had been quite passive. These additions also underscore the action of the creator god in human affairs, especially his support for the faithful even when confronted with the martyr's choice. Both prayer and hymn provide a not wholly appropriate note of repentance that may have originated in the synagogue's round of study and prayer. The tale of Susanna and those dealing with Bel and the Dragon inform us that both in his youth and in old age Daniel stood apart from all others as a skilled, insightful, inspired individual. A polemic against pagan idols, which has its roots in the words of the Second Isaiah and is related to themes in the Wisdom of Solomon and the Additions to Esther, informs these tales as well.

Finally, the Book of Jeremiah, too, inspired additions. The so-called Letter of Baruch, supposedly by the prophet's loyal scribe and companion, sounds a note of repentance and of trust in the deity. Idols are the focus of a rambling attack in the Letter of Jeremiah, an addition to the book that is based on Jeremiah 29. The Prayer of Manasseh stands in the same stream of concern, building on the notice in 2 Chronicles 33:11–13 that at the end of his life the evil king Manasseh had sought divine forgiveness for his sins. Since Manasseh had been accused of aping pagan ways, his repentance becomes an attack on alien deities and the religious practices linked with them.

These additions to Esther, Daniel, and Jeremiah offer insight into the way later generations preserved, utilized, and reformed their heritage to reflect their own piety and particular situation in life. Their background was a Judaism becoming increasingly defined in opposition to a dangerous pagan world. Because it was a context that called for trust in the deity even when his hand was not apparent, examples of the past were called upon to encourage and support the faithful in the present. Behind all this one senses a growing powerlessness as Jews faced alien forces that could be dealt with only by their god.

BIBLIOGRAPHIC NOTE

Major Jewish Sectarian Groups

Simon, Marcel. *Jewish Sects at the Time of Jesus*. Philadelphia: Fortress Press, 1967.

Pharisees

Baeck, Leo. "The Pharisees." In *The Pharisees and Other Essays*, pp. 1–50. New York: Schocken Books, 1966.

Black, M. "Pharisees." In *The Interpreter's Dictionary of the Bible*, vol. 3, pp. 774–81. Nashville: Abingdon Press, 1962.

Neusner, Jacob. *From Politics to Piety: The Emergence of Pharisaic Judaism*. Englewood Cliffs, N.J.: Prentice-Hall, 1973. An excellent introduction to the Pharisees.

Rivkin, Ellis. "Defining the Pharisees." *Hebrew Union College Annual* (1970), pp. 205–49.

————. "Pharisees." In *The Interpreter's Dictionary of the Bible: Supplementary Volume*, pp. 657–63. Nashville: Abingdon Press, 1976.

Sadducees

Sundberg, Albert D. "Sadducees." In *The Interpreter's Dictionary of the Bible*, vol. 4, pp. 160–63. Nashville: Abingdon Press, 1962.

Zealots

Farmer, W. R. "Zealot." In *The Interpreter's Dictionary of the Bible*, vol. 4, pp. 936–39. Nashville: Abingdon Press, 1962.

Merkel, H. "Zealot." In *The Interpreter's Dictionary of the Bible: Supplementary Volume*, pp. 979–82. Nashville: Abingdon Press, 1976.

Smith, Morton. "Zealots and Sicarii: Their Origins and Relation." *Harvard Theological Review* 64 (1971): 1–20.

The Book of Ecclesiasticus

Burkill, T. A. "Ecclesiasticus." In *The Interpreter's Dictionary of the Bible*, vol. 2, pp. 13–21. Nashville: Abingdon Press, 1962.

Skehan, P. W. "Ecclesiasticus." In *The Interpreter's Dictionary of the Bible; Supplementary Volume*, pp. 250–51. Nashville: Abingdon Press, 1976.

The Wisdom of Solomon

Hadas, M. "Wisdom of Solomon." In *The Interpreter's Dictionary of the Bible*, vol. 4, pp. 861–63. Nashville: Abingdon Press, 1962.

Reese, James M. *Hellenistic Influence on the Book of Wisdom and Its Consequences*. Rome: Biblical Institute Press, 1970.

The Book of Tobit

Wikgren, A. "Tobit, Book of." In *The Interpreter's Dictionary of the Bible*, vol. 4, pp. 658–62. Nashville: Abingdon Press, 1962.

The Book of Judith

Winter, P. "Judith, Book of." In *The Interpreter's Dictionary of the Bible*, vol. 2, pp. 1023–26. Nashville: Abingdon Press, 1962.

The Additions to Esther, Daniel, and Jeremiah

Moore, Carey A. *Daniel, Esther, and Jeremiah: The Additions*. Garden City, N.Y.: Doubleday & Co., 1977.

The books of the Apocrypha are also discussed in Otto Eissfeldt, *The Old Testament: An Introduction* (New York: Harper & Row, 1965); J. Alberto Soggin, *Introduction to the Old Testament* (Philadelphia: Westminster Press, 1976); Robert Pfeiffer, *History of New Testament Times: With an Introduction to the Apocrypha* (New York: Harper & Brothers, 1949); and Leonhard Rost, *Judaism outside the Hebrew Canon: An Introduction to the Documents* (Nashville: Abingdon Press, 1976).

15 THE THIRD CRISIS

Primary reading: 2 Esdras*

REBELLION AND MASADA

In the seventh decade of the first century of the Common Era tensions between the Romans and segments of the Jewish population in Palestine burst into open warfare. Rome had long regarded this part of its vast empire as one of the most troublesome posts to govern. On the demise of the Hasmonean dynasty, various types of supervision were attempted, sometimes using local Jewish leaders, sometimes sending appointees directly from Rome. That this leadership was not of the highest order is not surprising because the best men would not seek such a post.

At times the Romans were greatly insensitive to the feelings and practices of the Jewish population, allowing the presence of Roman troops with their military standards depicting various deities or religious symbols even within the temple. For their part, some Jews were insensitive to the difficulties of governing a vast and complex empire, while others were quick to exploit whatever provocation the Roman authorities might provide.

---

*Found in the Roman Catholic Old Testament and in the Apocrypha of Protestants and Jews.

As the middle decades of the first century passed, tensions increased until in 66 C.E. the flame of open warfare was ignited by the Zealots who banded together in a common cause. Briefly, the conflict was centered first in Galilee. When the rebellion collapsed in the north, Jerusalem was besieged in 68 C.E. That the city did not fall into Roman hands for two years does not mean that sides were evenly matched or that the outcome was ever in doubt. Rather the two-year span reflects internal political changes in Rome and a recognition that the Jews were themselves fragmented by the revolt. Even the Zealots were divided, and the Romans recognized that, given time, they would destroy themselves.

Much to the relief of the Romans, the Jews of the eastern diaspora did not enter the conflict. Apparently, some expected them to rise up and support the war for freedom in the homeland; even Rome feared that such an uprising might take place. But it did not, and the rebels' cause was severely wounded because within Palestine itself Judaism was divided. The Sadducees would not eagerly support a conflict in which they had little to gain and much to lose. Limited Sadducee attempts to control and moderate the conflict once it began were ineffective, and the sect lost credibility on both sides.

The Pharisees were divided as well. The Jewish historian Josephus, who would later identify himself as a Pharisee, was a man who for a time led the rebel forces in Galilee, who in ambiguous circumstances went over to the Roman side, and who at the end was working for the enemy. Even within the ranks of the Zealots there were bitter divisions. As the situation within besieged Jerusalem became increasingly desperate, suicidal skirmishes broke out over leadership and conduct of the war, and the Zealots' cause disintegrated from within.

By playing on these divisions and by steadily augmenting the pressure on Jerusalem, the Romans avoided an out-and-out battle. In time the city simply fell to them and they ravished it, focusing their attack on the temple. Destroying the temple and terminating its cultic round of service was probably a calculated act aimed at destroying Judaism, for in Roman eyes a diverse and scattered religious group that had no central temple or cult could not long survive. They must have hoped that, with the destruction of the temple, Judaism would just disintegrate and that Jews would be absorbed into the surrounding world so that there would be no need for wholesale extermination or the extensive dislocation of communities that had characterized Assyrian and Babylonian policy.

But resistance did not wholly cease with the fall of Jerusalem. Together with their wives and children, a small band of rebels occupied Masada, a stark mesa that rises about 1,200 feet from a point roughly two-thirds of the way down the western shore of the Dead Sea. Sheer on all sides, Masada provided an almost inaccessible place of refuge which had been elaborately built up by Herod, who had feared that he might need a secure place of retreat. On the site he had constructed palaces, living and working quarters for staff and servants, store-houses, a bathhouse, a cistern, and a wall surrounding the entire complex. But he had never had a chance to use his place of refuge, and these remains of Roman luxury had fallen into ruin by the time rebel fugitives from Jerusalem joined other Zealots there as the last vestige of the movement for national independence.

In 72 c.e. a large Roman force besieged Masada. A wall was built around its base with camps located at nine points, and a huge ramp was erected up the west side of the mesa, using Jewish prisoners taken earlier as the work force so that the defenders would have to destroy their own people if they wished to thwart the building of the ramp. When the summit was reached, those inside Masada were doomed.

On the final night, after moving speeches by the rebel leader Eleazar, the Zealots decided to take their own lives rather than fall into Roman hands and become slaves. After each man slew his own family, nine men were selected by lots to kill the rest. This done, one man killed his companions, then set fire to most of the remaining provisions, leaving just enough to show the Romans that not hunger but respect for their honor had driven them to this desperate act. Finally, the last man took his own life. When the Romans breached the defense wall in the morning they found only two women and five children still alive. It was a heroic end to a doomed cause and is movingly described by Josephus.

Although the Sadducees had not supported the war for independence, which they regarded as total folly, the defeat and the destruction of the temple dealt them a mortal blow. The temple and its cult had been the foundation of the Sadducee sect and the center of their religious identity, and with these gone their essence was taken from them. As individuals they no doubt lived on as Jews or Romans or both. The sect, however, did not survive the failure of the revolt, and Sadducees are heard from no more.

FAILURE OF APOCALYPTIC EXPECTATIONS

To what extent individual Zealots were informed by the apocalyptic vision is not known. Certainly a confidence in divine aid would have sustained one in a course of action that by any realistic standards was doomed, and a belief in an afterlife would have supported the martyrs at Masada. But we do have reason to believe that the Essenes interpreted the conflict in the apocalyptic framework, in terms of the war between the Sons of Light and the Sons of Darkness. Living in a state of constant alert, expecting their god to break into the course of history at any moment, the Essenes must have seen the war as the moment toward which all history had been moving—god's final encounter with the forces of chaos, darkness, and perversity. Their god would now bring a new creation into being; Israel would be reborn, and they were the holy seed from which their god's kingdom would emerge.

But when the Sons of Darkness won the war the theological heart was torn from the Essenes. Their story, visions, and hopes, the foundation for their pattern of life—all had been judged by the crisis of 66–70 C.E. and destroyed; the god of the apocalyptic vision seemed dead. Although details are lacking, it is known that in 68 C.E. the Qumran community was overrun by the Roman army, thereafter serving as the base for a Roman garrison that controlled traffic in the Dead Sea area. There is also evidence that some who had been at Qumran later hid at Masada. In any event, the Essenes as a distinct sect ceased to exist after 70 C.E.

Not all who were infused with the apocalyptic vision vanished, however. Some held on, and an attempt to reform and retain the essentials of this perspective is found in the complex Book of 2 Esdras. This book has at its core the work of a Jew who wrote around 100 C.E. (chapters 3–14), with two later Christian additions in the form of a prologue (chapters 1–2) and epilogue (chapters 15–16). In the core material Ezra reports seven visions that retain many of the apocalyptic elements, and an angel named Uriel offers various observations about the mysteries of creation and the deity's action in human history. Standing in the aftermath of the destruction of Israel the author laments:

> And after seven days the thoughts of my heart were very grievous to me again. Then my soul recovered the spirit of understanding, and I began once more to speak words in the presence of the Most High. And I said, "O sovereign Lord, from every forest of the earth and from all its trees thou hast chosen one vine, and from all the flowers of the world thou hast chosen for thyself one lily . . . and from all the cities that have been built thou hast consecrated Zion for thyself . . . and from all the multitude of peoples thou hast gotten for thyself one people; and to this people, whom thou hast loved, thou hast given the law which is approved by all. And now, O Lord, why hast thou given over the one to the many, and dishonored the one root beyond the others, and scattered thine only one among the many? And those who opposed thy promises have trodden down those who believed thy covenants. If thou dost really hate thy people, they should be punished at thy own hands.
>
> (2 Esdras 5:21–30)

At points Rome is bitterly denounced under the name of Babylon.

In its tones of anger, confusion, and terror this resembles the first response to the fall of Jerusalem in 587 B.C.E. in Psalm 137 and Lamentations. Once again theological foundations have been shaken, the old identities built upon them will not stand, and most of the same questions arise. Yet 2 Esdras reveals a strong conviction that the deity is somehow still in control and that the faithful will ultimately be delivered. The forces of evil and chaos will not win; the creative design of the deity must triumph. But hope seems less immediate here; there is a sober reluctance, born of bitter experience, to express hope in terms too concrete. Thus in vague but certain trust in some future act of the god the

Torah vision of the priestly document reemerges to temper the extremes of the apocalyptic vision, just as this vision had earlier given immediacy to the Torah promise.

Looking ahead a few decades we find that in some Jews the revolutionary spirit linked to the apocalyptic vision did not die. In 132 C.E. a man named Simon led a new strike for national independence, and he was given the title Bar Kokhba ("son of the star"), indicating that he was regarded by some as a royal or messianic figure who had come in the name of his god to free his people from Roman dominion. But Simon's war was doomed from the outset, and his fall three years later brought great suffering upon Jews who had supported his cause as well as upon those who had not. In Roman reprisals thousands were killed, their land was taken, and a cloud was cast over Jews in many parts of the world.

Wholly discredited, the apocalyptic vision apparently fell from grace in most Jewish circles. It is no accident that most Jewish apocalyptic literature was preserved in Christian circles (note the example of 2 Esdras), for Christians found it informative in their attempts to comprehend and express the meaning of the life and words of Jesus. In Christian hands, however, it lost its nationalistic thrust, for the Bar Kokhba debacle had given Christians all the more reason to sever their Jewish links if they wished to live at peace and gain a place in the Roman world.

Yet the very fact that there was a war between segments of Judaism and Rome in 132–135 C.E. indicates that Judaism had not disintegrated with the destruction of the temple. In spite of the demise of the Sadducees, the Essenes, and those who were called Zealots, Judaism survived both the tragedy of 66–70 C.E. and the ill-fated adventure of Simon Bar Kokhba. This was largely the accomplishment of the Pharisees to whom the tasks of leadership and rebuilding fell at the juncture of the first and second centuries.

TRANSFORMATION OF THE PHARISEES

Of the major sects within Palestinian Judaism, the Pharisees alone survived the tragedy of 66–70 C.E. with a Jewish identity intact. Although they were changed, they had come through with a strength and vision that they could now transmit to all Judaism. Not that some Pharisees had not been intensely committed to the rebellion. Some had taken an active part in the conflict; indeed, it was a later Pharisee, the great Akiba, who would designate Simon as "son of the star." But there were others who viewed such rebellions as a mad provocation of the Roman rulers, with whom one could live with some effort and understanding. Neither their attitude toward the rebellion nor their acceptance of the apocalyptic vision marked them as Pharisees, however. As a whole, they were defined by a particular life style, not by a specific set of political or religious beliefs, and this gave them the flexibility needed to confront the crisis.

According to tradition a Pharisee named Yohanan ben Zakkai was in Jerusalem during the Roman siege. Toward the end the Romans made the city an offer: if one bow and arrow were handed over, the people would be spared. The Zealots, torn by bitter rivalries, rejected any symbol of capitulation against the advice of Yohanan, who argued that a bow and arrow were nothing in comparison with a human life. Overruled, Yohanan fell under a cloud of suspicion; but since the rebels would allow no one to leave the city at this point he feigned death, was placed in a coffin, and was carried by his disciples to the city gate. When challenged by the men posted there, the disciples replied that they were removing their dead master's remains from the sacred city as the law demanded, and on this account they were permitted to pass. On meeting the Romans, Yohanan emerged from the coffin, greeted the enemy in the name of peace and of his god, and made clear to them that he and others like him were not opponents of Roman rule.

Yohanan then secured from the Romans the authority to establish an academy for study of the Jewish heritage at the coastal village of Yabneh (also called Jamnia) where Palestinian Judaism could be guided by Jews whom the Romans could trust. For their part, the Romans probably viewed as futile any attempt to perpetuate Judaism without a cult and temple but saw in this request an opportunity to demonstrate their good will and restraint. By this maneuver Yohanan brought the Pharisees back into the sphere of political activity. Failing in their earliest years to control the Hasmonean rulers, the Pharisees had withdrawn from overt political activity. But there was now a vacuum in the internal leadership of Palestinian Judaism, and this they moved to fill by working with Roman rule. In their view, a Jew could live under a tolerant foreign rule, and the Romans, when not provoked, now seemed willing to meet Jews halfway. In any event, this seemed the only realistic course open to men like Yohanan if Judaism were to survive.

But how could Judaism survive without a temple and the daily and yearly round of cultic worship and festivals? Of course, thousands of Jews had lived as Jews for centuries in the diaspora without access to the temple and its cult. But even for them there had at least been a temple cult in the homeland, however much distance and political barriers cut them off from it. Now there was no divine service. How would Judaism survive?

To this question Yohanan replied that study of the heritage, observance of the commandments, good works, and prayer were as effective a form of divine service as actual sacrifice. The Torah, especially in the hands of the Pharisees and their growing body of oral law, not only provided instructions for the temple cult but also a way of obedience that reached into every aspect of life at every moment. This, too, was divine service, and, by ordering one's daily actions, it would preserve a distinct identity. Again the Jew was to live in but not be a full part of the world.

Yohanan knew that the Jews had survived the destruction of their temple and loss of their homeland in 587 B.C.E. because they had found in their heritage a model for life in the wilderness, whether in exile in the east or scattered throughout the Roman Empire. Thus, as they had originated—without temple or cult, as wanderers and fugitives from slavery—so they would now live again in the wilderness with only a way of life and a promise. By taking this stand within the old Moses-Sinai story as it had been winnowed, reformed, and hallowed by centuries of interaction with new realities and crises, the Pharisees placed their own distinctive stamp upon Judaism.

Yohanan governed without formal title, office, or authority. Among the Pharisees, men like him, who were learned in the traditions of their people, skilled in interpreting the Torah and applying it to new situations, and who in their early years had lived at the feet of a master, were called rabbis. Their authority was not institutionalized or passed on through bloodlines; a rabbi might emerge from any class or setting if he had the needed determination and intelligence.

The Pharisees dominated Judaism after 66–70 c.e. because they were irrevocably tied to neither the temple nor the theology of the apocalyptic vision. They had respected the temple when it stood—it was, after all anticipated in the Torah—but they could survive without it. The synagogue, a place where one could study the heritage, pray, and offer praise to the deity, was their natural center, and there could be as many synagogues as were needed and wherever necessary. In this regard the Pharisees, alone among the Jewish sects in Palestine, had firm links with diaspora Judaism. With the loss of the temple, Jews throughout the world were once again bound together in a common life situation.

But even among the Pharisees the apocalyptic vision did not vanish; for it was Akiba who pronounced Simon to be a messianic figure, and the failure of his revolt brought trouble to Yabneh. In time the Pharisees had to move their academy north to the city of Usha in Galilee, but the fundamental course set by Yohanan was not abandoned and the formative influence of the Pharisees on Judaism did not abate. Before discussing further aspects of this influence, however, we must say more about a man whose life spanned the years of the revolt. We rely on his works for much of our knowledge of these events because he not only took part in them but recorded them in works that survive today.

JOSEPHUS

In discussing Judaism up to and through the revolt of 66–70 c.e. we have not focused on individuals primarily because glimpses into the personal lives of even the major figures of the period—Hillel, Yohanan ben Zakkai, Simon bar Kokhba—are lost to us. The one man who does emerge through an extended corpus of his own writings is Joseph ben Matthias, or as he is better known, Flavius Josephus, the Roman name he took for himself. The works of this historian often provide our only knowledge of the life and development of

Judaism from the Maccabees through the war with Rome, and they also tell us a great deal, if not always objectively, about the man who wrote them.

Born around 37 or 38 C.E., Josephus was of Hasmonean descent and of a priestly family, and he set out to study and experience all three major sects of Judaism in his day—Sadducees, Pharisees, and Essenes, even spending some time with an Essene hermit in the wilderness. In spite of his upper-class origins he finally chose the Pharisees as most representative of his vision of Judaism. Although he called himself a Pharisee and a loyal Jew, however, many of his fellows would have called him a shameless Roman collaborator and a disgrace to his people. From this distance one suspects that his identification with the Pharisees was based more on admiration than on emulation, tempered by the realistic recognition that they were the sole surviving force within Judaism after 70 C.E.

Josephus seems to have been a respected figure of authority in Jerusalem in the decades before the revolt. In 64 C.E. he was in Rome representing certain Jewish priests before Nero; some have suggested that he became totally enamored of Roman ways and culture at this time, though at the outbreak of the war he was in command of the Jewish rebel forces in Galilee, at that time the hotbed of revolt. An event then occurred that Josephus discusses more than once but that is nevertheless not clear to us now. In 67 C.E. Jewish rebels in the Galilean town of Jotapata were besieged by the Romans for a terrible forty-seven days. Only Josephus and one other man remained alive, and when Josephus was taken before Vespasian, the Roman commander, he predicted that his captor would become emperor. Two years later this prophecy came true, and Josephus took the name Flavius from the new emperor's surname. He also became a staunch advocate of the emperor, who in turn became his patron.

From the end of the war to the end of his life Josephus lived in Rome. With the aid of ghost writers skilled in Greek language and literary styles he wrote to recommend the Romans to the Jews, the Jews to the Romans, and himself to both. Four of his works have survived. In the *Jewish War* he describes Palestinian Judaism from the era of the Maccabees through the revolt, dwelling on the latter in some detail. This work, originally written in Aramaic, was addressed to Jews, especially those of the eastern diaspora, in an attempt to convince them that the destruction of the temple and general suppression of the revolt by the Roman army had been necessary because of a few Jewish fanatics who had managed to carry the day for a time; Rome, in his opinion, had exercised remarkable restraint.

In later Greek editions of this work he addressed Romans as well, saying that the unfortunate revolt had been sparked by only a mad few and that Rome must not judge all Jews in the light of this event. Indeed, in the view of Josephus, Judaism had much to recommend it to the Romans. As a tradition worthy of respect for its high ideals, ethic, inspiring history, and profound philosophical foundations it might even serve as a force for stability in the empire. Thus his longest work, *Jewish Antiquities*, surveys his people's history from the patriarchs to his own day, drawing heavily on the heritage as preserved in the Bible, often in its Greek form, but also on sources closer to his own time.

Against Apion attempts to counter more specific attacks against Jews with biting polemic force and bitterness. Apion was a Greek writer and teacher from Alexandria in Egypt whose dislike of Judaism had led him to write about it with scornful mockery and on one occasion to have brought charges against Jews before the Roman emperor. Finally, to a later edition of the *Antiquities* Josephus appended a piece now called *The Life* in which he defends himself, especially against charges arising out of the Jotapata affair and his sudden switch to the Roman side, though the defense leaves many questions unanswered.

Josephus is complex and intriguing both as a man and as a Jew. Although he became a thoroughgoing Roman who tailored his works to Roman literary tastes, his attachment to his people and heritage was such that he devoted his life's efforts to them. Although his vision of a Jewish life style did not prevent his living fully in the world at large, he was still a Jew, regardless of some of the charges leveled against him. In Josephus we see one Jew's struggle to survive the shattering tragedy of 66–70 c.e. with his identity intact; and though many would not approve his course, he not only succeeded but left the world richer for his efforts.

BIBLIOGRAPHIC NOTE

Moore, George Foot. *Judaism in the First Centuries of the Christian Era*. Cambridge, Mass.: Harvard University Press, 1962. Detailed and comprehensive.

Myers, Jacob M. *I and II Esdras*. Garden City, N.Y.: Doubleday & Co., 1974.

Neusner, Jacob. *First-Century Judaism in Crisis: Yohanan ben Zakkai and the Renaissance of Torah*. Nashville: Abingdon Press, 1975.

Rhoads, David M. *Israel in Revolution, 6–74 c.e.: A Political History based on the Writings of Josephus*. Philadelphia: Fortress Press, 1976.

Thackeray, H. St. John. *Josephus: The Man and the Historian*. New York: KTAV Publishing House, 1967.

————. Marcus, Ralph; Wikgren, Allan; and Feldman, L. H., trans. *Josephus*, 10 vols. The Loeb Classical Library. Cambridge, Mass.: Harvard University Press, 1926–1965.

Yadin, Yigael. "Masada." In *The Interpreter's Dictionary of the Bible: Supplementary Volume*, pp. 577–80. Nashville: Abingdon Press, 1976.

————. *Masada: Herod's Fortress and the Zealots' Last Stand*. London: Weidenfeld & Nicolson, 1966.

EPILOGUE TO PART 2

The failure of the revolt of 66–70 C.E. certified that Judaism was to remain in diaspora, and the debacle associated with Simon Bar Kokhba drove out whatever doubts remained. Jews continued to reside in Palestine, but Jerusalem and especially the ruins of the temple were declared off-limits by the Romans. Only once a year, on the anniversary of the tragedy of 587 B.C.E., were Jews permitted to go to the ruins and lament the destruction of the first and second temples. Although they continued to live in the ancient homeland, it was no longer theirs, and limited access to the sacred city was a constant reminder of that fact.

All Jews lived now in diaspora, which had not been the case since the first few decades of Babylonian exile. In terms of numbers, of course, Judaism had been centered in the diaspora from the time of its birth out of the ruins of old Israel, and for the first centuries after 587 B.C.E. the bulk of creative attempts that were to define early Judaism came out of the eastern diaspora. Following the period of Nehemiah and Ezra there had been a shift back to the homeland, but now centuries of dreams and life-giving hopes were shattered. Although the position of Jews and Jewish communities varied greatly throughout the Near East and

Mediterranean world, all defined their religious identities as distinct from their political loyalties to the land in which they resided.

That this became the accepted state of affairs for most Jews Yohanan ben Zakkai and his followers at Yabneh recognized clearly, and it allowed them to set the course that would define Judaism for centuries to come. We have already considered aspects of their work of preservation and redefinition following the failure of the revolt. Now we shall attend to the Pharisaic circles in and around Yabneh who gave final shape to the Hebrew Bible and whose work defined Judaism as a religion of the book.

FORMATION OF THE CANON

Amid debates and discussions at the Pharisaic academy at Yabneh, the extent and limits of the Hebrew Bible were defined and a particular type of authority was attributed to it. In this way a process of storytelling that had extended over centuries reached a climax, a process of identity formation that stretched back to the early days of the Israelite federation. Although these men recognized that they stood in a long line of forebears, they also knew that this was a turning point in the history of their people. Their work marked a new direction in the engagement between past and present that remains at the heart of the Hebraic religious heritage, and it is the most significant fruit of the Jewish response to the crisis of 66–70 C.E.

Continuing Development of the Tradition

Ancient Israelite and early Jewish religious tradition was bound together by a thread of storytelling in which two stories were told and experienced, reformed and recast, reaffirmed or rejected in a lengthy process of creative interaction between past and present. The story of the past, as known in cultic celebration, in theological and historical epic, behind and through prophetic oracle, was repeatedly brought to bear on the present in a continuing search for identity, directions, and a locus of authority. By those who perceived a present crisis as a judgment on the past, the past was at times rejected; others found in the past a basis for survival when death and chaos seemed to characterize the present order.

Both the content and form of the stories varied from one age and setting to another. The oldest creeds, for example, fixed the Moses-Sinai story in rough outline only. The Yahwist followed this outline but vastly expanded it, adding new elements as he liberated it from its cultic base and set it into the frame of the David-Zion complex. Other brief forms of the stories that existed at the same time are glimpsed behind the words of the prophets (see, for example, Amos 2:9–11; 3:1–2; Jeremiah 2:1–8; Isaiah 9:2–7 and 11:1–10).

In time the Elohist provided a distinct epic version of the old federation's story. This story prefaces a body of legal material in the early chapters of Deuteronomy and also served as a thematic guide for the extended reassessment of Israel's history that we call the deuteronomistic history. Some form of the Book of Deuteronomy was found in the temple in 620 B.C.E., when, serving as a spur to the reformation then under way, it received the stamp of royal authority. Deuteronomy reflects an early attempt to define Israel's normative story and the covenant obligations based in it with greater precision and detail.

In response to the crisis of 587 B.C.E. the priests of the early exile fundamentally reformed the ancient story, weaving the older epics of the Yahwist and Elohist into their narrative, and further defined the legal tradition as well. To Jerusalem in the fifth century B.C.E. Ezra brought this priestly document as a constitution, giving it a seal of validity in his role as a priest and Persian official. During the late preexilic and early postexilic period, too, the collections of prophetic oracles were shaped and the several books that bear their names were formed by means of a long and complex process. In the prophetic words of indictment, sentence, and renewed promise, Israelites and Jews found the words of their god addressed to them in ever new life settings, and they continually adapted and added to the original oracles so that the past again enlivened the present and the present shaped the past.

Throughout these centuries a gradual fixing and winnowing took place. On the one hand, the forms of the remembered past became increasingly more fixed and in these fixed forms received the semiofficial stamp of the governing authorities. On the other hand, certain materials of the past were sifted out or recast. What we now have of ancient Israelite and early Jewish tradition is but a small part of what was produced.

Some was not preserved because it served immediate ends only; some was lost in historical catastrophes (for example, the Chronicles of the kings of Israel and of Judah so often mentioned in 1 and 2 Kings or the old collection of songs called the Book of Jashar mentioned in Joshua 10:13 and 2 Samuel 1:18). But some material was rejected because it was judged to be wrong-headed. Once the crisis of 587 B.C.E. was seen as a judgment on the David-Zion story, for example, the old songs of Zion and of the house of David were rejected or recast; nor do we have a book of the prophet Hananiah.

In the last two centuries before the Common Era, in the Jewish community in Alexandria in Egypt, a rich body of materials was collected into a Greek translation of part of the surviving heritage from old Israel and early Judaism. The Septuagint contains the books that today comprise the Hebrew Bible, together with other books that today are found in the Protestant's Apocrypha.

The title Septuagint is often abbreviated as LXX because popular lore asserts that seventy scribes worked on the translation for seventy days and produced seventy identical results. Actually, however, the translation took decades. First the Torah was translated, then the so-called Former Prophets (Joshua through 2

Kings), then the prophets, and finally other writings. What emerged was a body of authoritative documents from the past that was found to address the present in meaningful ways.

In the Septuagint the remembered past was given a further degree of fixity and the winnowing continued apace, yet the situation remained fluid. On the one hand, for example, the discoveries in the caves of Qumran indicate that the Essenes regarded other materials as authoritative. Although for convenience's sake we today distinguish between "biblical" and "sectarian" scrolls, in doing so we impose a later division on materials that the Essenes would have bound together. On the other hand, the Samaritan community in the north seems to have regarded only the Torah as authoritative, exhibiting in this respect a radical winnowing of the heritage.

Even amid the fluidity, the Essene situation reflects a certain fixity as well, for in their commentaries, the *pesherim*, the past material is fixed and can only be cited; comments are added, but they remain distinct. The old tradition is not itself altered but is only interpreted. This was to be the way of the future as the form of the remembered past moved from a rough outline permitting endless variation to a document fixed in every word.

In this regard it is instructive to consider the legend in 2 Esdras concerning how the books of the Bible were preserved and retransmitted to the Jewish communities through Ezra. Addressing his god in lament, Ezra states that the darkness and confusion of his time have been augmented because "thy law has been burned, and so no one knows the things which have been done or will be done by thee" (2 Esdras 14:21). The reference is to the tragedy of 587 B.C.E. and to the destruction of the past, here envisaged as a set of documents already formed. The deity instructs Ezra to assemble five skilled scribes who are to reproduce what has been lost:

> So I took the five men, as he commanded me and we proceeded to the field, and remained there. And on the next day, behold, a voice called me, saying, "Ezra, open your mouth and drink what I give you to drink." Then I opened my mouth, and behold, a full cup was offered to me; it was full of something like water, but its color was like fire. And I took it and drank; and when I had drunk it, my heart poured forth understanding, and wisdom increased in my breast, for my spirit retained its memory; and my mouth was opened, and was no longer closed. And the Most High gave understanding to the five men, and by turns they wrote what was dictated, in characters which they did not know. They sat forty days, and wrote during the daytime, and ate their bread at night. As for me, I spoke in the daytime and was not silent at night. So during the forty days ninety-four books were written. And when the forty days were ended, the Most High spoke to me, saying, "Make public the twenty-four books that you wrote first and let the worthy and the unworthy read them; but keep the seventy that were written last, in order to give them to the wise among your people.

For in them is the spring of understanding, the fountain of wisdom, and the river of knowledge." And I did so.

(2 Esdras 14:37–47)

It should be noted that these books come directly from the deity; each word is literally that of the god. Clearly, nothing may be altered or changed, and there were ninety-four books in all. The twenty-four made public are those now in the Hebrew Bible; the seventy represent a body of esoteric apocalyptic material. Again, there is a degree of fluidity in the number of materials preserved and in their range, but there is fixity in their form and content.

After the crisis of 66–70 c.e. the tradition underwent further winnowing and fixation at Yabneh. We do not know all the details because no records were kept of the debates; at least, none has survived. But with the loss of the homeland, the destruction of the temple, and history's judgment on the apocalyptic vision, a careful restructuring and redefining of the remembered past seemed vital. Because the process had been well under way for centuries, the debates at Yabneh were in some respects simply a tying up of loose ends; but setting limits and constructing boundaries brought a vital new stage to the development of the Hebraic religious tradition.

Definition of Authority

The debates at Yabneh not only determined and certified the content of the Hebrew Bible but declared that no further items would be entered into it. As the legend in 2 Esdras reveals, it was decided to exclude any work that came after Ezra, for in his lifetime the Torah had become normative for the Jews in Jerusalem, and for this reason he is remembered as a second Moses. In the days of Nehemiah, Judaism had attained a stability that was not shattered until the days of Antiochus IV. Desiring to recapture that stability, the Pharisees at Yabneh returned to Ezra and through him back to their deepest roots in Moses and the Israelites encamped at the foot of Mount Sinai in the wilderness.

Hence works like Ecclesiasticus, 1 and 2 Maccabees, and Judith, which seem equal to older works in terms of content, perspective, and depth, were omitted. The fact that tradition linked Ecclesiastes with Solomon and set Daniel in the royal courts of Babylon and early Persia allowed the inclusion of these works, which modern critical study has assigned to a later period. Segments of the Septuagint excluded from the Hebrew Bible remained in use in Christian circles, and it was not until the sixteenth-century Reformation that Protestants redefined their Old Testament along the lines set by the Hebrew Bible. The Septuagint books excluded from the Hebrew Bible were later gathered together as the Apocrypha and these books remain part of the Old Testament of Roman Catholics.

The wording of each book was standardized as well. Among the Dead Sea

Scrolls, for example, different forms of the same books were found. Sometimes the differences were slight, but in other instances there were far-reaching variations involving variant orderings of material within a book (as in Jeremiah), differences in intent (as in Job), or additions and deletions (as in segments of 1 and 2 Samuel). Standard form was now given to each book.

Through their efforts the men at Yabneh provided Jewish communities throughout the world with a new and unifying center in the form of a book—better, a collection of books—that was fixed, defined, limited in range, and a finished product in the sense that no new materials were to be added. Although it might appear that this would end the dynamic, creative interaction between past and present, this was not the case, and the reasons are to be found in the very collection of books that the Yabneh circle provided.

The term *canon* was first applied to this collection several centuries after it was formed; earlier the material was said to "contaminate the hands"—that is, to be set apart as sacred and distinct from all other writings. *Canon*, however, is an apt designation, for it underscores the collection's intended function. The word comes from the Semitic word for a reed (*qaneh* in Hebrew), which was used both as a guide and as a whip. That is, a reed would provide a straight edge to guide a pen in drawing, but a herdsman might also use it as a whip to keep his animals moving ahead and in line. Hence a reed served both to guide and to chasten, to delimit and to drive on, and the canon was established to do likewise. It offered guidance that was rooted in the past, while this very past thrust one into ever new confrontations with the present and future.

The voice of almost every generation of ancient Israelite and early Jew is found in the canon, offering a rich and varied chorus, at points singing in harmony, at other points singing different songs. Although a pluralistic document, the canon is not an anthology of unrelated bits and pieces. It is a complex of attempts by people in varied situations and over many eras to express their understanding of their relationship with their god and to comprehend themselves as individuals and communities within a growing stream of tradition. At times the stream is wide, at other times it narrows; sometimes side channels cut off from the main branch, and more than once the waters back up upon themselves. Broadly, however, it is one stream in which generations found direction and limits, guidance and challenge. To preserve this enlivening dynamic the canon was formed.

The canon provides comfort when needed, judgment when appropriate, and a challenge always to confront the present and the action of the deity in its many forms, but it does not offer a tailored and unified theology or a set of codified practices to govern all possible situations in life. Within the Hebrew Bible is preserved rather the rich variety of Israelite and Jewish storytelling, of self-scrutiny, redefinition, and a search for identity and life.

Although the canon was closed, interpretation and reinterpretation did not cease. In Pharisaic circles a body of oral law took shape in which the Torah was endlessly reapplied to changing situations in life, so that new layers and levels would become apparent within the canon as it confronted these new realities. The Mishnah, dating from about 200 C.E., and the Talmud, from the fifth and sixth centuries C.E., are repositories of this continuing reinterpretation and reapplication of the heritage. The Christian's New Testament is likewise to be understood from one perspective as interpretation and application of his Jewish heritage.

Judaism and Christianity alike developed some methods of interpretation that may strike us as odd today in seeming to have so little relation to the literal sense of the text. But these methods demonstrate a continued enlivening encounter between past and present, and the process continues even today in the religions of the West. In shaping the Hebrew Bible the heirs of the early Pharisees directly confronted the crisis of the aborted revolt and of failed nationalism and assured that Jews the world over would always remain men and women made of words.

BIBLIOGRAPHIC NOTE

Freedman, David Noel. "Canon of the OT." In *The Interpreter's Dictionary of the Bible: Supplementary Volume*, pp. 130–36. Nashville: Abingdon Press, 1976.

Pfeiffer, Robert H. "Canon of the OT." In *The Interpreter's Dictionary of the Bible*, vol. 1, pp. 498–520. Nashville: Abingdon Press, 1962.

Sanders, James A. "Hermeneutics." In *The Interpreter's Dictionary of the Bible: Supplementary Volume*, pp. 402–7. Nashville: Abingdon Press, 1976.

———. *Torah and Canon*. Philadelphia: Fortress Press, 1972. An excellent introduction to the nature of canon and its authority.

Sundberg, Albert D. *The Old Testament of the Early Church*. Cambridge, Mass.: Harvard University Press, 1964.

GLOSSARY

Acrostic   A series of lines or verses whose initial letters form the alphabet, as in Lamentations 1–4 or Psalms 111, 112, and 119. Acrostics are, of course, lost in translation.

Amphictyony   A league of tribes or cities, usually with six or twelve members, bound by common allegiance to a deity and to the god's shrine. Many scholars believe that Israel formed an amphictyony in the federation period (1200–1000 B.C.E.).

Apocalyptic   A type of material that sets out the future course of history to the time when the rule of the deity and his people will be established and evil will finally be defeated. Usually presented as a vision granted to a notable from the past, it often employs strange symbols and numerical calculations. The fullest example in the Old Testament is Daniel 7–12.

Apocrypha   Books found in the Greek translation of the Hebrew scriptures made in the third to first centuries B.C.E. (the Septuagint) that were later rejected by Judaism but retained by Christians. At the Reformation, Protestants adopted Jewish practice with regard to these books, while Roman Catholic and Eastern churches retained them as part of their Old Testament.

Apodictic law Law stated in an unconditional manner without mediating clauses; for example, the Ten Commandments (Exodus 20; Deuteronomy 5).

Aquila A Christian who converted to Judaism and produced a highly literal Greek translation of the Hebrew Bible in the mid-second century C.E.

ASV Abbreviation for the American Standard Version, a highly literal translation of the Bible produced in America in 1901.

B.C.E.; C.E. Abbreviations for Before the Common Era and Common Era, used as nontheological replacements for B.C. and A.D.

Canon; Canonical A collection of writings to which a religious community attributes special, usually divine, authority. The Hebrew Bible is the canon of Judaism, while the Old Testament (in varied forms) and New Testament together form the canon for Christianity.

Casuistic Law In contrast to Apodictic Law, a term denoting case law, legal sayings with modifying clauses that often take the form: "If such and such is done . . . and this and that is the situation . . . then so and so must suffer a penalty" (for example, Exodus 22:10–17).

C.E. *See* B.C.E.

Chiasmus A literary crossover of the same or similar elements in a poetic unit, sentence, or larger block of material—for example, Isaiah 6:10 in which the sequence heart, ears, eyes in the first half becomes eyes, ears, heart in the second half.

Colon A single line of poetry, sometimes called a stich.

Commentary A discussion of one or more books of the Bible that treats linguistic, literary, formal, historical, religious, and theological meanings one unit at a time. Generally an introduction discusses the book as a whole. Many standard commentaries are cited in the Bibliographic Notes to this text.

Concordance An alphabetical listing of all the important words in a biblical translation, often giving the phrases in which the word occurs and including all references for the term, a useful tool in studying biblical themes.

Confession; confessional A statement of belief that forms the foundation upon which one's relation with a deity rests. In early Israel, confessional statements centered on the exodus and conquest, examples being found in Deuteronomy 26:5–9 and Joshua 24:2–13.

Covenant Code A title given to the self-contained body of laws and traditions found in Exodus 20–24.

D. *See* Deuteronomy.

Dead Sea Scrolls Papyrus and parchment scrolls and fragments written in Hebrew, Aramaic, and Greek, found in 1947 and later in caves near the northwest corner of the Dead Sea and said to be the work of a community of Essenes who occupied a nearby monastic complex now called Khirbet Qumran.

Decalogue   A Greek term denoting the Ten Commandments, found in Exodus 20 and Deuteronomy 5.

Deuterocanonical   A Roman Catholic designation for those books contained in the ancient Greek translation of Hebrew scriptures (the Septuagint) and considered canonical by Roman Catholics and Eastern Christian churches but excluded from the Hebrew Bible and Protestant Old Testament.

Deuteronomistic history   An extended review of Israel's history from the conquest of Jerusalem through its destruction in 587 B.C.E., found in the books of Joshua through 2 Kings (excluding Ruth) and set out in terms of standards presented in Deuteronomy.

Deuteronomy (D)   All or part of a scroll found during a reform of the temple carried out by Josiah in 620 B.C.E., Deuteronomy is one of the four strata comprising the Torah (Pentateuch).

Dittography   A technical term used in textual criticism for a copying error in which a letter, word, or line of text is mistakenly repeated.

Documentary hypothesis   A scholarly hypothesis suggesting that neither the Torah (Pentateuch) nor the Hexateuch is the work of one author (for example, of Moses) but that both represent a composite of four documents from several different periods: J (Yahwist, about 950 B.C.E.), E (Elohist, about 850 B.C.E.), D (Deuteronomy, about 620 B.C.E.), and P (the priestly document, about 550–450 B.C.E.). J and E were combined around 720 B.C.E., and D was added about a century later. P was added still later, giving final shape to the Torah.

Doublet   A term used in literary criticism denoting two or more versions of the same material; for example, Genesis 12:10–20; 20:1–18; 26:6–11.

E.   *See* Elohist.

Eisegesis   From the Greek *to introduce into*, this pejorative term refers to an interpretation that reads a desired meaning into a text.

El; Elyon   A Canaanite word for *god* and also the name of the father of the Canaanite pantheon, El Eyon was his designation in Canaanite Jerusalem, but he came to be identified with Yahweh when David made Jerusalem his city.

Elohim   The Hebrew word for *god*, used both of gods in general and of Yahweh, the god of Israel, in particular.

Elohist (E)   Denotes one of the strata comprising the Torah (Pentateuch); from the kingdom of northern Israel around 850 B.C.E.

Epiphany   A sudden, usually dramatic appearance of a deity, often accompanied by unusual events in nature (Exodus 19 and 24; Isaiah 6; Ezekiel 1).

Eschatology Traditionally this term denotes the doctrine of ultimate or last things. In biblical studies it refers to a dramatic reversal of the course of history such as that looked for by many prophets and depicted in later apocalyptic visions.

Etiology Refers to narrative that explains the origin or basis for a practice or phenomenon. For example, Genesis 32:22–32 explains how Jacob's name became Israel, why the site called Peniel was sacred, and what was the basis for a dietary practice.

Exegesis From a Greek term meaning *interpretation*, exegesis is a historical discipline that attempts to ascertain the meaning of a text by seeking the intent of the author/speaker and the likely impact of his intent on the reader/hearer. Once the original intent and impact of a text have been determined as fully as possible, other meanings assigned to the text by later readers are often considered as well.

Form criticism Form criticism, one of the methods employed in exegesis, seeks to isolate and define the typical structure and patterns in a given unit, noting especially repetitions of key words and formulas, and to place the unit in the life of a people by describing its typical social, legal, political, or religious context.

Former Prophets The books of Joshua, Judges, 1 and 2 Samuel, 1 and 2 Kings, which comprise the Deuteronomistic history.

Gattung A German term used in biblical studies to denote the type or genre of a literary unit.

Gemara Commentary on the Mishnah dating from the third through the fifth centuries C.E. The Mishnah and Gemara together comprise the Talmud.

Gloss A brief explanation of a part of a text, written above or beside a line and often later copied into the text as a part of it. Some have suggested, for example, that the word *Israel* in Isaiah 49:3 is a gloss identifying the Servant as the people Israel.

Habiru An ancient term denoting persons or groups who were outlaws in the sense that they were driven or had withdrawn from all social, political, and legal structures and obligations. Throughout the ancient Near East in the second and first millennia B.C.E. the Habiru appear as outlaws, slaves, merchants, mercenaries, raiders, and such. Some scholars link the term to the word *Hebrew*.

Haggadah Narratives dating from the first centuries C.E. that supplement and illustrate the Torah.

Halakah Rules and legal interpretations dating from the first centuries C.E. that apply the Torah to the lives of Jewish individuals and communities.

Hapaxlegomenon   From the Greek, meaning *a thing said once*, this technical term denotes a word that appears only once in the Old Testament and is for that reason difficult to translate precisely.

Haplography   A technical term used in textual criticism for a copying error in which a word, phrase, or line of text is omitted.

Heilsgeschichte   This German term, which can be translated *sacred history or story*, is used to describe Israel's understanding of its past in a confessional way. Thus, the escape from Egypt is not described simply as a flight of slaves but as the deliverance of the chosen people by Yahweh, in which they came to know and to acknowledge their god.

Hermeneutics   A term denoting application of the rules and principles used in interpreting ancient texts to a new and different setting; for example, applying the oracles of Isaiah of Jerusalem, originally addressed to the people of Jerusalem in the eighth century B.C.E., to modern Americans.

Hexateuch   The first six books of the Bible: Genesis through Joshua.

Hierocracy   A form of government in which religious figures are in authority, the term is used of Jerusalem and Judah after the building of the second temple in 520–515 B.C.E.

Historical criticism   Studying a text in the context of its time and place of authorship; seeking also to understand the persons, dates, and events mentioned in the text and the history surrounding them.

Holiness Code   The title given to the self-contained body of regulations found in Leviticus 17–26.

J.   *See* Yahwist.

JB.   Abbreviation for the Jerusalem Bible, a Roman Catholic translation published in English in 1966.

Kairotic   A Greek term describing a period of time as having special significance or potential, one that is later remembered as defining the identity of an individual or community. The exodus, for example, was a kairotic moment for ancient Israel.

Ketubim   A Hebrew term denoting the third segment of the Hebrew Bible: Psalms, Job, Proverbs, Song of Songs, Ecclesiastes, Esther, Ruth, Lamentations, Daniel, 1 and 2 Chronicles, Ezra, and Nehemiah.

KJV.   Abbreviation for King James Version of the Bible, published in 1611.

Latter Prophets   The books of Isaiah, Jeremiah, Ezekiel, and the twelve Minor Prophets.

Legend   A general term denoting stories about heroes, usually from the distant past, whose primary intent is not historical accuracy but entertainment, illustration, and instruction. Many of the accounts of the patriarchs in Genesis, of Moses in Exodus, as well as of Elijah and Elisha are termed *legends*.

Lexicon   A dictionary defining the Hebrew, Aramaic, and Greek words found in the Bible. Unlike a concordance, a lexicon is designed for those who wish to read the Bible in the original languages.

Literary criticism   A unit analysis that seeks to define literary type, the sources utilized in composition, the stages of composition, and characteristic rhetorical features.

LXX   Abbreviation for the Septuagint, the Greek translation of Hebrew scriptures done in the last centuries B.C.E.

Major Prophets   The books of Isaiah, Jeremiah, and Ezekiel; a descriptive term based solely on the length of these books.

Mari Tablets   A collection of historical, economic, and religious texts from the Upper Mesopotamian city of Mari which provide background for the eighteenth century B.C.E., the period to which some scholars assign the patriarchs of Genesis.

Masoretic Text (MT)   The text of the Hebrew Bible as given fixed form in the seventh through the ninth centuries C.E. and that stands as the standard text today.

Messiah   A title based on a Hebrew term meaning *one anointed and thereby set apart*, usually a king or priest. The term came especially to be applied to a member of the royal line of David and, in apocalyptic material, to the member of that line who would in the end restore the kingdom of Israel.

Midrash   A Hebrew term, based on a word meaning *to search out*, that is applied to commentary or interpretation of units of scripture. Collections of such interpretations are often called Midrashim, especially collections of Halakah and of Haggadah.

Minor Prophets   Prophetic books that were brief enough to be placed all together on one scroll: Hosea, Joel, Amos, Obadiah, Jonah, Micah, Nahum, Habakkuk, Zephaniah, Haggai, Zechariah, Malachi.

Mishnah   A collection of Pharisaic oral interpretations (Halakah) of the Torah that was formed and put into writing under Judah the Patriarch around 200 C.E.

NAB   Abbreviation for the New American Bible, a translation by American Roman Catholic scholars that appeared in 1970.

NEB   Abbreviation for the New English Bible, a translation done in England that appeared in 1970.

Nebiim   The Hebrew word for *prophets*, used to denote the second segment of the Hebrew Bible, which is made up of the books of the prophets.

NJV Abbreviation for the New Jewish Version of the Hebrew Bible, a translation that has been appearing in parts since 1962.

Onomastica Lists of names of different types of phenomena, such as items in nature, types of persons, occupations, or place names. It has been suggested that such lists were collected under the authority of Solomon (1 Kings 4:33) and that they stand behind the Yahweh speech in Job 38–39.

Oral tradition Material passed down through generations by word of mouth before taking fixed written form. Some scholars suggest that many of the stories about the patriarchs in Genesis, for example, had a long oral stage before taking written form.

P *See* Priestly document.

Parallelism A basic characteristic of Hebrew poetry in which the theme of a line is either repeated in different words (called *synonymous parallelism, see* Psalm 1:2, 1:5) or in which the opposite is given (called *antithetic parallelism, see* Psalm 1:6).

Pentateuch A technical term for the first five books of the Bible, also called the Torah.

Pesher A Hebrew term for a commentary on scripture, applied especially to the *pesherim* found among the Dead Sea Scrolls.

Peshitta The authorized translation of the Bible for the early Christian churches in Syria, done in the fifth century C.E.

Priestly document (P) The final strata comprising the Torah (Pentateuch), produced in exile and diaspora in 550–450 B.C.E.

Pseudepigrapha A term denoting early Jewish writings not found in the Old Testament or in the Apocrypha.

Pseudonymity The practice of ascribing a work to someone, often a notable from the past, who was not the actual author, as is the case with the Book of Daniel.

Ras Shamra Tablets A collection of texts, found in northern Syria and dating from about 1400 B.C.E., that reveal a great deal about the historical, social, political, literary, and religious situation in Canaan just before the appearance of ancient Israel.

Redaction Criticism A study method that seeks to define the methods and intent of editors as they compile and edit older sources—for example, those who collected and ordered the oracles of the prophets into the books as they now exist.

Redactor An editor; one who collects and shapes older, smaller material into larger, newer compositions.

Rhetorical criticism   A type of analysis that supplements form and literary criticism in not only studying the literary structures and techniques employed in a unit but in centering attention more on the distinctive than the typical, taking special note of the unique style of a given author or speaker.

RSV   Abbreviation for the Revised Standard Version of the Bible which appeared complete in 1957 as a revision of the ASV, which was itself a revision of the KJV.

Septuagint (LXX)   The Greek translation of the Hebrew scriptures traditionally ascribed to the reign of Ptolemy II (third century B.C.E.) and adopted as the Old Testament of the early Christian church. Later segments of the Septuagint were excluded from the standard Hebrew Bible (Masoretic Text) and today comprise the Apocrypha.

Sitz-im-leben   A German term meaning *setting in life*, used as a technical term in form criticism for the social context in which a typical unit was set and functioned.

Source criticism   Analysis of the sources employed in the construction of a particular literary unit. The four strata J, E, D, and P are the sources that comprise the Torah, for example.

Symmachus   A second century C.E. Christian who produced a free translation of the Old Testament from the Greek.

Talmud   A vast collection of Jewish interpretations made up of the Mishnah (itself an interpretation of the Torah) and the Gemara (commentary on the Mishna). There are two Talmuds, one from Palestine and one from Babylon, both shaped during the fifth and sixth centuries C.E.

Targum   The Targums are interpretative translations of the Hebrew Bible into Aramaic, having their origin in the early synagogue practice of reading the Hebrew, than translating it into Aramaic, with interpretative comments woven into the translation.

Terminus ad quem   A Latin phrase meaning *a fixed point to which* and denoting the *latest* possible date for something.

Terminus a quo   A Latin phrase meaning *a fixed point from which* and denoting the *earliest* possible date for something.

Tetragrammaton   A technical term for the consonants YHWH which make up the name Yahweh, the god of Israel. They are often translated Lord, reflecting the early Jewish practice of not pronouncing the sacred name of the deity.

Tetrateuch   A technical term denoting the first four books of the Bible.

Textual criticism   Study of the Hebrew Bible's early texts and early translations with the intent of establishing the text probably closest to the original, as well as noting the history of its transmission.

Torah   A Hebrew term that in its widest sense meant *teaching*, though it came in time to mean *law*, and was then applied as a title to the first five books of the Bible, which are also called the Pentateuch.

Tosefta   Additional oral-legal interpretation that supplements the Mishnah.

Tradition criticism   Study of the origins and development of a particular biblical theme—for example, the covenant relationship between Yahweh and Israel —as it appears in various parts of the Bible. For some scholars, tradition criticism centers exclusively on the early and oral stages of development.

Vaticinium ex eventu   A Latin phrase meaning *prophecy from the results* that is applied to events that are presented as foretold by a figure out of the past but that have actually already taken place. The visions in Daniel offer examples.

Version   In textual criticism a *version* is an early translation of the Bible, such as the Septuagint or the Targum.

Vulgate   The translation of the Bible into Latin done by the Christian, Jerome, in the late fourth and early fifth centuries B.C.E. *NOT TRUE* RES 10/31/83

Wisdom literature   Within the Bible, the books of Proverbs, Job, Ecclesiastes, Ecclesiasticus, and the Wisdom of Solomon are all classed as *wisdom*.

Writings   Within the Hebrew Bible, the Writings are those works not included under the Torah or Former and Latter Prophets.

Yahweh   The name of the god of ancient Israel and early Judaism, who was also called Elohim. In time, *Yahweh* was no longer pronounced by Jews, who used the title *Adonai* ("my Lord") or *Adon* ("Lord") in its place.

Yahwist (J)   The oldest stratum in the Torah, dated from 950 B.C.E.

NOTE: Most of the terms discussed here receive fuller treatment in articles in George A. Buttrick, ed., *Interpreter's Dictionary of the Bible*, 4 vols. (Nashville: Abingdon Press, 1962), in its *Supplementary Volume* (1976), and in Richard N. Soulen, *Handbook of Biblical Criticism* (Atlanta: John Knox Press, 1976).

INDEX